INSIDE EUROPE TODAY

INSIDE
EUROPE
TODAY

BY

JOHN GUNTHER

HAMISH HAMILTON

LONDON

First published in Great Britain 1961
by Hamish Hamilton Ltd
*90 Great Russell Street London WC*1
Second impression August 1961

Copyright © *John Gunther* 1961

PRINTED IN GREAT BRITAIN
BY EBENEZER BAYLIS AND SON, LTD
THE TRINITY PRESS, WORCESTER, AND LONDON

CONTENTS

MAPS

CHAPTER I

By Way of Introduction

TWENTY-FIVE years ago I wrote *Inside Europe*, which surveyed the tortured world of Europe in the late 1930's, on the eve of World War II, when the continent was dominated by three colossal tyrants—Hitler, Mussolini, Stalin. Now a quarter of a century has passed, the immediate upheavals and dislocations caused by the greatest war in history are behind us, and this is a good time to take a fresh look at Europe, its thicket of contemporary personalities, issues, forces, problems. How does the Europe of today compare with that of 1936? What has happened in a quarter of a century? What are the paramount, the fundamental changes?

Some in the realm of the obvious may be listed at once. The three big despots are no longer with us—nor are such smaller dictators as Pilsudski, Horthy, Metaxas, Kemal Atatürk, and various Balkan kings and kinglets. The Third Reich, which was to have lasted a thousand years, has been swept away into the ugly gutter of history where it belonged. The Italian monarchy has disappeared, and so have both the Third and Fourth Republics in France. England is revivified. There was only one Germany when war came in 1939 (and one was quite enough, thank you); today there are two. Nobody had ever heard the phrases 'Iron Curtain' or 'peaceful co-existence' in 1936; today we know them well. Nobody—except a handful of scientists—had ever thought of harnessing atomic energy as an instrument of warfare, and not one person in a million had ever heard the name Hiroshima.

But to proceed to other elements—

The most striking of all differences between the Europe of 1936 and that of 1961 is that a general war in the near future is unlikely. Even such an inveterate adversary of the Soviet Union

9   1*

as Chancellor Adenauer will tell you that Mr. Khrushchev has no present intention of making a war. But in 1936 everybody who had a milligram of insight knew that Hitler was inevitably bound to make a war. He wanted it, and nothing, not even the pusillanimity of Mr. Chamberlain, was going to stop him. The fierce threat of impending conflict, conflict that would spread throughout the whole world, to be made by a criminal lunatic who could not be reached by any instrument of reason, lay like a black, sinister shadow across every face.

Today, no equivalent threat exists. Mr. Khrushchev is a man who can be extraordinarily rude, crude, and disagreeable, quite capable of losing his temper, but he is not a madman. Such personal factors aside, Hitler could get what he wanted only by direct territorial aggression and open warfare. Khrushchev, in strict contrast, can get what he wants only by taking advantage, for his own purposes, of a period of peace. Hitler was spoiling for a fight—even at Munich; Khrushchev is spoiling for a *détente*—on his own terms, of course.

Another point is striking too. Hitler was capable of making the bloodiest, most unpleasant, and most disrupting war in history, but he was not capable of burning up the whole world at the push of a button. *If* war should come today—through strategic miscalculation or plain, stupid blunder—civilization might not survive. Never before in history has the possibility of such an obliterating catastrophe confronted mankind. So we have two overriding factors to consider, which to an extent complement each other. First, nobody actively wants a war (except possibly the Chinese), and, although the world situation is tense and harassing, open hot war is unlikely; but, second, if a general war *should* come, it could be immeasurably more disastrous than any other ever fought, because of the overwhelming fact that we have entered into the missile age.

Why, then, in view of the sombre shadow of megaton bombs, are today's Europeans not more frightened than they are? Why is western Europe booming, prosperous, and confident? One reason is optimism in a period of wealth—people don't want to face painful facts. Another is nuclear stalemate. We have today a world sharply divided between mutually exclusive groups, ourselves and the Communists, and the fact that each has the instantaneous capacity to destroy or reduce vitally the strength

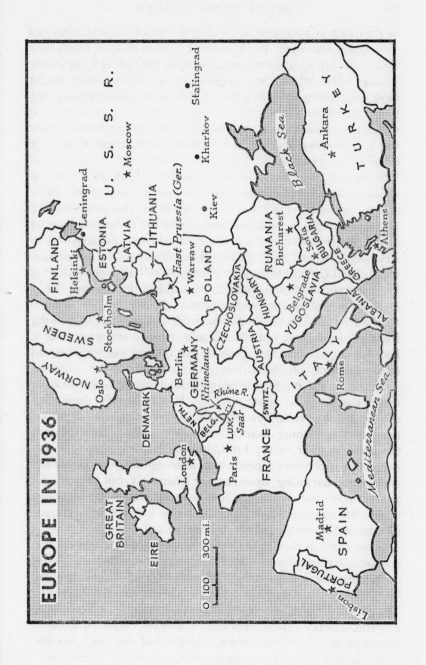

EUROPE IN 1936

of the other is a force which makes for peace. Neither side can
dare attack the other. But this also produces intense diplomatic
rivalry, which extends to sectors today, like Laos, Cuba in the
Western Hemisphere, and large areas in Africa, which would
have been thought utterly remote from the main struggle for
power in 1936.

Another fundamental, pre-eminent difference between pre-
war and post-war Europe is, of course, the Atlantic Alliance, a
corollary of which is the presence of substantial United States
military, air, and naval forces in Europe. This, as should be
known to us all, is a development not only of the utmost importance, but one which would have been thought literally
inconceivable by most Americans during the isolationist period
of our history, that is to say, the day before yesterday. The
Marshall Plan and ECA lifted western Europe off its feet; then
came NATO; military aid continues. If Europe today is
immeasurably different from pre-war Europe, a leading factor
is—only too obviously—the extension eastward of the American frontier. In 1936 Europe had a spongy fence known as the
Maginot Line; today it has American bases scattered over a
large area (whether wisely or not is another matter), and an
American army on the Rhine.

Finally in the realm of broad general considerations we have
the fact that, to be blunt, France, West Germany, Italy, and
even the United Kingdom are no longer great powers. This is a
development of magnitude, if only because it passes so much
responsibility for Western leadership to the United States,
which has not always proved itself to be fully seasoned and
mature in accepting such responsibilities. Since 1949, when
Russia built its first atomic bomb, this has been a two-power
world. In time, Europe itself (western Europe that is) may
become a new great power, if developments like the Common
Market continue to make for growth and coalescence, but this is
to look a long way ahead.[1] Also China may soon—uncomfortably
soon—become a great power of the rank of Russia and the
United States. But at the moment the world is polarized between
Washington and Moscow, and the most urgent and gravid of
all problems is to stabilize relations between them. In 1936, to
repeat, Europe consisted of a group of countries roughly equal

[1] For the Common Market, see Chapter XIX below.

in strength; in 1961, it is two parallel slabs of territory—one ours, one theirs—between two adversaries, the United States of America and the Union of Soviet Socialist Republics, which are not in true essence European powers at all.

SOME POINTS OF DETAIL—THE NEW EUROPE

Following are some details—political and otherwise—which illustrate further the differences between pre-war Europe and the Europe of today. Seldom has any quarter-century produced such seismic changes. I list these points without regard to order of importance.

Item. Three countries have gone down the drain—disappeared just like that—worthy, honest, and decent little countries too. They are the three Baltic states, Estonia, Latvia, and Lithuania, which were all absorbed by the Soviet Union in 1940. Also the Russians took substantial areas of Finland, Poland, and Rumania as well as part of East Prussia. One result of the penetration into Poland is that the Soviet Union has today a common frontier with Hungary, which was a matter of considerable convenience to the USSR when the Red Army brutally put down the Hungarian people's uprising in October, 1956.

Item. One new country has emerged—Cyprus.

Item. As everybody knows, East Germany, Poland, Czechoslovakia, Hungary, Rumania, Bulgaria, and Albania have become satellites of the Soviet Union—puppet states, although their degrees of subservience differ. Altogether a broad bloc of Russian-dominated territory stretches from the Baltic to the Black Sea and protrudes into western Europe as far as the Danube and Elbe. Something like 115,000,000 people have lost freedom, which constitutes as black a tragedy as any that has defaced modern times.

Item. Jugoslavia, under Marshal Tito, is a special case. It is Communist, but not a Soviet satellite. Tito is a 'national' Communist.

Item. Austria, forcibly incorporated into the Reich by Hitler in 1938, has become free and is now neutralized. The Russians withdrew from their zone of occupation in Austria in 1955; it was with this gesture that Khrushchev bought his way into the first Summit Conference in Geneva.

Item. Before the war dictators of varying colour ruled Germany (which included Austria after 1938 and Czechoslovakia after 1938-39), Italy, Spain, Portugal, Hungary, Greece, Turkey, the Soviet Union, Poland, and most of the Balkan states. Of these Germany (west of the Elbe), Italy, and Greece have become democracies today. Turkey deposed a semi-dictator, Adnan Menderes, in 1960.

Item. Only three countries have today the same rulers they had in the 1930's—Spain, Portugal, and Eire, which became a republic in 1937 and left the British Commonwealth in 1949. Franco has managed to hold on continuously in Spain since 1936, and Salazar in Portugal since 1932. De Valera in Eire had periods of being in and out of office. It is interesting that Spain, Portugal, and Eire are all Catholic and lie on the outermost fringes of western Europe.[1]

Item. Of the few institutions which have remained intact, or virtually intact, since the war one is the British royal family— also the Vatican. Another—at the extreme opposite pole—is the Communist party in the Soviet Union, although this has changed considerably since Stalin's day.

Item. As far as specific political events concerning individual European powers are concerned, the most important by far since the war is the reconciliation of France and Germany. The most important future *issue* is disarmament.

Item. Hitler murdered six *million* Jews, as revolting a crime as any in human history; as a result a new and odious word— 'genocide'—entered the world's vocabulary. Some Jews were lucky enough to escape from Germany before Hitler's mass exterminations began; others have left Europe since, and are now staunch, enlightened citizens of a brave new country, Israel. The fact that there are many fewer Jews in Europe than before the war has substantially changed the face of several countries, like Poland, and of several great cities, like Vienna and Berlin. They are the worse for it; a glow, a creative spark, a friendly leavening of earthiness and humour, have disappeared.

Item. The old League of Nations in Geneva is dead; the new United Nations in New York is very much alive, and day by day

---

[1] In passing it might also be mentioned that leaders of three of the four chief western European countries are practising Catholics—de Gaulle, Adenauer, and Gronchi.

plays a more pungent role in the affairs of the world. It is infinitely more powerful than the old League, if only because the United States is a member; also it owes much to the zeal, deftness, and indefatigability of its present Secretary-General, Dag Hammarskjöld. But it is certainly a very different organization from what was visualized by its founders in San Francisco in 1945. It has ninety-nine members now as against fifty-one at its first assembly, and whereas it was once dominated by the Western democratic powers these at the moment of writing have only a bare majority, if that. At least forty-two of its member nations belong to the Asian-African bloc, and at least thirty-five represent peoples who are black or brown.

Item. The European imperial powers—Britain, France, Belgium, the Netherlands—have lost most of their great colonial dependencies. More on this later. Britain has given up India, Pakistan, Burma, Ceylon, Malaya, the Sudan, Nigeria, and Ghana, among much else; France has lost Syria, the Lebanon, Indo-China, Morocco, and Tunisia; Belgium surrendered the Congo, with consequences still hot in the world's news; the Netherlands has lost Indonesia. Since the war no fewer than thirteen countries in Asia and twenty-two in Africa have become free; eighteen new African countries entered the UN in 1960; more will come. France is fighting a bitter war to hold Algeria. Anybody who would have predicted all of this in the 1930's would have been dismissed as daft. Think of the earnest, feckless debates in the British Parliament before the war on the Indian 'question'. Mr. Nehru was still in jail in the early 1940's. The emergence of the new Afro-Asian nationalisms is, of course, a profoundly seminal development. Europe is no longer imperial; the colonial era is just about wound up. What would the ghost of Kitchener say? Or of Henry Morton Stanley and King Leopold? Or Rhodes? Or Lyautey? Mr. Churchill once averred that he did not become Prime Minister to preside over the liquidation of the British Empire; but exactly that has happened within eighteen years.

Item. Communism appears to be immovably fixed in the Soviet Union, and, so far as we are able to say reasonably, in the satellites. But it has almost disappeared as a dangerous *internal* force in western Europe; this marks a striking change since the war, when the possibility of Communist advance to power was acute in both France and Italy. On the other hand, the Communist party is still the second biggest in Italy, and still has a large following in France; Communists dominate the largest party in Finland, and a Communist-front party is the second in Greece.

Item. Socialist forces are, *politically* speaking, generally weaker in western Europe than before the war, although Norway and Sweden still have socialist or labour governments, labour leads the government coalition in Denmark, and Austria is ruled by a coalition in which Social Democrats have an equal share. Socialists are the second party in both Belgium and the Netherlands, and are tied for leadership in Switzerland. But the Labour party in England has lost three general elections in a row, and so have the Social Democrats in Germany; by and large it seems that socialism is on the decline politically in most of industrial Europe, and the non-Communist left has lost much of its reformist fervour. Partly this is because of prosperity, partly because conservatives everywhere (especially in England) have stolen much socialist thunder. One eminent Belgian socialist told me with a resigned, cynical air, 'The best way for people to get social reform nowadays is to vote conservative.'

Item. Socialism may be diminishing as a political force, but *social changes* are advanced. Almost all European countries (except haunts of the backward like Spain and Portugal) subscribe nowadays to the major premisses of the welfare state within the confines of the free enterprise system. This, obviously, is because no government stands much chance of getting elected, much less of remaining in power, unless it assumes responsibility for citizens, to one degree or another, in health services, medical aid, old age pensions, unemployment benefits, and other forms of social insurance. Of course this is not new. The Scandinavian countries have been welfare states for a generation or longer, and the reforms of the Front Populaire in France began in 1936. Germany has had social security since Bismarck. But the movement for fully extended social services has been greatly accelerated since the war; the concept that all citizens must share in the proceeds of the national economy is almost universally accepted. West Germany spends not less than 30 per cent of its budget on social welfare (including housing); even Italy spends 17 per cent.

Item. Western Europe is having (at the moment at least) a substantial boom; times have seldom been better in England, France, West Germany, and Italy. Everywhere people appear to have money; this gives them bounce and zip; the outlook is vastly different from the 1930's, when the economy was stagnant. Need for economic and financial aid from the United States has disappeared—a cardinal development, which in a sense marks the end of the 'post-war' phase of European history, as several commentators have recently pointed out. Indeed, the United States, suffering from a severe drain in gold in 1960-61, is looking for help from Europe, instead of vice versa. Western Europe has at present a gross national product within 10 per cent of that of the United States, and by 1970 is expected to surpass it with £285 million against £264 million. No longer is Europe America's 'baby'; on the contrary, western Europe as a whole is steadily becoming more and more of a competitor in the realms of trade.

Item. Europe is confident; it's on the go; people circulate; try to get a hotel room or a table in a good restaurant anywhere from Stockholm to Madrid. Even the French have discovered the exquisite miracles of expense account economy. There is, however, an important qualifying point to make here. People spend money freely and Europe has a wealthy class, yes; but, in comparison to the late 1930's, there has been an enormous diminution in *privilege*. A profound social upheaval has taken place. This is the new world, and make no mistake about it— new, because the great bulk of citizens who were underpossessed, or whose immediate forebears were underpossessed, now have unprecedented opportunity for education, good jobs, security in old age, and social mobility. Of course millions of people are still poor—look at Spain or Greece. But in most of western Europe poverty is no longer associated with *class*. Society has become democratized. Taxation, particularly in England, has destroyed the easy possibility of inheriting vast wealth, on which privilege largely depended. An aristocracy still exists in England and elsewhere, and plenty of feudalism survives in Spain and Italy. But most of Europe is dominated today by the middle class, and, as the older generation dies off, this recruits itself more and more from the left. Most of the people with big money in Europe today are the new managers, the new industrialists, whose fathers may have been proletarian workers, not the surviving aristocrats. The concept that power is necessarily based on privilege is as dead as Louis XIV or Jack the Ripper.

Item. Naturally a good deal of what may vaguely be called 'Americanization' has smitten Europe, particularly in minor spheres. New hotels have bell captains and room service by telephone rather than by push-button; American-style filling stations dominate the roads, and towns have parking meters; railway trains like the new Trans-European Expresses, an off-shoot of the Common Market, operate on the model of American trains, with little nonsense about passports or Customs at the frontiers; American airliners fly everywhere; strip-teasers rule the night-clubs with gaudy lasciviousness; several European countries have picture and news magazines on the style of *Life* and *Time*; there are even places where American hard-cover books are occasionally to be seen; above all, cafeterias, auto-mats, and quick-lunch counters have come even to France, and citizens consume hamburgers, hot dogs, and chocolate frosteds. (But the French, even in cafeterias, manage to remain French; notice the trays of miniature bottles of Beaujolais, Médoc, or Chablis.)

Item. But to return to elements more basic. Europe has changed immeasurably, fantastically; but one thing has not changed. When I wrote *Inside Europe* a quarter of a century ago I began with Germany because Germany, the fiery heart of Europe, was the key to everything. It still is. But the Germany of today is rent in two; and there can be no stable peace in Europe, no permanent solution, until some kind of settlement is made of the German problem, so perennial, difficult, and exasperating. So, once more, we set off on a European tour with Germany as the essential first stop. Let us begin with Bonn, near the point where Julius Caesar and, some years later, the Ninth Armoured Division of the U.S. Army crossed the Rhine.

CHAPTER II

The Old Man on the Rhine

WHEN I saw Dr. Konrad Adenauer early in 1960 I thought that he looked fifty-five, although he was eighty-four. He has the agelessness of old Chinese mandarins, and, indeed, the cast of his features is faintly Chinese—broad cheekbones, taut ivory skin, eyebrows almost invisible, and a long nose pushed inward at the bottom, almost a tapir's nose. He looks so youthful, comparatively speaking, that the quaint legend has arisen that he had his face lifted. This is, of course, untrue, but he suffered severe facial injuries in a car accident many years ago, and had to undergo elaborate surgery, which accounts, among other things, for the Oriental slant of his glistening small eyes.

In any case Dr. Adenauer seems indestructible. This tenacious old gentleman was born in 1876, when Ulysses S. Grant was President of the United States, when Queen Victoria was only half way through her reign, and when Alexander II ruled Russia. His eyesight is still good; so is his hearing, and he still works a hard, lively day. He insists, however, on a sound nap after lunch, and, if he is travelling abroad and has a public function to attend, he sometimes asks for a bed in a room close to where he will be speaking, so that he can rest briefly before he appears.

Dr. Adenauer, the great years of whose career did not even begin till he was seventy-two, lives not in Bonn itself, the capital of the Federal Republic of Germany, as West Germany is officially called, but in Rhoendorf, a suburb a few miles away across the Rhine, where he has had his home for many years. Here fifty-four stone steps lead from the road to the gate of his villa, and these he climbs every day—well, not so briskly as a boy, but he does climb them, sometimes faster than his visitors. If the day has been exhausting, a turn among his rosebushes revives him, or a bottle of sound Rhine wine. He likes to play a game called *boccie* (an Italian version of bowls), and has alleys for playing it both at home and in the garden of the Chancellery, the Schaumburg Palace in Bonn. Altogether, Dr. Adenauer is an astounding physical phenomenon. His manner is still sharp, direct, and bold. People talk unendingly about what will happen in Germany when *Der Alte* dies, as if this were about to happen tomorrow, but it is quite possible that he still has half a dozen good years left in him.

Adenauer's basic sources of power are several:

First, the very fact of his age. He has become a kind of 'grand-father image'—not necessarily loved, because he is too severe, too obstinate, too authoritarian, too wily, to arouse much love. 'He is a grandfather who tells us fairy stories,' one of his political adversaries put it to me. Another said, 'He is not a grand-father image, but a *ghost* image.' Be this as it may, Dr. Adenauer, even if not loved, is almost universally respected and admired. He has a strong ethical appeal. Moreover, his age is a veneer, an armour, serving to make him untouchable. One of his major political opponents, a Social Democrat, told me that he no longer felt free to press him closely in a political attack; it didn't seem sporting to tilt the lance too sharply, even though the Chancellor is amply able to take care of himself in debate. Finally, one increment of age is, or should be, experience, and Dr. Adenauer has an unrivalled treasury of political lore to draw on.

Second, his *success*. Of course he has made mistakes, but in the eleven years of his rule, uninterrupted rule, he has transformed West Germany from a broken wreck, a shambles, into the most powerful, prosperous, and confident nation on the continent. This country has risen from complete destitution in 1946 to have a gross national product of £25,000 million in 1960, and its gold reserve, £764 million, is the second largest in the world. Its *total* reserves of gold and foreign currency amount to almost £2,500 million, and its industrial production has risen 85 per cent since 1953.

Third, American support.

Fourth, nobody else in Germany holds a candle to him as a political manipulator. There are plenty of able German politicians, but Adenauer puts them all into shadow—both members of his own party and the opposition. He is, be it remembered, not merely administrative head of the government but legislative leader as well, and his skill in both capacities is unparalleled. Important political changes may, however, be coming to Germany soon, and Willy Brandt, the socialist Mayor of West Berlin, is bound to be a formidable antagonist to the Chancellor in the elections scheduled for this year.

Fifth, Adenauer stands for what most West Germans seem to want today—peace, stability, rapprochement with France, and integration into Europe. Needless to say, these items are particularly welcome after the inadequacies of the Weimar Republic, twelve years of militant savagery under Hitler, and the catastrophe of World War II.

One eminent German told me, 'I do not like Adenauer. But he ended the tragic feud across the Rhine, and I will feel naked when he is gone.'

The Chancellor's chief quality, aside from durability, courage, and political sagacity, is probably his power of simplification. This is a trait somewhat unusual among Germans, but Hitler (whom Adenauer in no other way resembles) had it too. Hitler based almost the whole of his ferocious crusades on half a dozen points simply stated and easily grasped—*Lebensraum*, anti-Semitism, repeal of the Versailles Treaty, military might, and concepts such as '*Ein Reich, ein Volk, ein Führer*'. Adenauer is also a man of comparatively few ideas, and has a marked gift for making them clearly understandable to the people at large. He likes to explain his policies in the simplest terms, and is a man of reason, who can make long sentences short (another quality unusual in a German). One of his favourite maxims is, 'As soon as you are complicated, you are ineffectual.'

On the other hand, he has what I have heard described as a 'dark' mind. This does not refer merely to his conservatism, which is profound, but to his suspiciousness—his exaggerated sensitiveness to imaginary plots, conspiracies, and stratagems.

Dr. Adenauer once wrote a brief article for *Reader's Digest* in which he said that, when tired, he had learned that he could recuperate quickly by putting his feet in a basin of ice water, which drove the blood to his head. Another item that I find appealing is that he has a sweet tooth, and, during long cabinet meetings, nibbles at chocolate bars.[1] But no one should be misled by such trivialities. This is a man strong, unbending, and undivided, and the sub-surface hull of his character is impermeable.

*

The story of Adenauer's career is so well known that it hardly needs recounting. Three forces which helped to shape him—class, religion, geography—are fundamental. He came of middle-class stock (one of his grandfathers was a baker) with strong roots in the bureaucracy. He is, of course, a devout Roman Catholic, who likes to think that God is on his side and that God is a conservative. Above all, Adenauer is a Rhinelander, that is to say a German who can look back to a rich European as well as a purely Teutonic heritage. The story is always denied officially, but there seems good reason to believe that, after World War I, he joined the Rhineland Separatist movement briefly—that is, he was willing to give up Germany for France. As to his attitude towards Prussia and eastern Germany, the antithesis of the Rhineland, a favourite story about him is that, whenever he took the train to Berlin in the old days and crossed the Elbe, he would mutter darkly, 'Now we enter Asia!' He didn't go so far as to think that Prussia, Pomerania, Brandenburg and so on were actually populated by Mongol nomads, but, even then, he regarded the Elbe as what it is in fact today, a frontier.

Adenauer was born in Cologne on January 5, 1876, the son of a minor official. A dutiful student (but no blazing intellectual), he got a degree in law after study at several universities, and followed his father into the civil service, becoming a clerk in the Cologne Rathaus. He was thirty-eight when World War I broke out, and never saw military service. In 1917, aged forty-one, he reached the first climax of his career, and became Lord Mayor of Cologne. This post he held for sixteen uninterrupted years, until 1933; meantime, he became a leading member of the old Zentrum (Catholic) party. He lost his job as *Oberburgomeister* when the Nazis came into power, and, during the next grim years, was arrested twice by the Gestapo. Mostly, however, he sat out the Nazi régime placidly enough at Rhoendorf,

[1] Terence Prittie, 'Konrad Adenauer', *Atlantic Monthly*, September, 1957.

cultivating roses, about which he is erudite, amusing himself with various hobbies (he loves to tinker with antique clocks), and biding his time.[1] His personal life was happy. He has married twice, and is now a widower; he is the father of seven children, and has no fewer than twenty-one grandchildren. Twenty of these attended his eighty-fifth birthday celebration on January 5, 1961. One of his sons, Paul, is a priest, and lives with him today at Rhoendorf; another has followed in his footsteps (and those of his father) to become an administrative officer in the Cologne mayoralty.

When the Americans took Cologne towards the end of World War II Adenauer was called out of retirement and reinstated in his old post as Mayor of Cologne. This was in 1945, and Adenauer was sixty-nine. The Allies desperately needed 'clean' administrators, who had never had any dealings with the Nazis, and men of experience and stature were hard to find; Adenauer was a perfect choice, although he was thought to be somewhat old. But, when the Cologne area was assigned to British occupation, things did not go well, and, in fact, a British officer fired him for 'incompetence' in 1947. What this meant was that he was too authoritarian for the local British taste. Adenauer determined to go into national politics, and set out to create and build up the Christian Democratic Union, the party which he still leads today. He became Chancellor in 1949, as representative of a coalition which had a majority of only two in the Bundestag; he has won two general elections since, in 1953 and 1957. The last was called 'an Adenauer plebiscite'. His vote rose from 45·2 per cent in 1953 to 50·2 per cent, a bare majority but enough. Meantime, he was his own foreign minister from 1949 to 1955—and, as a matter of fact, still is, even if another man, the worthy but largely invisible Dr. Brentano, is titular holder of the post.

Adenauer has always thought, with his logical and somewhat pedantic mind, in terms of a fixed, strict timetable. First he sought to unify the three Allied zones of occupation in West Germany, as a bridge to freedom from foreign control; second, to consolidate the position of the new Federal Republic when it became a sovereign state on May 5, 1955; third, to regain the esteem of the victors in World War II, and become their firm

[1] Flora Lewis, 'Der Alte at 83', New York Times Magazine, January 4, 1959.

ally; fourth, to rearm West Germany and join NATO. All this he has achieved on schedule. The fifth great objective— reunification of the two Germanys—is not yet attained.

*

Dr. Adenauer has, of course, defects and limitations. His rule is almost defiantly personal, and he lays down the law to cabinet ministers in no uncertain terms; everything so largely depends on the will—or whim—of the Chancellor that nobody else dares to assert much authority; if an impending issue is important it is called a 'Chancellor question' and no one is allowed to touch it except Adenauer himself. As a result government is, as I heard a senior diplomat in Bonn express it, somewhat 'ram- shackle'. The head is strong, the legs weak. Liaison is faulty, and one ministry may be totally ignorant of what the next is doing in a common field.

One peculiarity about *Der Alte* is that he has little taste for economics, on which politics must so often depend. 'Somebody *must* go to the Chancellor,' one of his associates whispered to another recently, 'and tell him what a tariff *is*.' His indifference to economics in the abstract has not, however, kept him from being an enthusiastic advocate of the European Economic Com- munity, or Common Market, even though this brought him into sharp conflict with Dr. Erhard, his stout and emphatic Minister of Economics, who opposes certain aspects of the Common Market because membership means that Germany must raise some of its tariffs. This, Dr. Erhard thinks, will hurt German industry. But Dr. Adenauer overruled him, and Erhard sank—on this issue—like a pinnace in the wake of a battleship. One of the Chancellor's most trusted friends, Dr. Walter Hallstein, a former official in the German Foreign Office, is President of the Executive Committee of the Common Market organization in Brussels, and Adenauer helped put him there. Adenauer saw the Common Market as a supremely important instrumentation for furthering his dearest wish, the *political* integration of Germany, France, Italy, and the Benelux countries. He said to a friend recently, 'I want to stay alive longer for only one reason—to see a United States of Europe in my time.'

This statement would have been more in consonance with Dr.

Adenauer's inner beliefs if he had said, 'A United States of *western* Europe.' As is well known, the Chancellor's enmity to the Soviet Union is fixed, implacable and irreversible. A mild little joke is that his name is really John Foster Adenauer. To a great many liberal-minded people his ideas on Russia seem obscurantist and old-fashioned; he has little conception of some of the new forces that blow through the world. His mind, so his critics say, is not only closed, but sterile. It does not seem to occur to him that a third of the world is Communist, and that in the long run the alternative to war must be some kind of accommodation with the Soviet Union, no matter how brutal and ill-mannered its policies may be. De Gaulle in France and Macmillan in England both believe that a *détente* with Russia is essential, on decent terms, and, even after the failure of the Summit Conference in May, 1960, must be energetically pursued; but not Adenauer. The old man is as immovable as the Drachenfels forests near his home.

Be this as it all may be, Adenauer's contribution in his eleven years of power has been colossal. It was he, still full of sap and sting in his late seventies, who made possible an orderly transition from the Nazi régime to parliamentary government; he brought Germany out of an evil dictatorship, defeat, and burning chaos into the embrace of the democratic world. There had to be a bridge; and Adenauer built it. On top of this he made Franco-German rapprochement a living fact for the first time in more than three hundred years, and brought West Germany into the community of civilized nations. And at all costs he wants to keep his country from going down to ruin again.

CRONIES AND THE SUCCESSION

Adenauer, who is as gregarious as a sparrow, has hundreds of friends. Among them (something unusual in European politics except in England) are several of his sharp political opponents, like Willy Brandt. The inner circle, however, consists of a small group of men mostly old, rich, and very definitely on the conservative side. One is Hermann Abs, probably the most powerful banker in Germany; another is Dr. Heinrich Krone, parliamentary floor leader of the CDU—some observers would call him the Chancellor's closest political adviser. Another is Joseph

Cardinal Frings, the Archbishop of Cologne, a venerable churchman (born in 1887) who has been close to Adenauer for thirty
years or more; still another is Dr. Hans Globke, the Secretary
of State in the Chancellor's office, and a highly controversial
figure because, as a civil servant under the Nazis, he is said to
have written what is called the 'Commentary' on the Nuremberg
laws; his friends insist, however, that he used his official position
to do what he could for the Jews. Globke, who is sometimes
called Adenauer's *éminence grise*, has a grave manner, a cool
professorial charm, and a cautious eye behind shiny spectacles.
He was born in 1898, and is a jurist by profession. He told me
that he thought Adenauer's chief quality was his mastery of
political manœuvre. Then one should certainly mention Herbert
Blankenhorn, the Ambassador to Paris, and Felix von Ekhardt,
the Press chief of the government.

But the man closest of all is the celebrated Cologne banker,
Robert Pferdmenges, who is almost as old as Adenauer himself
—eighty-two. He was born of a Rhenish family of textile
merchants, and shares in almost every respect the Chancellor's
deeply ingrained feeling about the Rhineland and its tradition.
He went into banking as a boy, spent many years in London,
and after World War I became conspicuous as head of one of
the great Jewish banking houses of the day, that of Salomon
Oppenheim. He was close to Bruening in the pre-Hitler period
and spent some time in jail after the attempt on Hitler's life in
1944. After World War II he became president of the Oppenheim bank, and retired in 1957. Pferdmenges is almost as
internationally minded as Adenauer himself, and was one of the
early collaborators in the Schuman Plan, which led to the
European Coal and Steel Community. He is a Protestant.

None of these men could, it goes without saying, conceivably
become Adenauer's successor. The obvious immediate candidate
to carry on—assuming that the CDU stays in power—is Dr.
Erhard, despite his frequent vivid differences of opinion with
the Chancellor. After Erhard, the man next in line could very
well turn out to be the vigorous and comparatively youthful
Minister of Defence, Franz-Josef Strauss. More on both Erhard
and Strauss later. An important dark horse is Eugen Gersten-
maier, president (speaker) of the Bundestag. He is a strong
figure in the CDU, an exceptionally able if somewhat colourless

man, and a Protestant. He took part in the unsuccessful military conspiracy to kill Hitler in July, 1944. Uncertainty about the succession—and, after all, no one can get away from the fact that Adenauer is eighty-five, and not getting any younger—makes for a certain amount of restlessness. People chafe, but hold fast to what they have. Everybody in an important position seeks at all costs to hold on to his job, so as to be in conspicuous view in the event of the Chancellor's death.

BONN, A MOST PECULIAR VILLAGE

Nothing typifies the difference between pre-war and post-war Germany more sharply than the contrast between Bonn, the present capital, and that sleek, steely Sodom and Gomorrah of cities, Berlin. Nor can Adenauer be fully understood without appreciation of the atmosphere of Bonn. (Technically speaking, Berlin is still the 'capital' of Germany, and Bonn merely the 'provisional' capital and 'seat of government' of the Federal Republic, but Bonn is bound to retain its present status for a long time to come.) Bonn is the most powerful village in the world. Even the Germans call it a village, partly in derision, partly with affection.

Resting primly on the broad shoulder of the Rhine, Bonn goes right back to the Romans, in sharp contrast to Berlin, a Prussian outpost of comparatively recent origin. The Rhine has watered civilized territory for two thousand years. But the Romans gave up their encampment in Bonn, the story goes, because they couldn't stand the weather; then as now, this is a community where an oozy rain is frequent. The grey-green wooded hills across the river from Bonn, the backdrop of Adenauer's own hamlet of Rhoendorf, are as German as Hegel, *Lebkuchen*, or the goosestep. This is all Siegfried country. Here are the Venusberg and the Siebengebirge, weighted down with a thunderous mythology. Here, too, on the crest of Petersberg, some unfortunate recent history was made, which Europe is not likely to forget. Neville Chamberlain stayed at the Petershof Hotel when he came to Bad Godesberg (a village into which Bonn merges) to accept terms from Hitler, and later—the contrast is sharp—the same hotel became the first headquarters of the Allied High Commission.

Bonn has a charming pink and gold baroque *Rathaus*, dating from the sixteenth century; from its balcony Carl Schurz addressed his fellow-citizens before departing for the United States in 1848. Beethoven, as is well known, was born in Bonn, and Schumann died here. Both Nietzsche and the historian Jakob Burkhardt went to the University of Bonn, and Schlegel, the translator of Shakespeare into German, is conspicuously buried in the local cemetery.

But it was not history, nor the wonderful view of the river, nor literary or musical associations, that led Dr. Adenauer to choose this somewhat derelict little town as his seat of government. First, he lived in the neighbourhood, and did not want to move. In fact, the standard joke is that *Der Alte* chose Bonn because Rhoendorf, his home village, was *too* small. There were other reasons too. For one thing he wanted the capital to be small so that it would really seem to be provisional; for another, such obvious sites as Frankfurt were too deeply tainted with the immediate past; Munich was too Bavarian, and other big cities had too much left-wing proletariat. Adenauer wanted to be in a peasant neighbourhood on the conservative, Catholic Rhine.[1]

Bonn has grown a good deal since 1949, but it isn't what one would call a metropolis. The population today has been swollen by the government machine, and numbers 138,000, although many legislators refuse to live in it and simply hire a room during parliamentary sessions. The parliament (*Bundehaus*) was built out of a teachers' training college, and the new ministry of agriculture, appropriately enough, lies out in the moist fields surrounded by olive-green cabbage patches. Other government buildings are still makeshift. One recent visitor asked if there was any night life in Bonn. Reply: 'Yes, but she's gone to Cologne for the week-end.'

One pleasant thing about Bonn is its informality; officials are not only friendly, but, as in most small towns in non-Latin Europe, extremely accessible. Nobody stands on ceremony, even though this is the seat of government, and you can get practically anybody on the telephone. (No government car, incidentally, is allowed to wait for more than ten minutes when delivering a guest to a destination; to wait longer would tie up too many cars; economy and simplicity are watchwords.) Two

---

[1] *Germany*, by Joseph Rovan, Vista Books, p. 73.

other experiences remain with me. I looked at an item on the wine card of a Bonn restaurant; a wine was listed (Johannisberger Kochsberg, Trockenbeeren Auslese, 1937), priced at 240 marks (£21) a bottle; this, I believe, is the most expensive wine I have ever encountered in my life. Then in the washroom of a chic hotel I saw a plumbing fixture the like of which I have never seen before (or since): it was a kind of marble trough in the shape of a hopper, set into the wall waist high, with handles to grip and a gadget that turned on a shower. The attendant saw that I was puzzled, and told me what it was—an apparatus for gentlemen who dined too well to vomit into.

WHO RUNS THE FEDERAL REPUBLIC?

1. Adenauer and the Christian Democrat Union (CDU), which, with its associates, has 271 seats out of 497 in the Bundestag. The Social Democrats (SPD), the only important opposition party, have 169.

2. The great Rhineland-Ruhr industrialists. They support the CDU heavily, and have a massive lobby in the Bundestag; roughly seventy deputies are supposed to be direct representatives of big industry. It should not, however, be thought that the Chancellor is under the thumb of the industrialists. They are in his pocket more than the reverse. Nobody in Germany tells Adenauer what to do, not even Alfried Krupp. Some of the very biggest Ruhr magnates lean over backwards, as a matter of fact, to avoid intermingling at all with politics; they do not have too good a name in the Germany of today (many supported Hitler), and they know that if they become too conspicuous publicly they will have the Social Democrats snapping at their heels.

3. The *Länder*, or states which comprise the Federal Republic. There are ten of these, which are represented in the upper house of parliament or Bundesrat. Like American states they have a considerable local pride and identity as well as influence, and are autonomous in respect to a good many functions, for instance education. Three *Länder* have Social Democratic governments at present. Legend has it that the states were given so much power when Western Germany was set up for two reasons: first, the French thought at the time that an emphasis

on states' rights would reduce the strength of the central government, and they wanted a weak Germany; the second, not to be taken seriously, is that General Lucius Clay, who played a large role in this evolution, is a Southerner, and so naturally took a states' rights line. It is important to mention in connection with the *Länder* that Prussia, which dominated Germany for two hundred years, has been broken up. It no longer exists even as a place-name on the maps.

4. Both the churches—Catholic and Evangelical (Protestant). Sometimes people assume that because Adenauer is a Catholic the CDU is exclusively a Catholic party, like the Christian Democrats in Italy; this is not true. When *Der Alte* created the party he deliberately chose *not* to follow the example of the old purely Catholic Zentrum; instead he played hard for Protestant support as well. He knew that he had to have Protestant backing, for the obvious reason that Protestants comprise 51·1 per cent of the nation. Bremen, Hamburg, Schleswig-Holstein, Lower Saxony, and parts of Hesse and Northern Westphalia are all strongly Protestant. Today—an interesting phenomenon—an effort is made in high government circles to keep a close balance between Catholics and Protestants; if Mr. A. in a certain ministry is Catholic, then Mr. B., the next in line, must be Protestant, Mr. C. Catholic again, Mr. D. Protestant again, and so on down to the bottom. One tradition is supposed to be that the President of the Republic and the Chancellor shall always be of different religions, and this was true as long as Dr. Theodor Heuss, a Protestant, was President. His successor, Dr. Heinrich Luebke, is however a Catholic—he got the job in an emergency and in very special circumstances in 1959—and so, at the moment, both President and Chancellor are Catholic, but Dr. Luebke's term expires in 1964.

5. The trade unions, which present a mixed picture, and the agricultural vote, which is predominantly conservative. Farmers number about 12 per cent of the population of West Germany.

6. 'Senior citizens'—that is, the pensioned class together with hundreds of thousands of others who are 'beneficiaries of social security'. Most of these are zealous to protect their considerable rights and emoluments.

We should also have a word about the Press, which is exceptionally virile and, on the whole, a strong force for perpetuation of new democratic principles. West Germany has more than seven thousand publications (total circulation around 52·5 million), of which no fewer than fifteen hundred are newspapers.

★

It is, however, far from easy to list, much less appraise, all the forces at work in contemporary Germany. Nobody should be categorical. A chief reason for this is the astounding fact that approximately one out of every four West Germans is either a refugee or an 'escapee', and many of the recent arrivals are unassimilated. Of the total population of 53 million about thirteen million did not even live in West Germany before the war. Some, the 'escapees', were forced out of those territories, once German, which lie east of the Oder-Neisse line and which were annexed by the Russians and Poles (East Prussia, western Poland, Silesia, and so on) at the conclusion of the war; the indigenous German populations were weeded out to the last man and forcibly expelled. The others are the copious stream of refugees fleeing from the Communist régime in East Germany today, about whom more later. Obviously, the Federal Republic, with no fewer than thirteen million new citizens, is in a state of flux, of physical as well as emotional commotion, of unpredictably volatile development. Today's West Germany is a new country—and a frontier country at that.

CHAPTER III

Pressures in the Federal Republic

ON the face of it, Germany has changed more in the past quarter-century than any European country. Glance at a map of the vastly swollen Reich in Hitler's heyday; measure the shrinkage. Hitler's domain at its zenith extended from the Arctic tip of Norway to the Pyrenees, from the gates of Moscow and of Cairo to the Caucasus. The Nazi armies were, happily, eaten up or flung back, and today Austria is free, the Sudetenland has gone back to Czechoslovakia, and large territories have been lost in the east. Moreover, the German nation has suffered the dire, drastic fate of partition; there are two Germanys (or three, if you count the eastern areas now incorporated into Poland and the USSR). On other levels details may be cited in considerable number, like the disappearance of Prussia, which has, as it were, moved east. But, all this being granted, serious questions remain. Has Germany, the Germany of Adenauer and the West, *really* changed? Can any country *really* change? An answer might be: Yes—if the shock is severe enough. Certainly (as an example) Russia today is, to put it mildly, not the Russia of the Czars.

Everywhere I went in Germany I asked a series of associated questions. Do the Germans still venerate authority, and is the new democracy going to stick? What does the average German think of Hitler today? Is there any possibility of a Nazi revival? How nationalist is the new Germany? Is it conceivable that the Germans could make another war? All this adds up, of course, to the same general question—have the German people learned their lesson? Are they still incorrigibly aggressive, militant, and expansionist? Or has the catastrophe of World War II finally reformed and tamed them?

These are difficult questions, but I will do my best to give a fair summary of the answers I received.

DIVISIONS OF GERMANY

Formerly German

Hamburg

WEST GERMANY

Bonn★

Stettin

Berlin★

EAST GERMANY

Neisse R.

Oder R.

Danzig

Lithuania

East Prussia ★

★ Warsaw

POLAND

● Cracow

U.S.S.R.

Polish boundary 1939

● Lvov

CZECHOSLOVAKIA

SWITZER-LAND

AUSTRIA

HUNGARY

RUMANIA

0   100   200 mi.

Do the Germans still venerate authority? Yes. Chancellor Adenauer is something of an absolutist by temperament, and most Germans, with their innate respect for leadership and authority, admire him for this. On the other hand, as goes without saying, he is not remotely a dictator in the constitutional sense, much less a Hitler in personality. Moreover, a powerful and vigilant opposition, firmly committed to democratic principles and procedures, watches his every skip and jump. Whether democracy is going to hold on permanently in Germany depends to an extent on economic factors. Should the present boom, with all its sizzle and sparkle, collapse and a severe depression set in, almost anything might happen. So far—luckily—democracy and economic well-being have marched hand in hand.

One thing that killed the Weimar Republic, along with early economic difficulties and inflation, was the multiplicity of

2

splinter parties, which were a *reductio ad absurdum* of democracy; another was the abuse of presidential power. Today neither of these circumstances exists. West Germany has a healthy two-party system (the only two-party system in any important European country except England), and the president is a figurehead. Adenauer's CDU (Christian Democratic Union) polls roughly 50 per cent of the vote together with its Bavarian affiliate, the CSU; the Social Democrats (SPD) about 35 per cent. In other words, two very large, cohesive, and well-organized parties hold more than four-fifths of the voters of the nation. The two other parties represented in the Bundestag are minor—the Free Democrats (FDP) with forty-two seats, under a brilliant parliamentarian named Erich Mende, and the German Party (DP), a former partner in the Adenauer coalition which has now disintegrated. A complex organization with a stormy history, the Refugee party (BHE), sometimes known as the Bloc of Expellees and Victims of Injustice, got 5·9 per cent of the votes in 1957, but failed to win representation in the legislature. Similarly not represented is an extreme right-wing and semi-Nazi party, the German Reich party (DRP), which got less than 1 per cent of the total vote in 1957. The Communists got 2·2 per cent of the vote in 1953, but did not stand in 1957, having been outlawed as unconstitutional.

In a word, German citizens today have no political choice except among democratically constituted parties.

What does the average German think of Hitler? The majority, if I have gauged opinion correctly, thinks that he was a criminal or a lunatic or both; others avoid the question, and try not to answer it. Also there are some who, even if they won't admit it, approve of such Hitler feats as getting the French out of the Rhineland, repudiating the disarmament provisions of the Treaty of Versailles, and, on a different level, building the *Autobahns*; and there are no doubt others who would not condemn him today *if* he had won the war. He is resented not merely for the atrocious evil he did, but because he was a failure, a catastrophe. People say that he 'lost control'.

Age counts in this question. Citizens who were in their thirties and forties in 1933, when Hitler came to power, are twenty-eight years older today, and obviously comprise a generation that is going out. Hundreds of thousands of them had jobs under the

Nazis, whether they were ever actual Nazi party members or not; many still hold these jobs—as judges, bureaucrats, and so on, although the denazification process is supposed to have cleared out all those who were really malignant. But as recently as April, 1960, Professor Theodor Oberlaender, Minister of Refugees in the Adenauer cabinet, was forced to resign because of the accusation that, as a high Nazi official, he had been guilty of superintending a massacre of Russians, Poles, and Jews, in Lvov in 1941. After a prolonged investigation, initiated by the Adenauer régime to clear his name, he was declared innocent but has not as yet been received back into the government. At least one other conspicuous member of the present Adenauer cabinet was an important Nazi. But, to repeat, surviving Nazis represent a dying generation.

More significant, the youth of the country—those who were children during Hitler's years of power, or were not yet born, in other words the voters who will count most in the years to come—seem to be profoundly anti-Nazi. Present-day youngsters have, on occasion, been shown films of Nazi atrocities, and invited to listen to recordings of Hitler's ranting speeches in the Sportspalast. The films leave them horror-struck and incredulous; the speeches make them laugh. They can scarcely believe their ears.[1]

In school books, government pamphlets, state documents, and so on, the Hitler period is sloughed over. Sentences in official histories skip over measureless abominations, like the gassing of hundreds of thousands of innocent children, with phrases like 'A National Socialist rule of violence began when Adolf Hitler became Chancellor in 1933.' As a result many youngsters have had a hard time getting facts straight. If they asked their teachers what *they* did about Hitler, the teachers, if they were old enough to have held their jobs under the Nazis (and there are thousands of these), found it awkward to make any satisfactory reply. So, in general, they tended to ask their pupils to go to their parents for enlightenment, and the parents,

[1] In November, 1960, the government set out to educate citizens, particularly the youth, about the evils of the Third Reich by means of a series of twenty-six TV programmes which were based on film clips of Hitler in action. An audience ranging from eight to fifteen million is anticipated. New York *Herald Tribune*, November 2, 1960.

embarrassed too, often evaded direct replies. 'Were you a Nazi, father?' is not a particularly pleasant question to have to answer at the dinner table.

To recapitulate: Some Germans feel an acute, genuine sense of guilt and shame about Hitler, but others plead ignorance. I know a young man who lived within twenty miles of the extermination camp at Auschwitz when he was in his teens; he swears that he never knew it existed. Dr. Carlo Schmid, one of the best-known Social Democrat leaders today, who held an important administrative job for the *Wehrmacht* in occupied Belgium during the war and who is an enlightened man, told me that he had 'heard' of the Nazi concentration camps, but assumed that the total prison population was never more than about twenty thousand. When at last he learned details of what went on at Dachau and Buchenwald his thought was 'The Russians could do things like this, but not us.'

Is there any possibility of a Nazi revival? Very little. A period of reaction may come to Germany, but it would not be likely to take on overt Hitlerite form.

Fascism, by conventional definitions, comes to a country as the result of an interplay of several conditions: impoverishment of the middle class; inflation; weakness in the democratic structure; humiliation caused by military defeat; extreme nationalism; the rise of a strong demagogue; and fear of imminent Communism. The Reich was certainly defeated in 1945 and fear of both Russia and Communism are widespread today, but the other circumstances do not apply. On the other hand, the division of Germany into two segments is a constant irritant, and this could be an issue on which some future nationalist demagogue might easily wax fat, if unification is indefinitely postponed.

What, one may ask, about recent outrages against the surviving Jews in West Germany, swastika scribbling, offences against synagogues, and the like?[1] Such offences are, of course, odious and regrettable, but every responsible German I met insisted that they were the work of hooligans, and had little, if any, political significance. Swastikas have been smeared recently on synagogues in New York City, but nobody would say that

---

[1] Only about thirty thousand Jews live in West Germany today, less than one per cent of the population. The Jewish population in Germany in 1931 was 564,379.

this means that Fascism is on the rise in the United States. One interesting phenomenon is the Anne Frank cult. The play based on Anne Frank's tragic life and death has been a smash hit in the Federal Republic; young people in particular swarmed to see it, and were devastated by grief, shame, and the peculiar kind of masochism that seems to be fixed in Teutonic character. Similarly, a Swedish movie called *Mein Kampf*, which gives a full and horrifying record of Nazi atrocities, has been a sensational success. Of course, the Germans have always been a folk fascinated by their own past, even when trying to turn over a new leaf. William Bolitho once wrote that the typical German lives permanently in a state of neurotic siege.

How nationalist is the new Germany? Could it possibly make a new war? This, at last, is a question that one can answer with some assurance. *Nobody* in Germany, except possibly a few lunatics on the extreme right, wants a war. The last cost them too much. The country lost seven *million* dead. Moreover, the fact that they were beaten by the Russians as well as by the Western Allies, and suffered horrible losses *in Russia*, is peculiarly relevant. Wars lost in a Russian winter are not nice wars to remember. Then, too, Germans do, after all, live in the modern world and realize, even as do Britons, Russians, and Americans, that this is the missile age, and that a nuclear war might well end civilization. No country ever took such a beating —with conventional weapons—from the air as did Germany in World War II. Just look at Berlin, even today. Then consider that *one* hydrogen bomb carries as much destructive power as the entire bomb load dropped on Germany during the whole of World War II. The German citizenry is educated and well informed; such ominous facts are kept in mind.

Rearmament of the Federal Republic, after fierce international dispute, is a fact, yes, but the bill to create a West German army passed parliament only after a bitter struggle, and by a comparatively narrow margin against strenuous Social Democratic opposition. Militarism is not popular. Most youngsters seem to have little national sense, and some are almost defiantly pacifist. Most undergo their military service (which is limited to a year) grudgingly, and it has been impossible to build up an effective air force so far because so few young men are willing to volunteer to be pilots.

One reservation must, however, be made about all this. Certainly nobody in Germany has any territorial designs to the north, west, or south; aggression against Belgium or France or an attempt to regain the Sudetenland by force or to conquer Austria is almost unthinkable. The east is, however, a different story. Even so, it is unlikely in the extreme that West Germany would ever attempt to achieve unification by military conquest, if only because this would certainly induce Soviet intervention, and provoke a major war.

A final point is that, in theory, the Federal Republic officially considers that the territories east of the Oder-Neisse line, which are now incorporated into Poland and the USSR, are still a part of Germany.[1] German maps always assert that this lost area is 'Germany', with the explanation that it is merely under Polish and Russian 'administration' for the moment. Theoretically, a drive by West Germany to regain the imprisoned east beyond East Germany is possible; in practice it is out of the question, because East Germany would have to be conquered first. Authorities in Bonn will not say so publicly, but the Oder-Neisse line is no longer a vital issue, and this marks a salient change since 1945. In effect, the eastern provinces, which are now denuded of their Germans, have been given up for lost.

AMONG LEADERS

Of the men under Adenauer I met several; the most interesting, I thought, was Dr. Ludwig Erhard, the Vice-Chancellor and Minister of Economics who is the author of the *Wirtschafts-wunder* (economic miracle, i.e. German recovery). He is a very large, energetic man with a face almost the colour and, it seems, the size of a harvest moon; his tiny mouth looks like a hole drilled into a pumpkin. He is sixty-one. Dr. Erhard likes to eat and drink, is a vigorous conversationalist, and chain-smokes cigars in paper holders. During a conference, one of his secretaries supplies and lights these one by one. Although his background is Bavarian, Erhard is a Protestant. I asked him how he happened to get into politics. He replied cheerfully that an American jeep drove up to his apartment in Munich one

[1] So does the United States, which has never recognized the Oder-Neisse frontier.

morning in 1945, and without explanation carried him away. Dr. Erhard was a professor of economics, and thought that, for some mysterious reason, he was being arrested. No. The Americans had heard that he was one of the few economic specialists in the country who bore no taint of Nazism, and were carting him off to be a member of the new Bavarian government they were setting up.

Erhard is an old-fashioned free-trader in economic approach, and a passionately devoted believer in *laissez faire*. What he seeks to build up in West Germany is 'a socially minded free-market economy'. As things stand at the moment, he is the chief contender for succession to the chancellorship if Dr. Adenauer retires, as was mentioned in the preceding chapter, although quarrels between the two are frequent. For a long time the *Alte Herr's* choice as crown prince was not Erhard, but the Minister of Finance, Franz Etzel, because the latter is supposed to be more 'Europe-minded' than Erhard, and thus more to the Chancellor's international taste. But Etzel cannot even begin to rival Erhard as a vote getter, and has pretty much passed out of the picture. So has another man often mentioned, the able Ernst Lemmer, Minister for All-German Affairs.

What caused the economic miracle which Erhard has so brilliantly brought to pass? (1) Germans are a notoriously industrious people; they work hard, and are thrifty. Despair ruled the nation in 1946; hard work was not merely something expected of every citizen, but salvation—a way out of a stultifying blind alley. (2) Much of the pre-war German industrial plant was destroyed by Allied bombing, or dismantled by the French and British after the war; hence most German factories are comparatively new, built from scratch, and highly modern and efficient. (3) Marshall Plan aid poured roughly three billion dollars into the country. (4) The massive stream of refugees from East Germany and expellees from beyond the Oder-Neisse provided an almost inexhaustible labour market. Even today unemployment scarcely exists; in fact, labour shortage is acute. (5) Until comparatively recently Germany was disarmed and, like Japan, did not have to allocate a large percentage of its budget to armament.

*

Franz-Josef Strauss, the Minister of Defence, is a Bavarian, the son of a butcher, who was born in Munich in 1915. His wife is a brewer's daughter. Like Erhard, he is a large rotund man, and it has been said of him by his enemies that he is the only light-weight in Germany who weighs two hundred pounds. His record is by no means light, however. It was he who built up the new German army from nothing, and who has the responsibility for its co-operation with the American and other NATO forces on German soil.[1] Also Strauss made a fine rumpus by launching the idea, now quashed, that the Bundeswehr should establish bases and supply depots in Spain, largely because of shortage of space in the Federal Republic. Much controversy attends his person. Adenauer likes Strauss, but is inclined to think that he is too youthful for the succession at present, too rowdy, and too much wedded to Bavarian support.

If I were asked to sum up Mr. Strauss I would say that he is good-humoured, a realist, not taken in by pretension, clever, and ambitious. His face is bland, but he has a chin like a little round rock, and penetrating, widely set bright blue eyes. His devotion to the Chancellor is extreme, and he talks with reverence about what he has 'taught' the German people. Strauss genuinely feels that all countries, if they are to survive, must renounce the idea of exclusively national armies, and his major preoccupation is to put in order the German contribution to NATO, as well as to make the new German army an expert and efficient fighting force. One thing he is intensely proud of is that German detachments, in full uniform, conducted elaborate manœuvres recently on French soil, without untoward incident, and that Germany is to have bases for the new *Luftwaffe* in both France (on Corsica) and Italy (Sardinia).

ON THE SOCIALIST SIDE

One of the great men of modern Germany, the socialist leader Dr. Kurt Schumacher, died in August, 1952, and no one has risen to replace him except Willy Brandt, the celebrated *Oberburgomeister* of West Berlin, whom we will meet in the chapter following. Technically the leader of the Social Demo-cratic party today (on an all-West German basis) is Erich

[1] For Germany and NATO, see Chapter XVIII below.

Ollenhauer, a colourless personality who succeeded to Schumacher through seniority. But Ollenhauer has announced that he will not stand for Chancellor in the forthcoming federal elections, and Brandt is running instead. The Social Democrats have not been in power since the government of Hermann Müller in 1930.

Dr. Carlo Schmid, an engaging personality, is leader of the right wing of the party—and Number Two to Brandt. Though a socialist, he is about as Marxist as the Archbishop of York. Schmid is half-French, having been born in Perpignan of a French mother; his father was a German professor who was teaching there, and Schmid himself was a teacher for many years; in fact, he still maintains his classes in political science at Frankfurt. Schmid is sophisticated, cheerful, witty, and a resounding orator. Physically he is another stout man, a two-hundred-pounder like his political opponents Erhard and Strauss. If the socialists win he will presumably become Foreign Minister. I asked him how he had happened to enter public life; he answered that he was, so to speak, 'doing penance for Hitler'. Who, he asked himself after the war, was responsible for Hitler's rise? Not the great mass of citizens who hardly understood what *Mein Kampf* meant. The responsibility, he decided, belonged to those who *had* understood, but had not dared to oppose Hitler even so. So Dr. Schmid joined the Social Democrats to make amends, and since the war has sought to devote himself to the public good.

Another Social Democrat of consequence, who stands more or less on the centre, is a Bavarian aristocrat, Baron Waldemar von Knoeringen; on the left is Herbert Wehner, deputy chairman of the party, an ex-Communist who hates Communists today as only former Communists can. He was the son of a cobbler, lived some time in the USSR, as did many youthful German Communists, and subsequently worked in the anti-Nazi underground. Still another socialist leader is Fritz Erler, a former schoolmaster in his middle forties, who, if his party ever comes to power, will be Minister of Defence. He is able and attractive, and a man to watch.

The preponderant problem of the Social Democrats is, naturally, to devise means to increase their vote beyond the 35 per cent they now have. But this is no easy task; if the party

2*

goes further to the left, it will inevitably alienate middle-of-the road citizens whose adherence it must gain, but if it goes to the right it runs the danger of becoming almost indistinguishable from the Adenauer conservatives. One difficulty is that economic recovery under a *laissez faire* system took much wind out of socialist sails. The party is trying to cast off relics of Marxism, but has to do so slowly, because of its deeply entrenched leftist tradition. However, it discarded its long-held aim of nationalizing industry at the 1959 party congress, and went further towards a centre position in 1960. The present accent is, like that of Mr. Gaitskell's wing of the British Labour party, towards recognizing the necessity of change and the adoption of some system in which socialization and free enterprise are mixed. Also at the 1960 congress, held at Hanover in November, the German Social Democrats modified their traditional pacifist position. They do not want the German Army to have atomic weapons (a big issue), but pledged loyalty to NATO and the Western Alliance.

UNIFICATION PRO AND CON

The greatest issue in Germany is, of course, unification, that is the consolidation of West and East Germany into a single state. The present division of Germany with 53 million Germans in the west and 17 million in the east, separated by 825 miles of barbed-wire frontier straight across the belly of the country, is not merely a geographical and political outrage, an indecency, but something which far transcends the conventional evils of partition. What is at stake is, in effect, the right of seventeen million submerged East Germans to rejoin not merely their country, but the civilized world. Moreover, unification would end the insane anomaly by which the real capital of the country, Berlin, is not only partitioned itself, but lies in the Eastern Zone 110 miles behind the frontier, a beleaguered island totally surrounded by a sea of Communism. Consider what Americans would think if the United States were partitioned as Germany is, with one-quarter of the country—say, the Atlantic seaboard and part of the Middle West—firmly in Communist hands, controlled by Moscow, and with Washington, a city divided into non-Communist and Communist sectors, separated from Denver or Omaha by a belt of Soviet territory impossible to traverse except under severe restrictions.

A few years ago a public opinion poll in West Germany asked citizens what the paramount problem of the nation was. Forty-five per cent answered reconstruction; 15 per cent said unification. But now, with reconstruction accomplished, the figures have been reversed. Everywhere I went in Germany I saw men and women wearing a small metal badge in their buttonholes—a replica of the Brandenburger Tor in Berlin. This signifies membership in Unteilbares Deutschland—'Indivisible Germany'—an organization which crosses conventional political lines and is the largest, most consequential pressure group in the country. Hundreds of thousands of West Germans still have relatives in East Germany, and these are an important sector of its membership.

All this being said, it should also be said that, as I heard it put, unification, although a grave issue, does not seem to be a very *live* issue. Citizens pay lip service to it, but do little else. The general attitude is that unification must, of course, come in time, and so why not wait and hope for the best and assume that somehow, at some future undetermined date, the present absurd situation will end of itself?

But if you ask any West German politician, anybody at all, if it is correct to say that the Adenauer régime has become luke-warm on unification he will answer hotly, '*Falsch!*' (False.) I heard this innumerable times. The federal government considers itself to be the authorized caretaker of *all* Germans, particularly those in exile, almost—a peculiar analogy which several Germans expressed to me—as the Israeli government considers itself to be the caretaker of all Jews. But, in plain fact, there are many German citizens who, even if they do not dare to oppose unification openly, ask persistently what it will cost. For one thing everybody knows that the Russians would fight if West Germany attempted to absorb the east by force, and nobody wants a war. Then consider the fact that the Rhineland and Bavarian Catholics know that unification would drastically alter the religious balance of power in the nation, since East Germany is 81·3 per cent Protestant. Then, too, conservatives generally and the Ruhr industrialists in particular do not relish the idea of incorporating into West Germany seventeen million people who, even if most of them detest the Communist régime, have had fifteen years of socialist indoctrination, and who for the most part would probably take a strong left-wing position in a united Germany. Finally, to unify Germany will, for a period at least, be bound to lower the living standard of the West; unification will cost money, a lot of money, and may upset the *Wirtschaftswunder*.

Also, situated as they are in the heart of Europe, the Germans must take careful account of foreign attitudes. A reunified Germany might seriously interrupt West Germany's integration with western Europe, which most citizens would deplore. Today's Germans do not want to offend either the British or the French, and they know that the British in particular fear that a united Germany, seventy million strong, would be a formidable rival in the realm of trade. Nor do the French want to see seventy million Germans united as a military power. Moreover —just conceivably—a unified Germany with a strong leftist tinge might become an ally of the Soviet Union.

Within Germany itself, unification is still the principal issue between the parties. The Social Democrats favour it strongly for the same reason that some Adenauer conservatives tend to be cautious about it, namely, that it will change the religious pattern of the country in favour of the Protestants, increase substantially the power of the left, and perhaps serve to make the country socialist.

Meantime in both West and East Germany a new generation is growing up, and gradually the two German states are becoming more fixed as separate entities. To hundreds of thousands of young people in West Germany, the East is already a foreign country. At the same time, Communist power in the East holds the people down more firmly year by year, and does its best to break off liaison with the West. It is altogether possible, many percipient Germans think, that before long the question of unification may become almost as unreal as recovery of the provinces beyond the Oder-Neisse line; that, in a word, the present *status quo* is going to last. The western world must adjust itself to the fact that there will probably be two Germanys for a substantial period of time, tragic as this may be for millions of suppressed East Germans. This is the chief price the Germans are paying today for having started—and lost—World

War II. Partition is what Hitler cost them, and they will be paying this miserable tribute to him for a long time to come.

TWO QUESTIONS OFTEN ASKED

Why does not the United States make a peace treaty with the Federal Republic? That, technically, there is still no such treaty, although diplomatic relations have been normal since 1951, seems absurd. The chief reason is, obviously, that Germany is divided, and such an instrument, signed today, would fix the *status quo* officially, and make it impossible for the Germans to proceed towards unification. One consequence of this is that West Germany is not yet a member of the United Nations. It is a fully independent sovereign state, and as such has joined NATO, the Council of Europe, Western European Union, the European Coal and Steel Community, the International Monetary Fund, Euratom, the Common Market, and UNESCO, but it is still, idiotically enough, excluded from Mr. Hammarskjöld's UN. Countries like El Salvador, Mali, and Gabon are members of the UN, but not West Germany.

Why, inasmuch as the United States has recognized such Soviet satellites as Poland, Rumania, Czechoslovakia, Bulgaria, and so on, do we withhold recognition from East Germany? The answer is the same: to recognize the Communist régime would mean that we concede that it exists, which, technically, we do not, and would probably end all hope of the unification of Germany in the foreseeable future. United States policy is still based on the ultimate goal of a united Germany, but on terms which we know full well that the Communists will not accept.

CHAPTER IV

Berlin—Outpost and Pivot

WE—my wife and I—flew into Berlin from Frankfurt on a sleek
Pan American airliner over Communist territory for 110 miles
along one of the three carefully controlled air channels that give
the western world aerial access to the city. The trip is about as
adventurous these days as one from Milwaukee to Detroit. The
last time we made this journey the circumstances were quite
different—we flew in a stripped DC-4, sitting on fourteen
thousand pounds of coal, during the airlift in 1948.

Berlin itself is, to understate the case, also a long cry from the
Berlin of twelve years ago. Here, as in the Ruhr, the German
Wirtschaftswunder reaches climax. Berlin, which is still the
biggest industrial city in Germany, throbs, hums, and glistens.
The last time I strolled down the Kurfürstendamm it had the
vitality of a lump of putty; hungry people stood in line for
spoonfuls of naked corned beef out of a can; you could buy a
girl for a cigarette. But today the fashionable area of Berlin has
chic shops magnificently filled with merchandise from the ends
of the earth; restaurants and cafés are brilliantly ornate, and it
is a rare taxi which is not a Mercedes-Benz.

Nevertheless, plenty of traces of war, demolition, and
devastation are still sharply visible; Berlin was 60 per cent
destroyed by Allied bombing, and it has not by any means been
wholly rebuilt. Piles of sand-coloured rubble look like the long
rolling dunes, made out of debris from the mines, in Johannesburg. In the short drive from Tempelhof, the Berlin airport,
to our hotel we must have seen twenty gutted buildings. The
wreck of the old Hotel Eden, the haunt of pre-war movie stars,
still squats like a metal skeleton across the street from the shiny
new Berlin Hilton. The sombre ruin of the Kaiser Wilhelm
Memorial Church stabs bluntly into the sky at the top of

Kurfürstendamm; it looks like the stub of a broken tooth, and indeed the Berliners call it 'the unfilled molar'.

Ten minutes in Berlin will tell you why most Germans react with revulsion and fear to the thought of another war. The city has not yet cast off the shroud of the last one. Every third Berliner lost his home. Indeed, a proposal to rebuild and restore the Memorial Church was beaten down by the citizens; they want this gaunt horror to remain as it is in perpetuity—a monument to suffering, and a daily reminder of the corrosive ordeal Berlin went through.

As everybody knows, Berlin is a divided city. There are 2·2

million people in the western sector, and slightly over a million in the eastern. Before the war, the population was 4·5 million. The western sector covers 185 square miles; the eastern 155. The total area is three and a half times that of Washington, D.C.; this is a city with girth. The west is still divided into British, French, and American sectors (the American sector, eighty-one square miles in area, is bigger than Paris), but the frontiers between these no longer have the slightest significance; you can pass from one to another without knowing it. The Inter-Allied Governing Authority (Kommandatura) still exists, because the city is still, in theory, ruled by the so-called Berlin Declaration of the four victorious powers (US, USSR, Britain, and France) on June 5, 1945, but in actual fact West Berlin, composed of the American, British, and French sectors, and East Berlin, comprising the Russian sector, both have their own sharply different and separately functioning governments. Incidentally, West Berlin is not, technically speaking, part of West Germany, although it is completely integrated with it in economic affairs, currency, and so on; but East Berlin has been annexed to East Germany. Its leadership is sometimes called the 'Pankow' government, since the chief ministers live in a borough of East Berlin called Pankow.

West Berlin sends twenty-two deputies to Bonn, who can speak in the Bundestag but who have no vote, and the federal (Bonn) government maintains no fewer than fifty-four agencies in Berlin; it has more employees here than in Bonn itself, and Bonn helps support Berlin to the tune of not less than $500 million a year. But West Berlin is not *in* Western Germany, geographically or otherwise.

Of the original four-power government only four traces remain. (1) Spandau prison, where three celebrated Nazi war criminals are still incarcerated—Rudolf Hess, Baldur von Shirach, and Albert Speer. The guard changes among the 'occupying' powers once a month. Spandau is expensive to maintain, but the Russians don't want to give it up. (2) The Allied Air Safety Centre, which co-ordinates traffic in the three twenty-three-mile-wide air corridors leading into Berlin from the west. (3) An inter-zonal accounting office. (4) An inter-zonal travel office.

One curiosity is that Berlin is the only city in Germany where both the Communist party (the East German SED) and the Social Democrats (the West German SPD) vote. In the last election (1958) the Communists got only 1·9 per cent of the poll, a drop from 19 per cent in 1946. The socialists, under Willy Brandt, rule Berlin by a coalition, which suits their ends, although they have a clear majority (78 to 55) in the city council. The opposition consists of Adenauer conservatives, and the deputy mayor, who is the actual executive officer of the government, is a CDU man, Franz Amrehn.

The Allies maintain about eleven thousand troops in West Berlin—5,000 American, 3,500 French, 2,500 British. The Russians assert that they have no troops at all in East Berlin, but there are no fewer than twenty-two Russian divisions stationed next door in East *Germany*. (Of course NATO troops, largely American and British, are stationed in West Germany, but these are separated from West Berlin by a solid belt of Communist territory, whereas East Germany and East Berlin, under the Pankow government, are co-terminous and hence Russian troops in East Germany have instant access to East Berlin.)

Berlin is a divided city, yes—the most monstrous of aberrations. What would London be like if Westminster, let us say, were cut off from Chelsea by a barrier which was a line of demarcation between two utterly different and fiercely hostile concepts of government, society, and human values? In Berlin it is even impossible (except for certain official calls on the highest level) to telephone from the western sector to the eastern, or vice versa. A call between people a mile apart has to be routed via Frankfurt and Leipzig, over more than a thousand miles of wire. Even the water supplies are separate.

But although Berlin is a divided city, it is not altogether divided—an important qualification. Three municipal services are city-wide, serving both west and east. First, the sewer system, which is operated by the east; the west pays 100,000 marks ($25,000) a year for its share of the cost of maintaining it. Second, the S-Bahn or elevated railway, which is also run by the east. Third, the U-Bahn or subway, which is run by the west, although 140 cars are eastern-owned; for the use of these the west pays the east an annual fee. The S-Bahn and U-Bahn are crucial to the present situation. Buses and tram-cars stop at the frontier, and a passenger must change to a different vehicle, but traffic on the elevated and subway lines is (in normal circumstances) uninterrupted.[1] As a result, citizens can cross from west to east or vice versa practically without interruption or impediment, although occasional spot checks by eastern traffic police take place on the S-Bahn. Now, extraordinary as it may seem, there are about forty thousand Berliners who live in the east but work in the west, and who go back and forth every day; conversely, about seven thousand Berliners live in the west but work in the east. So almost fifty thousand citizens cross the line as a matter of course twice daily. One odd point is that two of the twenty-two West Berlin deputies to Bonn, including one member of the Adenauer government (Ernst Lemmer), live in the east; so do six members of the West Berlin government. The reason is simple enough: they lived in the eastern sector of the city or had property there long before partition, and do not want to move.[2]

Traffic exists on other levels too. The East German theatre is very good—also cheap; thousands of West Berliners cross every week to see a show or go to the opera, travelling mostly by the U-Bahn but sometimes by private car or taxi.[3] Conversely, thousands of East Berliners cross the line from east to west, quite apart from workers whose jobs make the trip necessary, in order to sight-see, go to western cinemas, admire such extravagant manifestations of western architecture as the new apartment blocks in the Hansa quarter, peek warily at the Hollywoodish splendours of the Hilton, and, most interesting of all, make use of the hospitable reading rooms of Amerika Haus. This, operated by the USIA in West Berlin, is the largest American information centre in the world. More than a million

[1] In August, 1960, the East Germans suddenly suspended east-west traffic in Berlin for a limited period—a 'baby blockade'—and then subjected it to new controls. But at the moment of writing the basic position which I am outlining has not been substantially changed.

[2] All the above refers to the eastern sector of *Berlin*, not the Eastern Zone of *Germany*. To proceed beyond East Berlin into East Germany, which it adjoins, is impossible without an East German visa, and these are sometimes difficult to obtain.

[3] When we were there seven theatres were open in East Berlin, offering a repertory which included, amongst much else, twenty-seven different operas, four plays by Shakespeare, and drama ranging from Aristophanes and Schiller to Gorky, Shaw (*Pygmalion*), and Bertholt Brecht. The fare in West Berlin was also good, but scanty by comparison.

Germans visit it a year, including—believe it or not—roughly 400,000 East Germans. One reading room is put aside exclusively for the use of Germans from East Berlin or the Soviet Zone, who use it (mostly to look at western newspapers and periodicals) at the rate of eight to nine hundred a day. They can—and do—attend English classes, go to cinemas (four fifty-five-minute shows a day), and enlist in discussion courses.

Now that financial aid is no longer necessary, the major American effort in Berlin is cultural. One important institution is RIAS (Radio in American Sector). This, founded in 1945-46, is the oldest functioning radio station in Berlin, also the biggest; it has correspondents in thirty-seven different countries, broadcasts twenty-four hours a day, and reaches between six and eight million listeners. As it was put to me, the American troops in Berlin guarantee (we hope) the physical security of the city; RIAS symbolizes freedom of expression and our will to stay. Its principal target is, of course, the Soviet Zone, although it reaches many listeners in West Berlin as well, together with a large number in Poland and Czechoslovakia as well as in friendly countries like Austria and France. But, to repeat, the main effort is to saturate East Germany, including the Soviet sector of Berlin, with American news, views, and entertainment. That this effort is remarkably successful is shown by the noteworthy fact that RIAS gets eighty-five to ninety thousand letters a year from listeners in Communist areas, in spite of censorship. The precision of the RIAS operation is remarkable. For instance it makes a particular point of broadcasting lessons to school-children; it has information about every textbook used in the East German schools and what, in general, the hours of class are—also how long it takes a child to travel home. Then, RIAS shoots forth a lesson designed to amend or counteract what has been taught. What makes this effort doubly interesting is, of course, that it originates in Berlin itself, in the very centre of the Soviet Zone.

All of this, including in particular the copious use of Amerika Haus by Communist East Germans, may seem to be like Alice in Wonderland, but it illuminates one of the most vital factors in the Berlin situation today. This city is the *only* point on the whole frontier between the Soviet world and ours which is, to a degree, open. Berlin is an aperture, an orifice, a slot, a perforation drilled in the curtain, useful not merely for observation, but as an indispensable escape hatch for refugees.

*

The refugee situation is, almost everybody will agree, the most interesting phenomenon in Germany. I am not discussing transients now, Berliners who cross back and forth daily as a matter of routine, but actual refugees. Roughly 3,350,000 residents of the Soviet Zone (East Germany) have fled to the Federal Republic since 1945. (These are not to be confused with the 'expellees', about nine to ten million, whom I have mentioned earlier, and who were ousted from the territories, once German and now Polish or Russian, *beyond* the eastern frontier of East Germany.) The number of refugees who cross over from East Germany to West fluctuates according to events; the count was 204,000 in 1958, 143,000 in 1959. The drop in 1959 was probably caused by a substantial improvement in economic conditions in the Eastern Zone, as a result of which fewer people felt impelled to get out. In 1960 the figure is rising again; about twenty thousand refugees crossed over in May, 1960, which would indicate an annual rate of 240,000.[1] The chief reason for this steep rise is also economic; the East German régime collectivized agriculture this year, and this has caused the bitterest misery, resentment, and despair.

Eighty per cent of East German refugees fleeing to the West come out through Berlin, because escape here is easier than at any other point on the frontier. Officially, the Federal Republic welcomes them one and all, but, in order to weed out possible spies and *agents provocateurs*, a careful screening takes place at the Marienfelde Reception Centre and elsewhere. Once cleared, the refugees are flown out (the only way to get them out) to Hanover, after which they proceed by rail or road to any one of the forty camps which are scattered throughout West Germany; in the end they are assigned to communities, and given jobs and, if possible, housing. The process is expensive and elaborate. Some refugees arrive at Marienfelde with nothing but the clothes on their backs; about half of last year's total were youngsters under twenty-five, some of whom were attempting

[1] *The Times*, June 2, 1960.

to evade *East* German military service. The flights out from Berlin are operated by Air France, British European Airways, and Pan American. (It is a curious item that Lufthansa, the German airline, is not allowed to fly into Berlin.) Pan American alone has fifty-four services into or out of Berlin every day.

Of the refugees over twenty-five many are intellectuals, including teachers, physicians, architects, other professional men. and so on—in fact the *élite* of the nation. One figure I heard on good authority is so remarkable that I can scarcely believe it—80 per cent of the senior staff of the University of Leipzig, formerly one of the great educational institutions of the world, has decamped. Many refugees leave their homes in East Germany with heavy heart. Not only are they giving up the intimate associations of a lifetime but they are depriving their own people, throttled by a Communist régime, of their services. Some communities in East Germany no longer have *any* doctors, dentists, or skilled engineers. Recently a middle-aged physician arrived at Marienfelde. He said, 'I have left four thousand people in my village without medical care. It is a tragedy. But I have had to come out with my family because my eleven-year-old boy is being taught by Communist teachers not to believe in God.'

One bizarre development is that the West German authorities, although they do not reject any legitimate refugee, sometimes deplore the extent of east-west traffic, and have even appealed to East Germans to stay where they are. A leader in this campaign is the Evangelical Church. The reason is not that West Germany is incapable of assimilating more refugees but that responsi ble West Germans, with their eye to future unification, do not want East Germany to be completely denuded of its bourgeois citizens, who still have an emotional kinship to the West. Also, from a humanitarian point of view, the loss to East Germany of doctors, teachers, and so on is viewed with distinct alarm.[1]

Why does the East German government allow such a prodigious leakage of population? Why does it not stop it by sealing the frontier between East *Germany*, where most of the refugees come from, and East *Berlin*? One reason is that this would mean that the Pankow government was barring its

[1] Sydney Gruson in the *New York Times*, December 4, 1960.

citizens from their own capital, a political impossibility. If an East German attempting to flee is caught by the police, he gets three years in jail, and his mother, if he has one, a lesser term; but the families of refugees who *do* get away are not arrested. Ninety-nine per cent of those who try to escape succeed. Once a refugee reaches East Berlin, the rest is (or was) easy. All he has to do is to take the U-Bahn or S-Bahn into the western sector. But why doesn't the East Berlin régime stop traffic on the U-Bahn, or at least police it effectively? Conceivably it could do so, but the procedure would be difficult and expensive and would disrupt the transportation system of the whole city as well as make it impossible for East German workers to move to and fro.

Now another most extraordinary and pressing point. Not only does a huge refugee traffic exist from East Germany to West: a substantial traffic also exists from west to east. Roughly fifty thousand *West* Germans fled to the East in 1959, incredible as this fact may seem; west-east traffic, depending on circumstances, reaches a figure that can be anywhere from a fifth to a third of east-west traffic. Of the fifty thousand in 1959 about two-thirds were what is known as 'redefectors', that is, men and women who had previously fled from East Germany to West but who then decided to return. I have never heard a completely satisfactory explanation for the movement of so many Germans, redefectors or not, from west to east. It is an extremely intricate phenomenon. Of course there are misfits in every society; even with the West German economy booming, some people do not have jobs they like. East Germany offers, in theory, unlimited secure jobs, good educational facilities (within the circumscription of the Communist system), exceptionally good social services, and plenty of economic opportunity; also it pays very high salaries to specialists, technicians, and professional men. Then there are many West Germans, particularly older people, who move for family reasons, or who want to see their old homes again. In any case the fact that fifty thousand Germans move from west to east every year seems to indicate that plenty of Germans do not care much for Adenauer or for political freedom *per se*, and do not value too highly the virtues of democracy—also that economic conditions in East Germany are much better than they were.

WILLY BRANDT AND THE BERLIN DEADLOCK

Willy Brandt, the *Oberburgomeister* or governing Mayor of West Berlin (in effect, prime minister of the West Berlin government), is one of the most attractive men I have ever met in public life. A friendly person, he projects candour and confidence, and is without a trace of humbug, the curse of most professional politicians. I have seldom known a man more satisfactory to interview; he answers questions straight on the nail, without pettifoggery or evasion, and is quick-witted, eloquent, and honest. He stimulates and gives out. To an extent he reminded me of Wendell Willkie, in both his abundant physical magnetism and square-jawed, tousled good looks.

Brandt, who as I have already mentioned is the Social Democrat candidate against the CDU in the 1961 election, stands on the moderate right wing of his party. Roughly his position is that of Giuseppe Saragat in Italy, or, to a degree, of Hugh Gaitskell in Britain. He is not particularly interested in theory; what does interest him is power. Let the SPD gain office; then it will be time to talk about controversial items in socialist theory. Brandt's sources of strength and qualities are several, like his youth (he is only forty-six), tough energy, and vote-getting appeal to the non-socialist middle class. Above all he is the man on the firing line, the man on the spot in Berlin, a city permanently in trouble, and the heart of the most dangerous crisis in the world.

Mayor Brandt was born in Lübeck, and purists in the German language sometimes scoff mildly at his accent, which has a salty Baltic tang (even as they laugh at Adenauer for his soft Rhenish purr). He managed to flee from Germany after the rise of Hitler, and, unlike most of his Social Democrat comrades who escaped to the south or east, went north and headed for Norway: he worked as a journalist, took Norwegian citizenship, joined the Norwegian resistance, and rose to the rank of major; after the war he returned to Berlin (in Norwegian uniform and with a handsome Norwegian wife), resumed German nationality, got a job in the Rathaus, and became a protégé of the late Ernst Reuter, the indomitable pro-western, pro-democratic Mayor of West Berlin during the airlift in 1948.[1] Brandt was never what

[1] Reuter was—interestingly enough—an ex-Communist.

the socialists call a 'Schumacher man', that is, a fanatic nationalist. Probably on most issues in foreign affairs his position does not differ greatly from that of Dr. Adenauer, though neither would like to hear this. He was beaten in his first try for the Berlin mayoralty, and won the second. He speaks excellent English, enjoys many friendships, and lives in a small flat in circumstances of the utmost modesty.

Again I permit myself a trite remark—what an odd, baffling, convoluted, mysteriously perverse people the Germans are! What prompts me to say this is that a principal point of Brandt's opponents in the present electoral campaign is the very fact that he fled to Norway and joined the anti-Nazi resistance there during the war. Today's Germany has, after all, repudiated Hitler. Dr. Adenauer and numerous others, like Dr. Erhard, who were anti-Nazi but who sat out the war in comparative tranquillity, are applauded; yet Herr Brandt, who risked his life in actual combat against the Nazis, is being called a 'traitor'. That he adopted Norwegian citizenship is termed a 'betrayal'. Nothing more odiously unfair can be imagined. Also a smear campaign was launched against Brandt by the CDU on the ground that he was illegitimate, which he has conceded in a perfectly straightforward fashion. His father deserted his mother shortly after he was born, and he changed his name to Willy Brandt many years later.

In an hour with us Mr. Brandt covered a wide range of topics. One of his special interests is education. Nothing is more remarkable in Germany, he thinks, than the profound, almost revolutionary difference between the present generation of youngsters and the last. Thirty years ago the youth of the land was almost insanely nationalist, but not today. Thirty years ago students fought duels; today they ride scooters, drink *espresso*, read paperbacks, and take holidays in France. Herr Brandt would like to see the level of teaching made higher—to get rid of the teachers who are old enough to have been Nazis during the war, and who still feel 'subjective guilt' about Hitler. He does not think that neo-Nazism, either among young or old, plays any role at all in contemporary Germany; in the whole of Berlin he doubts if there are more than two thousand people connected with any extreme rightist movement. Dr. Adenauer's greatest contribution, he considers, is that his government has, so to speak, *absorbed* the surviving Nazis, thus rendering them impotent.

Communism? 'It doesn't command one per cent of the electorate.' Anti-Semitism? 'Maybe we have here in Berlin gangs of hooligans; if a gang has thirty members it is a big gang and half a dozen of the thirty will be spies that we have planted there.' Unification? He smiled shrewdly: 'History does not recognize the word "never".'

About the position of Berlin Mayor Brandt seemed optimistic from a long-range point of view, although there are bound to be harassing incidents. But he does not think that the Russians will dare to impose another formal blockade, if only because 'even Khrushchev must have public relations advisers and to use the weapon of starvation against a city is not a technique that will gain him friends'—he does not want the Soviet Union to be more isolated than it is. However, if a new blockade should come, the Mayor says confidently that Berlin is fully prepared to meet it; no city in the world has such big reserves of coal, oil, food. As to Germany in general, the *Oberburgomeister* puts a certain amount of hope in the possibility of disarmament. The German problem and the security problem are inextricably mixed together. If Russia and the West could ever achieve some modicum of agreement on disarmament, this might reduce the necessity felt by both sides to keep troops on German soil. East Germany? The Communist régime, as of today, would not get 10 per cent of the vote in a free election. But this statement means little, since nobody is going to give the people a free election. As time goes on two contrary forces will gain ground: first, more East German citizens will want the truth, but, second, those who have roots with the past and know what non-Communist life was like will begin to die out.

A good many Germans, Mr. Brandt thinks, still feel torn between East and West. Nowadays young people in particular want to belong to the West, although many do not go quite so far as Chancellor Adenauer; but to some the East is a constant temptation, as well as threat. Citizens feel that they cannot sit for ever between the two forces; they must be on one side or the other. 'The struggle is not between the extremes at each end, but in the middle of the minds of men in the middle.'

*

The gist of the Berlin 'problem' is Soviet intentions. The Pankow régime in East Berlin is a thorn in the flesh of the West; but so is West Berlin a thorn in the flesh of the East. How, as one commentator put it recently, would Dr. Adenauer like it if Frankfurt or Munich were Communist islands in *western* Germany? The reason the deadlock over Berlin is so difficult to break is that both sides have so much at stake. Berlin is a massive prize in itself. Also the Communists cannot possibly consolidate their position satisfactorily in East Germany, which is as vital to Moscow, as, say, the Ukraine, so long as Berlin has a western sector which provides a loophole for the escape of East Germans. As long as West Berlin stands, the whole Communist tenure in Europe is insecure. The Soviet structure is not complete.

On the other side the importance of Berlin to the western world is only too evident. If Berlin falls, West Germany falls; I have even heard it said, 'If we are so weak as to allow ourselves to be dislodged from Berlin, we will lose all of Europe.' Much more is involved than turning over to the tender mercies of the Communists some two and a quarter million free Berliners, shocking a human tragedy as this would be. What is involved is not merely the honour of the United States, Britain, and France, but their security; loss of West Berlin would be an irreparably damaging blow to the whole of the democratic world.

But the dilemma remains—how is Berlin going to be held indefinitely? How can it be defended? How can an immense industrial city, with two and a quarter million people in the western sector, 'be held fast to the West when it is geographically separated from the West', and, in fact, completely surrounded by the East? Is Berlin worth a new world war? Would the French fight? Would the British fight? Would we?

These problems, as is well known, came to a head on November 27, 1958, when Khrushchev repudiated the four-power protocol setting up the mechanism of Allied control over Berlin, and issued a six-month ultimatum demanding a new status for Berlin as a demilitarized 'free' city. This, if such a status were established, would terminate four-power rule over Berlin, abrogate the Occupation Statute, and blow the whole position wide open. The East Germans would then control access to Berlin, and could claim that the Western Allies held their position in the city not by international agreement but on sufferance. The East German Communists would, of course, be under the guidance, or thumb, of the Russians all the time, but the Russians would pretend otherwise. And the East Germans could cut off Berlin, make a new blockade at any time, and control all communications, asserting that all this was now a purely internal German issue and that the western powers had no right to intervene or, for that matter, be in Berlin at all.

A seething crisis ensued, but the Allies stood firm, and Khrushchev never put his ultimatum into effect; in fact, he cancelled it. He did so partly because of fear of war, partly because he changed tactics and, playing hard for a Summit Conference, decided to be conciliatory. Such Soviet zigzagging is familiar. There followed Khrushchev's visit to the United States and his talks with ex-President Eisenhower at Camp David. What was said about Berlin at these talks is still a matter of dispute and varied interpretation. Then, eight months later, came the U-2 explosion which wrecked the Summit Conference in Paris in May, 1960. Following this it was almost universally expected that Mr. K., in his frantic rage, would unleash the East Germans and reimpose pressure on West Berlin. Instead, speaking in East Berlin immediately after the break-up of the Summit, he took a fairly moderate line. Here, as of the moment, the matter rests. Obviously Khrushchev still hopes for negotiation which, in one way or another, will modify the status of Berlin in his favour without risking war. One should not, however, discount the possibility of a new zigzag in Soviet policy, and a new harder line on Berlin at almost any time.

*

One more curious item demands mention. It is that, although East Germany (the Russian Zone) is, of course, a Soviet satellite and is recognized by the USSR as a sovereign state, the Russians *have never signed a peace treaty with East Germany*, even as the Western Allies have never signed a peace treaty with West Germany. Mainly (the subject is abstruse) the reason for this is that the Russians, playing for time and with a long-range end in view, are more interested in *Germany as a whole* than in their

East German puppet, and conclusion of a separate peace treaty with the East Germans would, of course, formalize and presumably make permanent the present fragmentation of Germany. What the Russians want ideally, obviously enough, is a united *Communist* Germany. The Allies, on their side, view with extreme distaste and alarm the possibility of a treaty between the Kremlin and the East Germans for several reasons, the chief of which is that this would end for the foreseeable future the possibility of any unification at all. Moreover, a treaty with East Germany would be construed, in various neutral or uncommitted states, as a signal victory for Soviet diplomacy, and recognition of East Germany by several other countries would probably follow. Khrushchev, however, must think twice about all this. Disadvantages to Russia, as well as advantages, might easily arise out of Soviet recognition of the East German régime. For one thing, as Mayor Brandt explained to a recent interviewer, the USSR would lose close contact with West Germany, the greatest of all European prizes. For another it would be put in a position whereby *Russia* could conceivably be involved in an open break with the West, or even warfare, by reason of some blunder made independently by the East Germans. Herr Brandt, talking to me, seemed to have two basic thoughts: first, that conclusion of a Kremlin-East German peace treaty was not imminent, and, second, that if it did happen it would not change the situation much. 'All that Khrushchev would be doing,' he said sagely, 'would be marrying himself.'

*

Now we must turn to the East, and inspect briefly the Russian sector, the Russian Zone.

CHAPTER V

Soviet Sector, Soviet Zone

We drove through Brandenburger Tor, the most conspicuous aperture in the frontier between the two Berlins, and swung into the Soviet sector along the Unter den Linden. The trees here, like those in the Tiergarten, were cut down for fuel during the last terrible winter of the war;[1] replanted, they reach a respectable height today, but seem thin. Every inch we drove made more dramatic the piercing contrast between the two Berlins. East Berlin has many fewer motor-cars, plain instead of sumptuous shops, and no chic restaurants or pavement cafés. Men and women dress more soberly, although they are not shabby. (I even saw one young lady with a handsome little poodle on a leash, which, if minor, was an unexpected note; in most Communist cities, pets are almost never seen—there isn't enough food to spare.) But the main element of contrast is that, almost at once, the visitor feels a curious, pervasive spiritual deadness. A bleak, joyless uniformity paints the whole community grey. This is Russia. Worse, it is a *German* Russia, and the combination of the two is almost too stifling to be borne.

Destruction here is immeasurably greater than in West Berlin. Buildings are shells, skeletons; large squares are still choked with broken rubble. One reason why the Berlin masters permitted their people to do little, until very recently, towards clearing up the mess, is that they wanted to teach a lesson—keep vividly alive memories of the war and the giant, ghastly toll it cost the German people. Russians do not by any means trust Germans. One striking detail is that one of the chief national holidays today in East Germany is May 8, the day of *Germany's* unconditional surrender.[2] Imagine a nation celebrating its own

[1] *Germany* in the Vista Books series, p. 140.
[2] Sebastian Haffner in the *Observer*, May 1, 1960.

defeat! But, of course, it was the Russians who devised this neat little subtlety. One impression likely to be gained by most western visitors, looking at East Berlin on a superficial level, is that here, once for all, the superiority of the free enterprise system to Communist economy seems to be overwhelmingly proved. Here, laid openly before the observing eye, are two adjacent segments of the same city; one is brilliantly thriving, bursting with vitality and wealth; the other seems sterile, derelict, drab, and poor. But it would be unwise to draw too firm conclusions from such evidence. First, West Berlin had the enormous advantage of sustenance provided by the Marshall Plan, which East Berlin did not. Second, East Berlin is not, in some ways, typical of East Germany as a whole; Leipzig and other cities are better off. Third, the Communists pay scant attention as a rule to the appearance of shops, the upkeep of buildings, and the like, except for demonstration pieces, and concentrate instead on what is not seen—and what really counts—the building up of heavy industry.

We saw what was once the Lustgarten (now Marx-Engels Square); explored an acre of ground-up rubble at the far end of the Unter den Linden; shopped in a big state-owned department store (dreary, dreary, but plenty of goods were on sale); saw everywhere the huge red and gold banners, often floating over totally destroyed areas, with their messages, JOINT PLANNING, JOINT WORK, JOINT GOVERNMENT, or FÜR FRIEDENSVERTRAG UND ENTSPANNUNG, FÜR DEN SIEG DES SOCIALIZMUS ZUR SICHERUNG DES FRIEDENS ('For a Peace Treaty and the Relaxation of Tension, For the Victory of Socialism through the Security of Peace'); passed down the Leipzigerstrasse, which was the biggest shopping street in Germany before the war, and which today is exactly nothing; surveyed the ruins of the lovely old Schauspielhaus; looked at the old Kaiserhof, of which one tottering wall remains; stared at Goering's enormous air ministry, which seems to be more or less intact; and saw the bunker on Wilhelmstrasse where Hitler died—a low, flattish, sandy hill covered with black oysters of rubble. This is all that remains of the Reich Chancellery. The principal showpiece is, of course, the Stalinallee, once the Frankfurterallee. The joke (in the West) is that it is the only street in the world that goes from nowhere to nowhere. This is where the *élite* of East Berlin lives. The pavement is three hundred feet wide, and the apartment buildings, of an ugly, fancy, cream-coloured brick, look like those in Moscow, and are stereotyped examples of Stalinist gingerbread architecture.

Returning through more acres of desolation we passed what remains of the Hotel Adlon, and could not resist a peek inside. This was once the king of all hotels, the original 'Grand' hotel, the father of luxurious hotels over half the world—where Escoffier invented *sauce diable*, and where Kaiser Wilhelm, no less, was a patron to the management. I suppose it was, all in all, the best as well as most magnificent hotel I have ever stayed in in my life. Today all that is left is a stairway, carpeted in grey linoleum, worn through in oval pools, which leads up to what was formerly the servants' wing, where a small dining-room holds six or eight tables. On floors above a few rooms are to let. A waiter saw me staring wide-eyed; he must have guessed my thought exactly, because he muttered, 'Not much to look at any more!' A plate of stale bananas stood on a window sill, with a solitary bouquet of stringy flowers. Everything did, however, seem to be clean, and the atmosphere connoted rebuilding and expansion soon to come. I saw a thin folio of single-page typewritten menus, and stole one. Samples of what is offered:

Italienischer Salat mit Toast	3.20 Ostmarks
(Italian salad with toast)	
Ungarischer Fleischsalat	2.55
(Hungarian meat salad)	
Rollschinken mit Butter und Brot	2.40
(Open ham sandwich)	
Heringsfilet in Sahne mit Äpfel und Zwiebeln	2.20
(Filet of herring in cream with apple and onions)	

Drinks are red wine, white wine (not otherwise identified), apple cider, milk, and coffee. Cream is 0.75 marks per portion, but these are Eastern marks, each of which is worth rather less than sixpence. Cheap! Louis Adlon would roll in his grave. He would roll in his grave, too, at the banner hanging on the Education Ministry directly across the street—FIGHT FOR A DEMILITARIZED FREE CITY OF WEST BERLIN!

*

East Germany is, in some respects, the most important Soviet satellite in Europe.[1] It is the only one (except Hungary and Albania) to be non-Slav, and is very close to the west geographically; in it are such cities as Erfurt, Weimar, Jena, Magdeburg, Dresden. East Berlin may look poor on the surface, but East Germany as a whole is prosperous, with a solid—and mounting—industrial output. The gross national product is going up at an annual rate of about 5 per cent, and was £6,450 million in 1958. Before the war the territories which comprise East Germany today supplied 55 per cent of all Germany's machine tools, 75 per cent of its textiles, and much of its specialized scientific equipment. It would be a grievous error to underestimate East Germany, or minimize the extent of its economic recovery or contribution to the Soviet sphere as a whole. The lift in living standards has been marked, particularly since the shift in emphasis towards the production of more consumer goods, which began with the new seven-year plan in 1958. In another sphere—military—East Germany has marked importance. Its army is tough and well equipped, and it has missile bases uncomfortably close to the frontiers of the free world.

Politically East Germany is called the 'model' satellite; this does not mean, however, that its leaders are nothing more than utterly subservient Kremlin puppets. If only because they are *German*, they have a good deal of will and initiative of their own; one should not forget that the Communist party in Germany was a substantial and powerful indigenous force before the war, and the present East German government inherits from this to an extent.[2] This country is not a façade or shadow state; it is a real country, and—one should always remember—it completely surrounds Berlin.

The government party is, in theory, a coalition between the Communists and left-wing Social Democrats, and is called the Sozialistische Einheitspartei Deutschlands (Socialist Unity Party)—SED for short. The Communists utterly dominate this so-called coalition. The leader is Walter Ulbricht, sixty-eight,

---

[1] Its correct name, self-given, is the German Democratic Republic (DDR). Officially, *West* Germany calls it 'Central' Germany, to differentiate it from the lost provinces farther east.

[2] Haffner, *op. cit.*

First Secretary of the Communist party and Chairman of the Council of State. The Prime Minister, Otto Grotewohl, a turn-coat Social Democrat, stands above him technically in the government structure, but has nothing of his power and banner-like prestige. Ulbricht, a carpenter by trade, who wears a beard like a badge and speaks German with a harsh Saxon accent, is a revolutionary of the old internationalist school, and spent many years in Moscow; he was—and perhaps still is—Stalinist to the core. Some people say that he is 'closer to China than to Moscow'. Be this as it may, he has survived every shift and turnabout in the party line in Moscow for years back, and Mr. K. apparently has complete trust in his reliability. All major policy decisions are, of course, made by the Kremlin, but Ulbricht is consulted closely. One point worth mention is that several conspicuous members of his government are ex-Nazis. Ulbricht is an interesting antithesis to fellow-Communists like Gomulka in Poland (or Tito in Jugoslavia) in that, although German, he has no discernible German national feeling; Gomulka is intensely proud of being an ardent Pole and Tito is above all else a nationalist Jugoslav; but Ulbricht's sole, unswerving allegiance is to the cause of Communism in universality—to the Party as an international revolutionary and conspiratorial instrument. That he has a Stalinist past does not worry Khrushchev in the least. Khrushchev likes, in fact, to have Stalinists on the borders of the Soviet empire, and moreover likes them to be as tough as possible.

*

Now a word of background. How did Ulbricht and his company reach power? We must go back to the end of the war, and several key dates are important. Ulbricht—incidentally, he speaks Russian fluently—belonged to what is known as the 'Gruppe Ulbricht', a civilian organization behind the Red Army; it was the first team of German Communist political advisers to reach Berlin and it immediately proceeded to estab-lish itself firmly in the Soviet Zone. But the Communists were faced with an awkward political situation, namely that the Social Democratic party (SPD) was deeply entrenched in the central and eastern regions of Germany, and had a membership of

680,000, which far surpassed Communist strength. Moscow
therefore worked for a merger between the KPD, as the
Communist party was then called, and the socialists, hoping
thus to absorb the latter. Schumacher and the orthodox Socialist
leadership opposed this manœuvre vigorously, and the Russians
got nowhere for a time. Then, with maximum adroitness, they
managed to strike a bargain with six or eight left-wing Social
Democratic leaders, including Grotewohl. They told Grotewohl
that, in West Germany, he could never be anything better than
a second to Schumacher and that if he changed sides, he would
become head of the first unequivocally socialist state in German
history. This Russian manœuvre succeeded, and on April 20,
1946, the KPD and defecting SPDs joined to form the Socialist
Unity party, under which name the Communists still rule East
Germany today. The socialists never got a chance to vote on the
merger on a country-wide basis, but in Berlin, where the
Russians could not prevent a free poll, they voted 87 per cent
against merging. Incidentally, the SPD has managed to keep up
a vigorous underground operation in East Germany ever since,
despite grave obstacles.

On June 17, 1953, Ulbricht faced his next crisis. His policy
had been to establish purely Soviet forms in East Germany;
the experiment didn't turn out well, and three powerful members of the party—including the head of the secret police, Herr
Zaisser, known as 'the German Beria'—rose against him.
Ulbricht, however, succeeded in crushing this revolt. Came
another crisis in February, 1956, after Khrushchev's speech to
the Twentieth Party Congress in Moscow, which down-graded
Stalin. A veteran Party member named Schirdewan rose in
East Berlin and demanded that Ulbricht, an obvious Stalinist,
be sacked. For a time Khrushchev appeared to back Schirdewan
but then wavered, so that Ulbricht was able to outride the storm,
and Schirdewan retired from the scene to become Chief of the
State Archives in Potsdam.

*

To resume: What is the reaction of the present-day East
German authorities to the refugee phenomenon? The leakage of
population is incontestably serious; the population of the

country has dropped about 20 per cent in a dozen years—from more than twenty to seventeen million, in spite of the considerable flow of 'counter-refugees' who, as noted in the preceding chapter, go in their remarkable way from West to East. The loss is felt most acutely in doctors, engineers, and skilled technical men. There is, however, no shortage of industrial manpower as yet. To a degree, the loss in population is a benefit; fewer people mean fewer mouths to feed, less consumer goods to have to produce. Of course, if the régime begins to feel a pinch, and under-production becomes a problem, it will act with the brutality of all Communist régimes, and simply enforce regulations whereby citizens will be rationed, i.e. given less to consume.

Apart from all this is another important factor, which derives from the nature of long-term Communist policy. It is that, even if the decamping of refugees is a serious matter, it is not worth closing the frontiers, abrogating the Occupation Statute, and causing a mountainous international crisis. The East German creed is identical with that of the Kremlin, namely that the whole world will be Communist in time. Therefore, since victory is 'certain', there is no need to hurry. The Kremlin leadership, as well as Ulbricht and the East Germans, hope that the West will sooner or later come to think of Berlin as a nuisance, decide that the position is hopeless, and, in a word, drop its guard.

What would a free vote in East Germany bring? Nobody knows, but West German authorities in general, including Dr. Adenauer and Dr. Erhard, think—as does Willy Brandt—that the Communist government would not get 10 per cent of the poll. There may, however, be a bit of wishful thinking in this. Some observers, while they are certain that a substantial majority would vote against the Communists, believe that this majority would be smaller than six or seven years ago. People, they say, are becoming more 'resigned'; they have been indoctrinated, stupefied, into 'resignationism'. One factor to be noted is that the East Germans are the only people in western Europe (except Spaniards and Portuguese, in a different category) who have been continually under totalitarian dictatorial rule since the early 1930's; they passed directly from Hitler to Stalin, without a moment's intermission, and any dictatorship that lasts uninterruptedly for almost thirty years can break the stoutest spirit. On the other hand, it should be remembered—to their honour—that the East Germans were the first people in the whole of the satellite empire to attempt to make a revolt. A valiant uprising took place on the Stalinallee on June 17, 1953—unarmed boys threw stones at Soviet tanks— and had to be put down by force of arms.

A final suggestive point is that, to an extent, the East German authorities cannot afford to dragoon or manhandle their population too unmercifully, because of the loophole of escape that West Berlin provides. If things get worse, more people will decamp. So again we see the vital, overwhelming importance of preserving West Berlin to the free world.

INTERNATIONAL

Now, quitting Germany, both western and eastern, for the time being, we should have a word about international considerations. Germany, cut in two and lying athwart the core of Europe, is, as is only too obvious, the heart of the European problem. Seen from outside Germany, this has two aspects. First, fear that Germany itself, particularly if reunited, might some day make a war. In the view of almost all experienced observers, this is not at all likely; but, after all, nobody can forget that Germany, within the last century, has launched no fewer than five excessively unpleasant aggressive wars, in 1864, 1866, 1870, 1914, and 1939. You just can't keep Germans down. Indeed, the decision to permit Germany to rearm, taken largely on American initiative early in the 1950's, was a harassing one, but there was no easy alternative. Our whole policy was predicated on the tenet that, no matter what the risk, we must build a defence in Europe against possible Soviet aggression. Second, fear that somebody else will make a war *about* Germany, particularly if it is not unified, even if nobody wants one. Hence have arisen any number of proposals for amelioration of the present fluid situation, ranging from the peculiar and ambiguous catch-all named 'disengagement', which in one form or other is supported by substantial left-wing sentiment over much of Europe, and which would presumably mean withdrawal from German soil of both NATO forces and the Red Army, all the way to the Rapacki Plan. This, suggested by Adam Rapacki, the Polish Foreign Minister, at the UN on October 3, 1957, 'associates disengagement with nuclear disarmament', and suggests setting up an 'atom-free' zone in Central Europe on both sides of the Iron Curtain.

Meantime, currents within the Federal Republic are susceptible of change. I have stressed in earlier passages of this book Chancellor Adenauer's devotion to European unity, and, in particular, to Franco-German rapprochement, as well as his spirited, unequivocal hostility to the Soviet Union. But the harsh pressures of time and circumstance may force new developments. For instance, the Adenauer-de Gaulle *entente* suffered damage, probably temporary, late in 1960 following de Gaulle's insistence on maintaining an independent nuclear deterrent, his refusal to integrate further French military forces with NATO, and his desire to change the structure of the Atlantic Alliance. As to Russia the *Alte Herr* still sticks inflexibly to his belief that Communism is incompatible with human dignity and that life without freedom is not worth having; nevertheless, he has lately adopted a line towards Russia strikingly more conciliatory than any he has ever demonstrated before. He went so far as to concede that Khrushchev is a quite different article from Stalin, that he pursues different goals for the Russian people, that he is 'a man with whom one can talk', and that a meeting between President Kennedy and Mr. K. might be desirable. Also he sent Berthold Beitz, who runs Krupp, on an unofficial mission to Poland in January, 1961, hoping thus to lay the ground for resumption of diplomatic relations between West Germany and Poland.

Nobody can measure at the moment the full significance of manœuvres like these. Basically, the policy of the Federal Republic remains unchanged. What the West Germans want is peace and unity. The problem is how to get both without sacrifice of security. Finally, one should take note of the fact that a certain amount of neutralist sentiment is visible in West Germany, although on a minor hypothetical level. Neutralization on the Austrian model might just conceivably become a future possibility, but this would necessarily have to be part of a general European settlement.

CHAPTER VI

The Person of de Gaulle

TWENTY-FIVE years ago I wrote in *Inside Europe* that whereas Germany was one person, Hitler, France was a whole lot of people. Today almost exactly the opposite is true, for although Adenauer is the dominant character in the Germany of 1961 the country is divided and there are a good many other consequential Germans in both West and East; but in France today nobody—nobody at all—really counts except Charles André Joseph Marie de Gaulle.

In 1936, when *Inside Europe* first appeared, Léon Blum, the socialist exquisite of the Ile Saint-Louis, had just succeeded the unspeakable Pierre Laval as Prime Minister; Laval was executed in 1945, and Blum, some of whose contribution still survives, died in 1950. There is no mention of de Gaulle in *Inside Europe*. He was at that time an inconspicuous colonel of infantry in his middle forties; few outside his immediate circle had ever heard of him. Within four years he was to become leader of the French nation in exile, organizer of the Free French, and commander of the Fighting French. By the end of the war he was a world figure—contentious, cranky, unpopular in many quarters, but a supreme, indomitable world figure just the same.

I have met General de Gaulle several times, dating back to London in 1941; if he chooses, he can be the rudest man alive. I will never forget an extraordinarily difficult interview I had with him in Paris in 1952, when he was out of power. He can also be winning. Whenever I have seen him I have gone away thinking that his chief characteristic is inflexibility. It is impossible to ignore his aloofness, his Olympian quality of detached grandeur. He is positively lunar, although not necessarily cold.

The General is somewhat stout these days, and looks, with his formidable height, like a slightly swollen obelisk. He is seventy, almost blind without glasses (as a result of cataracts), and is in quite good health.

De Gaulle is impervious to all except the closest of personal relationships, such as to his family, but he does have friends of course—old comrades in the Resistance, or men whose intellect he genuinely respects, like André Malraux, the author and art critic, who fought with the Loyalists in Spain twenty-five years ago, and who is his Minister of Cultural Expansion, and Louis Joxe, a former ambassador to Moscow and Minister of Education, who is now Minister of State for Algerian Affairs. But the President seldom unbends to anybody; his relation to his associates is almost that of a monarch, a somewhat arrogant monarch at that. Almost never does he take advice, and only seldom does he communicate his intentions to subordinates. Nobody has influence on him. 'The only trouble with the General,' one of his cabinet officers is reputed to have said on one occasion, 'is that he is not a human being.' A principal minister was once asked what French policy on a certain issue was. He replied, 'I know what it was half an hour ago, when I left the General. I do not know what it is now.'

De Gaulle is almost totally inaccessible to outsiders. Adenauer, a gregarious man at heart, will see almost anybody; so will Khrushchev, if it will serve a purpose; but de Gaulle is probably the head of state hardest to meet on the continent, with the possible exception of Dr. Salazar in Portugal. It is wrong, however, to assume that he despises people. It is simply, as one observer who has studied him closely for years put it to me, that he has a somewhat pessimistic view of human values. He hesitates to share himself, because he feels that humanity is weak, that it is the nature of man to be frail, and that even the best of men cannot be expected to live up to their promise. Therefore it is better not to trust human nature fully, not to give members of his entourage his unqualified confidence. This deeply ingrained characteristic in de Gaulle, which also serves to make him magnanimous when somebody does fail him, is probably the principal reason why nobody—not a soul—is in discernible view as his successor. Nobody is being trained to take on his responsibilities. There are some heads of state who persistently avoid having first-class men around them because of fear of being overshadowed; they are jealous of the man just outside the door, or enjoy playing one aspirant for power off against another. Stalin and Hitler were prime cases in point. This is not at all the reason for de Gaulle's diffidence. He has no jealousy of anybody, no fear of anybody else rising to the succession; what he does fear is that potential candidates for power do not have the necessary status or capacity. Quite recently a deputy to the National Assembly asked him point-blank what the future was going to be. De Gaulle replied calmly, 'Well, you will have to find another de Gaulle.'

This egoism is rock-like, unswerving from first to last, and almost sublimely absolute. Once, during his retirement, he was looking back to an early episode in his career and said, with perfect seriousness, 'Ah! That was when I *was* France!' As recently as January, 1961, when one of his friends suggested that he should thank those who had voted for him in the Algeria vote just concluded, he replied, 'How can France thank France?'[1]

I have heard it said that the difference between de Gaulle and Adenauer is that the former is a Frenchman, the latter a European. I do not think this is quite accurate. Certainly de Gaulle is a Frenchman above all else, and detests most aspects of supra-national policy, but in some respects he is a better European than Adenauer, because his arc is broader. Adenauer is, in fact, a kind of Eisenhower-era American. De Gaulle has a much bigger conception of Europe; he considers that it stretches to the Urals, and he was the first statesman after the crash of the Summit in 1960 to point out the absolute necessity (on acceptable terms) of seeking some kind of accommodation with Russia, no matter how disagreeable and aggressive Khrushchev was.

There has been some talk that de Gaulle will leave a testament, as Lenin did, listing and assaying various candidates for the succession. Commenting on this one of the wisest Frenchmen I know remarked, 'Nonsense! Kindly remember that this is France. When de Gaulle dies he will be dead, and no Frenchman would pay the slightest attention to any testament he leaves.' There are two things, somewhat paradoxical, that should always

---

[1] A different version of one of these anecdotes appears in Edward Ashcroft's 'Return of the Warrior', *Sunday Times* (London), May 15, 1960. Also see the New York *Herald Tribune*, July 12, 1960, and *Time*, January 20, 1961.

be remembered about France; it consists of 45 million people,
most of whom are (a) hard-headed realists, and (b) anarchists
at heart.

*

Anecdotes about de Gaulle are scarce, but one which demon-
strates nicely his attitude to France as well as his sublime
imperviousness has to do with a young man named Olivier
Guichard, a member of his secretariat. Not a political man,
Guichard is a kind of technician, and is one of a small group
close to the President; in fact, he lunches with the de Gaulle
family every day. De Gaulle, presiding at the lunch table, ladles
out the soup himself—the soup which is the mainstay of every
good Frenchman's principal meal. But Guichard, it happens,
does not like soup. At their first meal together, shortly after
de Gaulle moved into the Élysée, he turned to him with the
words, 'Guichard, will you have soup?' Guichard declined with
polite thanks, and this colloquy was repeated every day without
alteration for thirty days. On the thirty-first day the President
paused, became cognizant at last of the fact that Guichard did
not eat soup, and turned to him with a stern smile: 'Guichard!
How can France remain great if Frenchmen do not eat soup?'
The young man muttered some kind of apology in reply, and
de Gaulle, with noble mien, thereafter refrained from pressing
soup upon him, no doubt with an inward sigh at such lamentable
proof that France, even in his own household, was no longer the
France of Agincourt, Austerlitz, and Verdun.

One legend is that, on moving into the Élysée, the General
and Madame de Gaulle tactfully, quietly, eased out of their jobs
every person on the domestic staff—there weren't many—who
had been divorced. The General, a good Catholic, did not think
it proper that he and his family should be served by a divorced
person. Another is that exactly one vote was registered against
the General in his own village of Colombey-les-Deux-Églises
(population about five hundred) in the election which made him
president. The lone dissident was the de Gaulle cook. She
thought that moving to Paris and assuming the duties of
president would tire the elderly General too much.

The pattern of de Gaulle's thinking may be judged from these

3*

excerpts from a Press conference which he gave in Washington on April 25, 1960, during a visit to the United States. Of course, this took place before the Summit Conference:

Q.—Mr. President, do you anticipate another summit conference besides the meeting this year in Paris, perhaps in Moscow when President Eisenhower will visit Russia?

A.—If we do not wage war, we must certainly wage peace. In order to wage peace, we must negotiate. And in order to negotiate, we must meet together.

Q.—Mr. President, the curiosity of the Press is all-consuming. Who is your favourite French poet?

A.—My favourite French poet is the one that I am reading at the time that I am reading him. There are many whom I like and admire. I ask all of you for permission not to hurt the feelings of any of them—even those who have long been dead—by making choices.[1]

*

The outline of de Gaulle's career may be stated briefly. He was born in Lille on November 22, 1890; his father was a professor of philosophy at a Jesuit college; his paternal and maternal strains both represented the *petite noblesse*, and such qualities as rigidity, prudence, frugality, and correctness were born into him. Also born into him was a highly suggestive name—de Gaulle, which can be stretched to mean 'of France'. He decided to choose a military career, and was graduated with honours from Saint-Cyr, the French equivalent of Sandhurst. He had —ironically enough—a passionate admiration for his first commanding officer, Henri Philippe Pétain, then a colonel; he dedicated his first book to Pétain, and Pétain was godfather to his only son. Twenty-odd years later, the Vichy government headed by the miserable Pétain was to sentence him to death for treason. De Gaulle was a good officer, but rose slowly; and he was one of those comparatively rare birds among officers who realize that the pen is mightier than the sword. In 1934 he published *The Army of the Future*, which advanced the thesis that attack was better than defence—a most unorthodox view at the time, when France was crouching behind its supposedly

[1] *New York Times*, April 26, 1960.

impregnable Maginot Line—and appealed for the creation of a new type of highly mobile, mechanized army, which would be characterized by the mass use of large numbers of tanks. The French paid not the slightest attention to these views—but the Germans did. The book was, in fact, much taken up in military circles in Berlin, and de Gaulle, it might almost be said, was the unwitting father of the Nazi Panzer divisions which, when war came to the West in 1940, crushed France, the Low Countries, and the British expeditionary force with appalling speed. At any rate, de Gaulle's military theories were certainly proved right.

De Gaulle fled to London after the collapse of France and, on June 18, 1940, made one of the most celebrated speeches in contemporary history. He was unknown; he was forlorn and penniless; he was alone, a man without a country; and he was magnificent. His words, saying in effect that France had lost a battle but not the war, and that Frenchmen everywhere should rally to his standard (his opening words were, 'I, General de Gaulle . . .'), rang like trumpet blasts around the world. The subsequent years were stormy. He created the Free French movement; had grisly quarrels with the Americans and British during the Vichy period; suffered various ignominies in Algiers when the Allies could not decide to back him or not; entered Paris as a conqueror in 1944, and set up a provisional government; supervised the birth of the Fourth Republic; outlined a sensible policy for French Africa; went to Moscow (when the Americans and British were dawdling over recognizing his régime), negotiated a Franco-Russian treaty, and brought several French Communists into his government; was meantime denounced as a Fascist by the ill-informed; resigned office early in 1946 because the multiplicity of French political parties made government unworkable; stood in the wings for a while, and created his own party, the Rassemblement du Peuple Français; hoped to be called back to power, and was not; retired from active politics and buried himself for years at Colombey, biding his time, proving his mastery of French prose in a superb autobiography, and consolidating his long view of life; was called back to save the republic in the great crisis of May, 1958, when the army revolt in Algeria, led by the parachutist General Jacques Massu, came close to making civil war; took the prime ministership, superintended the formation of the Fifth Republic, and put this before the people; and finally became first President of the Fifth Republic and of the newly-formed French Community on January 8, 1959.

*

What does de Gaulle believe in most? First, of course, France. Second, himself, but as a symbol of France.

What does he want most? To restore France to indisputably accepted status as a first-class power, which it has not been since Munich. That is why he has been such a thorn in the flesh of NATO, and why he has insisted that France shall have its own nuclear deterrent.

What does he need most? Time. Yet he is over seventy.

What are the chief sources of his power, apart from such obvious personal qualities as endurance, an extraordinary logical mind, and intelligence?

First, his 'mystique', or identity with the spirit of France. The leader, the cause, the nation, have become one. He has a hand, it has been written, '*pure, sure, dure*'.[1] What Frenchman can resist him when he says that the three things that count most in leadership are 'concision, precision, decision'?

No man could be more gnarled with ego, but associated with this is a curious and altogether genuine humility. The French are not given much to writing fan letters, but after the Algerian crisis he received something like five thousand letters from citizens commending him and congratulating him on his return to power. He answered every one—*longhand*!

He memorizes his speeches, and can talk for an hour on the most difficult matters without departing from his text by a jot or tittle, and for some inexplicable reason the French admire this. He is called a '*cerveau*'—a brain. (Marshal Foch was similarly a *cerveau*, but not Joffre, Pétain, or Weygand.) His TV speech delivered on Algeria on January 29, 1960, was, a good many people of consequence believe, the best heard in Europe since the great Churchill speeches during the war. For pure and scintillating power of logic, it even surpassed Churchill. As is often the case, he refers to himself both as 'I' and in the third

[1] Sonia Tomara in the New York *Herald Tribune*, February 29, 1944.

person. His opening words were: 'If I have put on my uniform today to address you on television, it is in order to show that it is General de Gaulle who speaks, as well as the Chief of State.'

It was in this speech that he announced courageously that the Algerians would have 'the free choice of their destiny', and one passage is the following:

> Frenchmen of Algeria, how can you listen to the liars and the conspirators who tell you that in granting a free choice to the Algerians, France and de Gaulle want to abandon you, to pull out of Algeria and hand it over to the rebellion? Is it abandoning you, is it wanting to lose Algeria, to send there and to maintain there an army of 500,000 men equipped with tremendous amounts of *matériel*; to consent to the sacrifice there of a good many of our children; to pay out there, this very year, civil and military expenditures amounting to a thousand billion [old francs], to undertake there a tremendous programme of development; to draw from the Sahara, with great difficulty and at great expense, oil and gas in order to bring them to the sea?

Second, the fact that history has, after all, proved him right. He said that France would come back to life, and it came back to life. He said that the 'Algerian ultras' would come to order in 1958 and 1960, and they came to order. Moreover he was right *vis-à-vis* other *Frenchmen*; which means much more to the French than if he had merely been proved right as against such barbarians as the British or Americans.

Third, his disinterestedness. Almost every citizen knows that he cares for nothing except the public good. A friend put it this way: 'His patriotism is as indisputable as his prescience; thus he appeals not only to whatever instincts for gratitude that the French may have, but to their capacity for imagination.'

Fourth, the régime that preceded him was utterly discredited. He filled an arena desperately confused.

Finally, although de Gaulle's demerits and defects are obvious, there can be little doubt about the extent of his contribution. Of few statesmen can it be said that they saved a country: Lincoln was one; Churchill is another; but de Gaulle goes one better than them, in that he saved his country not once but *twice* in his lifetime—which must be one of the rarest phenomena in history. Without de Gaulle, there would have been no Free France in 1940; and without de Gaulle the country would probably have succumbed to civil war in 1958. Once Charles André Joseph Marie de Gaulle saved France from Germany, and once he saved it from itself.

CHAPTER VII

Changes and Perplexities in France

IT doesn't take long these days for a visitor to France to see that only two phenomena are major—a man, de Gaulle, and, second, a country, Algeria, which represents a stupendous and perhaps insoluble problem.

But something else should be mentioned too, which is that France is much more relaxed than it has been for years, despite the exacerbation of the Algerian crisis, worry about the army, and similar issues. Taxi drivers (of course, this generalization is too broad) smile rather than growl; chambermaids in the hotels actually seem pleased to make the bed; even head waiters are polite. Paris, which can be the most ill-mannered city in the world, has a new atmosphere of blandness and satisfaction.

One reason for the diminution of tension that most of France shows on the non-political level is, obviously, the boom. Never has the country, with its 45 million people, been so prosperous, though plenty of economic worries remain, and no one can know how long the present spurt will last. Another is that the sting of humiliation and defeat in 1940 has largely passed. Still another is the sense of contentment that has come with political stability under de Gaulle, even if his position has seemed to have become somewhat weaker lately.

As to the boom, the gross national product was an enormous £22,500 million in 1958, and it increases at an average annual rate of around 4·5 per cent. The rate of increase of industrial production is almost equal to that of Germany, and *per capita* income is higher than that of Germany, incredible as the fact may seem. Various contributing factors to the boom have been the stabilization programme (1958) which checked inflation, austerity, the creation of the 'heavy franc', expanding export trade, political confidence after 1958 which led to repatriation of huge amounts of gold held abroad, and a fairly tranquil labour situation. Also one should mention American aid, which by the end of 1957 totalled the not inconsiderable sum of £3,227,500,000.

France is, needless to say, still an extraordinarily homogeneous country—geographically compact, unitary, integrated, and solidly balanced between agriculture and industry. Think of the contrast it makes to Italy, which is still not a country at all in a manner of speaking, but a constellation of highly differentiated cities, each with its own striking individuality. Or compare it to Germany; France is like a diamond—a single stone, hard, polished, and sparkling—but Germany is a broken necklace or lopsided tiara. Or, to change metaphors, France is a glass of sharp, very dry and cold champagne; Germany is a keg of beer.[1]

France is, one might almost say, the union of ten million or so families into one family, with de Gaulle as father—at least for the time being. Or one might quote a well-known aphorism dating back to the days before World War I: 'Germany is a race; Egypt is a river; Austro-Hungary is a policy; Italy is a language; Britain is an island; France is a tradition.'

In what other ways has France changed since the war? For one thing the social structure is much more fluid. Frenchmen travel more; they are not so maddeningly provincial and insular as heretofore. Still, they can be insular enough. Men of substance no longer come home invariably to lunch (indeed a revolution!); all over Paris there are sandwich stands, milk bars, and the like. One of the most sumptuous restaurants in the world, Larue, has become a quick-lunch place, and on the Champs-Élysées is a real, live American drugstore, with live trimmings. Scotch whisky has become the most fashionable drink in upper circles. The French language has assimilated countless English words, like bestseller, sex appeal, garden party, brain trust, businessman, and cover girl. Solemn campaigns have been launched against alcoholism and prostitution.

The institution of the *dot* (dowry) still exists, particularly in

[1] One could pursue this little analogy further. Italy is red wine made mellow by the sun, but new, with dregs in it, and on occasion somewhat rough; Spain is vinegar; Greece fizzes like a warm bottle of soda pop; Russia is vodka, harsh, colourless, and potent; England is Scotch.

rural areas, but it is not universally maintained; young women live freer lives, and know the perilous joys of romantic love. Youngsters marry early; there are thousands of two-earner families. Thirty years ago it was unusual in the extreme for a girl to go to a university like the Sorbonne; today it is a commonplace. Then consider money. The old legend was that all bourgeois Frenchmen, at least those living in the country, hid their life savings, their capital, in a sock in the mattress; this prudent habit has not disappeared altogether, but it has become much modified. One reason is fear of further inflation. Citizens have entered into an era of consumer economy, and spend their money; one out of every nine Frenchmen has a car. They buy low-cost housing; they invest in industry, and go in for something hitherto almost unknown—instalment buying, though this is not so widespread a habit as in England. However, some French habits in regard to financial matters are still old-fashioned, to put it mildly. Most bills are still paid in cash, and many shops will not accept a cheque in payment for a bill; astonishingly few people have bank accounts. I know one editor of an important newspaper who still has no bank account at all. One reason for this is that the banks are obliged to report to the government every year on the financial position of their depositors, to the end that taxes may be fairly assessed; and, naturally, every Frenchmen worth his salt resists to the uttermost the idea of paying any income tax at all. (On the other hand, the idea that most French citizens live tax-free is certainly an illusion; taxes are high. They are often evaded, but it is difficult to negotiate them away altogether, as is a frequent happening in Italy.)

One immense and fruitful change is the lifting of the birth-rate. A keynote of pre-war France was sterility. But today, surprisingly enough, the birth-rate is soaring; this upward curve began immediately after the war in 1945, when French prisoners began to stream home by the hundred thousand. Similarly an increase in the birth-rate occurred in 1919-20, largely because of marriages deferred by reason of World War I, but this was temporary. The present rise, in contrast, has been continuous, so much so that in thirty years France will, statisticians assert, be the 'youngest nation in Europe'. France has been called the last empty country; it will not be so for much longer, and could in any case easily support a population of sixty or even seventy million as against what it holds today. The increase in birth-rate will inevitably cause grave social problems in time, particularly in education and housing. What caused the jump in birth-rate? Nobody knows; but one French commentator told me that it was an 'automatic' phenomenon associated with self-preservation; after the frightful losses of World War II there came a subconscious feeling of direct national need among citizens, a sense that the human energies of France must be restored, preserved, and multiplied.

RADICAL SOCIALISTS AND THE DEUX CENT
FAMILLES

The first two questions I asked when I arrived in Paris in 1960 were: 'What has happened to the Radical Socialist party?' and 'What happened to the *deux cent familles*?' In pre-war days France was run, if it was run at all, by an unstable combination of these two factors—the Radical Socialists, who were neither radical nor socialist, but who represented the solid block of middle French citizens who were the heart of the nation and who always voted against 'the church and the château'; and, second, the '*deux cent familles*', or two hundred families, who constituted the financial oligarchy centring on the regents of the Bank of France.

Neither is an important factor today, and this is what makes the biggest of all changes in contemporary France, next to the emergence of de Gaulle.

The Radical Socialists, the party of giants like Clemenceau and Herriot in their great days, were wiped out as a serious instrument by three factors:

First, Hitler. They were the root and pillar of the Third Republic; hence, when Hitler conquered France the party was discredited, and it never regained its place in the Fourth Republic, which ruled from 1946 to 1958. Of course, the moral collapse of the party and its diminution of prestige pre-dated the war; it was a Radical Socialist, Édouard Daladier, who betrayed the Czechs at Munich.

Second, internal dissension. This is a complicated story. Its gist is that Pierre Mendès-France, who was the Radical Socialist

Prime Minister in 1954-55, set out to reform the party, clear away its dead wood, and bring it up to date by eliminating the bureaucrats who ran the local machines. This caused furious resentment; the party split up, and Mendès formed a leftist splinter group of his own. Also one should mention the suicidal tendencies towards fragmentation which marked the French political system in former days. The Radicals were not exclusively responsible for this by any means, but they took a large share of the onus for the incessant rotation of cabinets that distinguished France before and immediately after the war.

Third, de Gaulle. The Fifth Republic came into being, and both Mendès (who was one of the most courageous premiers France ever had) and the conservative wing of the Radical Socialists lost much of their *raison d'être*.

As to the financial oligarchy, it still exists, but its power is much attenuated. This is not merely because it has become inherently weaker itself, but because the state has become so much stronger. The upper bourgeoisie hangs on to its wealth; but the real direction of affairs is in the hands of a new managerial caste. The government—the state—plays an enormously greater role in financial and industrial matters than before the war. It was, in short, nationalization which killed the old oligarchy. Few outsiders realize how much of the French economy has been nationalized. The state owns and operates the railways, coal mining, gas and electric power, the oil industry in part, the largest motor-car works in France (Renault), the five biggest credit banks, several of the large insurance companies, atomic energy, most of the aviation industry (for instance, Air France), the biggest steamship line, and, of course —from long back—tobacco, the Opéra, and posts and telegraphs.[1]

Much of this development came under de Gaulle in his first brief period of power in 1945-46. Also, semi-public companies have been of striking importance in the economic development of the former French dominions in Africa. Finally, government has, to an extent, control of a section of the Press. This dates back to events just after the war, when collaborationist newspapers were confiscated and their plants turned over to men of the Resistance.

[1] Steel, however, the most important item of all, is not nationalized.

These examples of nationalization are not quite so revolutionary as they may seem. For one thing state intervention in industry has a long and honourable history in France; a state, or rather royal, monopoly on the manufacture of such items as Sèvres porcelain, as an example, started centuries ago. For another, nationalization of some companies took place as a result of special circumstances; for instance, Renault was nationalized because it collaborated. For another, although various industries may be owned by the state, the management still has wide powers; several state companies are virtually autonomous, like Air France, and are certainly not run like ministries even though they are under theoretical public—not private—control. Air France is, incidentally, the largest airline in the world.

Another trend not generally appreciated abroad is the development of the social security system; next to England, Austria, and the Scandinavian countries, France is probably closer to being a full welfare state than any in Europe. Not only are ordinary benefits in force, but a variety of special stipends. As an example, the government pays an allowance to newly-weds, and the birth of children is handsomely subsidized. Social security includes 'housewife allowance', health insurance, and pre-natal care; parents get copious supplements to their social security for each child, up to 33 per cent of the father's salary for families with more than three children, and the state provides further handsome contribution to the support of children as they grow up. The more children, the bigger the benefits; perhaps this is another reason why the French birth-rate climbs.

Who does run France, if the Radical Socialists and the financial oligarchy count no longer? This is a difficult question, but three elements at least must be mentioned: (1) de Gaulle; (2) the civil service; (3) survivors of the Resistance.

POLITICS AND THE SUCCESSION

De Gaulle is, in some respects, in a curiously isolated position. The Fifth Republic took certain powers away from parliament, and established a semi-presidential system; deputies of several colorations have flocked to the President, like flies on a big stick of candy, but a varied assortment of non-de Gaullists and even anti-de Gaullists still exists. The recent referendum on Algeria gave the General a thumping vote of confidence—a round 75 per cent—but France is still France, which means that it is highly individualist within a common exterior, and political soloists are by no means inconspicuous.

In fact, if I may change the metaphor, the spectrum of French politics resembles a hazy rainbow continually in movement. Parties divide, subdivide, merge, disappear, and are reborn again. It is almost impossible to distinguish between some of the smaller splinter groups; some are not even splinters, but shavings. The nomenclature is inordinately confusing—there is a vast difference, for instance, between the 'Union for the New Republic' and the 'Unity of the Republic' group, both of which are represented in the Assembly, and some parties go by initials difficult to decipher.

Roughly in the centre is the new de Gaulle party, the presidential party, known as the Union for the New Republic. Its basis is purely personal, and at the moment of writing it commands 210 seats in a chamber of 552. Thus, to pass legislation, it needs help. Another important centre party is the well-known Popular Republican Movement, or MRP, which, together with something called the 'Democrat Centre', has fifty-seven seats. The MRP is a Catholic party, and, on the whole, firmly supports de Gaulle; it grew out of the Resistance, played a conspicuous role in the Fourth Republic, stands for NATO and the Common Market, and is thoroughly to the left on most social matters. It wants full social security, if only to wean workers away from the Communists, and, since it is strongly Catholic, it favours big families. Robert Schuman, the former foreign minister who was born in Lorraine and who is one of the fathers of the European Coal and Steel Community ('Schuman Plan'), is probably its most distinguished member.

To the right of de Gaulle the main force is the Independent and Peasants party, the second biggest in France (119 seats). Its secretary-general is a picturesque character, Roger Duchet; among its leaders are Paul Reynaud, the last prime minister of the Third Republic, and, very important, Antoine Pinay, a former premier and foreign minister, who was de Gaulle's finance minister until the President let him out in January, 1960. Pinay, who likes to think of himself as representing the average middle Frenchman, certainly hopes to return to power some day, and is busy playing the role of the forgotten man who hopes devoutly not to be forgotten. He was born in 1891, derives from the Rhône country, and spent many years as a leather manufacturer.

Politics on the right are, indeed, more a matter of personalities than of parties. Two men count aside from Duchet and Pinay—Jacques Soustelle and George Bidault. (Pierre Poujade, the demagogue who wants to abolish taxes, has become a dead letter, and does not rank in this category.) All the rightist leaders disagree violently except on one paramount issue, Algeria. They think that de Gaulle is being far too soft on Algeria, and want a much firmer line. The prospect that Algeria may be permitted to wriggle out of the French embrace appals them.

Soustelle, as is well known, was one of the men closest and most faithful to de Gaulle for many years. Formerly a man of the left, an archaeologist by training, he is both an intellectual and a man capable of action—sometimes erratic action. He served brilliantly in various cabinet posts (including Information, Overseas Departments, and Atomic Energy) and was a governor-general of Algeria, but was ousted from the de Gaulle party in April, 1960. He is reasonable on practically every subject in the world—except Algeria.

Bidault, born in 1899 (Soustelle is much younger), a familiar figure in contemporary French politics, once premier and foreign minister, was for years a pillar of the MRP, but departed from it, on account of Algeria, to take a right-wing position of his own. His new party, which consists largely of himself, is known as the Christian Democrats. But Bidault, who was once a professor of history, is important for two reasons: he led the Resistance within France during the war, led it well, and is still regarded as something of a hero; second, he gives the right a certain amount of intellectual prestige.

Turn now to the left of de Gaulle, excluding multifarious splinters. The left in general is, as of today, a somewhat etiolated force, but four centres of power exist. *First*, Pierre Mendès-France and his group of left secessionists from the Radical Socialist party. This is a small group, but Mendès, compromised as he is in some respects (he was prime minister at the time of Dien-Bien-Phu), cannot be ignored because he has outstanding ability, courage, and imagination and is trying to create a genuine leftist party—also because, after de Gaulle, Pinay, and perhaps Bidault, he is the only politician in France who has true national stature. The Mendès group now bands itself with a loose coalition known as the Union of Democratic Forces. *Second*, remnants of the old Radical Socialists and left Republicans (forty-three seats). One Radical leader of interest is the youthful—and engaging—Félix Gaillard, who was next-to-last prime minister of the Fourth Republic. *Third*, Guy Mollet and the orthodox right-wing socialists (forty-four seats). But Mollet works under several onerous handicaps; he was prime minister at the time of the Suez catastrophe, and, subsequently, deserted his own party in effect by accepting allegiance to de Gaulle; he was a minister of state in 1946, and agrees with him in the main on Algeria today. He disagrees with him, however, on recent developments concerning NATO and nuclear policy. Mollet is an intellectual, very bright, in his middle fifties, who has risen out of the working class. His father was a textile worker. *Fourth*, the Communists.

The Communist position is difficult to evaluate today, partly because of a new electoral law passed under de Gaulle, which, among other things, limits representation in the National Assembly to parties which have a minimum of thirty deputies.[1] At its peak—1946-47—the Communist party was the biggest in France; it had some 900,000 members, polled more than 5,500,000 votes—a flat quarter of the electorate—and had around 150 deputies. In the elections of November, 1958, its poll dropped sharply to 3,882,000 votes (18·9 per cent of the total), but this was still a sizeable figure; however, because of the way the electoral process has been applied, the party received only ten seats in the Assembly. What has hurt the Communists most is prosperity. It is difficult to get workers to man the barricades with insurrectionary zeal these days; on the other hand, the Communists were able to fill the Paris streets with a quite sizeable crowd during the Khrushchev visit in 1960. Another factor deleterious to the Communists is that they have become an *old* party. The leadership is pre-war. The Communists are, as it goes without saying, opposed to NATO, European

---

[1] The motive was, of course, to play down the curse of French politics, fragmentation.

integration, and the Common Market; they condemn de Gaulle in violent terms, but do not always specifically oppose him: for instance, in June, 1960, the party supported his offer to negotiate with the Algerian rebels. The biggest force behind the Communist party is the most powerful of French trade unions, the Confédération Générale du Travail, or CGT. The chief Communist leaders are still the veterans, Maurice Thorez, an old Stalinist who nevertheless has the confidence of the contemporary Kremlin, and Jacques Duclos, his Sancho Panza. Thorez, born in 1900, was the son of a coal miner; he led the Communists into the Popular Front government in the mid-1930's, and subsequently spent much time in Moscow.

PREMIER AND FOREIGN MINISTER

Michel Debré, the first Prime Minister of the Fifth Republic, was born in Paris in 1912; he is partly Jewish, being the grandson of a former Rabbi of Neuilly; his father was a distinguished professor of medicine and he himself, an intellectual by taste, is a Doctor of Law (University of Paris). Debré became a civil servant, joined the armed forces in 1939 and, when France fell, entered the Resistance. The de Gaulle magic touched him early, and he has been a fanatic supporter of the General for twenty years.

After the Liberation, Debré became a prominent figure in the Réassemblement du Peuple Français, and won a senate seat which he held for ten years, representing Indre-et-Loire. He became well known for a book attacking the Fourth Republic scathingly, and rose to be the chief de Gaulle spokesman in the senate. He played a leading role in the May, 1958, 'conspiracy', and, when de Gaulle took power, he was named Minister of Justice; it was he who wrote the constitution of the Fifth Republic and, when de Gaulle finally became President of France on January 18, 1959, he made Debré his first minister.

The Prime Minister is an absolutely honest man, something that cannot be said of all French politicians; his courage is marked, but he lacks political touch. Essentially, of course, he is a de Gaulle subordinate, nothing more or less. He does not tolerate criticism easily, and recently broke out with the angry remark, 'What other country would tolerate such papers as *L'Express*, *France-Observateur*, the *Canard Enchaîné*, or *L'Humanité*, which systematically denigrate the work of the government?'[1] A quick answer came from the *Canard*: 'What other country would tolerate M. Michel Debré as Prime Minister?' Debré, like many men of the Resistance, still maintains a somewhat conspiratorial air. One man who observes him closely calls his entourage a 'cryptocracy'. Each clique near the summit of power has its own active little network.

Apart from Algeria, Debré's principal recent preoccupations as Prime Minister have been in regard to French nuclear policy and the Franco-German rapprochement, including NATO. As to the former, France has, as is well known, set about to build its own nuclear deterrent, which, it is estimated, will cost the large sum of £462,000,000 up to 1965. The French have made three test explosions in the Sahara, and plans have been drawn for a small—and expensive—bomber fleet capable of delivering atomic weapons. De Gaulle insists on French possession of the bomb and means to deliver it for at least four reasons: First, to enhance French prestige by membership in the 'nuclear club'. Second, lurking fear of German rearmament, and worry that the Germans will, in time, be bound to have *their* nuclear deterrent. Third, resentment at American policy, which insists that the United States retain custody of American atomic warheads on foreign soil, which de Gaulle will not countenance. Fourth, unwillingness to be party to any future arrangement whereby a French nuclear striking force would be subject to international (NATO) control.[2] Debré has had a hard time putting the de Gaulle nuclear plan through the National Assembly, despite the President's prestige. The government narrowly escaped being beaten on several votes of censure, and the bill did not finally become law until after seven difficult weeks of exacerbated debate.

As to relations with Germany and NATO, the de Gaulle position rests mostly on his dislike of supranationalism. He certainly wants rapprochement with Germany, but on his own terms. Debré went to Bonn in October, 1960, to thrash out these matters—without concrete result—and de Gaulle himself has continued to flutter the NATO dovecotes. He wants 'a Europe

[1] *New Statesman*, August 13, 1960.
[2] More about these complexities in Chapter XVIII below.

of fatherlands', with national instincts stressed, less integration, the creation of a new 'European secretariat' to sit in Paris, and a veto on the use of nuclear weapons by any of the NATO powers. To some observers, this seemed to be 'a search for French national grandeur at the expense of Allied unity'.

Maurice Couve de Murville, the Foreign Minister, is, like Debré, a University of Paris LL.D. who worked for some years as a civil servant. He was born in Reims in 1907, and has variously been Director of Political Affairs at the Quai d'Orsay and Ambassador to Cairo, Rome, Washington, and Bonn. He became Minister of Foreign Affairs in the first de Gaulle government in 1958, to his own surprise, and has retained this position ever since. He is one of the very few members of the government who did not support de Gaulle during the war. He served under Vichy until 1943, as a civil servant, and then worked briefly for General Giraud, de Gaulle's detested competitor for supreme power. Couve de Murville, a somewhat colourless personality, is little more than an executant of Gaullist policies. He gets along well with Germans, and, during the period when the Franco-German rapprochement was at its rosiest, was called jokingly the 'Franco-German Minister of Foreign Affairs'.

LOOKING AHEAD

Should de Gaulle die tomorrow, almost anything might happen. One man's guess is as good as another's. If events proceed constitutionally, Pinay probably has a better chance to succeed than anybody else, because he has a strong following of his own, and, although on the right, might receive substantial leftist support because he would be regarded as a defence against more extreme rightists. Another possibility, but fainter, is a leftist coalition led by Mendès-France or even Mollet. Both these possibilities are, however, strictly contingent on evolution by legal means, and this may very well not happen. If de Gaulle should die or be somehow discharged from office *before* the Algerian war is settled, the possibility of a *coup d'état* is marked. Soustelle might try to seize power; he is quite capable of such an attempt, if he has army support. This might bring the Communists out on the streets, and could conceivably cause civil war. Most good observers think that, in the event of a supreme crisis, the army itself will try to take over, *at least if the Algerian war is still going on*. This is one reason why de Gaulle is so desperately eager to effect some kind of settlement in Algeria as soon as possible. Only he can make an Algerian settlement without civil war.

CHAPTER VIII

The Army, Algeria, and Africa

THE only thing which, at the moment, could upset the de Gaulle régime would be a critical worsening of the situation in Algeria. But the General handled the abortive uprising of January 24, 1960, with such dexterity and sureness of hand that another revolt by the 'ultras'—the last-ditch *colons*, or French settlers on Algerian soil—is unlikely, or at the least has been postponed. The attitude of the French Army is, however, ambiguous, and could lead to grave trouble. One reason why most reasonable Frenchmen hope that de Gaulle will hold on for another five years or so is that, if he dies with the Algerian problem still unsolved, the army might seize power by revolutionary means, as has just been mentioned, and, under some such officer as General Raoul Salan, make a military dictatorship.

This does not necessarily mean a Fascist or reactionary dictatorship, because the French Army in Algeria is a very peculiar army indeed. Salan himself is in Spain, as are Pierre Lagaillarde and others involved in the January revolt. Conceivably the army could install and operate a 'mixed' or even leftist dictatorship. The army is much divided. In the old days it was profoundly conservative, and the officer caste was largely Catholic. A young man could not easily get into Saint-Cyr unless he had recommendations from, first, the local *préfet*, who was apt to represent the gentry, and, second, the local *curé*. Thus officers were recruited largely out of the conservative class, and most of them stayed conservative, if not reactionary, all their lives—consider men like Marshal Juin.

But nowadays the conventional Saint-Cyr type of officer is dying out. Men who were captains or above in World War II have largely been retired; a new generation has come up. A strong proportion of officers—and men—who form the core of the army today are veterans of the campaign in Indo-China, and they learned much from it—quite apart from the humiliation of defeat. They studied the revolutionary military doctrines of Mao Tse-tung; they learned how effective guerrilla warfare could be when it was based on intimate contact with the local peasantry. Some French officers were captured by the Chinese; some were brainwashed. To almost all came the realization of the power of a people's army as distinct from a conscript army led by an old-style officer caste, and the perception that the French Army must renovate itself, move with the times. The bitter old joke was that France was perfectly prepared in 1914 for the war of 1870, and in 1940 for the war of 1914. This kind of quip does not go down well with officers today.

One peculiar point is that the army in Algeria does not particularly like or admire the French settlers, *colons*. Army men have made use of *colons*, and worked together with them on occasion, but there is little deep sympathy between them; they call the *colons* contemptuously the *pied-noirs*, black feet. One would normally expect army and settlers, two branches of the same root, to have close identity. But this is not the case, in part because the army is coldly aware that it is the *colons* who have been most responsible for poisoning relations with the indigenous Moslem population, and it realizes (after six years of war) full well that no permanent solution can come in Algeria if the Moslem population is flatly alienated. It wants to conciliate those Moslems with whom it is not actually fighting. After all, simple logic makes it obvious that it will be easier to stay in the country if the mass of Algerians are friendly.

But the army is suspicious of de Gaulle too. This is because it fears that circumstances may force him to give Algeria up, even against his will, and this is one thought that it cannot abide. Above all, the army wants to stay on in Algeria. This is the core of the whole army position. It is not a reflection of military colonialism, but of hatred of defeat. The French Army was beaten in France; it was forced to withdraw from Syria and the Lebanon; it was squeezed out of Morocco and Tunisia; it went through the catastrophe of Dien-Bien-Phu in Indo-China, and lost the whole French position in the Far East—the record is of unvarying retreat, retreat, retreat, and defeat, defeat, defeat. So the army says, in effect, 'Defeat no more! Here we are in Algeria, the last bastion, and here we stay!'

Meantime, serious tension continues to exist between extremist elements of the army and de Gaulle's civilian administrators. In January, 1960, the army first took the side of the rebellious *colons* who barricaded themselves in the streets of Algiers; then it receded when it became clear that almost the entire mainland of France stood solidly behind de Gaulle, and the *Putsch* collapsed. The de Gaulle government has done its best ever since to 'clarify' the situation by drawing army fangs, and a good many officers have been quietly eased out of the country, retired, or replaced.[1]

*

The Algerian war, the only hot war being fought in the western world today, began with a raid on French installations by a band of Algerian nationalists, probably not numbering more than five hundred in all, on November 1, 1954. The French thought of this—at first—as a minor, if irritating, stab in the back. Before long the stab was to become a gaping wound in the body politic of France, from which the nation might well bleed to death. The shock to Paris was so disconcerting because Algeria had for a long time been thought 'safe', although almost any sensitive visitor to Algiers in the early fifties did not have to look far to see that it was not. But the French put Algeria in an altogether different category from its neighbours Morocco and Tunisia, where nationalist sentiment had produced violent disorders. Algiers was—technically at least—an integral part of France itself, just like Normandy or Touraine, and an actual full-dress revolt there was 'unthinkable'—something akin to civil war.

One chafing factor was (and is) the fact, known to everybody, that Algeria contains not merely approximately nine or ten million Moslems but also one million French. A gruelling aspect of the problem has always been what to do with these million

[1] In February, 1961, General Jean Crépin, commander-in-chief in Algeria, was moved to another sphere and became commander of French forces in West Germany, replacing General Paul Allard, who had 'reservations' about de Gaulle's Algerian policy. Similarly, General Maurice Challe, the NATO commander for Central Europe, was replaced. Two generals now on top are fervent Gaullists, General Jean Olié, the new chief of staff, and General Fernand Gambiez, who has become commander in Algeria. *New York Times*, February 1, 1961.

white Frenchmen—*colons*, businessmen, officials, workers—who
live in the country. Sacrifice them? Leave them to the tender
mercy of those whom they call *sales arabes*? Transport them back
to France? Establish them in new careers, new livelihoods, on
the mainland? Or what? One could make a fine point here, and
say that plenty of the million white men and women in Algeria
are not truly French—many are of Italian or Spanish origin,
so much so that non-Arab Algerians almost seem to represent
some kind of new, mixed 'Mediterranean' nationality, with
Corsican, Sardinian, Basque, and Maltese elements. But all are,
of course, French citizens, and the problem of how to preserve
their interests justly, what to do with them, is inordinately
vexing.

The war has cost France—and Algeria—extraordinary losses
and dislocations. The French have been forced to maintain an
army in Algeria numbering 500,000; this makes—to put it
mildly—a serious drain on the national economy. Nobody knows
exactly, but probably the war costs the French exchequer
£700,000,000 per year. Moreover, casualties are unpleasant,
even though the fighting has, of recent months, died down a
good deal; French boys are being killed day by day, and the
average annual casualty list is about two thousand. On the
Algerian side total casualties are estimated by the French to be
about 210,000; by the Algerians, at a minimum of half a million,
including 150,000 dead. (French officers and men killed number
13,000.) Large areas of the country are still not safe for travel;
the local economy has been wrecked; and almost 1,250,000
Algerians have been forcibly 'regrouped' by the French
authorities into refugee centres. This enormous number of
people, more than 10 per cent of the total population of the
country, has been cleared out of areas which have been particularly troublesome or have given cover for guerrilla fighting;
whole districts have been physically emptied, wiped clean, of
human occupation. Finally, a quarter of a million Algerian
refugees have fled to Morocco and Tunisia.[1]

One remarkable thing is that the Algerians, despite unceasing
and relentless French pressure, including torture by the local
army and police, have not merely been able to maintain themselves as a guerrilla force seemingly impossible to expunge, but

[1] *World Today*, August, 1958, October, 1959, and March, 1960.

have created something akin to an actual government, although the French hotly deny this. The FLN (National Liberation Front), as the rebel organization is called, collects taxes and maintains local order of a sort. Probably its writ covers one-third of the country, although the French, of course, hold the vital coastal strip. Leader of the FLN is Ferhat Abbas, who is known as the President of the Provisional Government; his headquarters are in Tunis, or sometimes Cairo. Abbas is sixty-two, and was for some years a deputy representing Algeria in the French parliament; he belonged originally to the moderate wing of Algerian nationalists, and did not join the insurrection, of which he is now titular political as well as military leader, until 1956, when the revolt was two years old. He is often considered to be a front for more violent elements, and several sub-leaders—for instance, Belkasim Krim, the vice-premier—probably exert more power than he does. Ferhat is highly astute, emotional, and tenacious—an unusual combination. His wife is French, and he is supposed to speak better French than Arabic.[1]

The Algerian case, as outlined by Ferhat Abbas and his fellows, is quite simple: Algeria is the only Moslem country left in the world which is not free, and amply deserves freedom. International considerations have played a lively role in the evolution of the FLN. One is that Colonel Nasser, the Egyptian leader, whose hatred of France has been inflammatory since Suez, has backed the insurrectionists strongly. The French go so far as to say that the FLN could not 'exist' without Nasser. Still another is that Tunisia and Morocco, as would be expected, support the FLN to the limit in the UN, as do other members of the Afro-Asian bloc. Most important, the FLN seeks support from the Soviet Union and in particular the Communist Chinese. Ferhat Abbas has visited both Moscow and Peking (although the FLN is certainly not Communist), and late in 1960 Mao Tse-tung pledged 'total and unconditional' aid to the Algerians. A permanent Algerian mission has been established in the Chinese capital. Moscow, however, until recently at least, has blown both hot and cold. This is because the Russians, hoping to weaken NATO, have tended to support de Gaulle *vis-à-vis* the Algerians because he was anti-NATO. But lately Russian —as well as Chinese—arms are supposed to be reaching Algeria,

[1] *Time*, January 20, 1961.

and in October, 1960, Mr. Khrushchev (while at the UN) joined Mao Tse-tung in promising the FLN 'the utmost aid possible to help the Algerians attain freedom'.

Half a dozen possible 'solutions' of the Algerian problem, if you can call a poisonously destructive war a mere 'problem', exist in theory:

1. Complete French military victory, and restoration of the *status quo*. Impossible except at insupportable cost.

2. Complete Algerian military victory. Likewise impossible.

3. Partition, on the model of Eire, India-Pakistan, or Israel. Geographically unworkable.

4. Complete 'integration' of Algeria into France, which is the programme of the French right. But no one is willing to define 'integration' exactly. Everybody agrees that, if integration is to work, very large concessions will have to be made to the Moslem population, such as full political representation in Paris. The Arabs are promised 'equality', but what 'equality' is to consist of remains to be seen.

5. A policy of 'accommodation', which is the Gaullist formula.

General de Gaulle, assuming office as Prime Minister in May, 1958, spent eighteen months surveying the situation until he made up his mind—provisionally. (Of course, I am omitting much in this brief summary; for instance as early as October, 1958, he proposed terms of honourable surrender to the rebels, and in the same month set up what came to be known as the 'Constantine Plan' for economic rehabilitation in Algeria.) Then, on September 16, 1959, came a major policy enunciation —which went unprecedentedly far not merely in opening up the possibility of negotiations with the FLN but in promising Algeria concessions hitherto undreamed of. De Gaulle said, in short, that, once fighting had stopped, he would be prepared to grant Algeria the right of self-determination. In other words, he conceded that the country had the right to decide its own fate, and to choose freedom if it wished. But he insisted on a cease-fire and then a four-year 'cooling-off' period as a condition for elections. In these, when they were held, the Algerian population could pick one of three alternatives: (1) secession, i.e. complete independence from France; (2) autonomy within

4

the French framework; (3) *Francization,* or unity with France, that is, integration. But he did not use the actual word 'integration', which is a red rag to the Algerian nationalists. Of these alternatives de Gaulle himself favoured the second. It is also important to note that if Algeria chooses secession, the country will probably be partitioned; purely French areas will stay French.

The FLN decided promptly that the de Gaulle offer, sensational as it was, did not go far enough, and rejected it. The objections were that it did not define the terms of a cease-fire; it left France in control of Algeria for four years more, and there was no guarantee as to the circumstances in which the elections would be held. But if the FLN did not like the de Gaulle proposals, the army and the *colons* in Algiers liked them even less. The settlers in particular were outraged by the evolution whereby de Gaulle, who had come into power in 1958 to 'settle' the Algerian problem once for all by liquidating the war, was now opening the way to negotiations with the rebels, and even—insufferable insult!—making it possible for Algeria in the future to vote itself *away* from France. The January, 1960, revolt of the *colons* was the direct result.

On June 14, 1960, de Gaulle, a patient and reasonable man, tried again. He gave his personal guarantee that Algeria 'would be completely free eventually to choose its own future', and urged negotiations to discuss 'an honourable end to the war'. On June 24 the FLN accepted this new invitation and a two-man delegation representing Ferhat Abbas came to France. Conversations took place in secret at Melun, near Paris, but were badly managed and came to no result. The Algerian plenipotentiaries said that they were treated like 'prisoners', and were never even permitted to meet French negotiators of suitable rank.

*

After this events came thickly. Lines of division grew sharper in France. For a time de Gaulle stood roughly in the middle. Rightists pointed out that, if Algeria were lost, the economic results would be catastrophic on almost every level; for instance, it was calculated that Renault, the great motor-car works, would have to shut down two days a week. On the other side a variety of forces sought to influence the General. Roman Catholic cardinals, including the Archbishop of Paris, urged conciliation, almost at the same time that violent left-wing student demonstrations occurred, demanding a free Algeria. A formidable group of intellectuals, led by Jean-Paul Sartre and including men renowned all over the world, signed a 'Manifesto of 121' which went to the length of urging French soldiers in Algeria to desert.

On November 4, a new de Gaulle speech made a landmark. He still held imperturbably to his thesis that negotiations with the Algerian rebels could take place only if a cease-fire, on terms to be defined, came first, but he killed the possibility of integration as a solution once and for all. Indeed, he went so far as to say that 'an Algerian Algeria' with its own government and institutions, no longer under the control of metropolitan France, must be established, and that creation of an Algerian republic was inevitable. As a result the 'ultras' in Algiers rose again, but the rioting was quickly put down. De Gaulle himself visited Algeria in December to gain support for his solution, and on December 18 severe Moslem riots took place, with serious casualties. The army stood firm by de Gaulle, and for the first time in the history of the insurrection fired on European settlers.

A great public referendum, set up by de Gaulle, then took place on January 8, 1961. More than twenty million voters went to the polls in France, more than 2·6 million in Algeria. Voters were asked to answer yes or no to a double proposition on self-determination. The result was an overwhelming success for de Gaulle and the self-determination policy. He got 75·3 per cent of the vote in metropolitan France, 69·09 per cent in Algeria. Some 780,000 Algerians voted against the General. One reason for this is that a substantial number of Algerians are still, despite everything, not merely loyal to France, but actually serve as auxiliaries in the French Army. Algerians who were illiterate voted by colour: white for yes, purple for no.

Obviously this plebiscite ended the possibility of any purely 'French' solution, and once more preparations began for negotiations between Paris and the rebels. Glumly, thousands of *colons* prepared to pack up and retreat to the mainland, and the FLN announced promptly that it would offer special status to the Europeans who choose to remain if total freedom comes.*

*

One point not without interest is that the vast potentially-rich Saharan territories south of Algeria proper, and which were once considered to be part of Algeria, are not under discussion. The Sahara, no matter what happens elsewhere, is to remain indissolubly part of France. One reason why the French are determined to hold on to the Sahara at all costs is that large expanses in the desert are essential for nuclear testing; the other is, of course, that parts of the Sahara are full of oil. Production today is around eight million tons a year; this will have trebled in the next five years. Nationalist sentiment in the deep Sahara is negligible, and the FLN has little influence there at present.

* But elements of the army refused to accept the new situation. On April 22, 1961, four French generals, among them Salan and Challe, sought to seize power in Algiers by means of a military *coup d'état*. Paris faced the threat of attack by rebel parachutists. But de Gaulle stood firm, and the revolt ignominiously collapsed four days later. Even so, the possibility of furthur disorder cannot be altogether excluded.
—*Publisher's Note.*

MOROCCO, TUNISIA, AND BLACK AFRICA

Both Tunisia and Morocco won their independence from France before de Gaulle reached power, and entered the United Nations as sovereign states in 1956. This development, remarkable in itself, was made doubly remarkable by the speed with which it came. Everybody had known for years that Morocco and, more particularly, Tunisia, had well-organized and aggressive nationalist movements; but few observers, even as recently as 1952, so much as dreamed that freedom would be won so quickly. Yesterday (so it seems) Habib Bourguiba, the President of Tunisia, was a prisoner in French hands, and his country was erupting into a peculiarly unpleasant kind of chaos; Sultan Mohammed V of Morocco had been ejected from his throne, and was packed off to exile in Madagascar. Today each is head of an independent state, and the French position in the Mediterranean has been reduced to Algeria and the Sahara.[1]

[1] The Sultan died suddenly in 1961 as these pages went to press, and was succeeded by his son Hassan II.

It was not charity or submission to the will of the times that made France—which, to repeat, seemed as fixed in North Africa ten years ago as it was in Brittany—give up dependencies like Tunisia and Morocco without a struggle more prolonged than it was. One explanation is the Algerian revolt. The French knew well that, if this vitriolic insurrection spread both east and west to Morocco and Tunisia, all three states would probably be lost; so they decided to cut their losses, let Morocco and Tunisia go, and concentrate on trying to seal off and hold Algeria, by far the most valuable territory of the three and the one where the most Frenchmen live.[1] Another explanation is that the Tunisian and Moroccan nationalists took advantage of weakness in the French administrations on the spot, as well as a sharply divided political atmosphere in Paris at the time. Finally, Mendès-France took the lead in negotiations to free Tunisia.

In the old days, that is yesterday, just as in Algeria today, the classic French position was that it was impossible to surrender Tunisia and Morocco because to desert the *colons* there would be unthinkable. It is therefore illuminating—with Algeria in mind —to take note of what actually happened. In Tunisia about 100,000 of the 250,000 French *colons* have returned to France; those who chose to remain in Tunisia do not, surprisingly enough, seem to be voicing much complaint. One suggestive event is that many French landowners in Tunisia who returned to France were experts in the cultivation of sparse soil, and have brought their special agricultural skills, learned in Africa, to the mainland with good results. Particularly in parts of the south of France, where agricultural conditions roughly resemble those of Africa, this has been a fruitful development. As to Morocco the rush back to France was not so precipitate. The Sultan promised French settlers wide concessions in return for staying. Still, about 40,000 Frenchmen in Morocco, out of roughly 300,000, have returned to metropolitan France. But of course none of this, even if it seems to indicate that repatriation of the *colons* is not an insoluble problem, makes the Algerian situation less difficult. Algeria has, after all, a *million* Frenchmen, and to absorb and assimilate even a fair proportion of these into France will be a terrific task.

Freedom for Morocco, Tunisia, and Algeria was undreamed

[1] *World Today*, August, 1958.

of when I wrote *Inside Europe* twenty-five years ago. What has happened to *Afrique Noire*, Black Africa, French Africa below the Sahara, is even more sensational. These enormous groupings of territory, comprising the giant agglomerations once known as French West Africa and French Equatorial Africa (also the island of Madagascar), were—so it was thought—unshakeable pillars of the French Empire. But, during and after the war, it became clear that, in the long run, colonialism was doomed, if only for the practical reason that it was too expensive to maintain. De Gaulle had far-seeing ideas about this as far back as January, 1944, when he convoked a colonial conference at Brazzaville in Gabon, and promised the African peoples modification of the French bond in time. The next big step (to tell the story with maximum brevity) came in 1956, when the concept 'French Union' was invented under the Fourth Republic. This gave the French dependencies (they were no longer called 'colonies') a substantial advance towards autonomy. Then, soon after he attained power in 1958, de Gaulle took a really historic step. Under the Fifth Republic, the French Union became the 'French Community', the idea being that the French dependencies should evolve into an association of free states more or less like the British Commonwealth. He flatly offered all the French regions approximately the same choice as that which he was to give to Algeria later—to remain French, to secede, or to become self-governing states associated with France. Moreover, it was made clear that states which chose the third alternative could, at any time, advance further and declare their full independence.

Only one country, Guinea, voted for outright secession; promptly it became an independent state. It annoyed the French hotly that it did so. Apparently de Gaulle thought that nobody would take advantage of his magnanimity, and choose to cut the umbilical cord with France altogether. But, because of the example of Guinea and for additional reasons too complex to go into in this space, the other African states, having become autonomous members of the French Community, also decided to go the whole hog and advance to full independence. It was like a chain reaction. As a result all twelve of the remaining French countries in Black Africa became free by the autumn of 1960, although five also retain their membership in the French Community. The parade began with Madagascar, which became the Malagasy Republic; then Senegal and French Sudan amalgamated to form the Mali Federation.[1] Following in quick succession came French Congo, Chad, and the Central African Republic (formerly Ubangi-Shari), which coalesced into the new Union of Central African Republics but which retain their identities; the Ivory Coast, Dahomey, Niger, and the Voltaic Republic, which formed a loose grouping of free states called the Council of the Entente; Gabon; and finally Mauretania. In one wild week, eight different French dependencies became free. In all, France has voluntarily given up territory covering 3,014,317 square miles and containing roughly seventeen million people, without any trace of disorder between Frenchmen and African and without a shot being fired. And the United Nations has a covey of new black countries in its stout embrace.

This, to repeat, is an extraordinarily striking development; also healthy. The contrast to what happened in the Belgian Congo is significant. The French were not ideal colonizers by any means, but they gave a certain amount of education to their African peoples, made them citizens, allowed Africans to serve in the parliament in Paris, encouraged political advance to an extent, and, above all, did not go in much for segregation or colour bar; as a result, relations between France and Black Africa were (on the whole) harmonious, and when the French decided at last to get out they left an administrative cadre of educated African officials capable of carrying on. But the Belgians, in all their years in the Congo, built up nothing except what they called an 'economic base'. The Congolese had practically no training in citizenship, no advanced education, no experience of parliamentary institutions, no acquaintance with the techniques of democracy, no free Press, and no concrete practice in government; so strict had Belgian rule been that the very concept of nationalism was only understood in the most limited way. The French gave up Africa soberly, for realistic reasons, after a certain amount of tutelage and careful deputation of responsibility; the Belgians gave up the Congo overnight, long before it was ready for the soul-trying experience of self-government, and out of funk.

---

[1] Troubles, however, soon afflicted this new federation; it burst apart almost as soon as it was born, and became two separate states, Mali and Senegal.

CHAPTER IX

The Benelux Constellation

BELGIUM, the most highly industrialized state in Europe and one of the most densely populated, is a country sorely riven. One would not expect this—if only because the Belgians, an extremely sober people, have such a firm addiction to the bourgeois virtues; they are hard-headed, square-sided, and adhesively, stubbornly devoted to commercial enterprise and pragmatic results. This is a rich little country, which exudes industriousness; nobody wants to rock the boat. Even so, its politics are curiously unstable. Belgium had eight different governments in the six years between 1944 and 1950, and in the latter year, by reason of what is called the 'royal question', it came close to civil war. In the winter of 1960-61 came another period of exasperating crisis, when a strike caused by the government's austerity programme caused prolonged tension and disorder.

The deep, underriding cleavage in Belgium, which did not break off from the Netherlands and became a country on its own until 1830, is that between the Flemings and the Walloons. Belgium, though small, with nine million people, has two distinct components. The Flemings in the north number something over 50 per cent of the population; they are of Teutonic stock, and speak a German dialect close to Dutch. By and large they are less industrialized than the Walloons, poorer, and have a somewhat lower social status, although Antwerp, the chief Fleming town, as well as Bruges and Ghent, has a flourishing propertied class. The Walloons, on their side, are Celtic in origin, speak French, are tempted to look down on the Flemings, have a lower birth-rate, occupy the southern provinces of the country, and dominate industrial cities like Liége (in Flemish, Luik) and Charleroi. The capital, Brussels, lies between the two extremes, and partakes of both.

Another critical factor is religious. Belgium is overwhelmingly Roman Catholic, but there are Protestant elements both in urban Flanders and in the 'laïque' Walloon country. It is impossible to give exact figures, because no questions about religion are asked in the Belgian census, in order to avoid giving emphasis to separatist tendencies. Full religious liberty is guaranteed to all persons, and the state does not interfere in any way with the affairs of any church. An important issue is, however, that of state support of the church schools. The Socialist party vigorously opposes further state support of the 'free' or parochial schools, and wants to develop state (i.e. non-church) schools divorced from clerical authority. Finally, the division is sharp between the church party and the Socialists on the political level, even though most Socialists are Catholic. A final confusing point is that many good Catholics are vigorously anti-clerical.

Above all, the line between Flemings and Walloons is dramatized by language. Belgium is a bilingual state; it even has two official names—Royaume de Belgique in French, Koninkrijk Belgie in Flemish. All official documents, notices, signs, and so forth have to be in two languages, which makes necessary an immense duplication of effort and expense, and all children in the secondary schools are obliged to learn both. The Walloon population resents this bitterly, since French-speaking citizens don't see any point in learning Flemish, and the Flamands, on their side, dislike speaking French and even talk about the 'poison' of French culture.[1] The linguistic problem affects every level of society, although there are a surprising number of Belgians—above a certain age—who still speak only one of the two languages.

Following the strikes which disrupted the country early in 1961, and which cost more than £80,000,000, proposals were heard for a formal division of Belgium into a dual state, with the Walloons given autonomy. But it is unlikely that this will come to pass.

*

Behind all this are two other complicating issues, the so-called Royal Question and the Congo. Let us take them in turn.

[1] New York *Herald Tribune*, December 30, 1960.

Belgium is unique in that it has two kings, a father, Leopold III, and his son, Baudouin I. The father is, it is true, no longer on the throne and in theory plays no role in politics, but he is an essential ingredient to the story. To explain this we must go back a bit.

Leopold III, a thwarted personality, was born in 1901, and in 1926 married Princess Astrid of Sweden, Baudouin's mother. He acceded to the throne, in succession to his father, King Albert of the Belgians, in 1934. Astrid, who was a deservedly popular young woman, was killed in a motor-car crash in 1935, after she had been queen for only a year. Leopold was at the wheel of the car when the accident occurred—a severe traumatic experience. Leopold had always had strong political views. War clouds were mounting, and in 1936 he took Belgium out of its traditional alliance with France and England, hoping thus to buy off German attack. But on May 10, 1940, the Germans invaded Belgium for the second time in twenty-six years. Then, without consultation with the British and French who were desperately fighting beside the Belgian forces, and to their utter consternation, Leopold suddenly surrendered unconditionally to the Nazi invaders on May 28. No doubt patriotic motives influenced him; he thought that further resistance was useless. But it was passionately resented that he seemed to be taking a pro-German course and that, unlike Queen Wilhelmina of the Netherlands, he did not manage to get out of the country to become leader of an allied government in exile. His own cabinet, meeting in Paris, declared his action 'illegal and unconstitutional', and people said his father, the heroic Albert who had attempted to staunch the German avalanche so bravely in 1914, must be rotating in his grave.

For the next two years Leopold sat out the war in Brussels, technically a prisoner but allowed by the Germans to make use of the royal palace at Laeken, on the outskirts of the capital. In 1941 he married a young woman, Marie Liliane Baels, who was a commoner, and bestowed upon her the title Princess de Rethy. The marriage was morganatic, and was severely deplored by citizens who still had a close feeling about Astrid; moreover, the Princess de Rethy was accused—perhaps unfairly—of being pro-Nazi. Later in the war Leopold and his bride, with members of the family, were sent by the Germans for safe keeping, so to speak, to a lakeside resort near Salzburg in Austria, and a regent, Prince Charles, Count of Flanders, took over the throne. After the war Leopold sought to return to Belgium and resume his royal station; this provoked a savage, stubborn crisis. At last, on March 12, 1950, a plebiscite was held to decide the issue. Leopold won, but by a narrow margin. Protests against his resumption of the throne, mostly from socialists in the Walloon country, then rose so violently that the position became untenable; Leopold turned the crown over to his eldest son, Prince Baudouin, in August, 1950, after only three weeks of rule, and abdicated the next year. So Baudouin became king.

This young man was born on September 7, 1930. He is studious, diffident, and somewhat melancholy; in some respects he resembles his royal cousin, Otto Hapsburg, but has less charm. In 1960, after having been a bachelor king for almost a decade, he married Dona Fabiola de Mora y Aragon, a lady of the Spanish aristocracy slightly older than himself, and this match made a good impression if only because the country has been without a queen since 1935; citizens had more or less given up hope that the King would ever marry. Baudouin himself has not been particularly popular. First, his personality is somewhat dim. Second, he has several times taken a line of his own in domestic politics, a dangerous thing for a constitutional monarch to do. What role, if any, he played in precipitating the Congo catastrophe is still obscure. Third and most important, he still operates under the shadow of his father, Leopold III. For a time, Leopold and the Princess de Rethy actually lived with him in the palace at Laeken, and are now in a château nearby. Baudouin is passionately devoted to his father, and resents deeply the feeling of the country against him. Moreover, Baudouin gets along well with the Princess de Rethy, who is ambitious as well as beautiful. Belgians who dislike Baudouin— and Leopold—insist that the father and stepmother have a profound and perhaps pernicious influence on the youthful king. But Baudouin has supporters too. Several times recently public demonstrations have been held in Brussels, urging the King to dismiss Parliament and become a royal dictator.

Second, the Congo. Its loss has been a shock of the first magnitude. Belgium was like an iceberg. The exposed fragment of motherland, for almost half a century, got a large share of its wealth and substance from the huge submerged Congo mass. It is not too much to say that it was the Congo which made Belgium a first-class power. Quite apart from prestige there was the matter of hard cash. The Congo was as much controlled by Brussels as, say, on a very different scale, Gibraltar is controlled by London. Five enormous Belgian holding companies owned around three-quarters of *all* Congo business—a concentration of economic power unparalleled in the modern world. In all these five, the Belgian government itself held a very large interest, ranging up to 50 per cent. Details are abstruse, but, to cite one example, the Belgian government owns a two-thirds interest in the Comité Spécial du Katanga, which held 111,111,111 acres (the Belgians love neat figures) of some of the most valuable mineral property in the world. The CSK owns in turn about 25 per cent of the great company known as the Union Minière du Haut Katanga, one of the world's most formidably successful mining operations. Also tied into this structure is the fabulous organization known as the Société Générale de Belgique, a dominant factor in the entire Belgian economy. For decade after decade, profuse streams of wealth poured out of the Congo into Belgian coffers.[1] On the other hand the Belgians insist that the *present* economic importance of the Congo is not so marked as one might expect, and that its loss will mean a reduction in the national income of no more than 4·5 per cent.[2]

Why did the Belgians give the Congo up? Detailed analysis of these developments is beyond the province of this book, and we have not the space to go into them except in briefest summary. The overriding reason, as I have already mentioned in Chapter VIII above, was fear. The Belgians could not face the prospect that the Congo might become an Algeria. Pressure came from several directions. Belgian missionaries in the Congo, who are devoutly Catholic, wanted at all cost to avoid bloodshed. At the opposite end of the spectrum the powerful socialist trade unions in Brussels also warned the government of political consequences if unrest continued. Riots in Léopoldville (January, 1959) were unpleasant, but if they had occurred in British territory in Africa in the old days they would scarcely

[1] Some of the foregoing details are paraphrased from my *Inside Africa*.
[2] *New York Times*, January 1, 1961. Also see 'Why the Belgians Failed', by Claire Sterling, the *Reporter*, October 13, 1960, an illuminating account.

have turned the hair of a seasoned administrator. But the Belgians behaved with maximum nervousness, a year of tension followed, and the decision was taken to free the Congo. A round table conference took place in Brussels, at which various timetables for independence were suggested. Five years would have been a reasonable transition period. Instead, it was suddenly decided to give the Congolese their independence in six months!—on June 30, 1960—which was sooner than even the hottest nationalists expected. No one can possibly excuse the excesses which came in the Congo later, but the Belgians showed almost inconceivable lack of foresight in not realizing what would happen. They had, as we have just seen, given the Congo certain material advantages, but almost no higher education, no training in administration, and the scantiest of political tutelage. The Congo was still a tribal state—not a nation in the modern sense at all. The whole country, with a population of more than thirteen million, had no more than a handful of university graduates, and there was not *one* single native officer in the local defence force—which naturally mutinied. Of course the Congo had the basic, inalienable right to be free; the tragic error was to give it freedom without having taken even the minimum steps without which an orderly evolution to independent statehood was impossible.

Events in Katanga, where a pro-Belgian rump government emerged, are so fluid and confused at the moment of writing that it is difficult to assess them or forecast the future. Probably Belgian influence will remain paramount in this contested—and very rich—mining region.

PARTIES, POLITICS, PERSONALITIES

Three principal political parties exist in Belgium: the Social Christian, formerly known as the Catholic party, which won 47 per cent of the votes in the last general election (1958), and which has 140 seats in the lower house of Parliament; the Socialists, who got 35 per cent of the vote and have 84 seats; and the so-called Liberals, actually a party of the extreme right, who got 11 per cent and 21 seats. The government was a centre-right coalition of Social Christians and Liberals, with the Socialists (who held power alone from 1954 to 1958) in opposition.

The Liberals may, however, be dumped out at almost any moment, whereupon a Social Christian-Socialist partnership might take over rule.[1]

The Social Christians cover the arc from moderate right to moderate left; their glue is Catholicism, as it is in similar parties in Switzerland and Austria. This is predominantly a Flemish party, with its chief strength in Flanders. It has a strong left wing, which is closely tied to the Federation of Christian Trade Unions, the great Catholic labour organization. Also most of the Belgian aristocracy belongs to the Social Christian party, as do big business, the bulk of Flemish peasants, and workers who are practising Catholics. Traditionally this has been the Royalist party, and it supported Leopold hotly during the long kingship crisis.

The Prime Minister at the time of the strike was Gaston Eyskens, a middle-of-the-road Social Christian, who is a strong Catholic, a Fleming, and an intellectual by training and predilection. He was born in Louvain fifty-five years ago, studied in London and Geneva, did graduate work both at Columbia University in New York and at the University of Chicago, and became a professor. He won a master's degree at Columbia in 1927 for a thesis on, of all things, the economics of the Port of New York.[2] Eyskens, who is known as a rocker-along, a patcher-up, and who works a brutally hard day, entered politics back in 1934, suffered eclipse during the German occupation, and got his first big job as Finance Minister in a Catholic-Socialist government led by Paul-Henri Spaak, who later became Secretary-General of NATO. Spaak, a Socialist, is still the country's most distinguished citizen. More on him in Chapter XVIII below.

Second, the Liberals, who are to the right of the Social Christians. The leadership is divided about equally between Flemings and Walloons. Oddly enough, although on the extreme right, it contains abundant anti-clerical elements.

Third, the Socialists. This is an orthodox Socialist party affiliated to the International Confederation of Free Trade Unions; it is strongly anti-Communist, and resembles to a

[1] The government resigned in February, 1961, after a severe crisis caused by the great strike, and a new general election took place with indecisive results.
[2] *New York Times*, December 30, 1960.

degree the right-wing socialist parties in Austria, West Germany, and Italy. It bases its strength partly on the General Federation of Belgian Workers, the non-Catholic union which has a membership of 700,000. (The Catholic union, mentioned above, is slightly bigger.) Mostly, as is natural, the Socialists derive their support from the Walloon segment of the country, which is heavily industrialized.

The most conspicuous Socialist leader is Léo Collard, the president of the party, who is burgomaster of Mons. Born in 1902, he is, like Eyskens, an intellectual, and is a professor of international law by vocation. The boss of the socialist trade unions is André Renard, born in France. He was leader of the prolonged strike in the winter of 1960-61, which, as already stated, paralysed the country for a month, and led to the resignation of the government. Workers struck in protest against a complicated law—the so-called *Loi Unique*—which, aiming to reform the national economy, raised taxes and cut social security benefits.

The Communist party is legal in Belgium, but cuts no ice. It got less than 2 per cent of the national vote in 1958, a drop from 7·5 per cent ten years ago.

The only Belgian of note whose career goes back to pre-war days is the veteran Paul van Zeeland, a distinguished professor of economic science, banker, and former prime minister for long periods. He is a Social Christian, a minister of state, a good Catholic, a senator, a man of Flanders, and a graduate of Princeton.

*

Both the European Economic Community (Common Market) and Euratom, which we will deal with in a subsequent chapter, have their headquarters in Brussels. The Common Market establishment is imposing. As to economic matters, Belgium came out of the war in good shape, if only because the country was not devastated; in fact, Brussels, bursting at the seams with wealth, was the most glittering capital in Europe in the period 1946-48. Berlin and Paris were dead cities in comparison. Now the Belgian position, which is based on a processing economy, is less bright. For one thing critical troubles have come to the coal industry, especially in the Borinage district in the Walloon country. Coal mining, even though the coal was marginal, was the basic occupation of this important area, and considerable numbers of mines have had to be shut down. This has produced widespread social dislocation; whole villages have had to be abandoned and the populations absorbed in other communities.

Belgium is a charter member of NATO, but a good many citizens are half-hearted about it, like people in Scandinavia. The Belgians have always had a strong tradition of neutrality, and sometimes ask why the country should go to the formidable expense of supporting NATO fully if, in the event of war, it will instantly be overrun again as in 1914 and 1940. Of course the presumption is that, if a new war comes, the invader will not be Germany this time. In any case the Belgian defence budget is comparatively low in relation to its very high gross national product; man for man, the Belgians do not spend as much on defence as do the Dutch, although they are far richer. The Congo tragedy has played into this situation deeply, if only because Belgian resentment at both the United States and the United Nations has been acute. In August, 1960, Prime Minister Eyskens threatened to cut further the Belgian contribution to NATO. One sore point is the great military air base at Kamina in the Congo. Belgium, at the specific request of NATO, built, equipped and operated this base, which is believed to have the longest airstrip in the world, at a cost of £25,000,000, and is now obliged to give it up.

DUTCH TREAT

If Belgium, in a manner of speaking, has two kings, the Netherlands has two queens—the reigning monarch, Juliana, and her mother, Wilhelmina, who retired from the throne in 1948, but who is still alive and is known as Princess of the Netherlands. As a matter of fact, this is a country packed with duality; for instance, it has two names, Holland and the Netherlands (and a third adjective commonly describes it, Dutch). Also it has two capitals, Amsterdam and The Hague; the latter is officially known as the Seat of the Netherlands Government and Parliament. The only other countries with two capitals I can think of are Angola, Uganda, Bolivia, and the Union of South

Africa. Moreover, The Hague has two names; correctly it is called 's Gravenhage. The national currency is known as both *gulden* and *florin*, and, a last point, the country lives on two elements, land and sea.

The Netherlands has two queens, but, in contrast to Belgium, there is no 'royal question' on a similar level. Juliana is an exemplary character, loved and respected by her subjects; she was born in 1909, the daughter of Wilhelmina and Prince Henry of Mecklenburg-Schwerin, and in 1937 married a lively, outgoing young man, Prince Bernhard Leopold Frederik Eberhard Julius Coert Karel Godfried Pieter of Lippe-Biesterfeld. They have four daughters, no sons, and the presumption is that the next monarch will also be a queen; the House of Orange seems to go in for a succession of female heirs. Both Juliana and Bernhard can be regal if the necessity arises, but both make a point of informality. Certainly Juliana is the only queen I ever met in a kitchen. This was when she was visiting members of Bernhard's family in New York, and, at a small reception, happened to wander casually into the kitchen while guests were still arriving. As to Bernhard, he works hard at his job, is amiable, and has marked interest in aviation. His brother, Prince Aschwin de Lippe, is an expert in Oriental art, and is a curator at the Metropolitan Museum in Manhattan.

The Netherlands, a stout little country, has changed comparatively little since 1936. It is still remarkably homogeneous. There are no minority groups—except some thirty thousand Aboinese who fled from Indonesia in 1949—and religion, although a massive influence in the history of the nation, is not a separatist factor as it is in Belgium. The people are 42 per cent Protestant (mostly of the Dutch Reformed Church), 38·5 per cent Roman Catholic. The House of Orange is strictly Protestant. The country has few national resources, but its economic situation is good. The Dutch economy was wrecked and ravaged by the war, but this has had a counterbalancing advantage; new Dutch factories have been built from scratch, and are therefore more efficient and productive than those of Belgium next door, which pre-date the war. Rotterdam, which was gutted by the Germans, is now—after New York—the biggest port in the world; it handles more tonnage, as an example, than *all* French ports together.

There are several national issues:

1. The sea. The Netherlands has more than eleven million people in a land area less than twice the size of Wales; the density of population is more than eight hundred per square mile. Moreover, half the total area is below sea-level; hence it is necessary to construct and maintain dikes, which serve to keep the angry water out. But in 1953 came a flood disaster of cruel magnitude. The dikes were sundered by a North Sea storm, something like 400,000 acres of the country were flooded and made temporarily uninhabitable, and several hundred thousand citizens suffered. Ambitious reclamation projects have been going on for years. Land, the 'polders' dredged out from the sea, is being built out of water, protected by new dikes, and cultivated. The Zuider Zee is being drained and made into farmland; what was once a salt water gulf will become a new province of the country within the next twenty years. Furthermore a project was launched in 1956 to create another sizeable lake by damming the estuary of the Rhine. This is known as the 'Delta Plan'.[1] No wonder the aphorism is heard, 'God made the world and water, but the Dutch made Holland.'

2. NATO. The Dutch, who have good reason to know all about the horrors of war, are emphatic supporters of NATO and the Western defence system in general. This is the more remarkable because Dutch memories of Nazi Germany are still alive and bitter; even so, the practical-minded Hollanders, fully aware that no small country has much chance of survival except under collective security, have been willing to accept the rearmament of West Germany and West German membership in NATO. Their relations with the Federal Republic, if not cordial, are at least correct. In November, 1958, the Dutch decided to equip their forces with guided missiles, and to contemplate the building of a nuclear submarine. For these and other reasons, the Soviet Union frequently attempts to intimidate the Netherlands. In January, 1961, a Russian note to the Dutch government pointed out that it would be taking a 'terrible risk' if it made Dutch territory a base for American rocket weapons.

3. The Dutch are, of course, members of the Common Market, but would like to have cordial relations with the Outer Seven, a rival organization presently to be described, as well. The

[1] Cf. *An Atlas of World Affairs*, by Andrew Boyd, p. 60.

situation is the inverse of that of Switzerland, which belongs to the Outer Seven but has a lively trade with the Common Market too.

4. New Guinea. When the Dutch pulled out of Indonesia in 1949, the status of the great island of New Guinea, the second largest in the world, was left unsettled. New Guinea was not included in the transfer of sovereignty to Indonesia, but the Indonesians have claimed it ever since. The eastern half is, however, still administered by Australia, and the western half by the Dutch. The Indonesians take the line that the Dutch in West Irian, as they call this territory, occupy it illegally, and threaten to take it over. But the Dutch refuse to budge. This attitude is not so much a reflection of old-style colonialism as one might think. For instance, the Netherlanders have promised their segment of New Guinea self-determination after a ten-year period of tutelage, whereas the Indonesians, on their side, apparently intend to incorporate West Irian into Indonesia; it is the Indonesians who are the 'colonialists' in this case, rather than the Dutch. The Dutch area of the island, as big as France, is populated by people many of whom still seem to be living in the Stone Age; I have heard a Dutch sympathizer describe it as a 'worthless inferno'. It has some of the most impenetrable swamps—also mountain country—in the world, is still largely an untracked wilderness, and produces nothing of value. Among 700,000 people there are no fewer than four hundred different dialects. But the Dutch want to hold on for a variety of reasons. First, prestige. Second, a surviving overlay of bitterness *vis-à-vis* Indonesia—a delight in twisting Mr. Sukarno's ear. Third, religious impulses. The Calvinist tradition is strong in the Netherlands and many citizens feel that the Dutch nation has a duty to raise up the Papuans of New Guinea, educate them, before letting them go. Fourth, the New Guinea operation costs about £8,800,000 a year at the moment, a large sum for Holland, but it might turn out to be profitable in time.

5. The Koninklijke Luchtvaart Maatschappij, or KLM. This, the third largest airline in the world, is one of the few which operates at a profit; quite apart from this the KLM means a good deal to the Netherlands as a kind of imperial symbol— every Dutchman feels that it still carries the national flag bravely around the world even though Indonesia has been lost.

A prickly Dutch-American issue is that KLM has no landing rights on the West Coast of the United States, and wants these badly so that it can compete with other lines flying from Europe to California over the polar route. But for various reasons permission for this has not been granted by the American authorities.

*

The political structure of the Netherlands is intricate, but the atmosphere is quiet. Party antagonisms do not reach the pitch of those in Belgium, and stability is the rule. Queen Wilhelmina, who ruled for fifty-eight years, had only thirteen different ministries in the first forty years of her reign.

Today, however, there are five leading parties; this means that none is likely to get a clear majority, and government is by coalition. The present cabinet, which came into office in May, 1959, is composed of no fewer than four different elements, with the Labour (Socialist) party in opposition. Dominant in the coalition is the Catholic People's party, a centre group representing the Roman Catholic section of the population, with 49 seats in a chamber of 150; it governed in company with the Socialists from 1952 till 1959, but then the latter withdrew. Delicate and touchy manœuvres accompany the formation of Dutch coalitions. Once, eight years ago, it was necessary to have two foreign ministers in the government at the same time in order to maintain equilibrium. Two parties in the present coalition are Protestant—the Christian Historical Union and the Anti-Revolutionary party. The fourth member, the Freedom and Democratic party (Liberals), is arch-conservative. Catholics and Socialists run neck and neck. The Catholics, as just mentioned, have forty-nine seats; the Labour party forty-eight. This resembles strikingly the situation in two other worthy, small European democracies, Switzerland and Austria, where similarly the two principal parties run what is virtually a dead-heat.

The Communist party is legal, but has little power. It shrank from roughly 6 per cent of the total vote in 1952 to 3 per cent in 1959, and has recently split apart.

The Minister-President, or Prime Minister, is Dr. Jan Eduard de Quay, a moderate Catholic. In December, 1960, he threatened to resign over an issue having to do with government-subsidized housing, but after an eleven-day crisis resumed power with his cabinet unchanged. One curious point is that, by Dutch parliamentary practice, the Prime Minister is not allowed to speak on foreign affairs in Parliament or even at international conferences. Only the Foreign Minister, who is at present Dr. Joseph M. A. H. Luns, has the right to give pronouncements on prime affairs, although he is subordinate to the Prime Minister. This can produce complications. If, for instance, a meeting of foreign ministers is summoned in London by Mr. Macmillan or in Paris by President de Gaulle, Dr. de Quay must bring Dr. Luns along. The Dutch always send out first-class missions to foreign countries. They are represented at NATO and the UN by clever, sound, hard-working diplomats, and their embassy in Washington has been called the 'ablest' in the city.

THE PICTURESQUE DOMAIN OF LUXEMBOURG

Luxembourg, the area of which is exactly 999 square miles, lies between Belgium, France, and the Federal Republic of Germany, and is an interesting political curiosity. It has a well-established steel industry (for some years before World War II it was the seventh largest exporter of steel in the world), an extraordinarily high standard of living, a lively birth-rate, and no illiteracy. Its head of state, the Grand Duchess Charlotte, is the senior monarch—if you can call her an actual monarch—in Europe, and has reigned since January 9, 1919—more than forty years. Luxembourg has what is probably the best-known commercial radio station in Europe, and is trilingual; the people speak French, German, and the original language of the country, a Low German dialect called Letzeburgesch, which resembles Alsatian. The Luxembourgers, although there are only around 320,000 of them, are tenacious nationalists, and the motto of the tiny country is *'Mir wolle bleiwe wat mir sin'*, 'We want to remain what we are'.

When Luxembourg applied for membership in the old League of Nations in 1928 it had an army of exactly 250 men and two pieces of artillery. The armed forces are a bit bigger today, but still miniscule. Nevertheless, Luxembourg is an original member of NATO, and takes its obligations with seriousness. Luxembourg hoped to be the permanent headquarters of the Common Market, but this honour went to Brussels instead; it is, however, the capital of the European Coal and Steel Community, which is only fitting in view of its geographical position and flourishing steel industry.

The most distinguished citizen of Luxembourg is, by all odds, Joseph Bech, the President of the Chamber of Deputies. He was born in 1887, studied law at the University of Paris, and became a deputy to the Luxembourg Parliament back in 1914—just before the country was overrun by the invading Germans. He became Minister of Justice in 1921 and held office almost continuously until 1959, earning the title 'Doyen of European Statesmen'; he has several times been Prime Minister and Minister of Foreign Affairs, and led the Luxembourg government in exile from 1940 to 1945. He is a capacious individual, fond of life, who likes good food, wine, and company. One of his sons has become an American citizen.

The pattern of Luxembourg politics closely follows that of Belgium and Holland. The biggest party, with twenty-one seats in the lower chamber, is the Christian Social—a centrist Catholic party. Allied with it is the so-called Democratic party, which, like the Belgian Liberals, is strongly conservative and has an anti-clerical tinge. The opposition (seventeen seats) is socialist. The Communist party is legal, has a membership of roughly five hundred, and at present is represented by three deputies in a chamber of fifty-two. Manpower on a high political level is so short in Luxembourg that ministers double up on posts. Pierre Werner, a Christian Social, is both Prime Minister and Minister of Finance; Eugene Schaus, a Democrat, is Minister for Foreign Affairs and of the Armed Forces; another man holds the triple portfolio of Agriculture, Viniculture, and Education, and still another is Minister for Art, Culture, Transport, and Interior.

BENELUX ITSELF

I have asked several experts who invented the actual word 'Benelux', but never got a definite answer. It is an obvious enough abbreviation. The origins of Benelux go back to World War II, when Belgian, Netherlands, and Luxembourg leaders, exiled abroad, decided to strengthen their position by joining forces. But as a matter of fact Belgium and Luxembourg had established close economic ties long before this—back in 1921. The Netherlands joined the Belgium-Luxembourg combination in 1948, and a three-way customs union was formed. Since then the foreign trade of the bloc has doubled (and trade among the three member states has tripled), according to a recent statement by Pierre Wigny, the Belgian Foreign Minister. On February 3, 1958, the customs union agreement was expanded, and what is called the Benelux Economic Union, tying the three countries together even more firmly, was established; the system came into effect on November 1, 1960, and is to be valid for a treaty term of fifty years.

Already Benelux, considered as a unit, has a population of twenty-one million people, and is the fourth biggest 'power' in the world in volume of international trade. There are no customs formalities at all between Belgium and Luxembourg; one may cross the frontier without knowing it, and the currencies are interchangeable. Political contact among the three nations becomes closer steadily. Behind all this are some emotional complexities which, no doubt, will be fully ameliorated in time. Many Belgians, particularly the Walloons, are tempted to look down on the Netherlanders if only because the Netherlanders are almost indistinguishable from the Flemings, and many Protestant Netherlanders deplore Belgian clericalism. As to Luxembourg, it has been a little brother to the Belgians for centuries, and is closer to Brussels than it is to Amsterdam.

*

We turn now to the Mediterranean—and inspect for several chapters the southern tier of European countries.

CHAPTER X

Iberian Peninsula

PORTUGAL, one of the least-known countries in Europe, is an odd little place run by an even odder man. After twenty-nine years the remarkable Professor Dr. Salazar, the doyen of continental statesmen, is still in power, despite the recent bizarre affair of the *Santa María* and its oppositionist 'pirates'. The temptation is considerable to describe Salazar as a kind of Mussolini without castor oil, but the truth is more complicated.

As a matter of fact, although he decides everything that counts, the Portuguese Prime Minister came into office by perfectly legal means, never made a *coup d'état*, and has always ruled behind a façade of legitimacy. There is little overt terror in Portugal, and elections—of a sort—are held. In theory, Dr. Salazar could be dismissed at any time by Rear-Admiral Américo Deus Rodrigues Thomaz, the President of the Republic. But Thomaz is a figurehead pure, poor, and simple, and the chances that he might displace the indispensable Prime Minister are almost nil.

The gist of the matter is that Portugal under Salazar has most of the conventional stigmata of a dictatorship—a one-party system, suppression of free thought, a stifled opposition, rigid control of the Press, and an omnipresent if slightly comical secret police—but that procedures are mild on the whole. The state is organized on the corporative system, à la Mussolini, and Salazar is certainly the boss, but his régime is, as the Portuguese like to put it, 'authoritarian' rather than 'totalitarian'. Dr. Salazar does not believe in violence, and it would horrify him to be called anything but benevolent.

Salazar has named his corporative state the Estado Novo, and his party is the Uniao Nacional (National Union). There are two 'legislative' bodies, the National Assembly of 130 members, which is elected for a four-year term, and the Chamber of Corporations, a kind of advisory group of 135, whose members represent various economic, administrative, and cultural associations. In essence, a corporative system means that legislators represent professions and occupations as well as geographical districts.

Social ideals derive mostly from two celebrated Papal encyclicals, the Rerum Novarum of Pope Leo XIII in 1891, and the Quadragesimo Anno of Pius XI forty years later. These, in a nutshell, sketched out an elaborate social system, under the state, designed to encourage Catholic unity, uphold the sanctity of private property, and prevent economic friction and class war. Socialists have as a rule violently opposed them because, if implemented fully, they mean the end of trade unionism under socialist control, and deprive workers of their organizing power and right to strike.

Portugal is much softer in atmosphere than pre-war Italy or Franco's Spain, other corporative states. To an extent it resembles pre-war Austria, where the Quadragesimo Anno was also the theoretical basis of state policy, and where, one should remember, the system broke up in bloody civil war. The Portuguese experiment reflects the character of the people—generally bland, *gemütlich*, not given much to heroic extremes, and procrastinatory. Portugal, Dr. Salazar is convinced, is not yet ready for the responsibilities of democracy, and therefore he has to run it. Even the most upright, dedicated dictators base themselves on ego.

Strictly speaking, Portugal is an Atlantic power, not Mediterranean. The Atlantic bounds it on both west and south, and, as everybody knows, intrepid Portuguese seafarers performed prodigies of maritime exploration in the fifteenth and sixteenth centuries. Bartholomeu Dias rounded the Cape of Good Hope in 1488, and Vasco da Gama and other mariners touched on everything from Kenya to the Malabar coast. A double heritage comes out of this: (*a*) Portuguese relations with Brazil, a child now much bigger, richer and more potent than the mother; and (*b*) the Portuguese colonial empire, which, now that the British, Dutch, French, and Belgian imperial domains have been largely liquidated, is—extraordinary as this may seem—the biggest in the world.

Partly because of seafaring, partly because of the export of port, Portugal is Britain's oldest ally; this relationship was established by the Treaty of Windsor in 1386, and has stood up ever since. Portugal owns the Azores, which helps confirm its position as an Atlantic power; during the early part of World War II American planes would have been hard put to it to reach Great Britain if it had not been for the Azores. Portugal was theoretically neutral during World War II, but has been a member of the Atlantic Alliance and NATO since their foundation, and the Azores still has an American base. It is the only police state in NATO (with the possible exception of Turkey), and contributes little to it except geography.

The Portuguese entered the UN in December, 1955. Portugal has never recognized the Soviet Union and, like Spain, has no official contact with the USSR or the satellites.

The chief problem of the country (area 35,490 square miles, population 8,800,000) is poverty. A principal export is cork. Salazar has wrestled with economic difficulties in various ways. Portugal does not concede that the Soviet Union exists, but, on the Soviet pattern, it has instituted a series of six-year development plans; the present one runs from 1959 to 1964. The *per capita* income is still one of the lowest in Europe—about £82 a year—and social and other services are hopelessly archaic and inadequate. A good many tourists approach Portugal from Spain and are apt to think that, with its fresh scenery and pretty villages, it has a higher living standard than Spain. This delusion is caused partly by the fact that the Spanish territories adjacent to Portugal are the poorest in Spain, and so Portugal, in contrast, seems to be better off than it is. Another contrast is in the sphere of religion. Portugal is 97 per cent Catholic, but the Church is not such an overwhelmingly predominant factor as in Spain. Priests are not so conspicuous, and do not wear ostentatious dress; the Church in Portugal has nothing like the economic power of that in Spain, and Protestants are permitted to worship freely. As a matter of fact, Portugal and Spain do not resemble one another much, except superficially, even though they share the same peninsula.

Lisbon, like Rome and Kampala (the capital of Uganda), is built on seven hills, has distinctive charm, and is a very different article from Madrid. One curiosity is that its mellow suburbs contain a fabulous collection of ex-monarchs, royal pretenders, and their associates—all the way from former King Umberto of Italy to Magda Lupescu of Rumania, from the Count of Paris to the father-and-son team (Don Juan and Prince Juan Carlos) in line for the throne of Spain. Another is that Lisbon is an important post in the organization of Radio Free Europe, the American station in Munich which broadcasts to Russia and the satellites. Programmes do not originate in Lisbon, but it is vital as a relay point.

PERSON AND ATTRIBUTES OF DR. SALAZAR

Dr. António de Oliveira Salazar, a seminarian in his youth, was born on April 28, 1889. He was of humble peasant birth, the son of a farm worker; even so he managed to reach the University of Coimbra, where he won the degree of Doctor of Law. Then, giving up plans to enter the priesthood, he became professor of economic sciences at Coimbra, one of the oldest universities in Europe. His outstanding characteristic, unusual in a Portuguese, is asceticism. He is a bachelor, believes in discipline, earns £45 a week, lives in a three-room apartment, is frugal in the extreme, works fourteen hours a day, and only rarely sees outsiders. The number of interviews he has given in thirty years can be counted on the fingers of one hand. When, however, he does consent to receive somebody, his charm is marked. One recent visitor much impressed by him was Dean Acheson, the former American Secretary of State. His motto is, 'To study in doubt; to realize with faith.'

Salazar is, of course, a devout Catholic, and Portugal is certainly a Catholic country, but the Prime Minister is sometimes called, not altogether seriously, 'anti-clerical'. He is a man of state, not of the church, who firmly believes in the separation of church and state, and who does his best to keep the hierarchy in its place.

Salazar first came to public notice in 1926. Parliamentary government had broken down; there had been no fewer than forty governments in eighteen years. A general named Gomes da Costa made a revolution and inaugurated a dictatorship. Parliament was dissolved and a triumvirate of three military men—General António Oscar de Fragosa Carmona, Admiral

Mendes Cabecades, and da Costa—struggled for power. The national finances were in bad shape and one of the triumvirs, having heard that Salazar was a brilliant man with figures, suggested that he be called in to become Minister of Finance. Arriving in Lisbon, Salazar looked the situation over and, as a condition of taking the job, demanded complete control of the state budget. Da Costa refused, and the professor replied that he was perfectly content to return to academic life at Coimbra. Things in Lisbon went from bad to worse, the currency collapsed, and Portugal applied to the old League of Nations for a loan. The League refused to render assistance unless it could station an observer, with wide powers, in Lisbon; this suggestion affronted the national honour of the Portuguese and, as a way out, the suggestion was revived that Professor Salazar should take over.

By this time, 1928, the revolutionary triumvirate had broken up and General Carmona was President and dictator; he retained the presidency for twenty-three solid years, until his death in 1951. But Salazar, assuming the post of Minister of Finance in 1928, almost at once became the principal figure in the government; Carmona was merely the pompous, glittering front. Not only has Salazar been Prime Minister uninterruptedly since 1932, but he was Minister of Finance from 1928 to 1940, Minister of War from 1936 to 1944, and Minister of Foreign Affairs from 1936 to 1947; also he was Minister of Colonies for a time. Like Mussolini, he himself ran all the chief departments of the state.[1]

*

The party system in our sense does not exist in Portugal, but citizens sometimes run as independents against candidates of the National Union. Opposition does not exist formally under the dictatorship, but at least four different sources of political discontent are apparent, even though these are severely discouraged. There have been student demonstrations against Salazar on occasion, and once—back in 1937—an attempt to assassinate him.

[1] Cf. 'Portugal Today', by David Shillan, *International Affairs*, April, 1944; also *The Times*, May 5, 1936, and the *New York Times*, May 22, 1960.

The first dissident group today centres on a surviving handful of pre-1926 parliamentarians, who still command a certain respect. Second, elements in the army. Six army officers were among twenty-three men who were charged with plotting an armed rebellion against the régime in March, 1959. Third, a 'respectable' leftist group. Fourth, the Communist party. This, it goes without saying, is illegal, but it is well organized under the surface and aggressive, although small.

In 1958 came the remarkable Delgado affair. Humberto da Silva Delgado, an Air Force general who was Director-General of Civil Aeronautics, decided to run for President of the Republic against Admiral Thomaz, the National Union candidate. Delgado, be it noted, did not run against Salazar himself—only against the shadowy figurehead of the President. Nobody took the Delgado candidacy seriously until, to the stupefaction of citizens, the General acted as if this were a fair contest which he expected to win. There had been presidential 'races' before, but these were largely for form's sake alone. Moreover, Delgado openly criticized Salazar, made inflammatory charges about corruption and favouritism in the government, and said that, if elected, he would dismiss Salazar from the premiership. The upshot was that Delgado got an extraordinarily big vote—23·5 per cent in metropolitan Portugal, a bit over 25 per cent in the overseas territories as a whole, and not less than 35 per cent in Portugal's chief colony, Mozambique.

What was more embarrassing, Delgado (who once represented Portugal on NATO and in Washington) refused to keep quiet after the vote; in fact he insisted that he was the real winner, but had been counted out by fraud. Nothing, it seemed, would shut up this peppery little general. He even had the temerity to invite Aneurin Bevan, the British labour leader, to visit Lisbon for a series of lectures. This was too much. Delgado was arrested, and, after action by a disciplinary council of the army, was retired from active service on two-thirds pay. He was, however (the Portuguese are mild people), permitted to continue to use the title of general and even, on stipulated occasions, wear a uniform. But Delgado, refusing to accept rebuke, ducked into the Brazilian Embassy in Lisbon, and took refuge there. This caused a ferocious little contretemps in Brazilian diplomatic circles. Finally he was smuggled out of the embassy and flown to sanctuary in Brazil itself. One result of this fracas was a change in the law whereby presidents of Portugal (who are elected every seven years) will be chosen by an 'electoral college' hereafter, instead of by direct popular vote.

Then in January, 1961, came the freakish *Santa María* adventure. 'Pirates' boarded the Portuguese luxury liner *Santa María* (20,906 tons) when, on a Caribbean cruise with six hundred passengers aboard, it put in at Curaçao, seized it in melodramatic circumstances, and for twelve wild days held officers, crew, and company prisoner while they sailed in an eccentric course towards Recife, Brazil. These picturesque but not totally efficient desperadoes were not, of course, pirates at all, but anti-Salazar conspirators of the most gaudy dye. The leader was Captain Henrique Malta Galvao, an officer and man of letters who had once held an important post in Angola and who was subsequently imprisoned in Lisbon for revolutionary activity by the Salazar régime. He escaped, fled to Brazil, and established contact with Delgado. On the *Santa María* he said that he was acting on behalf of the 'National Independence Movement', headed by Delgado, who had set up a rump 'government', devoted to the overthrow of Salazar, on Brazilian soil.

American, British, Dutch, and Danish naval units, aircraft, and merchant vessels sought to track the *Santa María* down, without success. Dictator Salazar, violently embarrassed, asked the U.S. to arrest the ship, plant marines on it, and turn the conspirators (who, after all, romantic as their exploits were, had committed murder among other crimes) over to the Portuguese authorities. This the new American administration refused to do. At last, on February 2, while snowbound citizens on the Atlantic seaboard devoured every word about this exploit, which seemed to call forth memories of buccaneer days on the Spanish Main, Galvao and his men gave up, and surrendered themselves to Brazilian custody. Here, at the moment of writing, the story seems to end. But the episode had important repercussions in Portugal itself, by unleashing suppressed feeling against the dictatorship; Salazar—hit where it hurts most, in his prestige—had the most uncomfortable time he has known in almost thirty years.

*

The dictator is still doggedly active at seventy-two, though his days may be numbered now. One story is that he plans to retire at the end of Thomaz's term—1965. If the succession is legal, whoever becomes President of the Republic will appoint a new prime minister. Several candidates are spoken about. From the point of view of seniority and influence, the likeliest is probably Dr. Pedro Theotonio Pereira, a former ambassador to both the United States and the United Kingdom, who is now Minister of the Presidency in the Salazar administration. Another is Marcelo Caetano, Pereira's predecessor as Assistant Prime Minister, the Rector of the University of Lisbon; under Salazar he was the man who worked out the details of the Estado Nuovo corporative state. As to military men, General Julio Botelho Moniz, the Minister of Defence and head of the military establishment, is conspicuous.

To sum up: Portugal has changed little in a quarter of a century, and seems to be a backward, miserably poor relic off the track of most contemporary events.

PORTUGAL AND ITS COLONIES

The Portuguese overseas empire includes two enormous African territories, Mozambique and Angola, as well as smaller possessions scattered all the way from Portuguese India (Goa), to Timur in the south-west Pacific and the shiny, corrupt little enclave of Macao near Hong Kong. Another is the smallest colony in the world—the Fort of St. John the Baptist of Ajudá—on the Guinea coast in Africa. The Portuguese have held this remote outpost since 1680, and its population consists of one officer, the resident, and eleven men.

The Portuguese colonies are not, technically speaking, 'colonies', but are considered to be overseas departments of Portugal itself, as much a part of the country as Lisbon or Oporto. This status was given them in 1951, when Portugal itself was officially renamed an '*Afro*-European' power; the Portuguese saw the winds of nationalism rising everywhere and wanted to get away from the objectionable word 'colony'.

This terminological fiction does not alter much the realities of the situation. In effect, the overseas domains *are* colonies. Mozambique, Angola, and the rest are run by the Ministerio do

Ultramar in Lisbon, which in turn, like everything else in Portugal, is run by Salazar. A strong governor-general on the spot may influence policy to an extent, but Lisbon is the boss. The Portuguese overseas provinces, no matter what the window dressing is, are ruled exactly as Portugal itself is ruled, and the aim of the Portuguese administration is to perpetuate colonial rule for ever. The provinces have elections and send deputies to Lisbon, but there is no faintest thought of permitting the African population to develop towards freedom. The concept of self-government is utterly taboo; political organization is limited, and nationalism vigorously suppressed.

The Portuguese have been severely criticized in the UN and elsewhere for their perpetuation of colonial methods. In November, 1960, the Trusteeship Council of the General Assembly refused to accept the claim that Portuguese colonial territories were in reality 'overseas provinces', and directed the Portuguese government to report to the UN on affairs in each. Such information is required from all member states which still have colonies. Lisbon, of course, refused indignantly to accede to the request. The vote against Portugal (forty-five in favour of the resolution, six against, twenty-four abstentions) was a curiosity in that both the United States and the Soviet Union abstained, although for different reasons. Several states, even including Portuguese allies in NATO, voted against Portugal.

Angola and Mozambique, which I visited when I was doing roadwork for *Inside Africa*, are fascinating entities. Portuguese rule is a mixture of bad and good, mostly bad. Workers in Mozambique get an average wage of about one shilling a day, and in the whole of Angola, with a population of 4·5 million, there are probably not more than a hundred Africans with even a high school education. Forced labour, almost indistinguishable from slavery, is basic to the economy, education is starved, corporal punishment of a peculiarly vicious kind is the rule, and Africans have no political rights whatever. On the other hand, the Portuguese territories do not enforce segregation or colour bar, except in minor spheres, and the consequent result is an almost complete absence of racial tension. Lourenço Marques, the exceptionally attractive city which is the capital of Mozambique, is as relaxed as Johannesburg is taut, tortured, and explosive. Any Negro citizen of Portuguese

Africa can, with luck, become what is known as an *assimilado*. To do so he must fulfil four or five conditions—be literate in Portuguese, practise Catholicism, live in the European manner, give up polygamy, and attain a certain economic level. Then, on passing a test, he becomes a citizen with rights roughly equivalent to those of a Portuguese. In other words, the black man is enabled—presto!—to become white. But there are only about thirty thousand *assimilados* in Angola with its 4·5 million people, and only about six thousand in Mozambique, which has a population of 6·3 million.

The colonial issue has played nicely into Salazar's hand at home. Citizens say that Portugal is in danger, that their flag is threatened, that their good name has been defamed, and that they must rally around Salazar, their leader, in defence of their prestige. Opposition on other issues has been virtually eliminated—at least for the moment. Late in November, 1960, more than 100,000 men and women demonstrated in Lisbon in fervent support of Salazar and to protest against criticisms of Portugal at the UN. On the other hand, nationalist sentiment in Portuguese *Africa* is on the rise, and, following the *Santa María* incident, bloody riots occurred in Angola.

SPAIN: A FIVE-MINUTE GLIMPSE

Practically everything important in Spain today—except bullfights, the Roman Catholic Church, and the sublime lunar landscape under the high sky of Castile—dates from the Civil War. This served to sterilize Spain from the mainstream of European developments for a quarter of a century, produced grave economic stresses which still exist, and was the origin of the supreme power held by Generalissimo Francisco Franco. The Spanish Civil War broke out, as everybody above a certain age will remember, twenty-five years ago, when a rightist junta set out to overthrow the lawfully constituted government of Spain. It lasted from July 18, 1936, until March 31, 1939, and its wounds are not yet healed. Germany and Italy supported the rightists; the loyalist government came more and more under Soviet influence. Spain lost at least 700,000 killed in battle; cities were destroyed, industries wrecked, and agriculture starved. Some 250,000 Spanish citizens fled to France, and another quarter of a million spent terms long or short in prisons or concentration camps. At least thirty thousand were executed by one side or the other. Seldom in modern times has a country been more disastrously ravaged.

Today, it is hardly necessary to state, Spain is a totally different entity from that of 1936; the visitor does not hear gunfire in Toledo or Madrid. But it is impossible not to mention that, even today, the Spanish people are still deprived of even the rudiments of civil liberty, parliamentary rule, and democratic processes, as a result of the war. Of course, the case can be made that if Franco had *not* won the war, Spain might be Communist today, which would be a worse tragedy than the present situation. It is also true that Franco would not be dictator today except for the profuse help he got during the Civil War from his Axis partners, Hitler and Mussolini. Hitler and Mussolini are jackals now happily down the hatch, but Franco is with us still.

More than once during World War II Franco announced his 'absolute loyalty' to the Axis. On one occasion he stated that 'Germany's war against Russia was the greatest battle in history', and expressed pride that 'Spanish blood was flowing in this noble enterprise'. After the fall of France he met Hitler at the French border, smilingly shook hands with him, and then wrote later, 'Dear *Führer* . . . I stand ready at your side . . . and decidedly at your disposal, united in common historical destiny.' On the other hand, Franco never formally joined the Axis.

European memories are long; and Spanish leanings towards Hitler and Mussolini still rankle in some circles. Spain became a member of the UN in 1955, but is not yet a member of NATO, although the United States—perhaps unwisely—would like it to be. The reason why Spain is out is, clearly, that the small democratic governments in northern Europe, among others, will not countenance it as a NATO member. Spain itself would like very much to be inside the NATO structure, but will not apply for membership on account of the fear of being blackballed. Oddly enough, some loyalist refugees from the Civil War who live abroad—for instance in France—would *like* to see Spain in NATO, on the theory that this, in time, might liberalize the Spanish government.

*

Immediately after the Civil War came World War II. This meant that reconstruction of the devastated Spanish economy had to be delayed. Spain, with derelict and sparse resources, was thrown in on itself. After V-E Day came a moral boycott. Spain, a pariah, was attacked in the UN. It got no Marshall Plan aid. It was snubbed by most of the neutrals, and of course was violently condemned by the USSR and the Communist satellites. Even today there are no diplomatic—or other—relations between Franco's Spain and the Soviet bloc. I remember my surprise in Moscow in 1956 when, wanting to telegraph somebody in Barcelona on a personal matter, I discovered that this was impossible—also that there was no direct mail communication between the Soviet Union and Spain. Letters must be routed through a relay point in Switzerland.

As to the West, Spain remained isolated until 1953. Then came a salient event, the decision of the United States government to build, equip, and man a constellation of military bases in Spain. These were necessary because of the deteriorating political situation in Morocco, where American bases built only a few years before had lost some of their value, and because Spanish bases would be closer to Germany and the root of Europe.

The negotiations for the Spanish bases were, I was told by one of the men who conducted them, among the most difficult ever undertaken in a foreign field by the American government. Franco got a whopping price. The agreement provided for substantial American economic aid to Spain—£165,000,000 to begin with—and this sum has subsequently been copiously augmented. Including pipelines, naval stations, and miscellaneous investment, the American stake in Spain has become very large indeed. Both financially and otherwise, Spain was handsomely aided by the base agreements. The moral taboo was broken, and further contacts with the United States and Europe followed. Even so, the country must still tread warily in international matters. Not till 1959 did a British cabinet minister visit Spain officially; not till 1960, after a gap of twenty-seven years, did a Spanish foreign minister pay an official visit to the British government.

Spain, which has a population of roughly thirty million people, has had no boom comparable to West Germany and France, if only because it lacks basic economic elements. The average *per capita* income is miserably low—about £95 a year. The railways are probably the worst on the continent; most of the industrial plant is dated, and economy in some areas is at a standstill; and agriculture, the basis of the productive capacity of the country, has taken severe punishment. Social services do not come anywhere near the level of the rest of western Europe. There are about 300,000 unemployed, and industrial and other workers have recently suffered widespread reductions in take-home pay. On the other hand, there have been marked improvements recently on the financial side. A stabilization programme was inaugurated in 1959, which included devaluation of the peseta; as a result inflation has been checked. Also Spain became, in July, 1959, a member of the OEEC (Organization for European Economic Cooperation) and has received substantial loans from the Export-Import Bank.

General Francisco Franco, as I wrote in 1936 a few weeks after the outbreak of the Civil War, is a remarkable example of historical accident. Certainly he had had a brilliant career, and might in time have become head of state. But what pushed him into the foreground overnight was, first, the assassination of Calvo Sotelo in July, 1936, and then an aeroplane crash, three days after the war broke out, which killed General José Sanjurjo. Calvo Sotelo, a former Finance Minister, was to have been political chief of the rightist revolutionaries, and Sanjurjo was military leader. Franco, the Governor of the Canary Islands, stepped into his shoes, and instantly made a decisive impact by flying to Morocco, and, with the aid of Italian aeroplanes, transporting Foreign Legion and Moorish troops to the mainland. He became Chief of State a few months later.

General Francisco Franco-Bahamonde was born on December 4, 1892. His background was middle class. Entering the army, he rose swiftly; he was a captain at twenty, a major at twenty-three, and a brigadier-general at thirty-two—the youngest brigadier-general in Europe. The speed of this advance resembles that of General Douglas MacArthur. But Franco is an altogether different type of man. MacArthur, whatever his defects, has style, magnetism, talent for improvisation, dash, and an immensely forceful imagination. General Franco, who is small in stature, is pedantic, precise, grubby, and of limited

intellectual range. One of his nicknames in the early days was
the 'baby general'. Baby or not, he is probably even more of a
dictator and one-man boss in Spain than Khrushchev is in Russia.
He is Caudillo (Chief) of State for life, Leader of the Empire,
Commander-in-Chief of the Armed Forces, Prime Minister,
Protector of the Church, and head of the Falange party, the only
political party in Spain. He has absolute veto over legislation
prepared by the Cortes (parliament) and, unlike Khrushchev, is
one of the least collegial-minded of men.

The principal forces behind Franco are the army, church, and
propertied classes. One of his principal mechanisms for exercis-
ing authority—in civilian realms—is the Falange. This was not
a creation of Franco's, but was founded in 1933 by José Antonio
Primo de Rivera; its official name is Falange Española
Tradicionalista y de las Juntas de Ofensiva Nacional Sindicali-
stas, and it includes nationalist, monarchist, corporative, fascist,
and syndicalist elements. But it has little philosophical content
today and has, in fact, degenerated into being a kind of framework for the job-holding bureaucracy.

As to the Church, one might assume that the Franco government and the Roman Catholic Church are inextricably inter-
twined, but this is not quite the case. Church and state are, in
theory, one, but a considerable number of leading bishops, even
if they do not dare to express overt hostility, do not give more
than lip service to the Franco régime, partly because most of
them are inveterate monarchists. The late Pedro Cardinal
Segura y Sáenz of Seville, formerly the Primate of Spain, was a
persistent opponent of Franco's. The dictator's main support
comes from the extreme reactionary wing of the Church. Nor
does the Vatican—under Pope John XXIII—have relations with
Spain quite as inexpungeably intimate as heretofore. Franco
aside, the Church has always had, as everybody knows, special
and extraordinary powers in Spain. The Inquisition was not
formally abolished until 1931, and blasphemy was a crime until
the revolution made by the Popular Front. Today the Church
hierarchy and the religious orders, like the Jesuits, with their
enormous holdings of land and interlocking ownerships of mines,
industries, shipping, utilities, and transportation, still have
marked economic power, and the influence of the Church on
education is paramount. Even in state schools Catholic teaching

is obligatory. There are not more than 25,000 Protestants in the country (Spain is 99·98 per cent Roman Catholic), and the activity of these is severely limited. Protestants are allowed to worship in their own chapels (about 180 in all of Spain), but Protestantism itself is officially condemned as an evil. Protestants are not allowed to print or import Bibles, take commissions in the armed forces, edit newspapers, hold public office, or, most important of all, have their own schools.

The Franco dictatorship rules supreme, but plenty of surreptitious discontent is evident, even though the government mercilessly stamps out opposition. One root of dissent lies, oddly enough, within the Falange itself; there are many Falangists who consider that Franco has betrayed the original ideals of the youthful Primo de Rivera. Another is in the generation of youngsters who have grown up since the Civil War and are now at university age. They feel stifled and contribute abundantly to the pervasive sense of *malaise*—if not actual unrest—which becomes more conspicuous every year, even if it is largely unfocused. Censorship of Press and radio is still complete, but it is impossible to keep citizens from absorbing something of the intellectual drift of the rest of Europe, and people talk. Then, too, the classic separatist groups, the Catalans and Basques, still remain. Politically, opposition goes all the way from Catholic monarchists on the extreme right to the Communist party—illegal and underground, of course—and surviving remnants of the anarchists. One Catholic group is the peculiar organization known as the Opus Dei; another, led by José Maria Gil Robles, a pre-Civil War figure, is called the Christian Democrats. Then there are various shadow parties. Considering the severity of the dictatorship the amount of political fermentation that prevails is, in fact, astonishing. Probably, all in all, something between 80 and 90 per cent of the people as a whole oppose Franco, but they have no means of displacing him. However, occasional illegal strikes take place, although all strikes are strictly forbidden, and every once in a while announcements come that citizens have been arrested for subversive activity, and face trial by military tribunals. In contrast to procedures in Portugal, punishment is apt to be brutal. Spain, in short, is not in a healthy state. A magnificent country and a marvellous people are throttled by one of the shoddiest of dictatorships. Nor is Franco's position comfortable. The country may not blow up in his lifetime, but he is a man sitting on an outworn lid.

SUCCESSION

This is a live issue, even though Franco takes good care of himself and is in excellent health at sixty-eight; he likes to boast that his father died in the nineties.[1] The issue of succession revolves on the monarchy, and there are two principal candidates—a father and a son. The father, Don Juan of Bourbon, the Count of Barcelona, lives in exile in Portugal, and is forty-seven. He was the second son of the last king of Spain, Alfonso XIII, who fled the country in 1931. *His* son, Prince Juan Carlos de Bourbon, aged twenty-two, is the next in line. Technically Spain is not a regency, but merely a country with the throne 'vacant'. This means that, in theory, the field is open, and Franco alone has the power to make a choice.

Most people in a position to know think that he plans to pass over the father and give the succession to Prince Juan Carlos, but this is not certain. By terms of a law enacted after a referendum on the monarchy in 1947, no person may accede to the throne until he is thirty, which means that Juan Carlos would have eight years to wait. There have been strenuous fights between Franco and the boy's father over his education. Don Juan would like his son to continue to live in the comparative freedom of Portugal; Franco wants him in Spain. Father and son are, incidentally, not competitive; the point of view of the son is that his father 'is' the king, and the father does not want to stand in Prince Juan's way.

Franco has life tenure as Chief of State, but, of course, he could retire at any time. If he does not do so and does not name a successor before he dies, a Council of the Realm, consisting of the President of the Cortes, the Cardinal Primate, and the Commander-in-Chief of the Army, is empowered to choose as ruler 'any Spaniard of royal blood'. Both Don Juan, who is half English, and Juan Carlos are thought to be too 'liberal' and 'European' by many Franco people, and another candidate is

[1] 'Franco Ponders: What Kind of King?' by Benjamin Welles, *New York Times Magazine*, August 28, 1960.

Prince Xavier of Bourbon-Parme, a descendant of the Carlist branch of the family.[1] His chances are slim, however. No matter who gets the throne, a very large question remains. With Franco out, or dead, *who* will govern? As good a guess as any is that it will be the army.

---

[1] 'Spain and the Future', by Daphne Kirkpatrick, *World Today*, January, 1961.

CHAPTER XI

What's Going On in Italy

THE political situation in Italy today, which seems almost morbidly complex, can be described quite simply. No party is big enough to command a clear majority in the Chamber of Deputies; hence government, such as it is, must be carried out by coalition. Politics is a matter of simple arithmetic—how to count up to a majority. The resultant coalitions are usually patched together with very thin cement, and crack apart easily; crisis is apt to follow crisis, and governments are precariously short-lived as a rule, though not so short-lived as in pre-de Gaulle France.

The biggest party, which stands roughly in the centre, is the Christian Democrat. This, the Church party, is dominated by the Vatican. The Christian Democrats are not, however, a homogeneous or solidly cohesive group. The party has a right wing, a centre, and a left—all volatile and fluidly merging into one another. Altogether the Christian Democrats command, at the moment, 273 members of the chamber, which has 596 members in all; this means that the party is about thirty votes short of a majority. In order to rule, it must be able to pick up these thirty extra votes somehow, somewhere. Nor is it always sure of its own membership—at least 100 of its 273 members are, even if close to the Vatican, on the left.

How, one may ask, can members of a Vatican party be leftist as well as Catholic? How can an Italian political leader be a man of the Church and a man of the left at the same time, like Signor Gronchi, the President of the Republic? The answer lies mostly in the fact that Italy (no matter how brilliant its present spurt of prosperity) is still basically a poor country. A politician, to get anywhere, has to try to do something for the people, or pretend to, and, naturally, patriotic Italian Catholics want to demonstrate that they have as much interest in reform, which will improve the lot of the poor, as the Communists or socialists. The situation is roughly comparable to that of the MRP in France. Conversely, many Italian Communists are Catholics. More on this later.

To resume: if the Christian Democrats swing too far to the right, they are in danger of losing their left wing; this is also true vice versa. Yet, no matter how full of schisms the party is, it has to hold together; because if it did not, and actually did split up, the Communists would be the beneficiaries, a horrifying thought. Where, to maintain a majority, do the Christian Democrats go in order to obtain their necessary surplus votes? In April, 1960, after a crisis lasting sixty-three mortal days, during which Italy was without any government at all, they turned to the Neo-Fascists, an extreme right splinter group. But the Prime Minister who made this arrangement, a Christian Democrat named Fernando Tambroni, did not last for more than a few months; the left would not tolerate Neo-Fascists in the government, and that was that. Severe Communist-incited riots occurred. In July, 1960, when Tambroni fell, the Christian Democrats turned in desperation to three small parties of the centre—right-wing Socialists led by Giuseppe Saragat, Liberals, and Republicans—with a moderate left-winger, Amintore Fanfani, as Prime Minister. How long he will last no man can know, because his coalition is one of the most unnatural ever known in Italy. The Christian Democrats are first, last, and all the time the Vatican party; but the right-wing Socialists, Liberals, and Republicans (led by the doughty Randolfo Pacciardi, a former defence minister who fought with the loyalists in Spain) are vigorously anti-clerical.

Anti-clericalism, it should be added parenthetically, is perfectly respectable in Italy, particularly in upper circles; the House of Savoy itself was anti-clerical. Everybody knows the story of the Risorgimento; Italy was unified and made into a nation by men like Cavour, Mazzini, Garibaldi, who fought the popes, freed the Papal States, and set a new dynasty on the throne. Today the House of Savoy is gone, but anti-clericalism remains.

To the left of the Christian Democrats are the Communists (140 seats) and the left-wing Socialists (88 seats) led by one of the most remarkable of modern Italian leaders, Pietro Nenni. On most matters, Nenni and the Communists work together closely; for instance, Nenni opposes Italian membership in NATO, and openly commended the Communist-inspired riots which helped to overthrow the Tambroni government. Nevertheless, a major, permanent chord in Italian politics is an attempt to contrive a division between Nenni and the Communists, and thus bring the big Nenni bloc of deputies into alliance with the Christian Democrats. President Gronchi in particular favours this operation, and works unceasingly to achieve it; it is his dream. But there are two pressing obstacles. First, the Vatican resolutely opposes the idea, on the ground that it would 'respectabilize' Nenni, and give too much additional influence to the left; second, Nenni himself doesn't particularly want to be won over, because once he loses his alliance with the Communists his principal source of power will disappear.

So much by way of introduction. Let us inspect now the person of Signor Gronchi, who plays a key role in these developments.

SKETCH OF THE PRESIDENT

Giovanni Gronchi is an interesting man, not well known outside Italy. It is somewhat startling to consider that he sits where Mussolini once sat, and is head of the Italian state. In *Inside Europe* I described Mussolini as 'tempestuous and ornate . . . the most formidable combination of turncoat, ruffian, and man of genius in modern history'. Gronchi is far from being melodramatic, tempestuous, or ornate; he might be a character out of Balzac—provincial, guarded, somewhat grasping. Mussolini was built of steel and rubber, but was as hollow as a barrel; Gronchi is solid, but somewhat colourless. One may, indeed, think that the estimable Signor Gronchi cuts a poor figure compared to Mussolini—a stout little sparrow, if I may change metaphors, in contrast to a combination of eagle, peacock, and bombastic magpie. But let us remember that Gronchi was an under-secretary in the first Mussolini government back in 1922. And where is Mussolini now? The sparrow has survived to take the peacock's throne.

Gronchi, who was born in a small town, Pontedera, near

Florence, on September 10, 1887, looks a good deal younger than his seventy-three years—he is well preserved, still fond of the choicer emoluments of life, and fresh of eye and spirit. His father was a butcher (Mussolini's father was a blacksmith), and he grew up in the most crushing poverty (as did the Duce). He has always been a practising Catholic, and became interested in politics in his earliest days, because, as he says, he was not merely for the poor, but *of* the poor. He took a leftist position, and proved quickly that he had an astute eye for political manœuvre. Gronchi has always been a man who works best behind the scenes; he is a man of the corridors, not the balcony.

Incidentally, soon after arriving in Rome last summer, I passed through the Piazza Venezia, with its dazzling white monument to Victor Emmanuel II—which the Romans call aptly 'the typewriter', and which indeed, with its curving columns, does resemble some monstrous creation of Olivetti. I glanced upwards to the celebrated balcony of the Palazzo Venezia, where Mussolini made speeches and received the straight-armed acclaim of the mob. Here was his famous office, sixty feet by forty by forty. Today the Palazzo Venezia is a prosaic exhibition hall, and the balcony is hung with a blanket advertising a show. *Sic transit gloria.*

Giovanni Gronchi managed to work his way through the University of Pisa, and supported himself by a job in the composing room of a newspaper. He began adult life as a teacher of the humanities, joined the Partito Popolare, the Catholic reform party founded by the well-known Sicilian priest, Don Luigi Sturzo, and soon entered parliament. Mussolini, immediately after the March on Rome (1922), gave him a post as Under-Secretary of Industry; he was, however, never a Fascist nor a member of the Fascist party. Indeed, he left office the following year, in protest at the brutalities of the Fascist régime, and retired altogether from public life for twenty years.

He was forced to give up a teaching post at Pisa, but otherwise was not molested by the Fascists; he went into business, worked as a salesman for a paint and varnish company, and grew rich. Life began again with the Allied landings in Italy in 1943. One of his associates in pre-Fascist days had been Alcide de Gasperi, the tenacious, subtle-minded Catholic leader who sat out the *Ventenno* (Fascist era) in hiding in the Vatican library;

now De Gasperi called Gronchi back to Rome, and presently he became Minister of Industry.

By 1946 he was one of De Gasperi's right-hand men and a powerful leader of the left wing of the Christian Democratic party, which had emerged out of the Partito Popolare; in 1948 he rose to be speaker of the Chamber of Deputies. On April 29, 1955, he was elected President of the Republic for a seven-year term; he was a good candidate because the Christian Democrats wanted a man far enough to the left to win Communist and socialist votes. And, indeed, Gronchi was supported by both the Communists and Nenni socialists, because *they* did not want a reactionary. Signor Gronchi was the first practising Catholic to be head of the state in the history of Italy. Both his predecessors in the presidency (the monarchy was abolished shortly after the war) were anti-clerical—Enrico de Nicola, the temporary head of state in 1946-48, and Luigi Einaudi, President from 1948 to 1955.

I had a pleasant talk with Signor Gronchi in his official residence, the Quirinale Palace, which in the past has been the home both of the popes and the House of Savoy (not at the same time, I hasten to add); it is of unsurpassed magnificence. In a golden room, he was a figure in chiaroscuro—silver hair, pale blue eyes, grey suit, pale grey tie, black moccasins. The President is not interviewed often. During an hour, he smiled only once; this was when I asked him what had made him a politician. Politics, he implied, was something that gets into the blood of an Italian at a very early age, and never leaves. I asked him how Italy had changed since the war; he conveyed the impression that the answer was twofold—first, that a strong Christian-inspired party had risen to replace Fascism and the shambles of war; second, that Italy, with its fifty million people, was now a member of the Atlantic Alliance, a brother of the United States, and a vigorous partner in NATO. (Also he was quick to point out that it was not surprising for Italy to be a partner of the democratic West; after all, the Italians fought with the Allies in World War I.)

Signor Gronchi visited America early in his presidency; then, in February, 1960, he went to the Soviet Union, an unusual thing for an Italian head of state to do. One lively scene marked the visit. The obstreperous Mr. Khrushchev turned up at a reception given by the Italian Ambassador in Moscow for

President Gronchi and Giuseppe Pella, at that time his foreign minister, and, speaking before five hundred bewildered guests, suggested archly that Signor Gronchi become a Communist.

'Ours is the most democratic of all democratic régimes,' Mr. Khrushchev said. 'Under the capitalistic régime, the man who has more dollars is the most intelligent. Under the Socialist régime, he is the most intelligent who has more intelligence. Think again on this and you will become a Communist. . . .

'You must think about what I said—whether you want to remain a Christian Democratic President or turn Communist. In any case, whatever your decision, my feeling of respect for you will not be diminished. We must look forward for peace and friendship between our peoples.'

The toast finished, Mr. Khrushchev turned to Signor Pella, saying: 'I asked the President to become a Communist, but I was thinking of you, too.'

Then the following remarkable conversation took place before the gathering:

SIGNOR PELLA: It would be very difficult for the President to accept your proposal.

MR. KHRUSHCHEV: But I always propose difficult problems. And, moreover, I don't make proposals. I invite you. I accept you and I wish you all the best.

SIGNOR GRONCHI: I would like to present Premier Khrushchev with a good wish. Maybe some day, touched by divine grace, he will enter the Christian Democratic party.

MR. KHRUSHCHEV: I am for that party which gives the largest welfare to the people. If you do that, I accept the invitation.

SIGNOR GRONCHI: I count on this.

MR. KHRUSHCHEV: Yes, but first tell me how long the Christian Democratic party has existed in Italy.

SIGNOR GRONCHI: It has not existed as long as the Communist party.

MR. KHRUSHCHEV: Let us make a comparison. What has the Christian Democratic Party given to Italy? Are your symbol and flag on the moon?

SIGNOR GRONCHI: When you have money you can buy whatever expensive object you want. Thus, the comparison does not stand.

MR. KHRUSHCHEV: We do not sell ideas if they are not good. Ideas are not salami.[1]

[1] *New York Times,* February 9, 1960.

The Italians were furious, and considered the reference to salami to be in the worst of taste.

By tradition Italian presidents are supposed to be above politics—figureheads—but Gronchi has paid comparatively little attention to this tenet, and is steadily, if quietly, active in political manœuvre. As has been said above, his dearest wish is to draw the Nenni (left-wing) socialists out of the Communist camp, and link them to the Christian Democrats.

WHAT SURVIVES OF FASCISMO?

Very little.

A Neo-Fascist party does, however, exist, which commands about 5 per cent of the total votes, has twenty-four deputies in the present chamber, and can be a minor nuisance on occasion. Technically, it is against the law to be a 'Fascist'; hence, the party calls itself Movimento Sociale Italiano (Italian Social Movement), and is known by its initials 'MSI'. Members are nicknamed 'Missinis'; the leader is Augusto de Marsanich, who was an official under Mussolini. It was, as I have already mentioned, included in the short-lived Tambroni coalition.

Donna Rachele Mussolini, aged seventy, is still alive, as are four of her children by the late dictator—Edda, the widow of Count Ciano, who was executed on orders of his father-in-law during the last stages of the war; Vittorio, who lives in Argentina; Romano, now thirty-two, who is a jazz band leader; and Anna Maria, the youngest daughter. Anna Maria was married in June, 1960, to a night-club entertainer known as Nando Pucci; most of the family gathered to attend the wedding, as did various Neo-Fascist leaders. Pope John XXIII sent the couple a telegram of felicitation, but the event as a whole made only the slightest stir. To most Italians who are old enough to remember World War II the Mussolini family does not, to understate the case, call forth pleasant memories, and the Duce himself is glossed over with a shrug.

I heard one well-known editor say, 'The crime of Mussolini was not so much that he suppressed freedom, but that he did so little worth while with the authority he had. He might have solved the agrarian problem, and restored the south. Instead he was swept away by Hitler and silly, stupid dreams of empire. Churchill was right to call him a "utensil".'

Structurally, no evidences of Mussolini's corporative state remain, but a few miscellaneous Fascist laws are still on the books. One paradox is worth mention. The men who ran the Fascist régime were, by and large, educated under the democratic system which preceded it; today, the bulk of officials who are trying, against considerable odds, to make democracy work in Italy got their education under Fascism. But nobody wants a new dictator.[1]

*

A monarchist party also exists, devoted to the cause of King Umberto II, who has lived in exile in Portugal for the past fifteen years. A good many Italians are, at heart, monarchists, particularly in Sicily and the south, and the party has six seats in the senate (out of 250) and twenty in the chamber. Its direct influence is, however, negligible. For all practical purposes the House of Savoy is as dead as Diocletian. One point is that, if Umberto should ever by some almost inconceivable circumstance be restored to the throne, the first thing he would probably do would be to disavow the extravagant pretensions of his own followers, and rule in as republican a manner as possible. But he has about as much chance of becoming sovereign of Italy, as, say, Zsa Zsa Gabor has of becoming Queen of England.

SOME IMPORTANT PRESSURE GROUPS

First, Catholic Action. This, the lay arm of the Church, is a very potent force indeed behind the Christian Democratic party, and hence the government. It was led for some years by a physician, Dr. Luigi Gedda, and is the organization which gets out the vote. Catholic Action has some twenty thousand 'cells', firmly implanted in both urban and rural constituencies; its membership is about four million. One important personage is Giuseppe Cardinal Siri, Archbishop of Genoa, who is head of the

---

[1] A curious point is that General de Gaulle is somewhat unpopular in Italy because people fear that his example may point up the virtues of dictatorship even though he is not a dictator.

Italian Hierarchy of Bishops; I have heard him called 'the most powerful man in Italy', because he runs the internal mechanism of the Church. The 'line' is evolved in the Vatican, more or less, and reaches Cardinal Siri; he passes it down to the bishops, who in turn communicate it to the local parishes. Then it reaches Catholic Action, which instructs the voters.

There is, incidentally, extremely little direct contact between the Vatican and government on the official level. The Pope and Signor Gronchi do not sit down and put their heads together; in fact, they almost never meet. There are, it is clear, several wings in the Vatican of today, several factions; on one side the Siri conservatives, on another a more liberal wing centring on Cardinal Montini, the Archbishop of Milan. The Vatican, although it operates politically through Catholic Action, which is the main support of the government, does not always see eye to eye with the government. One point at issue is education. The extreme right wing of the Church deplores too active an accent on education, because (a) this may lead to apostasy, and (b) an educated *élite*, becoming the ruling class, might turn out to be anti-clerical and a competitor to the Church. A similar issue is social reform. Relief of the poor should come by way of charity sponsored by the Church, not through political action organized by the state, in the view of last-ditch reactionaries. 'Poverty must, unfortunately, be maintained because it breeds ignorance', is the way I heard one extremist express this view. Reaction tends to thrive on an ignorant electorate.

Second, the Communists. The Italian Communist party is, as is well known, the largest in the world outside China and the USSR. Moreover, with more than two million members and not less than 140 seats in the chamber, it is the second biggest party in Italy; in the last general election it polled more than 6·5 million votes. Moreover, as we know, it works in close alliance with the Nenni socialists, who have eighty-eight deputies and roughly four million votes; together, the Communists and Nenni-ists command 38–40 per cent of the electorate, the largest concentration of extreme left-wing power in the western world.

Until fairly recently the main Communist strongholds were North and Central Italy—the area of the old Papal States—but as prosperity has come to the north Communist strength has diminished there to a degree, and at present the main drive of the party is towards the feudal south. Here industrialization is beginning on a considerable scale, and the Communists hope to take advantage of it—also of the misery of the landless proletariat.

The leader of the Communist party is Palmiro Togliatti, born in 1893, a stand-pat Stalinist who has been a major figure in international Communism since 1919. Today, an exceptionally resilient and durable politician, he follows the Khrushchev maxims dutifully, and takes the 'respectable' and 'democratic' approach. It is seldom realized that the Communists participated in government in Italy up to 1947; the first four De Gasperi cabinets had Communist members, and Togliatti himself was, of all things, Minister of Justice. Another leading Italian Communist is the vice-secretary of the party, Luigi Longo; another, representing the left-wing trade unions, is Agostino Novella.

The question has been posed: How can an Italian be a Catholic and a Communist at the same time? Obviously, millions of citizens are both, as is easily proved by the fact that the country, 99·6 per cent Catholic, is also around 25 per cent Communist. One reason is that many Italian Catholics are not particularly devout in the formal sense; there are millions who go to church only half a dozen times in their lives, and do not consider that religious affiliation has anything to do with politics. Some even think that Communism is a kind of 'protestant' sect, or heresy, 'within' the Church, although no Catholic could ever harbour such a thought and still be a true believer. As to the Communists, they do not seem to care whether their members go to church or not, although technically they are supposed to be atheists.

One striking fact is that leading Italian Communists are seldom attacked personally by Church organs; the Vatican doesn't particularly want to alienate officially a quarter of the electorate. The chief cause of Communism in Italy is not, as might be supposed, poverty. Actually the lowest-depth Italian poor, like the peasants in Apulia and Calabria, are apt to be inert politically, and some are reactionaries. Communism is promoted by other factors, like the good Communist record in the Resistance. Another reason for Communism is emotional (as apart from economic) distress—resentment at the power of the Church and the doctrine that nothing matters in this life, but only in the hereafter, plus a feeling among the youth, particularly intellectuals, that only left-wing authoritarianism can remedy the ills of Italy, make a real land reform, assess and collect taxes honestly, and rid the country of feudal privilege.

Third, the great industrial companies of the north—Fiat, Montecatini, and similar agglutinations of economic power, which compose the General Confederation of Industry, known as Confindustria for short. This, however, does not in the ordinary run of events act as a single, cohesive pressure group; instead, individual industrialists are influential. The big industrialists, centred in Milan, control roughly 80 per cent of the newspapers of the country, and most of them support the Liberal party, the centre party which derives from Cavour. Its secretary, the youthful Giovanni Malagodi, is one of the liveliest, most sapient political personalities in Italy. But the Liberal party has no more than four seats in the senate, seventeen in the chamber.

One remarkable figure in the world of industry is Enrico Mattei, creator and head of the Italian State Oil Company, the ENI (Ente Nazionale Idrocarburi). Mattei, a leading Christian Democrat and a close friend of Gronchi's, represents the new managerial type of industrialists, who operates *state* enterprises. He was one of the comparatively few members of the Christian Democratic party to have played a brilliant role in the Italian Resistance, and this helped inaugurate his subsequent career. He became a deputy, and was given the job of liquidating an organization which Mussolini had founded to discover—if possible—petroleum resources in Italy and develop them. Nothing came of this. But Mattei, saying in effect that Mussolini may have been crazy about some things but could just possibly have been right about this, refused to abandon the project and discovered very large Italian resources, hitherto untapped, of natural gas in the Po Valley. Mattei then went into oil ventures on the Persian Gulf and elsewhere, petroleum sales at home, electronics, engineering, newspapers, housing, automation equipment, rubber fertilizers, motels, and much else. Recently he bought for the state a complete nuclear power station (he got it in England), and is now assembling it thirty miles from Rome—the first nuclear power plant in history to be 'imported'; also he worked out a transaction whereby he imports three million tons of Soviet oil a year for the next four years, in exchange for Italian engineering products. All his operations are by the state, although he is a highly individualistic tycoon with colossal power on his own.[1]

*

Two other pressure groups should be mentioned, the trade unions in the north, which are largely right-wing (non-Nenni) socialist in orientation, led by Giuseppe Saragat, and the small farmers, who are for the most part Christian Democrats. One interesting development in agriculture has been a shift from grain to cattle; Italy these days is full of something quite new —ranches. Also there should be a word about the Press, which has a virile tradition. Many of the leading newspapers of Europe have disappeared since the war, like the *Berliner Tageblatt*, the *Frankfurter Zeitung*, *Le Matin* and *Petit Parisien* in Paris, the *Pester Lloyd* in Budapest, and the *Neue Freie Presse* (Vienna). But two leading Italian papers have continued publication imperturbably and without the loss of a day since the era before the war, *La Stampa* of Turin and the *Corriere della Sera* in Milan, one of the foremost newspapers of the world.

FANFANI AND COMPANY

The new Prime Minister, Amintore Fanfani, a Christian Democrat of the left wing, has twice been premier before—for twelve days in January, 1954, and for six months in 1958-59. He has also held the Labour, Agriculture, and Interior portfolios, and in his previous prime ministerships acted as his own foreign minister. He is strongly pro-NATO and pro-American, and is a thorough integrationist as far as Europe is concerned. On the domestic side he has always taken a decided line towards support of the industrial working class and peasantry. Dr. Fanfani, short in stature and vigorous of manner, was born in Piave Santo Stefano, a village in Tuscany, in 1908. He went to a Catholic university in Milan, got a degree in economics, and became a professor of economic history; he has written several weighty

[1] *Economist*, November 5, 1960. Also see "Italy's New Caesar" by Robert Neville, *Harper's Magazine*, March, 1961.

books. Unlike De Gasperi and Gronchi, he fled Italy when the German occupation began, and lived in exile in Switzerland until 1945. Catholic Action, of which he is a prominent officer, led him into politics, and he has been a member of the Chamber of Deputies since 1948.

When the British Prime Minister, Mr. Macmillan, visited Italy in the autumn of 1960, he told Dr. Fanfani that he would like to hear some Italian songs. At once Fanfani marched to a piano and, in full voice, sang out 'O Sole Mio'.

Other tried—and somewhat shopworn—Christian Democrats are Antonio Segni, Giuseppe Pella, and Mario Scelba, the lively Communist-chasing Minister of the Interior. All three are former prime ministers. Segni, who is Foreign Minister in the Fanfani government, is a Sardinian by birth, who has had a long career as lawyer, teacher, and politician; he is seventy. One of his major interests has been agriculture, and he has always paid close attention to Sardinian affairs. Giuseppe Pella, a former foreign minister as well as prime minister, who is now Minister of the Budget, was born in North Italy in 1902; for many years he was a professor of accounting. Like so many of his colleagues, he came up in the party through Catholic Action.

*

I asked friends in Rome what would happen if the Fantani government, precariously situated at best, disintegrates. Reply: 'We will never have a dictator again—not a man on horseback. What we might well have is a man in a cassock, somebody like Salazar.'

BRIEF WORD ABOUT THE POPE

It would be difficult to conceive two churchmen more different than the new Pope, John XXIII, and his predecessor, the illustrious Pius XII. Pope John is stout, relaxed, fond of people, not given to ostentation, a peasant by origin, shrewd but not an intellectual, and, at bottom, not particularly interested in politics —much less in personal power. Pius XII, in sharp contrast, was an urban aristocrat, brilliantly intellectual, up to his neck in politics, lonely, lean and sharp as a razor, and an extraordinarily sophisticated character. He ran the enormous mechanism of the Vatican practically single-handed, made his own policy, and was at once a kind of king, president, and prime minister. Pope John XXIII, who was born Angelo Giuseppe Roncalli in 1881, gives the impression (I mean no disrespect) of being a saintly grandfather; when he acceded to the papal crown (1958) he was seventy-seven, one of the dozen oldest popes among the 262 since St. Peter. Roncalli was the eldest of twelve children, and grew up dirt-poor. He chose the name John after his father. He began his studies for the priesthood as a boy, got a degree in theology in Rome, and was ordained in 1904; he spent some years in administrative work in Bergamo near his birthplace, taught Church history, helped organize Catholic Action in the neighbourhood, and during World War I became a chaplain in the medical corps of the Italian Army, first with the rank of sergeant, then lieutenant.

One point of exceptional interest about Pope John XXIII is that, almost uniquely among pontiffs, he spent most of his mature years in non-Catholic countries, or countries where Catholics are a minority. After being consecrated as an arch-bishop in 1925, he went to Bulgaria as apostolic visitor; he remained there for ten long years, and then spent nine more as apostolic delegate to Greece and Turkey. Then came seven years in Paris, where he was nuncio, and where he was liked, admired, and respected by Catholics and Protestants alike.

Most observers in Rome competent to know think that Pope John wants to make the Catholic accent in Italian politics a little less openly marked, or, as the phrase goes, to 'depoliticize' the Vatican. He has certainly been a broadening influence. Unlike Pacelli, he likes to delegate authority, and is the least dictatorial of men. At his first consistory, in December, 1958, he named no fewer than twenty-three new cardinals; since then eighteen more have been appointed, with the result that the College of Cardinals today numbers eighty-six, the largest number since 1586. He cut the number of books on the Index Expurgatorius in half, from about 5,000 to 2,500, and has received cordially such conspicuous non-Catholics as Willy Brandt, the socialist Mayor of West Berlin, and Prime Minister Harold Macmillan. Then, in December, 1960, he had a long conversation with Dr. Geoffrey Francis Fisher, the then Archbishop of Canterbury; it was the first time that a pope and a head of the Church in England had met in 563 years.

Pope John, who was Patriarch of Venice after leaving France, is supposed to represent what is called the 'Venetian' wing of the Church in Italy, in contrast to its Roman wing. The Venetians have always been more 'open'. No doubt John XXIII was chosen for the papacy partly because he was venerable, and would obviously be what might be called an 'interim' pope; after the rigours of Pacelli, the powers-that-be in the Vatican wanted time to move around. Probably the most powerful cardinal, who, although on the right wing, was instrumental in the choice of John XXIII, is the Papal Secretary of State, Domenico Cardinal Tardini.

ALTERATIONS; ISSUES; CHALLENGES

Clearly, there have been striking changes in Italy with its fifty million people in the past quarter-century; the most important is probably industrialization. Whereas before the war Italy was roughly 60 per cent agricultural, 40 per cent industrial, today the reverse is almost true; more than 50 per cent of all Italian workers are engaged in industry. Moreover, the nature of industry has changed; the accent is no longer on small crafts but on mass production. This has produced a veritable revolution. Villages near Naples, which were as utterly removed from the twentieth century as hovels along the Nile a few years ago, have television sets and washing machines; today, citizens, instead of subsisting largely on *pasta*, have meat, sugar, coffee, commodities which were almost literally unknown (they are still unknown in some communities) twenty-five years ago. An energetic middle class is emerging, and the working class (in the north) is more prosperous than it has ever been before.

Another change is that a good deal of bombast, inflated national pride, departed with Fascismo. The country is much less touchy. One factor inducing this was settlement of the Trieste dispute, which is no longer a nasty little ulcer inflaming patriotic ego. Then, too, membership in the Atlantic Community has helped give a feeling of comfort, of solidarity, to those Italians who are interested in foreign affairs (there do not seem to be many), and so does membership in the Common

Market, which brings distinct economic gain. Finally, a fruitful rebirth in intellectual and technical realms is apparent, and Italians are rightfully proud of their brilliant recent accomplishments in industrial design, the world of fashion, architecture, and the films—consider the incomparable *La Dolce Vita*.

As to the Atlantic Alliance, one more word is in order. Seven Italian divisions are committed to NATO, and the United States has supported the Italian defence effort with direct military aid to the value of £645,000,000 so far—£49,000,000 in 1960. A principal NATO command is stationed at Naples, and the country has been armoured with American Jupiter missiles; the United States, however, retains custody of their warheads as is obligatory under American law. Curiously enough, I found more international evidence of NATO in Italian provincial towns like Pisa than in any comparable city in Europe; here were to be seen Dutch, Norwegian, American, and other uniforms. There are American installations in Verona, Vicenza, Leghorn, and other points besides Naples.

*

Italy is booming, yes; the gross national product rose last year by a remarkable 8 per cent as against 1959, and is about £10,000 million, triple the figure for 1946. The gold reserve is the third highest in the world (believe it or not) after the United States, and industrial exports amounted to £715,000,000 in the first five months of 1960, a rise of not less than 46 per cent over the year before. Nevertheless this is still a desperately poor country. There are still something like 1·7 million unemployed, large areas of the nation are still untouched by development, and nowhere in the western world, except perhaps Spain, is the disparity so sharp, so blatant, between rich and poor. In a recent year not less than 12 per cent of the total population of Italy was officially classified as 'totally penurious', with another 12 per cent 'in a state of poverty bordering on absolute penury'. Millions are undernourished. A recent survey of a rural district in Sicily showed that 80 per cent of habitations had no piped water or sanitation, that the residents were 40 per cent illiterate, and that infant mortality was 103·8 per thousand births, which is ten times the rate in northern Italy.[1]

[1] *Economist*, May 21, 1960. Also see *Italy*, by Paul Lechat, Vista Books, p. 142.

Italy is, in fact, two countries. The difference between the north and the *mezzogiorno*, as the south is called, is not like the difference, say, between Yorkshire and Sussex, or Brittany and Provence, or even Maine and Alabama. The Italian north and south are not merely two different countries; they seem to be countries on two different continents. Below Naples, Italy is Africa. In essence the problem of Italian poverty is the problem of the south—how to distribute the national income so that the south gets more. All manner of projects are under way, including an ambitious land reform. But difficulties are substantial. For one thing if the government (to put it crudely) takes too much money away from the north and gives it to the south it increases the danger of Communism in *both* areas—because the north will be weakened while at the same time industrialization in the south may open the way to Communist penetration.

The chief problem of Italy is certainly poverty; the second is political—how to make democracy work, how to make it secure, in a country so extraordinarily new (Italy has existed as a nation for only a hundred years) and non-unitary. Put in another way the question is how to make medieval Italy modern. If the government goes too fast towards reform, it risks reaction from the right; if it goes too slowly, it stimulates opposition from the left. One point I heard brought up a number of times is that Italy, like other countries which never had experience of the Reformation, has little tradition of the good citizen. Social conscience is at the minimum. People have allegiances to themselves, their families, their cities; but not much to the nation. What counts is private opportunity, private gain.

All this being said, something else should be said as well. Italy has troubles, and these may become graver in time. The country is unstable and large sections of the population are still blocked off from the light of modern times, but the country gives nevertheless an impression of extraordinary warmth and happiness as well as animation. This is a smiling country, the pleasantest of all European nations to visit or live in, no matter who runs it, how or why.

CHAPTER XII

Along the Mediterranean

On a map Greece looks something like a bunch of grapes hanging down into the water, and its correct name is Vasileion tis Ellados, or Kingdom of Hellas. It is the only kingdom surviving in Europe below Scandinavia and the North Sea countries. On its parched, chalky soil live approximately 8·4 million people, too many to support comfortably, and the chief problem of Greece is still what it was a quarter of a century ago, namely, that there are too many Greeks.

Greeks are both inveterate politicians and flaming individualists, and the old joke is that if there were only three Greeks left alive in the world, there would be four Greek political parties. They have always been adept at stratagem: the story of the Trojan horse is well known, and an ancient proverb says, 'After shaking hands with a Greek, count your fingers.'

No country so small—the area is less than that of Eire—has contributed so much to history. In a short blazing period that no erosion by time can ever erase the Greeks produced four of the greatest dramatists who ever lived, two of the greatest poets, two of the greatest historians, three of the greatest philosophers, and imperishable works of art beyond number. No two figures have ever carried conquest further than Venus de Milo and Alexander the Great.

Greeks add rosin to their wine, which makes it taste like turpentine. There are only 170 cinemas in the country, and the Crown Prince is known as the Diadoch. Civil servants are not allowed to strike or have subversive ideologies, and Greece contains twenty self-governing monasteries, the most famous of which is at Mount Athos. Greece lives on tobacco, dried fruit, marble, emery, olive oil, and sponges, among other things, but the trade balance is heavily adverse.[1] Perhaps because they are poor, the Greeks are extremely practical. During one period of inflation, they solved the currency problem by the simple but startling expedient of cutting all banknotes in half.

Greece has a king, Paul, and a queen, Frederika, who are no more Greek than I am, but they are greatly respected and liked by a majority of the Greek people. Paul, of German origin, is a bluff, extroverted character who took the throne after the death of his brother, King George II, in 1947. The queen, also of predominantly German stock, is a daughter of the Duke of Brunswick; she is called 'Frederika the Great' with affectionate admiration, and is known as 'the best man in the country'. She has the constitutional right to assume royal power in the king's name. When you have tea with Paul and Frederika, they are as cosy as crumpets.

The Greeks have, and always have had, a sublime vivacity. They are wonderful seamen, wonderful traders. Some 450,000 Greeks emigrated to the United States early this century, and there are few in the home country who do not have a sense of kinship with America. Greece doesn't rule the world any longer, but its contribution should be kept in mind. This is the country which invented political democracy, from this lump of frayed rock came the original impulses which led to the Magna Charta, the Bill of Rights, and the basic framework of American government—based on civil liberties and the right of every man to consider himself the equal of any other, even if he isn't.

KARAMANLIS, PERSONALITIES, AND POLITICS

One of the most interesting—and least-known—new figures in Europe is Constantinos Karamanlis, the Prime Minister of Greece, a man of the moderate right whose chief contribution so far has been to give the country political stability. Karamanlis has been Prime Minister for five and a half years, a tenure unmatched in Greece for more than thirty years. Greece is one of the most politically volatile of countries; once in the ornate public rooms of the Hotel Grande Bretagne in Athens I met three different ex-prime ministers in the course of one afternoon. Not long ago I asked an expert on Greek politics what made

[1] Made up in part by income from tourists and shipping.

Karamanlis exceptional. Reply: 'Exceptional? The only exceptional thing about him is that he's the best prime minister Greece
has had since the days of Lord Byron.' Karamanlis is a man from
the north. He was born in 1907, the son of poor parents, in
Macedonia. This in itself makes him unusual, because most
Greek politicians derive from Athens and the south. The fact
that he is a northerner contributes to his political prowess; he
symbolizes rural opposition to the centralism of Athens.
Northern Greece has never had much of a share in the political
pie before and Karamanlis has always made it part of his policy
to stand strongly for the peasants in outlying areas. Another
source of power is his modesty, a somewhat unusual quality
among Greeks. He can be forceful, opinionated, and impatient,
but he is an honest, modest man. A friend came to him after the
death of his predecessor, Field-Marshal Alexander Papagos, the
extreme rightist head of the Greek 'Rally', saying that the King
contemplated making him Prime Minister. Karamanlis said with
dignity, 'Kindly do not ridicule me. I am not worthy of the post.'

Karamanlis is a good-looking man, somewhat deaf. He studied
law at the University of Athens, and became a civil servant
(= politician). He began political life as a Populist, which
means Royalist, was elected a deputy in 1935, and has held
various cabinet posts; his success as Minister of Public Works
brought him to the King's attention. More obvious successors to
Papagos would have been Panagiotis Kanellopoulos, who is now
Deputy Prime Minister, or the most active leader of the Populist
party at the time, Mr. Stefanopoulos. But the King went over
the heads of both of these, and made Karamanlis Prime Minister.

Soon after assuming the premiership Karamanlis founded a
new party of his own, known as the ERE; the initials stand for
Ethniki Rizospastiki Enosis, or National Radical Union. But the
word 'radical' is misleading, since the party is heavily conservative. Karamanlis and the ERE got 47 per cent of the vote in
1956. Their majority was diminished in 1958, but the government still has 170 out of the 300 seats in Parliament.

The major element in the ERE programme is an attempt to
make government more efficient by decentralization and economic reform. A five-year plan (1959-64) has been launched—
again, as in Portugal, we have the spectacle of a passionately
non-Communist government employing procedures invented by

the Soviet Union—which, it is hoped, will be extended for a second period from 1964 to 1969. One illustration of public confidence is that coins have been minted in Greece for the first time in twenty years, replacing the filthy, tattered banknotes which had previously been used for even the smallest denominations.[1]

Opposition to Karamanlis extends from the extreme right wing all the way to the Communists. The Communist party itself was outlawed in 1947, during the Civil War, but in 1951 the Elleniki Demokratiki Aristera (Union of Democratic Left), known as the EDA (pronounced 'edda'), sprang up, and is a kind of holding company for the Communists. It is the second strongest party in Greece, and with its affiliates has seventy-nine deputies. The leader is Ioannis (John) Passalides, and it seeks to keep fresh in the public mind such facts as that 42,000 Greek Jews were killed in Hitler's asphyxiation chambers during the war. In the elections of May 11, 1958, it won 24·3 per cent of the popular vote, a steep rise, and, with sixty-one seats in Parliament, it is a force that cannot be minimized.

The Communists and fellow-travellers of the EDA do their best to make capital out of economic discontent. Of eight and a half million Greeks at least two million are either unemployed or underemployed; privation is acute, particularly in the rural areas, which contain 60 per cent of the population. The *per capita* income of the country as a whole is £100 a year, but of the agricultural districts only £63. The Greek national anthem begins with the words, 'I recognize you by the keenness of your spade'—a picturesque underlining of the importance of agriculture to the country. Greek politics have, as it were, been polarized since the war. The traditional parties have been squeezed out between Karamanlis on the right and the EDA on the left, which means that the only way to register effective opposition against Karamanlis is to vote for the fellow-travellers. The parties in between, including several with large power in the past, have all but disappeared. The Liberals under Sophocles Venizelos, a former Prime Minister and son of the great Cretan statesman of the twenties, still has twenty seats. But the Liberal Democrats under George Papandreou, another ex-Prime Minister, have shrunk to six; the Populists, led by Constantin Tsaldaris, the best-known Prime Minister of the

[1] *The Times*, May 16, 1960.

post-war period, to one; and the Progressives, established by Spyros Markezinis, the chief architect of the Papagos 'Rally', to one. A recent dramatic entrant to the local political scene is General George Grivas, who organized and led the terrorist underground, the EOKA, in Cyprus. But most observers think that Grivas, a thoroughgoing desperado in his prime and one of the leaders of the monarcho-fascist Greek underground during World War II, has pretty well lost his influence.

For a generation the chief political issue in Greece was the fierce struggle between monarchists and republicans. The anguish of this died with the accession of King Paul. Then came the Communist uprising and civil war. Today a principal issue— as in Scandinavia—is a tussle between NATO and neutralism. Karamanlis, who has paid one visit to America, is probably the strongest supporter of NATO in the whole Mediterranean area, and Greece is—on the surface—a loyal ally of the United States, but Greek relations with the Communist bloc are not altogether cool. Such leaders as Venizelos and Markezinis have visited Moscow recently, and Marshal Tito of Jugoslavia, who is certainly a Communist even though he just as certainly does not represent Moscow, has paid a state visit to Greece. Greece, Turkey, and Jugoslavia signed a defensive military alliance, known as the Balkan Pact, in 1954, but this is now pretty much of a dead letter because of the bitter quarrel between Greece and Turkey over Cyprus. Greek-Jugoslav relations are, however, close. An additional point is that 12 per cent of Greek trade is with Russia or the Soviet satellites, a fivefold increase in five years, and a new trade agreement with the USSR was signed in 1958. Greece, unlike Spain and Portugal, maintains perfectly correct diplomatic relations with all European members of the Soviet bloc except East Germany and Albania. Curiously enough, a state of war—dating from 1940—still exists between Greece and Albania, but this has not prevented co-operation between the two countries towards cleaning up mines which still lie in Adriatic waters.[1]

[1] One interesting point is that some 27,000 Greek rebels, who had fought with the Communists in the Civil War, fled to the neighbouring Balkan republics and elsewhere when the war ended, and still maintain Irredentist activity. One large community of Greek Communists lives today in Tashkent, in Soviet Central Asia. The official leadership of the Greek Communist party has its headquarters in Bucharest. *The Times*, May 4, 1960.

The United States does not maintain actual bases in Greece (as it does in Italy or Turkey) but has communications facilities at the Athens airport. To date American aid, both military and economic, pumped into the country has amounted to the tidy sum of £890 million. More than five thousand American government employees and their dependants, mostly military, live in Greece, which sometimes provokes Greeks on the neutralist side to protest about the American 'occupation'. The Greek government spends 28 per cent of its budget on defence, and Greeks who dislike NATO say that this is far too much.

Still another issue is the permanent struggle between ins and outs. Personalities count more than political conviction. Any government which has been in power as long as that of Karamanlis inevitably suffers a certain erosion, and there are always adventurers among Greek politicians who will make a deal with anybody, no matter what the issue, to gain power.

CYPRUS, AN ULCER REMOVED

Cyprus, the newest country in Europe, is also one of the oldest. Here the Goddess Aphrodite is supposed to have risen from the sea, and Greek colonizers seeking copper, the mineral which gives the island its name, made their first settlements here as far back as 1400 B.C. Cyprus became independent on August 16, 1960, and entered the UN shortly thereafter. One curiosity is its flag, which comparatively few people have seen so far; it depicts a map of Cyprus on a spray of green olive branches, and must be one of the few national flags in the world to contain a map.[1]

The population of the island is around 80 per cent Greek, 20 per cent Turkish. From 1878 until last summer it was a British colony. A confused triangular struggle for power after World War II led to a murderous insurrection and an even more murderously difficult political situation. The British were willing enough to get out, but not to give up their military bases on the island, which became of decisive strategic value after the evacuation of Suez. What the Greek Cypriots wanted was

[1] Queen Elizabeth and the Duke of Edinburgh touched briefly on Cyprus while *en route* to India and Pakistan in January, 1961. This was the first time a British monarch had visited the island since Richard Cœur de Lion in 1191. *New York Times*, January 21, 1961.

Enosis, union with Greece; the Turks on the island, fearful of their minority rights under a Greek régime, resisted this and demanded partition instead. The EOKA, under General Grivas, opened a vehement terrorist campaign, which the British authorities found it almost impossible to subdue. Relations between Greece and Turkey, each of which backed its Cypriot populations, deteriorated so severely that an open break seemed inevitable, and Greek relations with Great Britain suffered too—all of which was a grave embarrassment to Western defence plans in the eastern Mediterranean. Greece and Turkey are allies in NATO, but the Cyprus conflict made co-operation between them impossible.

Early in 1959, after extraordinarily difficult negotiation, an agreement between Britain, Greece, and Turkey was finally hammered out. The Greek government gave up its support of *Enosis*, and the Turks gave up partition. Instead it was agreed that Cyprus should become an independent republic in which the administration would be 70 per cent Greek Cypriot, 30 per cent Turkish Cypriot. On July 1 further agreement was reached whereby Britain retained its bases, but these are to be diminished in size; in return Cyprus is to receive financial help (twelve million pounds a year for five years) from the British Treasury.

Curiously enough, many Greek Cypriots are disappointed by independence; they had not wanted independence so much as *Enosis*—actual union with Greece itself. This is a case where nationalism, it seems, was thrust down the people's throat. Almost everybody, however, both on the Greek mainland and in Cyprus—as well as in Turkey and Great Britain—are relieved that the insurrection is over at last, and that the island is settling down.[1]

The President of the new republic is, of course, His Grace Mikhail Christodoulon Mouskos Makarios III, the Ethnarch (Archbishop) of Cyprus, shrouded by beard and black robes. Makarios, born in 1913, is, like Grivas, a Cypriot by birth. He rose swiftly in the ecclesiastical hierarchy of the Greek Orthodox Church, became a bishop at an early age, and was for many years the fountainhead of the *Enosis* movement. Plenty of people think that he is a Byzantine character, i.e. his approach to issues

[1] Lawrence Fellows in the *New York Times*, August 14 and 19, 1960.

may be sinuous. His patriotism is, however, undoubted. That he should have been willing, after so long a struggle, to give up *Enosis* and settle for the present arrangement still mystifies some of his supporters. The Vice-President, by terms of the independence agreement, is a Turkish Cypriot—Dr. Fazil Kutchuk.

Makarios is the only statesman in contemporary Europe to be both head of a government and head of a Church, which enhances his power and influence.[1] The Greek Orthodox Church is by far the most important political and economic force on the island. Four potential or actual sources of opposition confront the Makarios-Kutchuk team. First, on the Greek side, surviving EOKA extremists, but these have waned in strength since General Grivas returned to the Greek mainland. Second, the 'legal' Turkish opposition, which may be expected to watch Turk minority interests zealously. Third, irreconcilables among the Turks, who, like the Greek extremists, opposed the independence settlement and still hold out stubbornly for partition. Fourth, and most important, the Communist party.

This, known as the AKEL, is legal in Cyprus and has substantial strength, partly because of its close affiliation with the Pan-Cyprian Federation of Labour, which has about forty thousand members, is strongly left-wing, and normally commands about 25 per cent of the electorate. In the first elections after independence Makarios and the AKEL made a deal; as a result the first Cyprus Parliament consists of thirty members of the Archbishop's Patriotic Front, fifteen Turkish Cypriots, and five representatives of AKEL.

Both Greece and Turkey, the fathers of the new state, are members of NATO, but Cyprus is not and President Makarios has stated that his new republic will pursue a foreign policy independent of any military bloc. Neutralism is the order of the day. However, Cyprus has vital British military installations and, after much debate, it became a member of the British Commonwealth in March, 1961.

*

I visited Cyprus briefly during the war. With a friend I flew over from Beirut and we drove from Larnaca, an airport near

[1] Joe Alex Morris in the New York *Herald Tribune*, September 23, 1960.

the sea, up to the summer capital, Troödos, in the hills; never except in Peru have I seen such a piercing, dramatic contrast between two regions of a country only a few hours apart. The drive was like climbing a wall. At sunset we took a walk along what seemed to be a precipice, *above* a solid foam of clouds. Far below, near Paphos, was the place where Venus rose from the sea, and I thought of James Elroy Flecker's magical lyric 'The Old Ships' with its lines, 'black Cyprus ringed with a lake of fire'. Even then, the British were having trouble with Cypriot nationalists and revolutionaries, although I was told that the local population suffered unanimously from a disease known as Cyprusitis, or the desire to do nothing.

Also I remember vividly a constellation of youthful Hungarian girls who filled the derelict little night-clubs in Nicosia, the capital. The night-clubs may have been shabby, but the girls were not. There were about forty-five of them, deriving originally from Budapest in all its chic glory, who were stranded in Cyprus by the war. They were technically enemy aliens. They were also queens of the entire island after 6 p.m., *élite* of the *élite*. Those shining girls could, at one hundred yards, identify any kind of British or Allied uniform, and they knew the exact pay of every category of officer. All over the East they became renowned. Regiments came to Cyprus and went, and officers carried away with them to Baghdad and Khartoum and points beyond fragrant memories of Fräulein Lili or Fräulein Kathi. These pleasant kittens transformed Cyprus from a dreary, beleaguered island into a veritable haven of romance, making good the legend that this was indeed the birthplace of the goddess of love. I have often wondered what happened to those girls after the war. Probably some are grandmothers now.

COUP D'ÉTAT IN TURKEY

When *Inside Europe* first appeared in 1936 the extraordinary figure of Kemal Atatürk still utterly dominated Turkey. He was father of a reborn nation—at once a ruthless psychopath and a patriotic colossus. He picked up Turkey like a mangy dog and shook it into shape. Everybody knows that he abolished the fez, ended polygamy, turned the mosques into granaries, emancipated women, established a new capital at Ankara (replacing

Constantinople), Latinized the Turkish alphabet, stood off both the British and the Russians, and drove the Greeks mercilessly into the sea. Kemal died in 1938, largely as a result of debauchery. A few weeks before his last illness he said to a friend, 'If I can manage to live another fifteen years I can make Turkey a democracy. If I die it will take three generations.' Maybe he was right.

This roughneck totalitarian was always an innovator. Back in 1930 he did something which, so far as I know, is unique in the annals of dictatorship—he deliberately created an opposition by appointing to Parliament a handful of deputies who were instructed to vote *against* him. They were terrified, but would have been hanged, a worse fate, if they had not agreed to serve. The experiment was given up after a while, but it is worth mentioning because it marked the entrance into public life of Adnan Menderes, who ran Turkey much later—from 1950 to 1960. Menderes was one of the original group of men named by Kemal to 'oppose' him.

The man who took over from Kemal on November 10, 1938, General Ismet Inönü, is old now, but still plays a cogent role in the councils of the nation. For many years, under the name Ismet Pasha, he had been Kemal's right-hand man—if Kemal could be said to have had a right-hand man. He took the name Inönü when Kemal decreed that every Turk had to have a patronymic in the Western fashion; the river Inönü was the scene of his greatest victory in battle, during the Greek war in Anatolia in 1921. Inönü ran Turkey from 1938 to 1950. He was—and still is—a fascinating character. One of his characteristics is that, like his master Kemal, he is a recluse. As a general rule, when President, he never received anybody, even members of the diplomatic corps. (Once, though, during the war, I saw him with a team of friends at Taksim's, a celebrated Istanbul cabaret. It was as astonishing to run into him there as it would have been to meet King George V at the Folies Bergère.) His chief relaxation was his yacht, which was reputedly the largest and most splendid in the world at that time; it cost £1,250,000, and was a gift from Atatürk.

In 1946 Inönü decided that Turkey should have a chance to taste the democratic process, and he permitted the country to vote in free—well, almost free—elections. Two parties contested these: the Republican People's party, which under Kemal had been the only party in the country, and an opposition group, the Democratic party, which arose after Kemal's death. The joke was, 'The People's party stands for open voting and closed counting; the Democrats stand for closed voting and open counting.' Just the same the 1946 elections marked a signal advance. Out of a chamber numbering 468 the opposition Democrats got 60 seats. Their leaders were Celal Bayar and Adnan Menderes, the man whom Kemal had chosen to be an oppositionist many years before.

Fresh winds began to blow in Turkey after 1946. The door was opened. Having tasted democracy, citizens wanted more. The Republican People's party, after a generation of rule, began to unravel, and the Democrats rose steeply in strength; in 1950 came a new election, which they won handsomely—415 seats to 175. The venerable Inönü surprised everybody by accepting this decision with patriotic equanimity, although it meant the end of his years of rule, and he retired into the background. The Kemal era was no more. The Democrats who had been in opposition took over the government in an orderly transfer of power, and Bayar, who was the Front and figurehead, became President of the Republic. The Prime Minister was Menderes.

Extraordinary as it may seem, Menderes had never held public office before, although he was a deputy, and he must be one of the few men in contemporary European history who, by constitutional means, rose from being nothing one day to prime minister the next.[1] He was—and is—a peculiarly interesting human being; his chief characteristics are inordinate vitality, grasp of political organization, and extreme self-confidence and ambition. Born in 1899 of a rich landowning family, he was orphaned in early childhood; he was brought up by his grandparents, and studied at an American missionary school in Izmir (Smyrna). In 1916 he enlisted in the Turkish Army, fought the British in the desert campaigns of World War I, and distinguished himself in the subsequent brutal hostilities against Greece. Assuming power in 1950, Menderes ran Turkey with confidence and *esprit* for ten years. He was strongly pro-NATO, and became the chief American protégé in the Middle

[1] The *Observer*, May 29, 1960.

East. One thing that brought him down was excess. He wanted to be known as a great builder and indeed he worked hard to brighten the face of the nation. But his projects in Istanbul and elsewhere cost fantastic amounts of money; the country entered a ruinous inflation, and, when he fell, the public debt had reached the choice sum of £465,000,000.

*

The story of the *coup* which caused Menderes' downfall may be told briefly. Opposition to his régime climbed in 1959 and 1960; unwisely, he sought to throttle it. Former President Inonü went out into the hinterland to do some political speechmaking; Menderes sent army detachments to break up his cavalcade. This was severely resented, both because it was an affront to Inonü, seventy-six years old and the foremost living Turk, and because it brought the army into politics. The country seethed and simmered. Menderes in mid-April (1960) suspended all political activity for three months, which seemed to presage a reversion to dictatorship, and set up a special commission to 'investigate' the opposition. Newspapers were suppressed, editors jailed, and university professors discharged. As a result severe rioting broke out on April 28. On May 5 mobs of students attacked Menderes himself in Ankara and shouted for him to resign; he yelled back defiantly, 'Kill me! Kill me!' Then on May 9 occurred an event the significance of which was not fully understood at the time; the commander-in-chief of the ground forces of the Turkish army, General Cemal Gursel, resigned his post.[1]

In the early hours of May 27, 1960, the army struck in a smooth, bloodless *coup*. Bayar, Menderes, the entire cabinet, a round dozen high military officers, and no fewer than 400 of the 406 Democratic deputies to Parliament were arrested. General Gursel became acting Prime Minister and at once set up a largely civilian government, but it soon became clear that an army junta ruled behind the scenes. Apparently ex-President Inonü had nothing to do with all this, and knew nothing of the *coup* beforehand. From first to last, although bitterly opposing the Menderes régime, the veteran statesman insisted that the

[1] Don Cook in the New York *Herald Tribune*, May 8, 9, and 10, 1960.

Republican People's party must not seek to return to power except by constitutional means. But army informants told him what had happened at 5 a.m. on May 27, and the conspirators gave him hourly reports on the serpentine course of events thereafter.[1]

This was the third *coup d'état* made by the army since the 'Young Turk' revolt of 1908. It was not, however, caused exclusively by military discontent. Certainly the army was the force that tipped the scales, and when it decided that Menderes had to go he went, but other factors also played a role. One was an irritable and pervasive restlessness on the part of outs who wanted to be in—also intellectual fermentation by editors, teachers, students, and the like. Another was a peculiar situation involving urban citizens versus the peasants. Turkey is predominantly an agricultural state, but from the beginning of time workers on the soil have got the short end of the stick. Menderes genuinely wanted to improve the position of the peasants, and sought to syphon economic power out of the cities in order to give relief to the impoverished peasantry. This the powerful city interests resented. Still another source of dissatisfaction was corruption, which was copious. And still another was resentment at American influence in Turkey; Menderes was attacked for being a 'puppet' of NATO and the Americans.

General Gursel, who elevated himself to become the new chief of state, was born in Erzurum near the Soviet frontier in 1895, and has been a professional soldier all his life. During World War I he fought against the British at the Dardanelles. He was commissioned a lieutenant in 1914, but did not rise to become a brigadier-general until August, 1946. Until the *coup* in 1960 he was practically unknown outside military circles, and his fellow-officers describe him as being slow in talk, somewhat lethargic, but all in all an extremely hard-boiled citizen.

The junta behind Gursel, which calls itself the Committee of National Union, is split into two wings, moderate and extremist. It had at the beginning thirty-eight members. The number was lately—a pregnant development—cut to twenty-four. On November 13, 1960, Gursel announced that he had dismissed fourteen of its members on the ground that they were endangering the 'national interest'. The most conspicuous of those purged

[1] Michael Adams in the *Guardian*, June 2, 1960.

was Colonel Alsapan Turkes, who, in fact, was the actual author of the *coup*—the man who engineered it and then persuaded Gursel to be its front. Gursel, a stolid man of the centre, did not want to be pushed further left by the Turkes faction. This evolution provides a striking contrast to what went on in Egypt after the moderate Neguib, spurred by the radical Nasser, seized power in Cairo in 1952. In Egypt the extremists won in the end and Neguib was eliminated. But in Turkey the Turkish equivalent of Neguib fired the man equivalent to Nasser.

General Gursel has abolished all political activity in Turkey for the moment, which was exactly what Menderes had sought to do, but he has repeatedly promised to restore democratic procedures as soon as possible, hold free elections at the earliest moment, and re-establish full civilian government. But obviously this is a revolutionary situation—Turkey is in flux. One man to watch is Major-General Cemal Madanoglu, who is still a prominent member of the Committee of National Union although he was closely associated with Turkes. Another is Selim Sarper, a distinguished career diplomat who became Foreign Minister, and replaced a man, Fatin Rustu Zorlu, who was particularly hated. Sarper is a firm friend of the United States. He was successively Ambassador to Rome, the UN, and NATO before assuming his present post, and is a kind of weather-vane. If he goes, it will indicate that the Turkish revolution has become anti-American.

Bayar, Menderes, and several hundred of their associates went on trial in November, 1960. Altogether the Gursel régime has made 1,087 political arrests, and the first trials provided high and fancy drama, which convulsed Istanbul. Bayar, who is seventy-six, was charged with corruption having to do with an Afghan hound which he received as a state gift and then sold to the Ankara zoo for £785. Menderes, according to reports of the trials, was accused of various financial irregularities which involved vast sums of money, and it was alleged that he had ordered an Istanbul gynaecologist to kill a premature child born to his mistress, a lady named Iyhan Aydan. She is a former singer with the Ankara state opera, and has been Menderes' close friend for the last nine years. Both Bayar and Menderes were cleared of these particular charges but, at the moment of writing, still face the death penalty for alleged crimes more politically substantial, like conspiracy against the welfare of the state.

*

Turkey is, as is obvious to anyone who looks at a map, an essential linchpin in the Allied defence system. It is the bridge between Europe and Asia, between the Mediterranean Sea and the Black, and is the only power to be a member of both NATO and CENTO, the pact linking Turkey, Pakistan, Iran, and Great Britain in a mutual security arrangement. The headquarters of CENTO (Central Treaty Organization), formerly known as the Baghdad Pact, are now in Ankara. Once Iraq was a leading member.

The United States maintains an important base, equipped with missiles, on Turkish soil, as well as a radar station, and it was from Turkey that the ill-fated U-2 set out in May, 1960, on the first stage of its flight over the Urals. American personnel in Turkey totals not less than 14,642 persons, of whom 13,876 (including dependants) are military. The Turkish Army is powerful, well equipped, and well trained; it numbers 470,000 men and is by far the biggest European national force linked to NATO. Largely it was built up by munificent American aid, although—aid or no aid—the Turks are always sturdy in military fields. But the United States has poured more than £1,000 million into Turkey since 1947, and of this roughly two-thirds was for military purposes.

One reason why Turkey has, for many years, been a good ally and presumably a good investment is its traditional fear and hatred of Russia. Official relations with the Soviet Union are quite correct, but to most Turks the USSR and all it stands for are anathema. The Communist party was outlawed as far back as 1924, and its influence is negligible.

The United States has been severely criticized on occasion for pampering the Turks. The great Italian newspaper *Corriere della Sera* wrote on May 3, 1960:

> The Menderes government is kept in power by American aid . . .
> whatever aid the U.S. gives to Turkey is well given and Turkey
> deserves it, but there is a limit beyond which even the best of allies
> must call a halt. . . . That limit arises the day the recipient govern-

ment oppresses the freedom of its people. . . . The U.S. has lately suffered two serious experiences, those of Cuba and Korea. By supporting Batista, the United States forfeited the friendship of the Cuban people . . . in the Republic of Korea the U.S. waited until the last moment before giving up Syngman Rhee.

Joe Alex Morris, Jr., wrote in the New York *Herald Tribune* on May 31, 1960:

The revolution which snuffed out the ten-year-old régime of Premier Adnan Menderes last Friday can be ranked with Korea as a case where the United States and the West all too uncritically accepted, financed, and supported a government just because it was on our side.

There is no evidence so far that the new Committee of National Union has shifted Turkish policy away from support of NATO and the United States, but—to repeat—Turkey is in revolutionary flux and nobody knows what may or may not happen tomorrow. General Gursel announced immediately after assuming office that he did not contemplate any change of policy *vis-à-vis* the United States, but he can hardly be thought to be as 'dependable' as Menderes. It is lucky for the Western Allies that the Turks have such a lively hostility to the USSR. One lesson that may well be drawn from all this is that it is always dangerous for a democracy, like the United States, to become too closely involved with a dictator or semi-dictator, no matter how convenient this may seem to be. It is the people who count in the long run, and no régime is worth supporting if it keeps citizens down, if only for the simple reason that they will kick it out in time.

CHAPTER XIII

Austria Felix

YEARS ago I wrote the following in a magazine article:

> Vienna, which is the capital of Romance as well as of Austria, is the city of Maria Theresa and Metternich; of the greatest Brueghels in the world and the finest Jan Vermeer; of 10,000 dark blondes who walk in the spring rain in the Prater, and of aged and brittle countesses in high reception rooms; and of *Ochsenmaulsalat*, whipped cream, and beer. . . .
>
> The best things in Vienna are water, beer, and coffee. The water is superlative. It comes from Semmering, sixty miles away in the Styrian Alps, and is ice-cold from the tap, so that the glass mists even on the hottest summer day. In the outskirts of the town are the *heuriges*, small wineshops located in the vineyards which surround Vienna. But the supreme Viennese contribution to human civilization, next to Mozart, is the coffee house. . . .

Und so weiter!

Strange to say, most of this description still applies. But three profound changes have come to Austria since the shattering events of a quarter of a century ago, such as the civil war in February, 1934, and the subsequent assassination of Dr. Engelbert Dollfuss, the midget chancellor: (1) alteration in the character and atmosphere of Vienna itself; (2) neutralization of the country; (3) political rule by a coalition which has held office since 1945 and which performs the complex miracle of uniting in earnest fraternity the two leading political parties—clericals and socialists—which for many years snapped savagely at each other's throats.

*

Let us discuss these phenomena in turn.

Vienna's staple charms, as I have indicated, still remain. This is a city which knows how to enjoy life to the full, and the whole town gasps if the Burg Theatre gives a sloppy performance; the glories of Austrian baroque are still radiant, and the Hofburg and Ballhausplatz, where I watched in the streets on July 25, 1934, while Dollfuss was being murdered by the Nazis inside, still retain their delicate magnificence; most of the rubble left by the war has been cleared away and the Ringstrasse no longer looks like a face with every other tooth missing. But there is a difference—chiefly because Vienna no longer pretends to be imperial. For four hundred years it was not only the capital of the leading power of Central and South-eastern Europe but also of the whole Germanic world; today with most of its cosmopolitan lustre gone, it is settling down quietly to its contemporary position as a fascinating—but minor—provincial city.

Early in the nineteenth century, Vienna was the third largest city in Europe, second only to London and Paris. Even in 1920 the population exceeded 2·2 million; today it barely tops 1·6 million.[1] Despite this, one of the basic paradoxes of the old Austrian situation still remains—the disproportion between the size of its capital and its countryside. Vienna, a swollen head with a gaping maw, as I once put it, is attached to a dwarfed and shrunken body. Austria as a whole contains no more than about seven million inhabitants, and is about the size of Scotland combined with Northern Ireland. An old joke about two Viennese is to the point. One says, 'Let's get some exercise and take a walk around Austria.' The other replies, 'No—I don't want to get back before lunch.'

One striking point is that the Jewish population has shrunk from about 300,000 in the mid-1930's to roughly 30,000 today. In the old days Vienna was not only made variegated and colourful by citizens who derived from the succession states, Hungarians, Czechs, Slovaks, Dalmatians, Transylvanians, Slovenes, and so on, but it was, from the point of view of basic culture, incontestably the Jewish capital of the world. This was the city of Freud, Adler, Schnitzler, Egon Schiele, Kafka, Werfel, Felix Salten, Mahler, Max Reinhardt, Stefan Zweig, Hugo von Hofmannstahl, Wilhelm Stekel, and other distinguished Jews without number in the world of the arts, letters, and science.[2]

[1] M. S. Handler in the *New York Times*, August 2, 1960.
[2] Arthur Koestler in the *Observer*, October 18, 1959.

But Hitler killed the Jews off, and as a result the Vienna of today gives a note of intellectual drabness, of sterility. Not only did 90 per cent of Viennese Jews flee or die; those who survived went through an experience fully equivalent in horror to that which descended on their fellows in the Reich. Let me quote from a passage in *Inside Europe* which describes their plight immediately after the *Anschluss*, the union of Austria with Germany:

Jews [in Austria] were barred from being real estate agents, travelling salesmen, and accountants. They were forbidden to enter the Stock Exchange (which suffered a severe slump); they were forbidden to go to their safety deposit vaults without police escorts. Landlords were asked to expel Jewish doctors, and it was established that Jews could not live in flats with windows facing main streets. All Jews with property of more than 5,000 marks had to declare it, even if this were held abroad. Jewish children were not allowed to go to state schools or universities, and Aryan servants were not permitted to work in Jewish households. One law forbade Jewish doctors the right to practise, except those who had had war service, in which case they were allowed to serve only Jewish families; another made it an offence for any doctor to receive foreign medical books or periodicals written or published by Jewish concerns, which automatically cut German medicine off from a vast scientific literature. Another law obliged every Jew to adopt the name Sarah or Israel, while Jews born thereafter had to be restricted to a given list of first names.

Two marvellous Viennese institutions are still intact, though they were badly hit by the war. One is the Opera, now sumptuously rebuilt; the Austrian taxpayer subsidizes it to the tune of £1,400,000 a year, and it is worth every penny of this. The other is the magnificent series of *Gemeinde* houses, the municipal dwelling blocks built by the socialist administration in Vienna after World War I. In 1934 I watched several of them being bombarded and shot to pieces by the Heimwehr artillery, but they have long since been rebuilt and are functioning as before. Vienna, which still has a socialist administration, is one of the best-run municipalities in Europe, and the welfare state reaches an apogee here unmatched in Europe except in Britain and Scandinavia.

*

Second, neutrality. Austria, like Germany, was occupied by the Allies and passed under four-power control in 1945; Vienna, like Berlin, was divided into American, British, French, and Soviet sectors. But the Austrian occupation was avowedly temporary, and national elections were permitted to take place as early as November, 1945. These established the coalition government which has been in power ever since, and which from the beginning represented the country as a whole. The geographical divisions did not become solidified, as in Germany, and there has never been a problem of Austrian unification.

The occupation régime lasted for ten years, until the Russians withdrew in 1955, whereupon Austria emerged as a totally free, united, and neutral state. The Russians got a substantial price for withdrawal, £53,000,000 worth of supplies from Austrian industry and ten million tons of oil paid over a period of years. But the real reason the Soviets agreed to withdraw was political, to counteract West German affiliation with NATO. Also they were consumed with desire to meet Eisenhower and the Western leaders at the first Summit Conference, which was held at Geneva in the summer of 1955, and to attain this they were willing to give up Austria on the understanding that it would be neutralized. The Austrian Treaty was signed, with considerable fanfare, on May 15, 1955; Eden, Dulles, and Molotov were among the signatories.

The treaty came into effect in July, 1955, and the last occupation forces—American, British, French, and Russian—left in October. Curiously enough, nothing in the treaty itself mentions Austrian neutrality. As a sop to their pride, the Austrians themselves were permitted to declare their neutrality. This was done by means of a constitutional law passed on October 26, 1955, which provides for perpetual neutrality of the Austrian state and pledges the country never to join any military alliances or permit the establishment of foreign military bases on its territory. The pledges of the treaty are taken with extreme seriousness. For instance, Austria has not joined the Common Market, out of fear that this might prejudice its neutrality; it is, however, a member of the Outer Seven.

During the Lebanese crisis in July, 1958, U.S. military aircraft had to fly over Austria to get to Beirut in a hurry. The American authorities were punctilious in asking for permission for each flight, but the haste of the operation produced a certain amount of confusion and a few Air Force planes passed through Austrian air space without getting the required authority. In each such case, the Austrian government registered an immediate sharp protest, even though its sympathies were altogether on our side. A more important, as well as picturesque, 'violation' of Austrian neutrality came during the visit of Mr. Khrushchev to the country in July, 1960. The irrepressible Russian Prime Minister tossed his weight about in his usual blunt, spiky manner, and made several provocative speeches. As a British observer put it, he was giving a muscular bear hug to a timid neutral which did not want to be embraced. He declared that the Soviet Union would respond with armed action in defence of Austria if anybody else violated its neutrality, and that the American missile bases in Italy were a source of grave danger to the country; if, he went on, US missiles directed against the USSR or its satellites passed over Austria in the event of war, the Soviet Union would consider this a violation of Austrian neutrality and would act accordingly. The tart Austrian reply to this was to the effect that they did not want any outsider to 'interpret' what they thought their neutrality ought to be.

*

Finally, domestic politics. Ever since 1945 Austria has been ruled by a remarkable coalition of opposites, which has given the country complete political stability for fifteen years—half a generation. The coalition consists of two elements of almost exactly equal strength. First, the People's party, which derives from the old Christian Social party (*not* socialist) of pre-war years; Dollfuss and Schuschnigg were among its leaders. Its initials in present-day Austria are OeVP. It has always been strongly conservative, its basic support lies in the countryside, and it has marked clerical overtones. Second, the former Social Democrats, now known simply as the Socialists—symbol SPOe—with their strength in the intelligentsia, the labour movement, and the towns. In 1945 the two attained practically identical strength, and this ratio has never altered. For instance, in the elections of May, 1959, the Socialists got 44·8 per cent of the vote, the People's party 44·3 per cent. The People's party have seventy-nine seats in the Nationalrat (Lower Chamber of

Parliament), the Socialists seventy-eight. No election has ever been closer—except possibly the Kennedy-Nixon race in America in 1960.

The remarkable thing in Austria in 1959 was that neither party wanted particularly to win, or at least to beat the other by a substantial margin. The coalition suits almost everybody, and few wished it to be upset by a heavy preponderance of votes to either member. Jobs are based on a system, scrupulously regarded, which is known as *Proporz*. If the top man in a government department belongs to the People's party, the next man must be a Socialist, and so on down the line. The President of the Republic is a Socialist, but the Chancellor is of the People's party. Socialists hold the vice-chancellorship and the ministries of Foreign Affairs, Interior, Social Welfare, Justice, and Communications; the People's party have Education, Finance, Agriculture, Trade, and Defence. This evolution is the more extraordinary in that, a scant twenty-five years ago, Christian Socials and Social Democrats were—as I can attest from some anguishing personal experience—the bitterest of enemies. Interestingly enough, two actors in promoting a truce between them immediately after the war were two correspondents in Vienna, John MacCormac of the *New York Times* and M. W. Fodor, who for many years represented the *Manchester Guardian*, the *Chicago Daily News*, and other newspapers in Austria. MacCormac and Fodor went to the Chancellor of the time, Leopold Figl, a homely Christian Social who was president of the Austrian Farmers' Federation and whose nickname is 'Papa Potatoes', at a wine-tasting festival, and sought to explain to him how inestimably valuable it would be if the two major parties could make peace—especially in view of Soviet occupation of part of the country. Figl replied, 'Impossible! Those Socialists shot at us as if we were rabbits!' A few days later MacCormac and Fodor met a group of Social Democratic leaders in Grinzing, the suburb of Vienna renowned for *heurige* and its associations with Beethoven, and here too pleaded the desirability of coalition. The Social Democrats, who hated the Christian Socials with just as fixed and ferocious an enmity as vice versa, put their heads together and unexpectedly agreed. The two correspondents then went back to Figl, and negotiations began.

A third party exists in Austria, the FPOs or rightist liberals, who have eight seats in the lower house; it stands on the extreme right, and derives most of its strength from ex-Nazis. The Viennese don't like to admit it, but there were plenty of Austrian citizens who welcomed Hitler and who were vigorous, enthusiastic Nazis before and during the war.

At the other extreme are the Communists. The party is legal in Austria, but is so weak that it has no representation in Parliament. Even in the Soviet occupation zone, it got less than 5 per cent of the vote in November, 1945. In the last general election (May, 1959) only 3·3 per cent of the total vote of the country was Communist.

Why has the coalition worked so well? First, mature and intelligent leadership on both sides. Second, the only alternative would be a return to pre-war bitterness and instability. The Viennese, even if given to *Schlamperei* and *Gemütlichkeit*, have a rare quality among peoples, that of being able to learn from experience. Pain hurts.

SOME PERSONALITIES

The President of the Republic, a Socialist, is Adolf Schaerf, who was elected for a six-year term in 1957. Largely his importance is titular. His office is supposedly removed from partisan politics, but he has been an influential factor in the smooth, stable running of the coalition. Schaerf, a jurist by profession, was born on April 20, 1890, in a Moravian village which was then located in Czechoslovakia. He arose from working-class parents, studied at the University of Vienna, practised law, and acted as secretary of the Social Democratic parliamentary group from 1919 to 1934. He was imprisoned by Dollfuss when the Socialists were brutally suppressed in the early 1930's, and then again by the Nazis after *Anschluss*. He isn't Jewish, but is proud of the fact that he speaks Yiddish. His personality is reserved, and his tastes intellectual.

Julius Raab, leader of the People's party, has been Chancellor since 1958. He was the son of an engineer, and was born in 1891 in Lower Austria. He worked for an architectural company, and, interested in politics from an early age, organized units of craftsmen and engineers into a Christian Social Artisans' League. A

Heimwehr leader (but on the mild side) in the pre-war years, he became a member of Dr. Kurt Schuschnigg's last government. He has always been strongly Catholic and conservative. In October, 1960, something almost unprecedented happened; Austria had a sudden political crisis, caused by disagreement over the budget, and Chancellor Raab resigned. President Schaerf refused, however, to accept his resignation, the issue was patched up, and the cabinet resumed activity without alteration. Raab has several times used the threat of resignation as a political weapon, and the Viennese call him ironically the 'perpetually retiring' Chancellor.[1]

The leading Socialist from the point of view of seniority is the Vice-Chancellor, Bruno Pittermann. Oddly enough for a politician in a country as Catholic as Austria, he is a practising Lutheran. Dr. Pittermann, the son of a wagonmaker, was born in 1905; he is both a Ph.D. and LL.D. from the University of Vienna. A teacher, he lost his job after *Anschluss*, and spent some years in private law practice. Pittermann is strongly pro-American, and as far as social theory goes, stands on the right wing of the Socialist party; his views are roughly akin to those of Hugh Gaitskell and Willy Brandt. His wife is Jewish, and he speaks English, French, Yiddish, and Italian.

Another distinguished Socialist, with a shrewd and lively mind, is Dr. Bruno Kreisky, the Minister of Foreign Affairs. Like Schaerf, he has been jailed twice—both by the Dollfuss dictatorship and the Nazis. He is the son of a banker, and his wife is Swedish. He is an exceptionally able man. Like most Austrians, Kreisky is, although officially neutral, vehemently pro-American. Few Austrians will forget that U.S. aid to Austria totalled £533 million between 1945 and 1953. Another attractive and important personality is Dr. Reinhard Kamitz, the Minister of Finance.

*

On occasion people ask about Otto Hapsburg, the pretender to the old imperial throne. Recently he came into the news because

---

[1] In the spring of 1961 he did resign—not for political reasons but because of his age. Dr. Alfons Gorbach was scheduled to succeed him as Chancellor. Gorbach is a 62-year-old lawyer from Styria who lost a leg in World War I and spent no fewer than eight years in Dachau, one of the worst Nazi concentration camps.

of agitation to return former Hapsburg estates, which were confiscated in 1918, to the family; they cover some forty thousand acres, and are lucrative. Otto, who was born in 1912, and whose full name is Franz-Josef-Otto-Robert-Marie-Antoine-Karl-Maximilian-Heinrich-Sixtus-Xavier-Felix-Renatus-Lud-wig-Gaetan-Pius-Ignaz-Prince of Hapsburg-Lorraine, was the son of the last Austro-Hungarian Emperor, Karl, and Zita of Bourbon-Parme. He has always been intelligent, sensitive, and good-looking, and, unlike most princelings, he got a sound education. As a practical politician he must know that the prospect of reviving the Austro-Hungarian monarchy is as impossible as reviving the Egypt of Cheops, King Tut, or Lord Cromer, but he continues to stand for the re-creation, in some form or other, of economic unity along the Danube. Otto, although a citizen of Austria, is not allowed to live in or visit the country by terms of the Hapsburg Exclusion Act, and, as recently as October 1, 1960, the Socialist party reiterated its determination to keep him out. He lives with his family in Bavaria, a few miles from the Austrian frontier.

AUSTRIA, ITALY, AND THE TYROL

A prickly little dispute about the South Tyrol has been endemic between Austria and Italy since the war. Alto Adige, which is what the Italians call the area, was part of Austria until the end of World War I, and it still contains a substantial German-speaking citizenry. The Austrians assert that the Italians, who want to Italianize the region as thoroughly as possible, have persistently obstructed a 1946 agreement which guarantees the population certain minority rights and privileges, such as using the German language in communications. The Italians, on their side, accuse the Austrians of forming an Irridentist movement in Bolzano (Bozen), where the German-speaking Italians are a majority. All this came to a head at the UN in October, 1960. The Italians refused to countenance autonomy for Bolzano, charging that, if this were granted, Austria would proceed to take the area over. As a matter of fact, during the Hitler era, the South Tyrol *was* separated from Italy and returned to the Reich, but it reverted to Italian suzerainty immediately after the war. Italy declined to negotiate at the UN, but said that it would be

willing to let the International Tribunal at the Hague adjudi-
cate the matter; Austria refused this offer, on the grounds that
the dispute was political, not juridical. After strenuous argument
a provisional agreement was reached whereby both sides agreed
to open bilateral talks, hoping thus to thrash the matter out.

ANOTHER NOTABLE NEUTRAL

In some ways Switzerland is more neutral than Austria, in some
ways less—if the concept 'neutrality' is capable of qualification.
Swiss neutrality derives from the Congress of Vienna, which
established the frontiers of the nation in perpetuity in 1815 (they
have not changed by an inch since), and thus predates that of
Austria by 140 years. Switzerland, like Austria, has not
joined the Common Market, because this is supposed to have
political undertones, but instead—again like Austria—is a
member of the Outer Seven as well as of GATT, the General
Agreement on Tariffs and Trade. Austria is a member of the
UN; Switzerland is not. The Swiss do, however, belong to
several UN agencies. Also Switzerland is a member of the
OEEC—Organization for European Economic Co-operation—
although it has never asked for (or needed) any external financial
aid. Neither Switzerland nor Austria belongs to NATO. One
interesting point is that the Swiss, although their sympathies
are, of course, close to the West, have recognized Red China,
and the Communist Chinese maintain a busy small mission in
Berne.

Switzerland (area 14,944 square miles, population 5,210,000)
maintains a first-class, well-trained small army, because the
Swiss believe not merely in neutrality but in armed neutrality.
In both world wars, they went to extravagant lengths to guard
themselves against attack, and protect their mountainous but
vulnerable frontiers. The Swiss Army, unit for unit and man for
man, is one of the two or three best in Europe—probably as
tough as the Turkish. I have heard a patriotic Swiss say that, if
his country should ever by some fantastic mischance become
embroiled in war with France, the Swiss forces could easily
reach Cherbourg in three days.

Switzerland, the oldest republic in the world, is, as everybody
knows, indissolubly well integrated, despite the extraordinary

fact that it is quadrilingual. Seventy-two per cent of its people have German as their principal language, 20 per cent French, 6 per cent Italian, and a little over 1 per cent Romanish. In contrast to Austria, which is overwhelmingly Roman Catholic, Switzerland is 58 per cent Protestant, about 41 per cent Roman Catholic. The country is governed by a peculiar system. The Federal Assembly elects seven men, each of whom administers a government department, to a Federal Council for four-year terms; these choose a president and vice-president out of their own membership to serve a one-year term. The federal councillors, once chosen, are usually re-elected time and again, and rotate annually to the presidency; but the President, having served one year, cannot succeed himself except after an interval. This device ensures continuity and stability. One curious point is that no federal councillor is supposed to travel abroad while holding office, but of course this rule is sometimes broken.

The President for 1960 was Max Petitpierre, a Radical Democrat who was also President in 1950, 1955, and 1960, and Vice-President in 1949, 1954, and 1959. He has been chief of the Federal Political Department, that is Minister of Foreign Affairs, since 1944. Also—maybe a bigger job—he has twice served as president of the chamber of commerce for the watch industry. Petitpierre, who rose out of a background of wealth and, in so far as there are any aristocrats in Switzerland, of aristocracy, was born in Neuchâtel in 1899. He studied law at Neuchâtel, Zürich, and Munich, won a doctorate in 1934, taught law for a time, built up a handsome legal practice, published several technical books, and in 1937 entered politics. He is thoroughly pro-American, but has never visited the United States. His wife, whom he married in 1928, is a sister of the well-known writer Denis de Rougemont. Dr. Petitpierre has very definite ideas, both theoretical and practical, about neutrality. He likes in particular to stress what he considers to be the difference between neutrality and 'neutralism'. The latter, a negative concept, does not attract him.

The Swiss government is a four-way coalition, consisting of Social Democrats, Radical Democrats (a moderately progressive bourgeois party), the Christian-Social party (Catholic conservatives), and the Peasants, Artisans and Middle Class party, an offshoot of the Radical Democrats, but more conservative. Four other parties, all small, compose the opposition. As in Austria, the Social Democrats and the Christian Socials run neck-and-neck; the former have fifty-one seats in the National Council, the latter forty-seven. Moreover, the Social Democrats in Switzerland run a tie with the Radical Democrats, who also number fifty-one. The Communist party is legal, and has three seats out of 196.

One curiosity is a fight over woman suffrage which goes back many years; Switzerland is one of the few countries in Europe in which women do not have the vote. The Social Democrats in particular support woman suffrage and propose to introduce it every year; but each year conservative elements in the Council combine to beat it down. Feeling against woman suffrage is so strong in some parts of the country that a political organization of *women* has been organized to oppose it.

The temptation is considerable to think of Switzerland as consisting of nothing but Alps, timepieces, secret bank accounts, and milk chocolate. One point often neglected, as the British historian H. R. Trevor-Roper pointed out in his *Men and Events*, is the hospitality the Swiss have always given freely to political and other refugees—a characteristic somewhat surprising in view of their hard-headedness and self-sufficiency in other matters, and their tendency to play everything absolutely safe. But the list of writers, revolutionaries and men of talent who have found harbour in Switzerland is long and uniquely distinguished. It runs from Calvin to Charlie Chaplin, and includes Rousseau, Voltaire, Mussolini, Lenin, Arthur Koestler, and Thomas Mann.[1]

*

We re-enter now the grand line of European politics and affairs, and turn to England.

---

[1] But people who abuse Swiss hospitality or violate its neutrality get short shrift. For instance, a Frenchman who represented extremist Algerian reactionaries was summarily expelled from the country in January, 1961.

CHAPTER XIV

England, the Most Important Country

I n England in 1936 the somnolent, bulldog-like Stanley Baldwin was Prime Minister, and Neville Chamberlain, who was once described as 'a good town clerk in a lean year', was his Chancellor of the Exchequer. They led a so-called 'National' government, and Ramsay MacDonald, the Socialist leader and 'boneless wonder', was Lord President of the Council. Winston Churchill had been out of office since 1929, and chances seemed slim that he would ever return to an eminent position. However, I wrote at the time that 'most people agree that in a great upheaval he would emerge as Britain's national leader'. They did not have long to wait.

Harold Macmillan, in those remote old days, was an inconspicuous back-bencher, unnoticed except for occasional somewhat eccentric deviations from the orthodox Conservative line; the late Aneurin Bevan was familiar, but few would have predicted that this inflammatory bad boy of the Labour movement (as he was called then) would turn out to be the most effective Minister of Health in British history, and, before his tragic death, a potent and beneficent force for solidarity in the Labour party. Hugh Gaitskell was completely unknown politically in 1936; he was only twenty-nine. Others conspicuous on both sides of the House today—R. A. Butler, Duncan Sandys, Peter Thorneycroft, the Earl of Home (pronounced 'Hume'), Selwyn Lloyd, Harold Wilson, Michael Foot, Richard H. S. Crossman —were still playing with water-wings, not yet ready for the swim.

And where today are the titans of 1936, the towering Whitehall giants of the days just before the war? Alfred Duff Cooper, peppery and poetic, is dead; Lord Halifax is dead; Sir Samuel

Hoare is dead; so is Sir John Simon, of whom it was written that, playing golf, he putted around bunkers; so, on the Labour side, are Sir Stafford Cripps and Ernest Bevin. Anthony Eden was killed by Suez in 1956, but is still alive.

Ahead—in England early in 1936—were the abdication crisis, which aroused so much emotion and was so steeped in day-to-day, hour-to-hour intolerable suspense that those who lived through it will never forget it; also Munich; also sixty-eight months of total war; also the Labour governments of Mr. Attlee, who has become one of the most urbane and seasoned of elder statesmen; and the burgeoning glory of Winston Churchill. Dominant issues in 1936 were Hitler, unemployment, and India. Now Hitler is a lump of cinder, unemployment has largely been swallowed up by the contemporary expansion of industrial power, and India is free. Who remembers, incidentally, that Mr. Churchill spent a good part of his ten years in the wilderness (1929-39) fighting tenaciously against Indian independence? It was one of his more formidable vagaries. But he spent the same amount of time seeking with grim eloquence to awaken his countrymen to the deadly menace of the Nazis, and devoted himself as well to the most pleasant and rewarding of all occupations, the composition of good books.

HOW ENGLAND HAS CHANGED

On a minor level—or perhaps not so minor—there are all manner of differences between Great Britain in 1936 and Great Britain (population 51,680,000) now. Politicians refer to their colleagues by their Christian names on TV, and the prostitutes are off the streets. Cambridge has abolished Latin as an entrance requirement (so has Oxford for science students), and standards of the popular Press (to my mind, at least) have grossly deteriorated. The House of Lords has life peers, chosen on a non-partisan basis—this reform was put through not merely to make it easy to kick people upstairs and cover up men who had been a failure in the Commons, but to give the Lords more vitality, more relevance to the life of the nation. Girl students at Oxford may apply for insurance policies against pregnancy (if the newspapers are to be believed), and points of demarcation between the two great political parties have been much whittled down. The terminal age for compulsory education has been lifted from fourteen to fifteen, an important advance, and naked strip-tease shows, presented all over the West End of London to 'club' audiences, do a business of five million pounds a year or more. The youth of the land betrays a distinct note of irreverence towards the mysterious entity known as the Establishment, the angry young men are angry because they have less to be angry about, and tourists may enter the sacred precincts of almost every country house in England by paying a small fee. Often this is the owner's private enterprise; collecting the tourist fees can be a big business. Other owners of ancient aristocratic houses get financial assistance from the National Trust, usually on condition they admit visitors. Sometimes the Trust, a non-government agency, buys an estate, allowing the owner to occupy it for life; occasionally the state takes over a home or part of its contents, in lieu of death duties. Hundreds of thousands of trippers pay a 'bob a nob' to get a peek at Knole, Hatfield, Cliveden, or other resplendent ancestral piles.

Another important item is racial tension. This was virtually unknown before the war, if only because Negro communities were scant; recently, considerable numbers of Jamaicans and other West Indians, perhaps 100,000 in all, have settled in England, as well as 55,000 Pakistanis, Indians, and Africans, and unpleasant race riots have occurred; the most violent was in the Notting Hill Gate district of London in 1958. (Similarly in France, racial prejudice, hitherto unknown, has begun recently to assert itself, but in France the targets are not Negroes, but Algerians, Arabs, and others brown-skinned.) Another item in England is emigration. About 230,000 Britons left the home country in 1957; this figure has now tapered off to an average of about 140,000 a year. Most emigrants go to Canada or elsewhere in the Commonwealth. Still another item is vociferous public discussion of a subject traditionally hush-hush—homosexuality, a widespread ailment in England. A recent letter to the *New Statesman*, signed by three persons, begins, 'We are homosexuals and we are writing because we feel strongly that insufficient is being done to enlighten public opinion on a topic which has for too long been shunned.' In 1957 the Wolfenden Report recommended that 'homosexual behaviour between consenting adults in private should no longer be a criminal offence.'

But an attempt to put this proposal into the statute books was roundly defeated in the House of Commons in June, 1960.

Other conspicuous phenomena of change demand more extended word.

First, social fluidity. It would be a gross exaggeration to say that class distinctions in England no longer exist—indeed, they remain sharper, deeper, than in any other country in the world *in certain spheres*—but speaking in general caste is nowhere nearly so important as it was before the war. The social structure is much less rigid, less arbitrarily and unalterably fixed. The days when a political or colonial appointment could be made without reference to experience or merit are as dead as those in America when Commodore Vanderbilt made his celebrated remark, 'The public be damned.' One example of the way emphasis has shifted is that, in the thirties, roughly 65 per cent of all students at Oxford and Cambridge had been preceded there by their fathers, elder brothers, or other relatives. Today, the proportion is reversed. Another is that, in the old days, a youngster had little chance for a post in the Foreign Office if he did not have a private income; this may help a candidate today but I am assured that it is certainly not the *sine qua non.* Again, social patterns have changed vastly in industrial and 'county' areas. Before the war, if a boy's father was a coal-miner or textile worker, the chances were that the youngster would follow him in this occupation; only exceptionally gifted, aggressive, or lucky people emerged from their environment. But today countless young men and women climb out of their backgrounds with comparative ease. Again, in Victorian days if a villager did not tug his forelock to the local squire, in an automatic gesture not merely of respect but of subservience, he was out of bounds; today, country folk may still respect and even be fond of members of the local hierarchy, but few have marked class-consciousness, or are obsequiously subservient.

Three factors, it would seem, have led to the fluidity of much of contemporary British society. One is, of course, education; the great universities have been pretty well democratized, and the public schools (Eton, Winchester, Harrow, et cetera) have scholarships for working-class boys—although the public schools are still, by and large, cloisters of the privileged and still have massive influence in important circles.[1] Another is TV, or, as some British call it, 'the telly'. Since channels are few and choice of programmes limited, this can go a long way towards shaping a homogeneous society. But most important of all is money. The virtual end of unemployment has literally transformed England. In general, the poor have become richer to an extent; and certainly the rich have become poorer. Death duties (which, incidentally, were first brought in by a Tory government many years ago) rise to 80 per cent on an estate of a million pounds; no factor, not even the income tax (which goes up to 17s. 9d. in the pound), can be more levelling. Only 800 people in the whole of England keep out of earnings more than six thousand pounds per year, and only 17,600 keep more than four thousand pounds—believe it or not. Most rich people live on their capital.[2] Class, in the long run, depends on hereditary factors, but *heredity without money* means (again in the long run) the end of class.

Second, it seemed to me visiting England in 1958 and again in 1960 that there has been a diminution in the respect generally accorded the royal family. Here we tread on delicate ground. I do not mean that the Queen and Queen Mother are not loved and revered loyally by the immense majority of the population— they are—but that the *institution* of monarchy is regarded with a perspective sharply different from that of former years. Writers both Tory and Labourite, like Lord Altrincham and Malcolm Muggeridge, have made vivid adverse comment on royal prerogatives and attributes.[3] The marriage of Princess Margaret provoked a good deal of gossip, particularly at the dinner tables of the established *élite,* of a scabrous kind that would have been unthinkable a generation ago. The *New Statesman* printed a profile about the royal bride which, though not unfriendly, was not conventionally respectful and which dealt with her not merely as an example of royalty but as a human being with human frailties. 'She has . . . few real

---

[1] But this, I am told, is much reduced nowadays, to speak generally, in the civil service, science, and industry; it is still conspicuous in the City and the armed forces.

[2] An important point is that there is no capital gains tax in England. See Virginia Cowles, *No Cause for Alarm,* p. 108.

[3] True, the controversial Mr. Muggeridge was, as a result, barred from the BBC for a time.

resources with which to face life.' Members of the Labour party asked pertinent questions in the House about the sum allotted for decorating the London streets for the wedding (£25,000), and the cost of the honeymoon cruise on the royal yacht *Britannia* (£40,000). In general, however, few British citizens resent what the royal family costs them, and almost everybody loves frantically the public festivities that come with such an event as a royal wedding. 'After all,' one sound businessman remarked to me, 'we pay those people [the royal family] £600,000 a year, and the least we expect is a good show for the money.'

A poem entitled 'The Epistle to the Philistines', by the distinguished playwright John Osborne, appeared in *Tribune*, the left-wing Labour weekly, on May 13, 1960, in ironic celebration of the royal marriage. I do not think it could have been printed anywhere in England a few years ago. Here are excerpts:

> Grace be to you and peace from Our Gracious Lady and all princes and others who have smiled on us from carriages and high places.
>
> I rejoice to bring you tidings of humble men elevated, for it is now said by their fruits ye shall know them and not by their roots.
>
> Inasmuch as the old and once established religion was unsatisfying to the people . . . the new gospel has been pronounced and taken root long since. . . .
>
> They need not to think of the morrow nor to think at all, for they see clearly as through a glass coach. . . .
>
> This is the doctrine that shall be spread abroad, for it is revealed of Grace, and shall be known as Justification through the Defender of the Faith and the Ministry of Works. . . .
>
> For Her sake you shall diligently come and go forth, you itinerant painters and wall paper pickers;
>
> You gown sellers, fashion setters, you play makers and play fakers;
>
> You poets and Rolleiflex flickers;
>
> You breathy column sisters and microphone prelates; you dancing rogues and morning coat vagabonds. . . .
>
> You knights and cringers; you pinched conformers; and indeed all you exquisite things.
>
> You shall be called henceforth the New Set, for many are sybarites but few are chosen;

The Queendom shall be yours, and it will come soon; and the day shall come when we are all Queens, each and every one of us.
Therefore rejoice, take heart and be diligent. Thy Queendom Come.

Buckingham Palace has, it would seem, become distinctly aware of marked alterations in public opinion about the court. In the summer of 1960 occurred an event literally unprecedented —the Queen and the Duke of Edinburgh attended a reception given by Lord Astor of Hever deliberately planned so that they should meet—guess what—a group of journalists.

Third, the boom. Harold Macmillan won the last election largely by the slogan 'You never had it so good', and 1960 was an even better year than 1959—in fact, probably the most prosperous in recent British history. Britain, like France and West Germany, has entered with a rush into a dazzling era of consumer economy. Everybody, it seems, has money—moreover, spends it. Wages have gone up, and never before has the working class had such spending power; also inflation has been kept within bounds. One conspicuous point is the relative affluence of young people; boys just out of school can get eight pounds a week at their first jobs, or even more, and a late-teenager is scorned by his fellows if he hasn't good-looking clothes. These youngsters belonged, let us remember, to a *rationed* generation; they were the hardship kids who grew up in a privation economy, who subsisted year after year with only the most meagre apportionment of shoes, butter, motor cycles, meat, radios, what not—and now they are bursting out.

Wealth makes for relaxation, and Britain is a relaxed country at the moment; also it makes for mobility. One conspicuous point is the enormous increase of instalment-buying—hire-purchase or 'H.P.' as the British call it, or, somewhat cynically, 'the Never-Never'. This puts merchandise within the reach of almost everybody, and it is another cogent reason why classes are being levelled out. As one friend put it to me: A person can, after all, only drive one car at a time (no matter how many he may happen to own), and a garage mechanic with a second-hand Ford can, with reasonable luck, get as far along the road as a duke in a Jaguar. A family in Whitechapel can install a heating system on hire-purchase, and may even be better off than the duke from the viewpoint of simple bodily comfort, because even a wealthy duke cannot easily afford central heating for a castle with 150 rooms.

A minor—but suggestive—point has to do with motor-cars. When the council houses, local housing developments, were planned and built (practically every town and village in England has one), nobody dreamed of the new age dawning, and little— if any—provision was made for garages. Nobody dreamed that the average working man or labourer would ever be able to afford a car, much less need a garage. So today even the newest housing developments almost everywhere in England are a tangled mass of parked cars jamming up local highways and village lanes. Roads are a big issue in England, as is traffic control. (Roads should also be a big issue in France, but are not; France has an excellent secondary road system, but few throughways like those in Italy and Germany.)

Mr. Macmillan has a variety of nicknames in the Press. Perhaps this is a result of his popularity, even among those who criticize him severely. He has been called Mac Wonder, Mac Shuffle, Mac Master, Mac Bland, Mac Martyr, Mac Whim, Mac Jingo (during Suez), Mac Artful, Mac Whirl, Mac Jekyll, Super Mac, and even Tar-Mac, 'the great arterial engineer'. This last came after a bizarre snafu in relation to a road called the Preston Bypass.[1] Roads, parking, and traffic congestion are, to repeat, pressing issues.

The British boom is a boom, yes, a great big spanking boom, but this is not to say that there are not worries in the economic picture. I have said that unemployment has 'largely' been absorbed, but stubborn small pockets still exist in localized areas in the industrial north and Scotland. Still, the ratio of unemployment to the total work force is only about 1·5 per cent, and the difference is that of day and night between 1960 and the 1930's, when unemployment was the most harassing of all national problems, apparently insoluble, and one which threatened to stifle the entire economy. The other principal contemporary worry has to do with exports. Britain is a trading nation; it must import food (about half its total consumption) or starve; and imports must be paid for. Exports have been holding up well, but imports are rising twice as fast; the adverse balance of trade is bigger than at any time since 1957, and the trade

[1] *New Statesman*, January 31, 1959.

deficit was running to £75 - £80 million a month in 1961. The main reason is probably the paradoxical one of too much prosperity—that is, the colossal demand by Britons in Britain for British consumer goods, which means that manufactured articles which normally went abroad are now absorbed at home.[1] To check this process the government has taken several steps, like lifting the bank rate, squeezing credit, and trying to keep hire-purchase in bounds by direct controls.

Fourth, nationalization and the welfare state. About one-fifth of British industry is now under public control. Most of the manufacturing industries, on which British trade largely depends, have not been nationalized and probably never will be, as Drew Middleton has pointed out in *These are the British* (p. 98); steel was nationalized by the Labour government, and then denationalized, i.e. brought back to private ownership, by the Tories. Roughly one-seventh of the steel industry is, however, still state-owned, and the list of other industries, services, and the like which remain firmly nationalized and under public control is formidable—the BBC (dating back to 1927); the railways; most (but not all) civil aviation; some (but not all) trucking and transport; the Bank of England (1945); coal, of supreme importance (1947); gas and electricity; and cable and wireless communication as well as domestic posts and telegraph. Then, too, one should mention subsidized housing, the National Insurance Scheme, which provides social security on an extremely advanced and comprehensive basis, and, above all, the National Health Service. The health programme was, incidentally, originally proposed not by Labour but by the Tories, but it was the first Attlee government which put it through. Nowadays, the National Health Service, despite the ferocious controversies which attended its birth, not only works efficiently, but is overwhelmingly popular with the rank and file of citizens. About 65 per cent of its cost comes directly from the Exchequer. Indeed, the fact that a Briton does not, in the normal course of events, ever have to pay more than nominal sums for doctor, dentist, or medicine throughout the whole course of his life, from birth to the grave, has played a cogent role in the

[1] Another factor is the development of small-car manufacturing in the United States, which has severely hurt the lucrative British export of cars to America. *Time*, July 16, 1960.

current boom and the increase in national purchasing power. This is because of the elementary fact that the share of the family budget that formerly went to medical care can now be spent otherwise, on anything from breakfast bacon to hi-fi. The ghastly financial drain caused by severe or prolonged illness is now all but eliminated, which is not only a good thing of itself, but releases immense funds for other use. This is a point obvious enough, but not one always realized. Another point is that, as a result of the National Health Service, citizens do not hesitate to go to a doctor *early*, and this has saved many lives.

The Macmillan government is, of course, a Conservative government, but on most issues stands (to American eyes) a bit left of centre. In fact the Macmillanites are called 'Left Conservatives' by Tories to the right of them, or even, a favourite phrase, 'Pink Conservatives'. The root of the Macmillan policy is to play politics like chess, and, at all costs, to hold on to an impregnable position in the centre; to do this the Prime Minister has to have a certain amount of left support. Some observers thought that, after the third straight Conservative victory in 1959, Macmillan would veer to the right, if only because he *is* a Conservative and it was presumably safe to do so politically; however, he continues to hold to a slightly left-of-centre position. This infuriates the Labour party, and makes it difficult for the Labourites to wage a winning electoral campaign; the Tories have filched their thunder. Moreover, on two issues—further nationalization of industry and defence—the Labour party is itself bitterly divided. Mr. Gaitskell, one of the most enlightened, intelligent, and patriotic of men, has to spend much more time and energy fighting one wing of his own followers than in confronting Macmillan and the government.

Fifth and finally, Britain is no longer a great power. It is most certainly at the top of the second rank of powers, but it is not on the level of the Soviet Union or the United States. And perhaps this is the most profound, the most noteworthy, of all the changes mentioned in this chapter, since for roughly a hundred years Britain *was* incontestably the chief power in the world, and it is no small thing for a great power to stop being one. Moreover, the British Empire (as apart from Commonwealth) has all but ceased to exist, a development so remarkable that we must look into it in more detail.

EXIT EMPIRE

On November 10, 1942, Mr. (as he then was) Winston Churchill made a celebrated speech at Mansion House in which he said defiantly, in his iron-chinned way, that he had not become first minister of the Crown in order to preside over the liquidation of the British Empire. But today, fewer than twenty years later, one of the most astonishing evolutions in history has produced exactly this, as I mentioned in an earlier passage of this book. The liquidation of the Empire, the possibility of which Mr. Churchill so intensely deplored, and which he did not believe for a moment could conceivably occur, is close to being a fact.

Since the war the following British dependencies, once marked so proudly in pink on every schoolboy's map, have become free.

	Population	Area in square miles
Asia		
India	420,000,000	1,269,640
Pakistan	86,167,000	364,737
Burma	20,856,000	261,789
Ceylon	9,361,000	25,332
Israel	2,062,900	8,048
Jordan	1,600,000	37,000
South-east Asia		
Malaya	6,698,000	50,680
Mediterranean		
Cyprus	549,000	3,572
Europe		
Eire	2,800,000	26,600
Africa		
Egypt	25,000,000	386,110
Anglo-Egyptian Sudan	10,225,912	967,500
Ghana (formerly the Gold Coast)	4,900,000	92,000
Nigeria	34,600,000	373,250
British Somaliland	600,000	68,000
TOTALS	625,419,812	4,102,376

A word or two of qualification is in order. Egypt, to speak technically, became a sovereign state as far back as 1936, but Britain held close strings to it, and British dominion there was reasserted in no uncertain terms during the war. Suez reverted to Egyptian control in 1954. The Anglo-Egyptian Sudan was not, officially speaking, ever part of the Empire, but to all intents and purposes this great country was a British satrapy (and a model satrapy, too) until signature of the Sudan accord between Britain and Egypt on February 12, 1953.

Another point—of singular weight—is that, following a subtle constitutional evolution and because of the inherent far-sightedness of British rule, most of the newly free countries, although they rank incontestably as sovereign states, retain close economic and political ties to Britain, and are loyal members of the Commonwealth, which developed out of the Empire. The Union Jack no longer flies over them, they no longer have British governors, but association with London and most other members of the Commonwealth remains cordial and intimate. An exception is Burma, which overtly seceded from the Commonwealth—also Eire.

All this—the giving of freedom to more than 600 million people—is, to repeat, astonishing enough, if only because it has happened with such extreme rapidity. Moreover, the movement is by no means concluded. The pace of dissolution is, in fact, quickening. Sierra Leone, on the west coast of Africa, has just attained freedom, and Tanganyika, on the east coast, will probably achieve complete self-government within two years. Kenya and Uganda are almost certain to follow Tanganyika. The Central African Federation (Southern Rhodesia, Northern Rhodesia, Nyasaland) is tormented by constant crisis; the ruling whites (who can be just as nationalist as blacks) want full independent Commonwealth status, and the Africans in Nyasaland cannot be held much longer within the brittle, unworkable frame of the Federation. On the other side of the world the West Indian Federation is progressing, with some uneasy fits and starts, towards complete self-rule. Then consider outposts like Singapore, for which an entirely new kind of status has been invented by the elastic British, and Malta in the Mediterranean, where nationalist sentiment mounts fiercely. Finally, Zanzibar in the Indian Ocean. Here too nationalism steadily becomes

7

more articulate, and the situation is exacerbated by propaganda and political infiltration by the Communist Chinese. Going, going, gone! This is the gist of the imperial story from the plantations of Malaya to the northern deserts of Nigeria, with their incomparable lunar remoteness, from lush Caribbean islands next door to the United States to the seared, broken uplands of Tanganyika.[1]

What has caused this evolution, this giving away of what seems to be a quarter of the earth? There are obvious reasons, as I wrote in *Inside Africa*, all the way from Woodrow Wilson, who announced in Paris in 1919 the doctrine of the right of small nations to self-determination, to abstract considerations in the realm of ethics—that colonialism is morally wrong, un-workable, and as archaic as slavery. Also, in several areas, the British were forced out. They gave up most of their vast terri-tories for the simple and primitive reason that, once an undeveloped community becomes educated to the ways of the modern world, it will be impossible to suppress nationalism except at an exorbitant cost in money, manpower, arms, and blood. But there are other factors, too. For one thing Britain, alone among colonial powers, had as its professed object the systematic—if gradual—training of colonial wards towards eventual self-government. I do not mean to overstate idealistic factors; 'eventual' is the key word; nobody expected the flood of self-government to come with such a rush. Another factor is the good old British doctrine, once expressed to me by Ernest Bevin, the late Foreign Minister, of 'Give—and keep!' That is, by getting out in time, by fulfilling the nationalist aspirations of colonial peoples early rather than late, the British hoped shrewdly to retain political dominance and economic advantage. It hasn't always worked out that way. Britain, for instance, certainly does not dominate Mr. Nehru's India. But British relations with India are infinitely better, smoother, more fruitful, than before the war, and British trade with India has actually increased—by a lot.[2]

[1] Even St. Helena (population 4,682, area 47 square miles) has a lively nationalist movement.

[2] In 1938 exports to India were £33·8 million, imports from India £49·9 million. Corresponding figures for India and Pakistan in 1959 are £204 and £168 million.

The question may well be asked, 'But are the underdeveloped colonial peoples really *ready* for self-government? Should they not have further tutelage?' Of course (consider the Congo) several are not ready; most still need political advice and economic aid. Nevertheless, the fitness question is totally irrelevant; it comes too late; it bears no relation to the present situation: whether the colonial peoples are ideally ready for independence or not they intend to have it, and cannot be stopped from getting it. The real issue is how to continue tutelage *after* independence, how, in a word, to give the newly free states, who may carry a large burden of hatred for their former colonial masters, confidence in the good will, imagination, and capacity of the Western democratic world. The alternatives are chaos, collapse, or Communism—perhaps all three.

*

The man who, at present, is actively in charge of the large process of liquidation, dissolution, of the remains of the British Empire is a remarkable young Scot, Iain Norman Macleod, who since 1959 has been Secretary of State for Colonies. Mr. Macleod is an able citizen—cheerful, supple-minded, bright as a new coin, confident, and, in the best sense of the word, tough. He first came to prominence by taking on no less a personage than Aneurin Bevan in a debate on health matters, and, even though Bevan, the best debater in the House after Churchill, was speaking on chosen ground, the youthful Macleod annihilated him.

A Highlander by descent, he derives from the Macleods of the island of Lewis; his father was a doctor, and his background is middle-class. He went to Fettes, a well-known public school in Edinburgh (though he happened to have been born in England), and then Cambridge; he told me that his chief interests at Cambridge were bridge and the stage; he liked to act. Politically, in his own words, he was 'somewhat pink' as a young man. His father was a liberal. Came the war, and Macleod suffered a severe leg wound in France. He was assigned later to a staff college, rose to be a major, and landed in Normandy with his regiment on D-Day; he was a combat officer on the beachhead, and saw much action until the end of the war. Subsequently he served in Norway.

After the war one of Macleod's passions continued to be bridge, also chess. He was good enough to be captain of England's bridge team, and earned a living as bridge correspondent of the *Sunday Times*. His book, *Bridge Is an Easy Game*, was published in 1952. His other passion became politics. He decided, by a process of careful ratiocination, to become a Tory (he likes to think of himself, not as a stand-pat 'conservative', but as a *Tory*, which in England connotes something different), and got a job with the Conservative party brain trust, organized by R. A. Butler; presently he became head of its Home Affairs Research Department. Macleod was elected to the House of Commons in 1950, and had a sensational rise. Within two years he achieved cabinet rank as Minister of Health, an almost unprecedented record. In 1955 he became Minister of Labour and National Service and then, in 1959, Colonial Secretary. Until Mr. Macmillan named him to this post he had never paid much attention to colonial affairs, and had never spoken in a colonial policy debate.[1]

That Macleod is a coming man is conceded by everybody. He might well have become Foreign Secretary in the cabinet shake-up in the summer of 1960, but Macmillan felt that perhaps he was rising too fast and, anyway, he still had a lot of work to do with the colonies. His chances for the prime ministership some day are excellent, although, if Macmillan retires, his immediate successor would probably be somebody with more seniority, like Butler. But Macleod is only forty-seven, which is practically babyhood for a British politician, and he can afford to wait. When he became Minister of Health at thirty-nine, one of the youngest cabinet officers in history, somebody protested to Mr. Churchill, 'Macleod is too young to be eligible.' Churchill's pungent reply was to the point: 'He's too eligible to be too young.'

HOW ENGLAND HAS NOT CHANGED

One could mention a number of minor items. Just as the institution of the concierge will most certainly outlive any convulsion

[1] Similarly, Mr. Selwyn Lloyd, when he became Foreign Minister, had never taken part in a foreign affairs debate, and (he once told me) did not even know exactly where the Foreign Office was at the moment of his appointment.

that may ever befall France, no matter what, so one may assume that the more resplendent London hotels and shops will continue—till Doomsday or even beyond—to have commissionaires, often with pointed waxed mustachios, who wear smart uniforms and service medals. Similarly, one may take it as an article of faith that never, never, never will there ever be a spot of dust on the sleek flanks of the Rolls-Royces lined up outside Claridge's. Other changeless factors are—of course— ivy on village walls, the open forum in Hyde Park, pubs, letters to *The Times*, severe standards in the courts of law, the cathedral close, and tall women who like to shoot and hunt. And no doubt Britons will continue forever to agree that politics are the first profession of the land, respect venerableness in public office, and produce gifted men thick with eccentricities—take Field-Marshal Lord Montgomery as an example, who said after a recent visit to several citadels of Communism that 'The only place you hear talk of war today is in the Western Hemisphere.'

But something more important, more germinal, should be mentioned too. As a youthful British friend of mine put it, England is still a country with a conscience—provided that conscience does not interfere with more than a reasonable share of economic well-being. No country in the world has such a zealous pride in civil liberties, and this is still probably the only nation capable of going to war on behalf of another, as it did in 1914 for Belgium and 1939 for Poland—though other motivations also played a role. Britain is still an intensely virile nation in the realm of ideas, it still respects the nonconformist conscience, it still has a lively political capacity for protest, and it still believes in right.

CHAPTER XV

Defence and Nuclear Disarmament

Two large issues in England today are defence—including NATO, United States bases, and the peculiar empyrean catch-all known as unilateral nuclear disarmament—and the Common Market. Both merge into general European considerations, and both demonstrate profoundly the differences between pre-war Europe and the Europe of today—in fact, NATO (at least what NATO symbolizes) and the Common Market are probably as significant as any changes that have come to the continent in the past quarter of a century.

Defence is a difficult subject in England. One may begin with the premise that the country is, from an abstract point of view, indefensible in the missile age. As a target, Great Britain is a sitting duck. No important country in the world is more vulnerable to atomic attack. For one thing Britain is small, with a highly concentrated population (seven-tenths of its people live in three huge metropolitan areas); for another, it is no more than a stone's-throw from the nearest Soviet missile bases in East Germany. One calculation is that no more than sixty megaton bombs, which could be dumped on England in a matter of minutes, would destroy it. All this has, as a natural result, produced repercussions in the national consciousness. A visitor can spend months in Italy—as an example—and never hear a single word about thermonuclear warfare or about the bomb; nobody gives the idea even a passing thought. But the opposite is true in England. Not only do the British fear the Soviet Union; so—on a different level, of course—do they fear the Pentagon. Also China. Once after lunch in the House of Commons my host waved good-bye with the words, 'Well! I'll hope to see you soon again—that is if the Chinese don't get the bomb and blow us all up tomorrow morning!'

Real and pressing as fear of nuclear destruction is in England, the government is neither willing nor able to spend exorbitant sums to fend it off. The total British defence budget is only about £1,600 million, or approximately 10 per cent of American defence expenditure. The United States at the moment is spending more on rocket research and development *alone* than Britain spends on its entire military establishment—land, sea, and air. Of course, the British have conventional as well as nuclear military expenses to support. So does the United States, but because of their geography the British give conventional forces and weapons—tanks, infantry, et cetera, for use in limited warfare—a high priority. Incidentally, National Service (conscription) ends in Britain in 1961.

In April, 1960, came a crisis—which reveals much—over a non-conventional weapon known as the Blue Streak. This was an IRBM, or Intermediate Range Ballistic Missile, with range enough to hit easily important targets in the Soviet sphere. But it was usable only from a fixed launching pad, and it became clear that, by the time it could become operational, it would be totally obsolete. Short-range Soviet missiles would, it was calculated, be able to destroy the fixed and therefore identifiable Blue Streak pads before the weapon could get off the ground. Another disadvantage was that Blue Streak used liquid fuel. Nevertheless, very large hopes had been placed in it, and its preliminary development cost £65 million, a tidy sum for England. To complete the project would have cost between £500 and £600 million. Announcement, made in the House of Commons by the Minister of Defence, Harold Watkinson, that Blue Streak was to be scrapped produced a tumult. George Brown, the Labour party specialist on defence, called it 'the biggest ministerial collapse of modern times', and it was commonly said that this marked the 'end' of the British attempt to create its own independent nuclear deterrent. However, the Macmillan government weathered the Blue Streak storm.

The key to much is the phrase 'independent nuclear deterrent'. This means, in short, power to retaliate by means of nuclear weapons whether or not the country is supported by allies. It was not quite correct to say that the Blue Streak, had it been pursued, would have been the only such deterrent in British hands. Britain has an extremely well-developed and skilfully run atomic establishment, and produces its own A- and H-bombs. The nub of the matter is how to deliver them. To this end the RAF has a small long-range bomber force, the equivalent to an extent of the Strategic Air Command (SAC) in the United States, consisting of aircraft, the 'V'-bombers, which are capable of carrying weapons with atomic warheads. These, at present, are the only independent nuclear deterrent the British have. And, compared to American and Soviet equipment, this force is insignificant. The word 'deterrent' is full of pitfalls. Can a country be a great power in the modern age unless it has its own independent nuclear deterrent? A great national debate is taking place in Britain at the moment on this issue. The Conservative party, of course, supports a deterrent, but powerful elements in the Labour party, focused mostly in the trade unions, are emphatically opposed. They stand for unilateral nuclear disarmament, as we shall presently see.

Quite apart from the savage split it has caused in the Labour party, the deterrent issue is exceptionally thorny. With Blue Streak gone and the V-bombers not altogether adequate, what is the British deterrent to be? Or, to put the question in somewhat different terms (the words are Mr. Watkinson's), what is to be the independent British contribution to the 'deterrent power of the West as a whole'? Also, how is Britain itself to be defended? Suppose there should come some rupture in the Anglo-American alliance? Suppose some future government should take Britain out of NATO? As far as the situation today is concerned, it is totally clear that British deterrent power must rest on continuing close association with the United States. One plan is to purchase from the United States the Skybolt missile, which operates from air to ground; a plane delivering a Skybolt can let it loose a thousand miles from the target, and presumably return to its base unscotched. But Skybolt does not even exist at the moment except on paper, and will not be ready until 1964 or later. Already, however, details have been worked out for 'integration' of future American and British Skybolt teams, and the Victors, the latest version of V-bombers, will presumably be equipped to carry Skybolts, though not all experts agree that this is possible. Second, Britain may set out to build atomic submarines capable of carrying the Polaris, or may make other use of the Polaris missile, the solid-fuel IRBM developed by the U.S. Navy, from mobile carriers. But a full Polaris programme would be fantastically expensive.

*

On April 15, 1960 (Good Friday), some twenty thousand Britons set out from the village of Aldermaston, the site of a nuclear research establishment, and marched on London, fifty-five miles away. They were well organized, cheerful, and full of spirit under their banners, BAN THE BOMB and NOBODY CAN IGNORE US NOW. Reaching London on Easter Monday in good formation, the marchers, who made a column four and one-half miles long and whose number had been considerably augmented by enthusiasts who joined them *en route*, held a remarkable demonstration in Trafalgar Square, in which seventy-five to a hundred thousand citizens participated. The leader of the march was Canon John Collins, a prominent Anglican churchman and Precentor of St. Paul's Cathedral.

This was the third of the annual 'peace marches' under the banner of Unilateral Nuclear Disarmament. The first was greeted as a kind of weird joke; the second as a somewhat odd example of British idealism-*cum*-eccentricity; this third march had to be taken more seriously. For one thing the organization and weight of numbers were impressive. For another the marchers were not exclusively left-wing intellectuals, anti-Gaitskell Labourites, Communists, pacifists, teenagers, or assorted crackpots; included was a scattering of sound, sober, nine-to-five white-collar workers, representatives of the professions, and respected figures from academic life. Among avowed unilateralists are such renowned figures as Bertrand Russell, J. B. Priestley, Commander Sir Stephen King-Hall, and Professor A. J. P. Taylor.

Indeed, the Campaign for Nuclear Disarmament, as the movement which sponsors the Aldermaston marches is officially called, has become one of the most powerful pressure groups in England; I heard it said that it was the only organization in the country that could put fifty thousand people on the streets on a day's notice. Its immediate political significance is that it has come close to wrecking the unity of the Labour party. Hugh Gaitskell has, for a year, been fighting for his political life against the 'unilateralists', as those who stand for British renunciation of the bomb call themselves, even though they do not include more than a quarter or at most a third of labour voters; this is because several prominent members of the parliamentary Labour party, as well as trade union leaders like Frank Cousins, have adopted the unilateralist position. One union after another—twenty-three in all at the moment—have swung around to the Cousins line, and hope to make unilateralism the official party doctrine. More on this later.

How, it may well be asked, can any responsible or patriotic Englishman take up unilateralism, and thus plead for immediate British abandonment of all nuclear arms without regard to consequences? How, in the present burning state of the world, can they bear to leave the United Kingdom defenceless except for conventional weapons? But this is just the point. The major hypothesis of the unilateralists is that, by renouncing nuclear weapons and scrapping the present stocks of A-bombs and H-bombs and means of delivering them, also of withdrawing from NATO and abolishing American bases, the country will not be made weaker, but stronger. If, they reason, Britain takes the lead in nuclear disarmament and has no nuclear weapons whatever, and is freed from any association with NATO or the United States, it is unlikely that Russia will ever bother to attack her, since the Soviet Union has no serious quarrel with Great Britain *per se*; in other words, as I heard it put, 'the best way to attain security is by total weakness.'

The Gaitskellites, on their side, think that this is a policy of utter madness, or even worse. One interesting point is that the late Aneurin Bevan strongly took the Gaitskell side on this, and, had he lived, might have been of inestimable value to the official Labour leadership in the present fight. Bevan said that unilateral nuclear disarmament would mean that any British plenipotentiary would go to future international conference tables 'naked'.

One objectively-minded Labour MP who vigorously opposes nuclear disarmament told me that the unilateralists are composed of six main groups: (*a*) genuine idealists; (*b*) 'practical' pacifists, including many churchmen, who want to neutralize

Britain; (c) Communists and fellow-travellers; (d) woolly-minded escapists, whose only solution for the intolerable pressures of today is to stick their heads in the sand—ostriches; (e) anti-Americans; (f) people who fear West *German* rearmament. A strong body of British opinion still hates and fears Germany. The argument is that, at all costs, Germany must be kept from the capacity to produce its own atomic armoury. Only four countries in the world today have the capacity to make nuclear weapons—the United States, the USSR, Britain, and France. (Red China may, of course, at almost any moment become the fifth.) The argument of the unilateralists is that if West Germany creates its own nuclear plants other smaller countries will follow suit, and the position will be soon reached whereby some insignificant madman in some insignificant country like (to pick at random) Paraguay could be in a position to start wholesale nuclear war by accident and incinerate the world. The *only* means of preventing this (so say the unilateralists) is for a major power, like Britain, to take the lead and voluntarily give up nuclear weapons, in the hope that, first, other nations will follow this example, and, second, that it will open an avenue to over-all disarmament by international agreement.

Some Labourite leaders, like the taut and perspicacious Michael Foot, are convinced that in four or five years (if the world lasts that long) unilateral nuclear disarmament will inevitably give them a triumphant issue, one on which they can win the next general election and sweep Macmillan from office.[1] England is a country where the latent force of idealism, no matter how eccentric, can never be ignored, and where it may spurt to the surface at almost any time. Moreover, the basic concept of neutralism has a powerful appeal to many. Needless to say a Labour victory with the party pledged to unilateral nuclear disarmament would pose severe problems for the United States. It would probably mean the end of NATO and the American defence position in England and perhaps in all of Europe. Many left-wing unilateralists dislike and fear American bases in England almost as much as they hate the bomb.

One of the first repercussions of the RB-47 incident in July, 1960, when an American reconnaissance plane was shot down

[1] *New York Times*, June 26, 1960.

by the Russians in Arctic waters, was a march organized by the Campaign for Nuclear Disarmament to Brize Norton, the United States base in Oxfordshire from which the ill-fated RB–47 took off. The episode was minor in itself, but demonstrated anew the fact that American bases in Britain can be made use of as a domestic issue. Following this, angry crowds in Coventry attempted to break up a public meeting at which General Lauris Norstad, the American Commander-in-Chief in Europe, was the speaker. Then came sharp demonstrations in Scotland when it was announced that Holy Loch, in the Firth of Clyde near Glasgow, was to become a base for American submarines equipped with the Polaris missile. Signs were waved in Glasgow and London, 'Yankees—take your rockets home!'

The unilateralists say, in short, 'Why should Britain risk being destroyed because of a quarrel between Russia and the United States? Let's be neutral.' On the other hand there is no reason to assume that neutralism in England is going to win.

*

At this time, American forces exist in Britain on three levels. *First*, the long-range bombers of the Strategic Air Command: these are strictly an American force, and have no connection at all with NATO. The SAC does not, however, keep many of its operational bombers on bases in British territory, which are considered to be too vulnerable; mostly such bases are used for training flights. In theory, the United States would have to procure British permission before launching any SAC planes from British bases if war should break out.

Second, tactical fighter-bombers, attached to NATO and theoretically under the command of the Supreme Allied Commander, Europe (SACEUR), who is at present General Norstad, at his headquarters (SHAPE), near Paris.[1] These squadrons were formerly stationed in France but had to be transferred to Britain and West Germany when General de Gaulle refused to permit them to remain longer on French territory. This was because they are equipped to carry weapons with nuclear warheads, over which the United States retains authority, and de Gaulle, as we knew well, would not coun-

---

[1] 'SHAPE' stands for Supreme Headquarters Allied Powers, Europe.

tenance the presence on French soil of an atomic stock pile or
nuclear weapon-carriers not subject, in the last analysis, to
exclusive French control.

Third, the Thor missile sites. Along the east coast of Britain
are a number of Thors, perhaps sixty, the IRBMs developed by
the U.S. Air Force; these are kept in permanent readiness, and
are aimed presumably at various key targets in Russia and the
satellites. These weapons (range about 1,500–1,800 miles) are
under a peculiar system of dual control, and operate under what
is called the 'double veto' system; the Royal Air Force operates
the actual installations, but authority over the warheads themselves is exclusively American. To fire a Thor, two men—a
British officer and his American counterpart—both have to turn
keys. Each carries the vital key around his neck. A somewhat
terrifying photograph of the Thor control board, with one
button ominously marked 'War-Peace', appeared in a French
magazine recently; it was picked up and reproduced on the
front page of the *Sunday Times* in London and then appeared in
Time in the United States. Once the two keys are inserted in the
proper slot, an automatic fifteen-minute count-down begins; at
the conclusion of this, the Thor fires. That a photograph of this
sensitive and complicated device should appear openly in the
European Press made American observers unhappy, and created
some nervous talk in England as well. People could not help
thinking that, despite the dual-control system, somebody some-
day might push the fatal button by mistake.

Following the RB-47 incident Mr. Macmillan faced intense, if
polite, hostile questioning in the House of Commons. Labour
members wanted to know whether the British government had
been informed in advance of the American reconnaissance flight
from Brize Norton. It had not. The upshot on the American side
of the Atlantic was that the United States categorically promised
to inform the United Kingdom in advance of any reconnaissance
flights hereafter by American pilots taking off from British
soil.

American bases and depots in England include installations
at Chelveston, Bruntingthorpe, Upper Heyford, High Wy-
combe (headquarters), Brize Norton, Fairford, Greenham
Common, Blackbushe (U.S. Navy), Alconbury, Molesworth,
Sculthorpe, Lakenheath, Mildenhall, Bentwaters, Woodbridge,

Wethersfield, Denham, and South Ruislip (headquarters).[1] Originally, as everybody knows, American bases were set up in Great Britain, with the warmest and most grateful British co-operation, in World War II; they were shut down after the war, but reactivated in 1948 as an answer to Soviet policy, during the crisis over the Berlin blockade. This occurred, it is important to note, when a Labour government was in power. Also the decision to build British A- and H-bombs was taken under the régime of Mr Attlee. Americans may be suspicious of the nuclear disarmament wing of the Labour party, even if it is noisier than its strength merits, but the official leadership of the party has always been committed to the Atlantic Alliance and is firmly pro-American.

*

The total of American forces in Great Britain today is about 50,000, mostly Air Force. American military personnel in other European countries numbers roughly 10,000 in Spain (mostly Air Force, but also naval detachments), 40,000 in France (chiefly ground support troops), 10,000 in Italy (mixed between Army and Air Force), 10,000 in Iceland and Greenland, and 190,000 in West Germany (divided between Seventh Army and the Air Force). In addition, the U.S. maintains the Sixth Fleet in Mediterranean waters, with 25,000–35,000 men—very important. Thus the total US numerical strength in Europe is around 330,000. Italy and Turkey have Jupiter missiles (the U.S. Army IRBMs), and Italy has short-range tactical missiles as well, with their warheads under American control.

A PROPHECY

My friend the late Anne O'Hare McCormick, than whom no journalist can be more sorely missed, said after V-E Day that, to her mind, World War II brought two overriding lessons. First, nobody will ever attack Russia by land again; second, the British will never fight another war. Prophets are often wrong, but this remark should go on record.

[1] The *Observer*, July 17, 1960.

CHAPTER XVI

Macmillan

WHEN Harold Macmillan became Prime Minister in January, 1957, to the surprise of practically everybody in the United Kingdom except himself, British fortunes and prestige were at their lowest ebb for a generation. The grim fiasco over Suez had split the country; Anglo-American relations were the worst since 1776 or thereabouts; the Commonwealth was restive and alarmed; morale at home was cracking, and a flight from sterling threatened; the Tory party was frustrated, leaderless, and discouraged.

Today, some forty-eight months later, developments have come that are little short of phenomenal. Suez left a lurid scar, but the wound has healed; relations between London and Washington are harmonious and fruitful, and Britain has the largest gold stock in its history; above all, the Rt. Hon. Maurice Harold Macmillan, Prime Minister and First Lord of the Treasury, is undisputed leader of his party, widely popular and respected in the country at large, and at the peak of his considerable powers.

In a preceding chapter I listed some of the Prime Minister's remarkable collection of nicknames. A favourite five years ago was 'Mr. MacMothballs'. Today the newspapers call him 'Non-stop Mac' and 'Go-getter Mac'.

Mr. Macmillan, a complex character who is half-Scot, half-American, would be the last man to assert that the contemporary rise in the British position has been due exclusively to himself. But he contributed strongly to it, and he symbolizes a new spirit in the Tory party. Interestingly enough he himself has undergone an evolution not unlike that in the country itself. Success has brought him confidence.

When he became Prime Minister, he was no more than a

shadow to the great mass of the public—moreover, with his walrus moustache, an enigmatic, old-fashioned, and almost comical shadow. As often as not he seemed paralysed by diffidence or inertia, like a parody of the Edwardian county gentleman. The change to the revivified Macmillan of today did not come overnight. In fact, the first months in office were heavy going—for himself as well as for those around him, who despaired at his inability to 'communicate' himself to the public. At one point, not too long ago, the polls called him the most unpopular Prime Minister since Neville Chamberlain.

Although he is a profound Conservative in most of his instincts and leader of the Tory party, Macmillan is by no means an orthodox Tory. He spent more than twenty years in rebellion against stand-pat party principles, flirted with socialism, and was once called a 'dangerous' left-winger. No British politician has much future these days unless he pays lip-service at least to the principles of the welfare state, and Macmillan's conscientiousness, idealism, and 'pink conservatism' have contributed substantially to his rise, as well as such factors as dexterity and cleverness. I asked one of his best friends how he accounted for the slow but emphatic change in the Prime Minister, his transformation from a private into a public person.

Answer: 'As a matter of fact, Macmillan has never been a "private" person. He has been in public life for well over thirty years. He was relatively unknown, but not "private". What happened when he became Prime Minister was that he wanted to sit down for a while and get his bearings. He knew that there were certain tasks to be tackled, and that he had to tackle them. He said to himself, "If I'm any good, it will show in time." He started doing things that were bold and imaginative, and people began to realize that here was a man of unusual vigour, competence, and intelligence.'

Then, in May, 1958, came Macmillan's appearance on Edward R. Murrow's TV show, 'See It Now'. For many months the Prime Minister had resisted doing anything on TV; he was loath to be interviewed, and he hated radio. (He has no radio or TV in his country house, and, so far as I know, there is no TV in Downing Street.) Then he awoke, overnight, to find himself a television star. His dry, understated personality, originality of view, candour, modesty, and quiet good humour became for the first time apparent to millions, both in England and the United States. Nobody could say that Murrow 'made' Macmillan, but he gave him a big lift upwards so far as public relations are concerned, and the Prime Minister, gratified and astonished, said later that the show was worth five by-elections.

OUTLINE OF THE RISE TO POWER

The bare bones of Macmillan's career can best be put on display by mentioning some of the influences that helped shape him.

First, his Scots background. His paternal great-grandfather was a crofter (tenant farmer) on the island of Arran; his grandfather, Daniel, grew up in the most pressing poverty. But Daniel was enterprising enough to make his way down to England, where he became a book salesman. Then, with a brother, he set himself up in a bookshop in Cambridge, and eventually moved to London and founded (1843) the great publishing house of Macmillan, which is still one of the foremost in the world. Maurice, the Prime Minister's father, joined the family business after having been a music student and teacher. He was a somewhat unworldly character, diffident, introspective, and religious.

Harold Macmillan's mother was an American, Helen (Nellie) Belles, the daughter of a Kentucky doctor who practised medicine for many years in a small town in Indiana. A woman of commanding grace and push, she married an artist named John Bayliss Hill in 1874, at eighteen; he died a few months later, and Nellie made her way to Paris to study music, an adventurous thing for such a young woman to do in those days. Here she met Maurice Macmillan, and they were married in 1883. Harold, their third son, was born in 1894.

The Prime Minister always revered her. He told me, when we talked in Downing Street not long ago, that she had been by far the strongest influence on his life. Like Franklin D. Roosevelt's mother, she adored her son, but took no nonsense from him. She wanted him to be ambitious, she wanted him to be a success, no matter how he might cultivate a languid pose. Whether, when she died in 1937, she could have guessed that he would ever be Prime Minister is open to question. One important point is that Nellie was an ardent Francophile. Harold was made to learn French in the nursery before he learned English, and he has been fond of things French ever since.

Macmillan narrowly escaped death in an air crash in North Africa in 1943; he woke up in a hospital, badly burnt, without any idea of what had happened to him. His first words were, 'Tell my mother that I'm alive and well.' She had been dead six years.

Undiscriminating writers on Macmillan talk about his 'aristocracy', as if he were a Churchill or Salisbury. Indeed, he married far up into the aristocracy and many of his attributes are aristocratic, but he is not an aristocrat by birth at all. He comes of peasant Scots blood mixed with middle-class American stock, and is mostly a product of what has been aptly called the 'commercial intelligentsia'.

Second, education. Probably Macmillan is the best-educated Prime Minister since Balfour or Asquith fifty years ago, although he is not an intellectual of their standing. He went to Eton and Balliol College, Oxford, loved the classics, and was a good (if somewhat lazy) student. Once, during World War I, he was seriously wounded and cut off from his troops; his men found him in a shell hole reading Aeschylus in Greek.

Today, he is still inveterately bookish. Returning recently from Australia on the first all-Commonwealth tour ever taken by a British Prime Minister, he amused himself by reading all fourteen volumes of Froude's *History of England*. When John Hay Whitney, the former American Ambassador to the Court of St. James's, met him for the first time he was busily occupied with a history (in French) of the Quai d'Orsay. When he was exhausted after one long cabinet session a colleague asked him what he was going to do to relax; his somewhat defiant answer was, 'Read a *good* novel!'

Actually, however, the Prime Minister does not read much fiction these days, although he is—and always has been—a Trollope addict. He told me that he turns more and more to history and biography. He likes long, pithy lives—particularly about illustrious predecessors in British history—full of documents. These tell him the whole story, and he can proceed to make up his own mind about the issues involved. The day I met him he was reading a life of Palmerston.

He likes Latin, and sometimes bewilders people by making jokes in Latin, or scribbling Latin puns on official minutes.

Third, World War I. Young Macmillan left Balliol to take a commission in the Grenadier Guards, and served in France for several years. He was wounded three times, and his last wound —a shattered pelvis—kept him in bed for twenty months. His friends thought that he would never walk again. The meditation forced upon him by this prolonged immobility, as well as the suffering it caused, cut a strong groove in his character. He served ably, but was never decorated or even mentioned in dispatches. He did not, in his younger days, seem to leave much of a mark on his contemporaries, either at school or in the army. Memoirs of the period, even by those who knew him well, seldom refer to him.

Fourth, marriage. Macmillan went to Canada in 1920 as an A.D.C. to the Governor-General, the ninth Duke of Devonshire, and married his daughter, Lady Dorothy Evelyn Cavendish. This was an epochal event. At once he entered the patrician inner circle. Queen Alexandra came to his wedding, and so (and this may have pleased him more) did Thomas Hardy.

The Devonshires have proliferated for generations through the tight upper fabric of British social, political, and court life, and, on entering politics, Macmillan found that he was related by marriage to no fewer than sixteen members of the House of Commons. Later it was calculated that he had blood ties with seven out of the nineteen members of the cabinet, and with no fewer than thirty of the total number of men (eighty-five) in the government.

The Macmillan situation *in re* his relatives was soon compounded. After a cabinet reshuffle in November, 1960, Julian Amery, his good-looking son-in-law, became Secretary of State for Air, and Lady Dorothy's nephew, the eleventh Duke of Devonshire, became Parliamentary Under-Secretary in the Commonwealth Relations Office. At least three other men with ministerial rank were related either to the Prime Minister or his wife. David Ormsby-Gore, the able Minister of State for Foreign Affairs, is the brother-in-law of Maurice Macmillan, the PM's only son, who is also in the Commons. When these appointments were announced, Hugh Gaitskell, the leader of the Opposition, commented good-humouredly, 'The Prime

Minister has staunchly refused to allow any unfair discrimination against his relatives.' Other comment was a bit stiffer, and the *New Statesman* (December 10, 1960) acidly pointed out that the Macmillan government contained one duke, one marquess, six earls, two viscounts, and no fewer than seven barons.

To resume: Lady Dorothy Macmillan has, on her side, never been particularly fond of politics; she has a green thumb and likes gardening better. The Macmillans have four children and twelve grandchildren, on all of whom they dote; one entire floor of the family house in Sussex is made up of nurseries.

Fifth, business. Macmillan went into the family publishing business in 1924, and for many years, with his elder brother Daniel, was joint managing director of the company. As a publisher, he paid more attention to business than to the editorial side; nevertheless, he was active on the literary front as well. One of his decisions was to publish *Black Lamb and Grey Falcon*, by Rebecca West, even though it was a thousand pages long, in a period of acute paper shortage. Another interesting Macmillan decision (not made by Harold himself, however) was to print *Gone with the Wind*, which came over from the American branch of the house, in an edition of—three thousand copies! The British did not think it would sell.

Publishing made Macmillan a rich man and he has been a millionaire for well over twenty years, partly through inheritance, but mostly by reason of profits made by his own endeavour. His son, Maurice, followed him into the firm, but is equally busy in politics.

The Macmillan roster of authors through the 118 years of the company's existence is impressive; Henry James, Shaw, Wells, Kipling, Yeats, and a multitude of other distinguished men were all published by Macmillan at one time or other. The company had a special penchant for poetry, and also—oddly enough—for left-wing economists and historians, like J. M. Keynes. Keynes's *Economic Consequences of the Peace* was a celebrated Macmillan best-seller, as was H. G. Wells's *Outline of History*.[1]

Sixth, politics and public affairs. Macmillan felt, in the good old British way, that it was his duty to fulfil his obligation to

---

[1] In the U.S.A., but not in England. A different publisher put it out in England. Today the British and American Macmillans have no connection.

the community. Besides, he wanted to get ahead, and to enter politics was the natural thing to do. He stood for Stockton, an industrial and shipbuilding constituency, in 1923, soon after his return from Canada, and lost in his first run—by seventy-three votes. But he ran again the next year, won handsomely, and has been in the House of Commons—with interruptions—ever since.

Stockton taught him a lot, particularly in the depression years. Later he moved on to a safer constituency, Bromley. Unemployment was an agonizing problem, and young Macmillan came to grips for the first time in his life with the common man. In the mid-1930's he wrote a book, *The Middle Way*, which caused a considerable stir although it was unreadably dull; it advocated a kind of modified New Deal for England, and Macmillan became anathema to the hard-shell Tories. He replied in kind, and some of his remarks, criticizing the Conservative leadership of the time, are still quoted. He called the Bank of England a 'permanent tyranny', talked with contempt of 'casino capitalism' and 'the aristocracy of second-class brewers and company promoters', and said that members of the Conservative front bench were 'disused slag heaps'.

He even went so far as to vote against his own party on a matter having to do with unemployment relief, and on one occasion campaigned momentarily for a Socialist against one of his own Tory colleagues. For a time he advocated a coalition with labour, and talked of building up a 'synthesis between socialism and capitalism'. He hated avaricious plutocracy, and wanted a decent minimum standard of life for all.

Meantime, foreign affairs came to dominate British politics. During the Baldwin-Chamberlain period Macmillan pursued an independent line. He 'refused the party whip', which was tantamount to temporary resignation from the party, because he favoured sanctions against Italy during the Ethiopian war, and vigorously (although politely) opposed Munich and appeasement. Altogether he spent long years in the 'wilderness', snubbed by the Tory leadership, and never got a ministerial post until 1940, when he was forty-six.

Then success came fast. Winston Churchill became Prime Minister, and in 1942 sent him to Algiers as Minister Resident; here he formed friendships with two men whom he had good occasion to work with later—Dwight D. Eisenhower and Charles de Gaulle. One reason why Churchill gave him the Algiers job was that he had been, in a modest way, a Churchill 'man'; another was that he knew French so well. The nursery pays off.

Macmillan then became Secretary of State for Air, and after that Minister of Housing; this was a lesser job, but he worked at it loyally and was a marked success. There followed terms as Minister of Defence for six months in 1954–55, Foreign Secretary from April to December, 1955, and Chancellor of the Exchequer from December, 1955, to January, 1957. In all these posts his tenure was short, and in none did he make much of a record, except housing. He was a disappointing Foreign Minister, and left little mark on the Treasury. How, then, did Harold Macmillan happen to become Prime Minister in January, 1957, when Anthony Eden resigned?

Historians will be writing about the minutiae of this for a long time to come, and the story is too complex to go into in short space. Churchill and Lord Salisbury, who was at that time the *éminence grise* of the Conservative party, put in for Macmillan as against R. A. Butler, his principal rival. The Tory rank and file thought that Macmillan was safer, more resolute, and had more stamina, although he was still an eccentric character, an odd type, to many.

Macmillan's role in the Suez fiasco has aroused bitter controversy. First, he was a strong backer of Eden's ruinous policy of going into Suez by force of arms. Second, he was the most influential minister to urge withdrawal when it was seen that the military adventure was a fiasco. His main motive, his friends say, was not so much worry about the reactions to Suez in America, Russia, or the Commonwealth, but fear that the disaster might cause a run on sterling. As Chancellor of the Exchequer, he had every right to weigh this consideration heavily.

A somewhat cynical observer put it this way when the grisly affair was over. 'After all, we have to have a leader. And we might as well have one who leads both ways. Macmillan led us into Suez, and then led us out again!' Later, a jingle was composed:

When Eden bombed that old canal,
Our hero Mack the Knife,
Said I'll stick by you,Tony,
And be your friend for life.[1]

PERSONAL

Macmillan is a tall man, taller than most of his photographs
indicate—about six foot one. For some years he cultivated what
can only be called a 'droopy' look; the joke was that Eden was
a rabbit trying to look like a man, Macmillan a man trying to
look like a rabbit. He has large hands, and a softish handshake.
One of his peculiarities is that his handwriting is very small, and
his secretaries have a hard time deciphering it.

He has a perceptive face, longish greying hair brushed back
in a pompadour, and luminous dark eyes. The lids are heavy,
and hang sharply down at the outer corners; he has sometimes
been called 'the hooded wonder'. His manners are, of course,
effortlessly good, even bland. One of his ministers told me that
his chief single source of power was his calmness, that he was
'unflappable'.

Macmillan is notorious for being the worst-dressed man ever
to sit in Downing Street. He hates to go shopping and, as
Franklin Roosevelt did, likes to wear tweed jackets thirty years
old. His attitude towards dress has been called 'appalling', and
he has not bought a new suit in years. Instead of a waistcoat,
which is considered to be *de rigueur* in British official life, he
usually wears an old cardigan sweater which he may, or may not,
remember to button. Instead of a hat he prefers a tweed cap,
which looks like something that might have been discarded by
Sherlock Holmes.

He eats abstemiously, and at formal parties seldom does more
than nibble; his favourite dish is cold meat. Also he is fond of
savouries, the sharp combinations of cheese, eggs, bacon, mush-
rooms, or anchovies that the British like to serve after dessert.
He smokes anything, preferably a pipe. He is one of those wise
men who think that alcohol is a benign substance, if only because
it loosens the tongue, and he drinks in moderation.

He is healthy, sleeps well, and, although obviously a sensitive

[1] New York *Post*, June 13, 1960.

person, does not seem to have a nerve in his body. No matter how late it may be, he always reads for an hour before going to bed. He seldom takes holidays, and in his first eighteen months as Prime Minister had exactly seventeen days off. Unlike almost all Englishmen of his class, he is not much interested in sport or games, although he likes the outdoors—trees particularly—and sometimes has time to shoot. He shoots left-handed, and is a tolerable shot.

Some people think that the Prime Minister gives forth a note of sadness, as if he were nursing a secret sorrow, and he is certainly not what anybody would call an ebullient man. He has charm, but this is on the quiet side. He has, however, an alert sense of humour, and loves to make jokes, some of them very sharp.

The word 'shy', which is sometimes applied to him, demands qualification in the case of Macmillan. He hates hurly-burly, never slaps backs, and dislikes contact with people he does not know, but in his own circle is far from shy. What he likes best in the world, next to England, books, gossip, and his family, is conversation, and he is a fast, fluent talker.

Occasionally he would go to fashionable London cocktail parties before he became Prime Minister; he would stand alone in a corner as a rule, polite but miserable, until somebody came up who interested him. He can run into an old acquaintance at a club, and, if full of his own thoughts, not even recognize him. Then he will, as it were, wake up, and call out a greeting. Macmillan's mild adventures in various clubs give rise to almost as many anecdotes as his bookishness. Time and time again, members of the Beefsteak (a dining club) or Buck's are astonished to see the Prime Minister walk in unannounced and alone. He sits down at the common table, greets those present, and joins the talk.

Macmillan believes in a certain amount of privacy and formality, however. One member of his cabinet, whom he likes and does business with daily, and with whom his official contact has been of the closest for several years, has never once been invited to Birch Grove, the Macmillan house (with two thousand acres) thirty-eight miles from London. Only two or three senior ministers and members of his secretarial staff are, as a matter of fact, close to him. One colleague whom he likes greatly and depends upon is Lord Mills, former Minister of Power and now Paymaster-General; another is Edward Heath, former chief whip and now Lord Privy Seal.

I asked somebody who has known Macmillan all his life if he had ever thought that he would be Prime Minister. The answer was suggestive. 'No. But now that he is Prime Minister, it seems natural that he should be.'

In a recent speech, Macmillan said, 'When you are a Prime Minister everything becomes a bit larger than life.' He proceeded, 'It's really quite surprising. A week's holiday with one's in-laws becomes a life addicted to shooting on ducal grouse moors. A couple of week-end study groups with one's colleagues becomes country house government. A modest cheerfulness becomes a reckless flippancy. But don't mistake me. No politician would feel happy without this sort of thing.'

Some people say of him critically that he is an 'actor', and that much of his life has been a series of poses. Indeed, he has cultivated an air of off-beat cynicism, perhaps to save himself from disappointment; he is not so much of a cynic as he pretends to be, but part of what began as a pose has stuck. There is something curiously unreal about him, as if he were not made of real flesh and blood; he seems masked. One politician told me, 'What I'd like most in life is a solid week with the Prime Minister alone. Then perhaps I would really know what he is thinking.'

A prominent Labour MP was asked recently to name Macmillan's outstanding characteristic, and replied, 'Pomposity!' Another answered, 'Superciliousness'. Others think, beyond this, that his chief defect is lack of deep inner conviction, that he is too detached, too clever. Macmillan, on his side, has often seemed to be unwarrantably rude to Labour members. This is not good policy, because the Opposition will always be there the next day; it divides the country; moreover, to show disrespect for the Opposition is to show disrespect for the House of Commons itself, the symbol and repository of all that is best in British democracy.

THE PRIME MINISTER AT WORK

Remarkably enough, Mr. Macmillan has no office in the business premises of Downing Street—not even a desk! He works on a long table, which can seat about twenty men, in the ground-floor cabinet room. Upstairs he has a small study, and it is true that this does contain a small, fragile desk of sorts, but it is not at all the kind that an important executive would be expected to use. I asked him what on earth he did with his papers, since there were no drawers or filing cases anywhere, and he replied airily that 'they went into boxes'.

The Downing Street establishment is small, and the Prime Minister's secretariat does not consist of more than seven or eight people, most of them youngish civil servants. Macmillan was stupefied, on a recent visit to Washington, at the size and ramifying extent of the presidential establishment. The British procedure is much less complex and grandiose.

Moreover, the atmosphere at No. 10 is astoundingly informal. A bobby stands at the door; otherwise there are no precautions that one can see, no security check of any kind. The Prime Minister is mildly formal during actual meetings of the cabinet (which normally take place twice a week), but otherwise he is almost disconcertingly casual, relaxed, and family-like. Macmillan seldom rings for anybody. Instead he scurries out into the tiny rooms that house the staff, wanders around alone like a mother hen pursuing chicks, and says to somebody, 'I'm having trouble with this memorandum—please help me draft it.'

The doorway leading from the office of the principal private secretary to the cabinet room has tacked on it a note in the Prime Minister's handwriting: 'Quiet Calm Deliberation Untangles Every Knot.' This is from the Gilbert and Sullivan operetta *The Gondoliers*, and Macmillan put it up there with his own hand to indicate that this should be the mood of the entire establishment. Once, years ago, the author of *Tom Brown's School Days*, Thomas Hughes, came on hard times and wrote to the Macmillan company for a job. The reply by Harold Macmillan's grandfather laid down certain conditions, one of which was that the firm expected every employee 'to do the day's job in the day'. The maxim has been carried over to rule Downing Street today, and the PM tells his staff about it any time that anybody will listen.

I asked him if he liked being Prime Minister, and he answered with an emphatic, cheerful affirmative. He has a philosophic attitude towards the unfolding of history. I asked him how he

took the load off, and he indicated lightly that he had others to
do that for him—which was a nice little compliment to his able
secretaries. In fact, Macmillan takes decisions easily, without
weighing inconvenient or embarrassing consequences too much,
and is an excellent leader of a team. 'If you take all decisions too
seriously, you never take them,' he says to friends. His favourite
phrase is, 'Let's think it over', and he never lets himself be
over-pressed.

He gets a dispatch box full of papers every night, and works
on them after dinner—sometimes while relaxing with his family.
Most ministers 'play the box' with a group of secretaries standing by, to whom they dictate instructions. Macmillan—as a rule
—prefers to do this work alone. He writes a minute on each
paper in red ink (only the Prime Minister may use red ink on a
cabinet document) ordering whatever action he recommends.
Sometimes he writes a thousand words or more of these minutes
a night, which is a lot.

I came in to see the Prime Minister at three one afternoon,
and was told that I would have fifteen minutes with him. I left
Downing Street around five—two hours later! The Prime
Minister (like Roosevelt) likes to talk. When I was ushered
casually into the cabinet room, with its stimulating historic
associations, Mr. Macmillan reached out to grasp and show me a
silver candlestick he had just received. It had previously
belonged to five other prime ministers—Walpole, the younger
Pitt, Peel, Disraeli, and Lord Rosebery.

Mostly, at the beginning, he talked about British history, the
British past. (He did not mention his exertions as Prime
Minister; among other things he had travelled eighty thousand
miles in eighteen months, not bad for a man of his age.) He took
me out into the garden, told an anecdote about Mr. Gladstone,
and hustled me around No. 10 and the adjoining No. 11,
residence of the Chancellor of the Exchequer, pointing out
various associations. Then we scooted up to the Treasury Board
Room, in an adjacent building, where the cabinet once met with
the monarch in the chair. The custom had to be given up after
Queen Anne—because George I, her successor, did not understand any English!

Macmillan talked about how difficult it is to take adequate
notes on a telephone conversation, probably because you do not

see the person you are talking to; how newspapers in London once printed editions all night; about Russian policy in Central Asia before World War I, and much else concerning Russia, including details of a trip he took there, as a tourist, in 1929; about what a wonderful face Disraeli had; about the proper pronunciation of Polish names; about the joy of rereading old books instead of taking a risk with a new one; about Asquith, Lloyd George, Nehru, Adenauer, Father Knox, and Lytton Strachey; above all, about England in the years just before 1914 —the glow and throb of the England that was, the gallantry and peculiarly innocent ardour, valour, of those lost, silken, quivering days, and how a whole generation was cut off, sacrificed, exterminated.

At the end I asked him what he believed in most. I have asked this question of many eminent men and have had a vivid anthology of responses. The Prime Minister might have replied England, himself, the Anglo-American alliance, change, standards, the august routine of old-style aristocratic life, or the people. His answer was God.

TO SUM UP

Mr. Macmillan is, like all prime ministers, a complicated human being, but one of his principal assets is that his approach to a problem is almost always direct—refreshingly so. Three items come to mind. First, the Prime Minister became convinced early in 1959 that the international situation was deteriorating so seriously and at such a pace that something must be done at once to stop the possibility of open conflict; so he decided to go to Moscow himself, have a look around, and investigate the possibility of getting along with Mr. Khrushchev. Second, he took an eighteen-thousand-mile trip through Africa in January, 1960, and, visiting the Union of South Africa, made one of the best speeches of his life there, referring to the 'strength of African national conscience', and accepting it blandly as the most natural of facts that 'a wind of change' should be blowing through the continent, even though he knew that this would meet sharp disfavour from his audience. Third, after the collapse of the Summit in the summer of 1960, he tried once more to unravel the international log jam over Russia. Khrushchev was at his most provocative in relation to the RB-47 incident, the Congo, and disarmament. Macmillan sat down and wrote him a personal letter which contained the phrase, 'I simply do not understand what your purpose is today.' Seldom has a communication about great political affairs been addressed to a Russian premier in such personal, informal language, and it had an immediate effect.

There are negative things to say about Mr. Macmillan, but nobody can doubt that he is a man of profound good will.

CHAPTER XVII

The Establishment and the Opposition

I LIVED in England for six months in 1958, and I don't think I ever heard the word 'Establishment'. Then, when I returned to London in 1960, it seemed to be on every other lip. Actually the term was invented some years ago by Henry Fairlie, a provocative columnist and TV commentator, in an article in the *Spectator*. As a matter of fact, the elusive concept that Mr. Fairlie sought to define is no new thing in England. I myself, feeling my way towards the same idea and trying to analyse what ran England, called it (with no originality whatever) 'an inner circle' back in 1936. Those I nominated as immovable members of this included Stanley Baldwin, Lord Tyrrell, Geoffrey Dawson of *The Times*, Lord Salisbury (father of the present one), Montagu Norman, then governor of the Bank of England, Lord Derby, and Sir Maurice Hankey.

But I added that no two observers would agree on the names to be included, Baldwin aside. One should never be tempted to think that the ruling classes in the United Kingdom comprise a body which could meet in a room, elect a chairman, or otherwise perform the organic functions of domination. England possesses no tight, close oligarchy like that represented in pre-war France by the regents of the Banque de France. The 'ring' is not a ring. Indeed—I am still paraphrasing what I wrote in 1936—the overriding strength of the British ruling classes is its fluidity. It is quite possible to belong to one of the oldest families in the British Isles and yet not be 'in'. Brains are certainly not the sole criterion of entrance, nor is wealth, nor is position, although all three will help.

How, then, does one define the inner circle, or Establishment?

Who *does* run England? Mr. Fairlie's definition emphasizes a desire to perpetuate forms, with 'reverence for the orders, privileges, and mysteries of a conservative society', and he adds that the Establishment is *not* a 'power *élite*'. For instance, a big newspaper publisher can exert enormous power but would no more be accepted by the Establishment than Heliogabalus. I doubt that any member of the Labour party would consider himself to be an authentic member of the Establishment, even while in office. Also one must think in terms of religion; almost all in the Establishment pay at least formal allegiance to the Anglican Church. I do not think that there are any Jews in the Establishment, and Roman Catholics are few and far between. Incidentally, there are twenty-two Jews in the House of Commons today (total membership 630). Only two of these are Tories. There are five million Roman Catholics in the country but only twenty-five Catholic MPs—fourteen Tories, eleven Labour.[1]

Nor does membership in the Establishment necessarily depend on class, or even money. Class does not matter as much as one might think. If a poor boy out of the Midlands rises to be Speaker of the House of Commons or Secretary of the Cabinet he will be 'in', no matter how humble his origin. Conversely, the richest blueblood in the City may be out. A poet, like John Betjeman, may well be regarded as a highly important (if irreverent) Establishment voice, and scholars, if, for instance, they happen to be masters or dons in a distinguished Oxford or Cambridge college, are often favoured. In a way institutions are more important than individuals. Institutions, after all, persist when men are gone. But *some* individuals will remain members of the Establishment for ever, even when they have lost political power, like the present Salisbury. Another point to make is that almost anybody who enters the Establishment has, even if not rich, been a success in whatever his field happens to be. Above all, it is an organization of those who have *arrived*.

Anyway, omitting names, I will risk severe argument and rebuke by listing those who, by reason of their position, have almost automatic membership in this indefinable holy of holies. First, the Prime Minister. Second, the Permanent Under-

[1] *Sunday Express*, May 15, 1960. The Jewish population of Britain is about 400,000.

Secretary of the Treasury, who is head of the civil service. A flamboyant Foreign Minister or a stuffy, docile Chancellor of the Exchequer may very well not be 'in', but it would be impossible to keep the head of the civil service out. Third, the Archbishop of Canterbury, and possibly the Archbishop of York as well. Fourth, the governor of the Bank of England. After this the field becomes somewhat more open. Most people would certainly include the editor of *The Times*, the head of the BBC, the private secretary to the monarch and a scattering of Fellows of All Souls, the post-graduate Oxford College, restricted to fifty scholars of outstanding intellect. Also, distinguished economists are apt to be included, though no economist today has the rank of Sir Josiah Stamp, as an example, before the war. One might even throw in a hostess or two.

But again one must urge caution; these elevated figures do not sit down in a room together, have a cosy or conspiratorial drink, blackball aspirants, or make policy. Far from it. Several wings of the Establishment do not like other wings, and have small contact. It is all very mysterious, like so much in England—a country given to stylistic enigma. For instance, I was enchanted to hear, on the most expert authority, that the recent election for the Chancellorship of Oxford University, in which Mr. Macmillan vanquished Sir Oliver Franks, the former British Ambassador to Washington, was a *defeat* for the Establishment, not the opposite. But of course Mr. Macmillan is titular head of the whole Establishment, the whole bag of tricks. How then could his election (by the narrow margin of 279 votes) be regarded as a defeat? The answer seems to be that the masters, fellows, dons, and so on at Oxford form their own special rarefied segment of the Establishment, and hotly wanted Franks, one of their own, for the job as against a rank outsider—on academic terms—like Macmillan.

Certain cardinal events become landmarks in the evolution of the Establishment, on which it stands fast. One was the abdication crisis in 1936. The Establishment, personified at that time by Mr. Baldwin and the then Archbishop of Canterbury, preferred to have Edward VIII leave the throne rather than accept Mrs. Simpson as queen. So Edward—and Mrs. Simpson—went. Another was Suez. The Establishment was badly shaken by this, but held firm. I have met eminent members of the Establishment who like argument and even, in their strange British way, welcome defeat once in a while. Their theory is that 'it is good for the Establishment to realize that it is not omnipotent'—even if it runs the country!

A BOUQUET OF CONSERVATIVES

After Macmillan the most important Tory is certainly R. A. Butler; the most interesting, to many minds, is Iain Macleod, whom we met in a previous chapter. Others? Among coming men Peter Thorneycroft (once Exchequer, now Aviation) is probably the most attractive. Duncan Sandys (formerly Defence, now Commonwealth Relations) is probably the toughest and most obstinate; Selwyn Lloyd (formerly Foreign Affairs, now Chancellor of the Exchequer) the hardest-working and sharpest-witted; the Earl of Home (Foreign Affairs, but stranded in the Lords) the most courteous; David Eccles (Education) the least popular; Lord Mills (Paymaster-General) by all odds the closest to the Prime Minister; John Hare (Labour) one of the most promising; Harold Watkinson (Defence) the least colourful; Lord Hailsham (Science), about whom we shall have a word below, the most brilliant; Enoch Powell (Health) the most dedicated and possibly the most courageous; Christopher Soames (Agriculture) one of the pleasantest; Ernest Marples (Transport) the most dramatic; and Reginald Maudling (Board of Trade) the most engaging. After a recent debate he said, 'I hope to go down in history, if for nothing else, as the man who proposed to Parliament what should be the size of a double Scotch.'

Richard Austen Butler, known universally as 'Rab', was born in India in 1902. His father, the late Sir Montagu S. D. Butler, was governor of the Central Provinces at the time, and had also been Master of Pembroke College, Cambridge, and Mayor of Cambridge. Young Butler had a surpassing academic career at Cambridge, and started life as a don; a shy man as well as an intellectual, he has always liked academic cloisters. Mr. Butler holds three posts of large consequence today: Home Secretary, Leader of the House of Commons, and head of the Conservative party. When he was passed over for the prime ministership in

8

favour of Macmillan, the blow was bitter. Like Macmillan and
Macleod, he stands slightly to the left of centre; in fact it was
he, more than anybody, who was responsible for working out
new Tory policy, and he believes firmly that 'planning, public
ownership to an extent, and some features of the welfare state
are inevitable features of modern managerial societies'. Moreover, it was Butler who 'gave Macmillan his brains' (as the
naughty phrase has it), and he has even been called a 'secret
socialist'.

He lives in Essex, has always had a strong interest in agriculture, and has represented a safe rural constituency since 1929.
In the mid-thirties he devoted most of his interest to India and
foreign affairs, and was a right-hand man to Neville Chamberlain in the Munich period. David Lloyd George once called him
'the artful dodger'. This was not a fair comment. I remember
having a long talk with Mr. Butler the week the war broke out
in 1939, when he was Under-Secretary of State in the Foreign
Office, and I have never forgotten his skill in answering questions, his clarity and forthrightness.

Butler has always been fascinated by planning. Under
Churchill he became President of the Board of Education in 1941,
which meant that he was not in the mainstream during the war.
The story is that Butler thanked him when he was given this
post, and Churchill replied, 'Thank me! I meant it as an insult.'
But, of course, this is an apocryphal story. Butler did well at the
education post, and successively became Minister of Labour,
Chancellor of the Exchequer, and Home Secretary in January,
1957. Recently he said that he wanted a policy which would
'conserve, unite, and construct'. When I saw him last year and
asked him what the great changes in Britain had been in the
past quarter-century, he suggested two—the virtual end of
unemployment and the fact that the difference between the
Conservative and Labour parties had been much trimmed down.[1]

Another bright brain in the cabinet is Lord Hailsham. Born
Quintin McGarel Hogg in 1907, the son of a celebrated British
jurist and an American mother, Hailsham succeeded to his
father's peerage in 1950—which abruptly cut off his House of
Commons career. He resisted to the uttermost being elevated

---

[1] Cf. the *Observer*, March 16, 1952, and the *News Chronicle*, September 21,
1955.

to the Lords, and in fact sought legal sanction for continuing to sit in the Commons even though, through no fault of his own, he had become a peer. Had Hailsham been able to remain a commoner he would certainly have been—and still would be—a weighty candidate for prime minister. Late in 1960 an analogous situation arose on the Labour side of the House when Anthony Wedgwood Benn succeeded to his father's peerage, and automatically became Viscount Stansgate. Benn, too, resisted to the uttermost being elevated to the Lords by the accident of heredity, and fought a vivid campaign—unsuccessful so far—for the right to renounce his title. On occasion British politicians have to pay for the traditions without which they would not be what they are.

Lord Hailsham had a brilliant career at Eton and Christ Church, Oxford, became a Fellow of All Souls, followed his father's footsteps in the law, and rose to be a Queen's Counsel in 1953. Meantime he had, inevitably, gone into politics, and after robust service in the war, was successively First Lord of the Admiralty, Minister of Education, Lord President of the Council, and finally Minister for Science. This, a new post, and one which most European governments do not have, is an experiment. Hailsham has a small staff—one story is that the whole personnel could fit in a bus—which is responsible for working out and co-ordinating the government's science policy. Science, like defence, is an acute preoccupation in Britain today —indeed, the two subjects are, as elsewhere, heavily intermingled.

Hailsham, when I talked to him, indicated his belief that two of the profound changes which distinguish the England of today from that of former years are, first, the fact that foreign aid is no longer necessary, as it was in the immediate post-war period; second, that class differences have been immeasurably reduced.

Both Butler and Hailsham, for different reasons, are disappointed men. But both have a lot of good old-fashioned British stiff-upper-lip-ism, and would never dream of showing it.

GAITSKELL AND THE OPPOSITION

I have mentioned Mr. Gaitskell a good many times in the three preceding chapters, and now we have the pleasure of describing him further. Few leaders of the British Labour party have ever found themselves in a more difficult position through no fault of their own. Possibly Mr. Gaitskell's days as leader are numbered, which would be a grave—perhaps irreparable—loss to both his party and country. What has hurt him most, quite apart from fissures within the party, is the fact that Labour has lost three general elections in a row, though Gaitskell was not leader at the time of all three; even so, it is no easy thing for a leader to carry on after even two losses—ask Adlai Stevenson— and the Labour party is particularly vulnerable because it lacks any vital, overriding issue.

Hugh Todd Naylor Gaitskell, born in 1906, comes of pleasant middle-class stock; his father was a member of the Indian Civil Service. He went to Winchester like so many other leading members of the Labour party (e.g. Richard Crossman), and New College, Oxford, where he won first-class honours. He became a socialist partly under the stimulus of the General Strike of 1926, went into teaching, and in short order became head of the department of political economy at University College, London. His wife, a warm-hearted and vivacious young woman with keen political sense, has been of great service to his career. They live in a comfortable house in Hampstead, and have two daughters. The Gaitskells are happy people, interested in every aspect of life, and gregarious. At Gaitskell parties, which are cheerful, modest, and totally informal (Mrs. Gaitskell does the cooking), one may meet people ranging from Oxford eggheads to penurious young artists. Gaitskell, a man packed with curiosity, has a wide intellectual scope. Once in New York, after he had delivered the Godkin Lectures at Harvard, a group of friends met him hoping to ask him questions about British politics; Mr. Gaitskell didn't mind being questioned, but he turned the tables on the group by asking a lot of penetrating questions himself—about the state of the American novel.

But we must resume description of his political career. On the outbreak of the war he went into the civil service, like his father and brother, and became principal private secretary to Hugh Dalton, the Minister of Economic Warfare. Soon he became a kind of white-haired boy to Dalton, and went with him to a post in the Board of Trade. In 1945 he was elected to Parliament, and soon gained a junior post in the Attlee government. He became

Minister of Fuel and Power in 1947, though he had only been in the Commons for two years. Seldom has a rise been so rapid. A brief period as Minister of State for Economic Affairs followed, and in 1950 he became Chancellor of the Exchequer, the youngest Chancellor (forty-four) in half a century.

Controversy now began to attend his person. There came a series of vivid quarrels with Aneurin Bevan, one of which began when Gaitskell, in the interest of a rearmament budget, imposed a small temporary health service charge; the ferocious and magnificent Bevan denounced him as a 'desiccated calculating machine'. Gaitskell replied in kind. The Chancellor took, by and large, a middle position in the party, and was a bridge between right and left wings. He became party treasurer in 1954, and then, when Mr. Attlee retired in December, 1955, was elected leader.

One of his outstanding qualities is clarity of mind; he has an unrivalled capacity to outline a problem with lucidity and precision. Beyond this he has vast energy, an almost boyish eagerness for experience, and marked courage—besides which he is one of the most generous of men. Nor can anybody deny his dialectical skill. Some people may think that he is dry, but he is a formidable debater, as anybody will have gathered who happened to hear him on an NBC programme in New York early in 1961, when, in a panel discussion on foreign policy, he extinguished some formidable opposition.

Gaitskell is a practical man; this, among other things, led to the celebrated crisis over 'Clause Four'. This—to concentrate an exceptionally difficult subject in the briefest space possible—is the 'nationalization' clause in the party constitution written in 1918, which calls for the nationalization of industry, i.e. the common ownership of the means of production, distribution, and exchange. Gaitskell's opinion was that such a broad commitment no longer fitted the circumstances of post-war affluent society, and that it was a ruinous albatross hung around the party's neck. His attitude, more modern and moderate, is that 'both public and private enterprise have a place in the economy'. The Gaitskell opponents, representing several intermingled forces within the party, held that this was a betrayal, and that Labour must stick to an old-fashioned, doctrinaire concept of orthodox socialism and public ownership, even if this meant that it would never win an election again. They called Gaitskell's general line

—towards modernizing the party—'treason'. This argument struck so deeply on both sides because, obviously, it brought up the vital issue of what *is* modern socialism. Somebody quipped, 'Hugh doesn't realize how *conservative* the Labour party is!'

*

Now to carry on the angry story of the Labour party split from the point where we left it in Chapter XV above. The pressing and painful issue is, of course, unilateralism and nuclear disarmament. The quarrel exists on several levels, but, to oversimplify, its main focus is a struggle between elements in the TUC (Trades Union Congress) and the parliamentary Labour party. To understand this we must have a preliminary word about the Labour party in general. It is not, like the Conservative party, a unitary organism; on the contrary, it is a movement rather than a party, an amalgam consisting of several loosely associated units—the TUC (which is composed of 185 separate unions), the constituency Labour parties, one for each parliamentary district, the Co-operatives, and finally the parliamentary Labour party itself, which consists of the 258 Labour members in the House of Commons.

The trades unions, with about 9·7 million members—not all of whom, however, are affiliated to the TUC—and with funds of around eighty million pounds, are so important because, historically, they have always been the essential base of the whole Labour movement; the party was merely 'the political arm'. Also they constitute a major source of funds in the constituencies and in Parliament; a percentage of the funds of most unions—which derive from the dues of members—is assigned to the party for political purposes. Some unions are called 'dictatorship' unions, some 'democratic'. Among the biggest are the Transport and General workers Union, once dominated by Ernest Bevin and now run by Frank Cousins, which has more than 1·2 million members; the Amalgamated Engineering Union, the executive of which has been heavily infiltrated by Communists; the National Union of Mine Workers; the National Union of General and Municipal Workers; the three railwaymen's unions; and the Union of Shop, Distributive, and Allied Workers. Each union holds an annual meeting in the spring or summer, and an Annual Congress of the whole movement follows in the autumn. Voting at this takes place by bloc, which means that the leader of each casts the entire polling power of his union without the necessity of holding a referendum within its ranks. This system has often been attacked for being undemocratic. Its adherents say in rebuttal that the head of the union has, after all, been elected democratically, and casts his vote, representing the union as a whole, very much as presidential electors in the United States cast the votes of states.

Union after union during the course of the last year took up the cause of unilateralism, nuclear disarmament. I have sought to explain the reasons for this above. One curious point is that, although individual unions went unilateralist in large number, its general council or executive did not; out of its thirty-six members only seven are unilateralists. Another curiosity is Communist influence, which is all on the unilateralist side. *Politically* the Communists play no role in Great Britain whatever; the Communist party did not poll more than thirty thousand votes, an infinitesimal segment of the electorate, in the last general election (October, 1959), and did not get a single candidate into Parliament. Yet its influence is considerable in several unions, like the engineers and electrical workers. Strangely enough, some Conservative industrialists like to have Communists in their plants; Communist shop stewards are efficient and hard-working.

The ruling organism of the TUC, its annual congress, met on the Isle of Man in September, 1960, and Cousins, confirming his revolt against the Gaitskell leadership of the party, introduced a resolution demanding 'complete rejection of any defence policy based on the threat of nuclear weapons' and unilateral disarmament, i.e. the end of NATO and US bases. What happened then was, to say the least, confusing. One picturesque detail is that the Amalgamated Engineering Union, the second biggest in the country, voted both ways. So, in a manner of speaking, did the congress as a whole. The Gaitskell adherents carried one resolution (4,150,000 votes to 3,406,000, a slim margin) to keep the nuclear deterrent and continue to permit the presence of American forces in Great Britain as long as necessary, but were beaten in another—by a much larger majority—which called for rejection of any policy 'based on the threat of the use of nuclear weapons'. As a result, nobody quite knew what was what.

Then came the annual conference of the Labour party itself at Scarborough in October. The parliamentary Labour party— itself torn—had whittled out a compromise and adopted a pro- gramme agreeing to the abandonment of an independent British deterrent, but pledging fulfilment of British obligations to NATO 'while pressing for a reduction in dependence on nuclear weapons'. This was not enough for the TUC unilateralists, and Cousins won 'the battle of Scarborough'. Several resolutions tell the story. One introduced by the engineers which flatly demanded the unilateral renunciation of 'the testing, manu- facture, stockpiling and basing of all nuclear weapons in Great Britain', was passed—but by a small majority, only 340,000 votes out of some six million—and a second, submitted by the Transport and General Workers Union, which went even further, was carried, but only by about 40,000 votes.

Gaitskell had two choices as a result: he could either resign from leadership of the party and retire to the back benches or fight. He decided to 'fight and fight and fight again to save the party we love', and said that he would devote the entire rest of his career, if necessary, to force a reversal of the Scarborough decisions. His opponents in the parliamentary Labour party thereupon set out to depose him. Their justification was that his leadership had been repudiated at Scarborough, and that he no longer represented the views of the party as a whole. His answer was that he was the servant of the parliamentary Labour party, all of whose members had been elected, not of the TUC bosses—moreover elected on a platform that had included firm support of NATO. The man who sought to wrest the leadership from Gaitskell, and who stood against him in the PLP caucus, was Harold Wilson, a member of the Labour 'Shadow Cabinet' who was destined to be Chancellor of the Exchequer if Labour is returned to office. Gaitskell won by 166 votes to 81. This would seem to be a comfortable margin, but on the other hand it indicates that a third of the membership of Gaitskell's own party in the House stands against him. No situation could be more difficult. One curious point is that Wilson, a shrewd politician, is *not* a unilateralist.

An astounding number of personal cross-currents cut into this struggle. Some MPs oppose Gaitskell on unilateralist grounds, some on Clause Four, some on no issue except pique. Emmanuel Shinwell, who was once Gaitskell's superior in the Ministry of Fuel and Power, and Herbert Morrison (now elevated to the Lords as Lord Morrison), whom Gaitskell beat for the leadership in 1955, dislike him on personal grounds. The Labour party has several organs. One is the National Executive, elected by a complicated process and headed at present by Richard Crossman, which has, at the present moment, a small Gaitskell majority. Another is the so-called Shadow Cabinet, chosen by Labour's MPs out of their own membership. At least two members oppose Gaitskell—Wilson and Fred Lee—but the rest support him. Unalterably on his side are George Brown, the deputy leader of the party, Denis Healey, who is scheduled to be Foreign Minister in a Labour government, James Callaghan, the official spokesman on colonies, and Patrick Gordon-Walker, former Minister for Commonwealth Relations.

One ardent unilateralist is Anthony Greenwood, son of the late Arthur Greenwood who was a distinguished cabinet minister during the war; he has been an MP since 1946 and a member of the National Executive since 1954. Another is Michael Foot, who recently won Aneurin Bevan's old seat at Ebbw Vale. Mr. Foot, whom I have heard described as 'the most troublesome man in England', derives from a distinguished Devon family, liberal by tradition. Aged forty-seven and on the extreme left wing, he is one of three remarkable sons of Isaac Foot, a lawyer and former Liberal MP. One brother is Sir Hugh Foot, a sound and courageous colonial administrator who was the last governor of Cyprus; the other, named Dingle, is a Labour MP. Michael Foot is director of *Tribune*, the chief unilateralist organ, and a very bright young man indeed. For many years he was closely associated with Bevan, but split away from him when Bevan patched up his quarrel with Gaitskell and, in Foot's view, moved 'right'. Another associate is a man equally radical, Ian Mikardo, who lost his Commons seat in 1959.[1]

*

[1] Their followers are sometimes known as Footmiks. *Sunday Times*, May 29, 1960. Also see the *New York Times*, November 11, 1960, and the *Observer*, November 20, 1960.

What manner of man is Cousins? He was born in Nottingham-shire in 1904, the eldest of ten children and the son of a miner; like Aneurin Bevan he worked in the pits as a child, managed to get some education, and then emerged. For some time he was a lorry driver, and this led him into union activity in the middle 1930's. Cousins has always been a convinced socialist, and is a fanatic adherent of Clause Four; only recently did he become interested in international affairs and an addict of neutralism. Cousins, an undeniably able man, has a genius for organization, is a good performer on TV, and carries several chips on his shoulders. He has never stood for Parliament, and has been General Secretary of the Transport Workers and a member of the General Council of the TUC since 1956.

What makes Cousins important is his considerable feat in transforming the Transport Workers from a right-wing union, once utterly dominated by Ernest Bevin and his successor Arthur Deakin, into a left-wing organization—this is the biggest development in British labour since the war. He has been called 'the most modern and most sophisticated of union leaders', but if a Labour government, dominated by his influence, should ever come to power, this might well separate Britain from the United States and be a disastrous blow to the western world.

In strict contrast to Cousins, George Brown, the deputy leader of the party in succession to Aneurin Bevan, is on the right wing, and, although he has a trade union background and is a member of the Transport Workers, takes a strong pro-Gaitskell line on most issues. Brown, who is forty-six, was born in Southwark, the son of a lorry driver, and left school at fifteen —a completely self-made man. He is a strong personality, colourful, ebullient, and full of punch. He gets on well with Cousins, but admires Gaitskell greatly as well, although he may think that he is a bit too 'intellectual' on occasion. Mr. Brown had a famous tiff with Khrushchev when the Russian leader visited London in 1956, at a Labour party dinner at Claridge's; Khrushchev at last found a man in the free world who could answer him in words he understood. Khrushchev accused the British of having been soft on Hitler, and Mr. Brown, in no uncertain terms, told him off.

Harold Wilson, who contested for the leadership against Gaitskell late in 1960, and who despite this is still a member of the Shadow Cabinet, is a Yorkshireman, the son of a chemist, born in 1916. He went to Oxford, and has always been interested in business. He cut his teeth (as did Gaitskell) in the Ministry of Fuel and Power in 1943, entered Parliament in 1945, and rose to be President of the Board of Trade in 1947. He was close to Aneurin Bevan for some years, is sometimes called a fence-sitter, and on most issues takes a moderate left-wing line. Mr. Wilson has several times visited Moscow on business trips, and can regale listeners, as I will attest, with wonderful tales about his encounters with Mr. Mikoyan.

LIBERALS

The little joke has been whispered that a person can be a Liberal of any colour these days provided that it is violet. This refers, of course, to the well-known fact that, since Megan Lloyd George left the Liberal party in 1955, its undisputed *grande dame* is Lady Violet Bonham-Carter, the eldest daughter of the renowned Liberal leader and Prime Minister in World War I, the Earl of Oxford and Asquith. Lady Violet is the wife of the late Sir Maurice Bonham-Carter, and is a great lady indeed. The present leader of the party, Jo Grimond, married in 1938 Laura Miranda, a daughter of the Bonham-Carters, and a son, Mark Raymond Bonham-Carter, is a leading member, although he lost his seat in the Commons in 1959. Indeed, what survives today of the Liberal party is largely a Bonham-Carter family affair.

Mr. Grimond was christened Joseph but calls himself Jo. A Scot, he was born in 1913, has represented Orkney and Shetland since 1950, and became leader of the parliamentary Liberal party in 1956. Few characters in British public life are more attractive; Grimond has magnetism, charm, good looks, and a lively mind. He went to Eton and Balliol, had a good war record in the Scotch Yeomanry, and became a barrister. He does a considerable amount of political writing, and writes well. So does young Mark Bonham-Carter (born in 1922), who, incidentally, was educated in part at the University of Chicago, and married a daughter of the late American publisher Condé Nast. Recently he has been writing lively polemics in *Encounter*.

The Liberals, who descend from the full weight and majesty

of Mr. Gladstone, have only a miniscule six seats in the House of Commons today. However, they got 1,640,000 votes, or 5·9 per cent of the electorate, in 1959, and were the only party with a bigger vote—small as it was—than in the previous general election. One should also point out that the Liberals, running 221 candidates in all, got second place in no fewer than twenty-seven contests in addition to those they won; they led either Labour or the Tories in twenty-seven constituencies, even though they did not get enough to win. Whether the party can ever be revived as a real force is doubtful. But most Liberals feel—rightly—that there should be room in Britain for a genuine middle party opposed equally to extreme conservatism and the Labourite left wing. What Grimond wants is a 'broadly based, progressive party', with 'co-ownership' as a substitute for nationalization,[1] and the party stands firmly against neutralism and the unilateralists.

[1] *New York Times*, September 15, 1959.

CHAPTER XVIII

A Word on NATO

WE turn now to NATO. The present fashion is to doubt its efficacy and repeat the tart words of General de Gaulle that it is 'a structure which was designed to meet conditions which no longer exist'. That is, it was set up in 1949, before anybody realized the full implications of the nuclear age. Few people anticipated that the Soviet Union would soon have the bomb, and would proceed to build operational ICBMs (Intercontinental Ballistic Missiles) which could cross oceans in a trice, as well as rockets capable of kicking up dust on the moon. Nor did many people—to descend to a homelier level—think in terms of ground troops supported by nuclear arms. Nuclear considerations have completely altered not merely strategical patterns, but tactical patterns. Walter Lippmann wrote in June, 1960: 'We refused to look at the stark and dominating fact that once the Soviet Union had become a nuclear power, the peripheral countries were defenceless.'

The original idea of the North Atlantic Treaty Organization, the full name of NATO, was to create an international military force which could, in an emergency, stop the Russians on the ground or at least delay them significantly if they attempted to march across Europe. And as a matter of fact NATO still has considerable value as a shield, as well as a sword. It has never come anywhere near reaching the strength designed for it originally, ninety-six divisions, and, going all out, the Soviet Army, with its atomic-equipped, missile-armed, and highly mobile forces, could quite possibly reach the Atlantic Ocean in a matter of weeks. Even so, NATO commands substantial power; its forces are small, but well trained; they might slow up a Soviet advance to an extent, force the Russians to bring up reserves, and deny to them territory which the Red Army hoped to occupy at once, on the theory that, in such a case, we would not dare to bomb the civilian populations friendly to us in West Germany, the Low Countries or France.[1]

Then, too, NATO still has psychological and political importance. After all, this alliance has held together for twelve years against obstacles harassing in the extreme. No similar international force, representing fifteen nations scattered over half the earth, has ever been created in peacetime.[2] One of the headaches is a fantastically cumbersome and involuted command structure—the wry joke is that never in history have so few been commanded by so many. Another is the fact that the organization does not operate as a functioning military establishment except during manoeuvres, and still another is that several countries have not, to put it charitably, contributed much to the organization as a serious military force.

Finally, there have been embarrassing political difficulties over the length and breadth of Europe. One, already mentioned in this book, was the virulent quarrel between Greece and Turkey over Cyprus, which for a long period made effective co-operation in the eastern Mediterranean impossible on any level. Another is the question of admitting Spain. Another is a long-standing quarrel over the command position in Portuguese waters. Still another, much more important, is the role of France. General de Gaulle, seeking as we know an independent nuclear deterrent of his own, and irritated at what he considered to be intolerable slights on the part of the United States and Britain, not only drove our tactical bombers off French soil, but withdrew the French Mediterranean fleet from NATO. De Gaulle's grievances are several. First, he considers that the US favoured Great Britain, but snubbed France, in exchanging nuclear information. The American reply to this was that they did not trust French security. Second, he felt that France was being slighted in the responsibilities of command. SHAPE is headed by an American, General Lauris Norstad; of the three primary commands under SHAPE the northern, with head-

---

[1] For some of the background of this section I am indebted to the conversation of Hanson W. Baldwin, military correspondent of the *New York Times*.

[2] The original NATO signatories numbered twelve—Belgium, Canada, Denmark, France, Iceland, Italy, Luxembourg, the Netherlands, Norway, Portugal, the United Kingdom, and the United States. Greece and Turkey came in in 1952, and West Germany in 1955.

NATO IN EUROPE

quarters in Oslo, is British, and the southern (Naples) is American. The French have the vital centre, however (Fontainebleau). Still another (the Mediterranean command at Malta) is British. The Supreme Commander, Atlantic, is an American (Admiral Robert L. Dennison, stationed at Norfolk, Virginia) and the Allied Commander-in-Chief, Channel, is British (Admiral Sir Stanley Power at Portsmouth). Third, resentment that large segments of the French Army fighting a desperate war in Algeria are still technically assigned to NATO, whereas American, British, and other European components of the NATO forces 'take it easy' along the Rhine.

Early in 1961 NATO had twenty-one and a half divisions in western Europe—against Soviet strength which would probably amount to a minimum of one hundred divisions at the outbreak of hostilities. The NATO breakdown is the following: five

USA divisions, three United Kingdom (reduced recently from four), seven German, and two each from France, Belgium, and the Netherlands. The half-division represents a Canadian detachment. Five more German divisions will, it is hoped, be inserted into the structure by the end of 1961; this is the fondest dream of Franz-Josef Strauss, the German Minister of Defence. Then in addition one should mention NATO forces other than those on the West German front—twelve divisions in Turkey, seven in Italy, five in Greece, one each in Denmark and Norway, and a few troops in Portugal. In addition—adding up the whole —we must mention again the US Sixth Fleet, headquartered in Naples, multitudinous and elaborate air installations all over West Germany, and the Jupiter bases in Italy and Turkey.

One detail not without significance is the rise of several able and expert German military men to important posts in the NATO structure. One is General Adolf Heusinger, Chief of Operations of the German Army towards the end of World War II, and now Inspector-General of the Bundswehr. In December, 1960, Heusinger became head of the permanent military and policy planning group of the North Atlantic Treaty Organization, with headquarters in Washington, replacing a Dutch general. Heusinger, never a Nazi, was standing immediately next to Hitler on July 20, 1944, when military conspirators attempted to assassinate the *Führer* by means of a bomb. Heusinger was not party to the plot, and was badly injured; but, many years later, he gave public approval to it. Another is the celebrated General Hans Speidel, who, under French over-all command, is Commander, Allied Land Forces, Central Europe. This is a stout and brilliant officer. He was Field-Marshal Rommel's Chief of Staff for a time, played a large role in attempting to repel the Allies in the Normandy invasion after D-Day on June 6, 1944, and, to his everlasting credit, was the officer who in the last days of the *Götterdämmerung* refused point-blank to obey Hitler's orders to destroy Paris.[1] Speidel, who is a Ph.D. and was once a professor of military history, is also the kind of general who does his own scouting by helicopter. It is, of course, almost too obvious to mention that, having fought against Americans, British, and French in sustained combat only sixteen years ago, General Speidel now heads part

[1] William L. Shirer, *The Rise and Fall of the Third Reich*, p. 1085.

of an international force containing American, French, and British contingents. Boys from Picardy, Kansas and Lancashire have a German as their commanding officer.

*

But we must return to the essence of the new NATO story, namely the transformation of its military arm into a force equipped with nuclear weapons. This has drastically changed the picture almost everywhere overnight, and dominates every contemporary consideration. Points to make:

1. German and other NATO detachments in western Europe are equipped with weapons capable of discharging missiles, but do not possess the actual nuclear warheads. All such warheads are, by American law, the exclusive property of the United States and rest strictly in American custody. *American* detachments on German soil have weapons with nuclear warheads; German detachments do not. On the face of it this would seem to make for a strategical nightmare of no small dimension, in that, in the event of attack, it could well be assumed that the enemy would instantly strike at those NATO divisions *not* capable of nuclear retaliation. But in practice this doesn't matter much. American detachments are closely interlocked with those of other nationalities all along the line, and, moreover, each German division has a number of troops specifically trained in the use of Long Johns, a short-range mobile nuclear rocket designed for tactical use in ground warfare. These can be made nuclear in a matter of minutes by attaching the atomic warheads. Also one should mention that the nuclear armoury is varied. Available are Corporals and Sergeants with a seventy-five-mile range, as well as Davy Crocketts, the smallest nuclear weapon yet developed, which can be operated by two soldiers and can be used at practically point-blank range.

France has, since de Gaulle set out to build his own deterrent, its own nuclear stockpile free from American control. The Germans, so it seems, are on the whole delighted—*at present*—that they do not have the responsibility of maintaining their own nuclear storage depots. What the Germans want at the moment is not so much nuclear arms themselves as independent means to deliver them, i.e. modern bombers. The German air force is still puny, and, by terms of the agreements which permitted Germany to rearm, the country voluntarily pledged itself not to manufacture long-range bombers or nuclear arms. However, the contingency may easily be foreseen when, in the near future, Germany might ask to be relieved of this renunciation and feel compelled to set out to build its own nuclear armoury, although this would provoke fierce opposition in Great Britain, Scandinavia, and the Low Countries, as well as in some circles in West Germany itself.

2. New and immeasurable headaches have arisen in such areas as command responsibility. Suppose, for instance, through accident or otherwise, hostile action begins on a strictly local basis with none but conventional weapons. Should the NATO forces retaliate by *nuclear* means, and discharge A-bombs—or even H-bombs—on a small, limited target? But, if this is not done, horrible as it would be to do it, do we not take the risk that the enemy on its side may, at any moment, progress from using conventional to nuclear weapons and destroy *us*? In general the policy has been set up that the NATO forces, on a tactical level, will reply to an attack by conventional means with nothing but conventional weapons—at least until the situation clarifies.[1] In any case, nuclear weapons may not be used without express order from the President of the United States.

3. Most experts seem to agree that, if war should come, it will be a very short war indeed—either because it will be severely localized at the outset, or because it will expand into a full-dress nuclear affair with strategic bombing which will annihilate everybody at once. One NATO plan is known as MC 70. It has been drawn up on the basis that a European war will not last more than thirty days, and that it is useless to store supplies and equipment for troops for more than three months.

4. Who pushes the button? Who, rather, is empowered to make the supreme, final decision to employ nuclear arms if a local conflagration spreads? Is it some officer in the field? Is it General Norstad in either of his capacities—Commander-in-Chief of the U.S. forces in Europe as well as Commander-in-Chief of SHAPE? Who recommends action to the President of the United States? Will the British Prime Minister be consulted? Can the decision be made by the NATO Council, its political

[1] Don Cook in the New York *Herald Tribune*, December 11, 1960.

element, or by the civilian secretary-general? I had a long and friendly talk in Paris with Paul-Henri Spaak, who held this post till recently, but if he knows who the ultimate button-pusher is, he didn't tell me. In fact, I have never been able to get a satisfactory answer to this question. Will everybody consult together? If so, they will, in the event of an extreme emergency, have to consult in a hurry. British calculations are that a Soviet short-range missile, the Golem, can reach British targets from its pads in East Germany in three minutes.[1]

5. All of this and much else came to a head late in 1960 when General Norstad outlined in detail a proposal which had been simmering for some months—to ameliorate some, if not all, of these confusions by the drastic step of turning NATO itself into an independent nuclear power. NATO, as a unit, would get its *own* nuclear armoury, and thus become—after the United States, the United Kingdom, Russia, and France—the fifth nuclear power in the world. One aspect of the proposal was that five Polaris submarines should be assigned to NATO. There were several motives for this development. One is that NATO does not have sufficient ground troops, and that the character of war has irremediably changed. Another is the hope that such a step would keep the French from pushing further with their independent deterrent (the French do not have as yet the capacity to deliver strategically the bombs they produce) and also—looking at the future—discourage the Germans from embarking on nuclear production of their own. Germany is, as has just been mentioned, forbidden at present to develop her own nuclear weapons, just as it is forbidden to have a strategic air force, but this prohibition may not last for ever.

The Norstad plan could not, it seems clear, be adopted without amendment by Congress of the Atomic Energy Act, under which the United States is forbidden to share nuclear weapons with anybody else. Another difficulty, particularly troubling to the British, is that each of NATO's fifteen members would, presumably, have to be consulted before any decision to use the projected stockpile could be taken, and this might be a laborious procedure. Also the British want to differentiate with careful discrimination between NATO itself and SHAPE, its military arm. They do not want to put the supreme question of war,

[1] Philip Deane in the *Observer*, September 17, 1960.

peace, and possible nuclear obliteration in the exclusive hands of military men; they want a *political* as well as military decision. On the whole the British are inclined to rest content with the present situation whereby US strategic (i.e. long-range or intercontinental) weapons cannot be discharged except on the authority of the President in Washington. The British Labour party in particular does not want any possible contingency to arise whereby some individual representative of a NATO power could cause thermonuclear war without consultation. But the French, and possibly other powers, do not want the whole responsibility to rest with the United States, if only because of apprehension that the President may not give permission to unleash the US nuclear armoury in defence of *Europe* unless the actual territory of the *United States* is attacked.[1] This is one reason why de Gaulle wants his own deterrent. I have listed other reasons in Chapter VII above.

ONE OF THE GOOD MEN OF EUROPE

Paul-Henri Spaak, a rotund, gregarious, and cheerful personality, succeeded Lord Ismay as Secretary-General of the North Atlantic Treaty Organization in December, 1956. In this post he has needed both his weight (which is over fourteen stone) and his agility. The SHAPE generals knew how to get along with Ismay; but Spaak was a different article. It would be difficult to determine whether Spaak carries more authority than Norstad, the boss of SHAPE. In theory neither is subordinate to the other. Roughly, Spaak occupies the same position as does Hammarskjöld in the United Nations, and Norstad, wearing his NATO hat, is the equivalent of a UN task force commander. But, as mentioned before, Norstad is not only military head of NATO but also Commander-in-Chief of US forces in Europe, and this gives him additional authority.

Somebody once called Spaak, who is sixty-one, 'a perfect Belgian', because his father was Flemish, his mother a Walloon. For several generations the Spaak family has been distinguished; one of his grandfathers was a prime minister, and his father is a well-known man of letters. His mother, a firm socialist (as is her son), was the first woman ever to be elected to the Belgian senate.

[1] *New Statesman*, December 17, 1960.

Politics—in particular the labour movement—took hold of Spaak early. He started political life on the extreme left, led demonstrations in the streets, and was once injured in a riot. He entered Parliament in 1932, became Foreign Minister in 1936 (and remained Foreign Minister off and on for almost twenty years) and, in 1939, became the first socialist Prime Minister in the history of Belgium—also the youngest. He managed to flee the country when the Nazis overran it, and took a leading role in the fight which forced Leopold off the throne.

But the principal thing to emphasize about Spaak is his authentic internationalism. He led the Belgian delegation to the San Francisco conference in 1945, and then became the first president (1946-47) of the United Nations Assembly, immediately after its birth. He was one of the creators of Benelux, and was in the thick of the evolution which produced the European Coal and Steel Community and the Common Market.[1]

---

[1] Mr. Spaak resigned from his NATO post in February, 1961, as these pages go to press, in order to return to Brussels and take over leadership of the Socialist party there.

CHAPTER XIX

At Sixes and Sevens

To explain the evolution and functioning of the European Economic Community, or Common Market—sometimes also called 'The Inner Six'—we must go back a bit into some complicated recent history and define terms briefly.

Soon after the war Jean Monnet, a French economist and man of affairs of great vision and discernment, suggested to Robert Schuman, Foreign Minister at the time, that pooling of the iron, coal, and steel resources of France and Germany would not only be a logical step towards bettering the economy of both countries, but could have immeasurable importance in leading to political rapprochement. Schuman, who was born in Lorraine and who had actually served in the German Army in World War I, has always been an international-minded man, and caught on to the idea at once. After all, there is no difference between French and German coal or iron under the crust of the earth; veins in subsurface mines know no frontiers. Moreover, the Saar, Lorraine, and the Ruhr complemented each other perfectly in natural resources. On May 9, 1950, Schuman formally proposed the creation of a common authority for French and German coal and steel; difficult and elaborate negotiations thereupon began. The project was extended to include Italy, Belgium, the Netherlands, and Luxembourg, and on April 18, 1951, a formal treaty—on the governmental level—was signed in Paris setting up the European Coal and Steel Community (ECSC). Monnet became first president of its High Authority, or governing body, and by the summer of 1952 the organization, with its 'capital' in Luxembourg, began to function. Almost from the beginning it was successful. All partners gained. A common market for coal, iron ore and scrap was opened in 1953, followed by one for steel. The remarkable thing about the ECSC was that

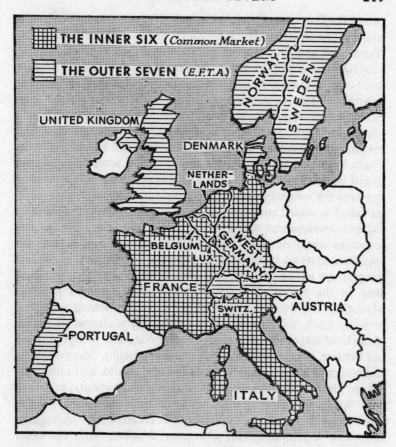

THE INNER SIX (*Common Market*)

THE OUTER SEVEN (*E.F.T.A.*)

NORWAY

SWEDEN

UNITED KINGDOM

DENMARK

NETHER-LANDS

BELGIUM

LUX.

WEST GERMANY

FRANCE

SWITZ.

AUSTRIA

PORTUGAL

ITALY

it was, in the true sense, supranational, not merely international, because the signatory nations agreed—in several spheres—to surrender actual sovereignty to the new organization, and it was given the power to tax. Besides the Monnet-Schuman concept included creation of a common assembly, or parliament, and this held its first session in Strasbourg in September, 1952, with Paul-Henri Spaak as its first president.

Monnet and his colleagues, ambitious idealists all, soon set out to enlarge their concept. At the same time others, on a higher political level, were also working strenuously for European integration, like Adenauer and René Pleven, the French Prime Minister. Soon arose a proposal to form what came to be called the European Defence Community; this was an attempt to make German rearmament possible within a general European framework and give it more palatability by creation of a single, international European army. But the EDC was killed (August, 1954) by the French parliament, largely because it still had substantial fear of Germany. Monnet thought that the next development should take a different tack, and that it was a mistake to try to create political or military unity without first establishing a sound economic base. He and Spaak put their heads together, and conceived the idea that something fruitful might be done in the field of atomic energy. This was a promising area for several reasons. No single country had what could be called a vested interest in the atom, the whole new field of nuclear development was a dramatic challenge, and the smaller countries could not possibly afford the expense of setting up establishments to harness nuclear power by themselves. Hence the concept of doing what had already been done for iron and steel in the realm of atomic energy rapidly gained ground. Meantime the Benelux economic union was working well. So, in June, 1955, the foreign ministers of the six member states of the Coal and Steel Community met at Messina, Sicily, to work out further steps towards European integration. Monnet, who had resigned his chairmanship of the High Authority in order to devote himself exclusively to these new developments, together with Spaak and others, influenced the meeting stoutly. As a result two new organizations were created, the European Economic Community or Common Market, and Euratom (pronounced 'You're at 'em') or European Atomic Energy Community.[1] After arduous work—and somewhat to everybody's surprise—formal treaties were signed at Rome on March 25, 1957, setting up both the new agencies, and these came into operation as soon as the treaties were ratified.

The new 'European Community', as it is officially called, thus consists of three different but closely interlocked instruments—the ECSC for coal and steel, the Common Market, and Euratom. In a sense they are all the same organization, and the six member states are the same in each—France, West Germany, Italy, Belgium, the Netherlands, and Luxembourg. Let us proceed.

[1] Monnet himself chose the phrase 'Common Market'. Others wanted 'Single Market'.

THE COMMON MARKET ITSELF

This has two main aspects. First, the member states, which represent a total population of 170 million and comprise one of the richest concentrations of industrial power in the world, agreed to lower tariff barriers *as between themselves*, and thus eventually convert France, West Germany, Italy, and the Benelux nations into an integrated free trade area, like the United States. The idea is that a purchaser in Germany, say, will be able to buy French goods at approximately the same price as in France, as one may buy California fruit or wine in New York at the same price as in California. The diminution of tariffs is to proceed by degrees, and it was originally thought that it would take from ten to twelve years before tariffs of the member states could be reduced to zero. The process began with a modest 10 per cent cut on January 1, 1959, a year after the treaty went into effect; another 10 per cent cut came in the summer of 1960, and a third on January 1, 1961. It is now anticipated that tariffs will reach zero by 1966. Second, the member states agreed to make their tariff rates *uniform vis-à-vis non-member states*. In other words the Six will behave, on external trade matters, like a single country. To effect this, countries hitherto sharply protectionist, like France, will lower their tariffs; conversely countries which have leaned in the past towards free trade, like Belgium and the Netherlands, will have to raise them.

Beyond this, and omitting details in such realms as agriculture, quotas, and so on, the Common Market has highly significant overtones. What really counts is that the most ardent backers of the Six, like Monnet and Adenauer, hope that the organization will become the nucleus of a future United States of Europe, no less. Any country may join.[1] Already the Common Market has made lengthy strides. Its secretariat in Brussels, headed by Professor Walter Hallstein, has grown into an elaborate organization. Trade has gone up spectacularly—29 per cent as against last year within the borders of the Six, 8 per cent as between the Six and the outside world. Italian steel production has increased fourfold. Zealots talk about such future

[1] In January, 1961, arrangements were made to admit sixteen African states which attained independence in 1960.

developments as a common motor-car licence plate for citizens of all six countries, a common currency, and even common citizenship.[1] In theory frontiers will disappear, except emotionally: the line between France and Germany, or France and Italy, will mean no more than those between Vermont and New Hampshire, or Kent and Sussex.

The British were invited to attend the first discussions leading to formation of the Common Market in the summer of 1955, but snubbed them. Then, as it became increasingly clear that this revolutionary project was actually going to work, they became more interested, and offered tentatively to join both the Coal and Steel Community and Euratom. This offer was declined; the Common Market powers said that Britain must join the Six without reservation, and become a full member of the EEC. This, for a variety of reasons, the British felt they could not do. For one thing they have played balance-of-power politics since the babyhood of the nation, and felt a subconscious emotional hostility to this new, powerful, solidly integrated bloc of European powers across the channel. For another, they could not join the Six without sacrificing trade relations with the Commonwealth, which is the source of roughly 40 per cent of all British trade. For instance, Britain imports most Commonwealth goods, particularly foodstuffs and raw materials, duty-free under the Imperial Preference System, but if it joined the Six it might be obliged to put a tariff on such imports, which would make it difficult for the Commonwealth countries to compete against European suppliers.

However, the British soon found out that, even if membership in the Six might cost them a good deal, they were also losing a good deal by staying out, because the Common Market is in a position to damage severely their export trade to *Europe*, a highly important item in the British trade position—particularly in a period when imports, as was mentioned in a preceding chapter, are rising faster than exports. Some unpleasant problems had to be faced. How were the British going to continue to sell machinery to the Netherlands, say, if mutual tariff arrangements made by the Six made it cheaper for the Dutch to buy analogous machinery from Germany or France? How can

[1] Already secretariat members' cars in Brussels have their own number-plates, blue with the letters EUR followed by a number.

they sell motor-cars to Belgium or Italy, against a tariff wall, if these countries can buy competing French cars, as an example, duty-free?

For good or ill the British decided, after prolonged hesitation, that their best move would be to set up a rival European trade apparatus. This is known as the European Free Trade Association, and is called the EFTA or Outer Seven. It comprises Britain, Switzerland, Austria, Portugal, and three Scandinavian countries—Sweden, Norway, and Denmark. The treaty setting up the Outer Seven was ratified in May, 1960. Like the Six, the Seven plan to abolish all internal tariffs as between themselves within a period of years, and the first cut came promptly on July 1; external tariffs (against outsiders) are, however, not to be modified. This, presumably, is to ensure that Commonwealth goods and raw materials may still enter Britain duty-free or at very low rates. One incidental point is that whereas all members of the Six are also members of NATO,[1] three of the Seven are neutrals—Austria by the terms of its peace treaty, Sweden by its own inclination, and Switzerland by determination. The Seven do not have so strong an underlying political motivation for cohesion and instinct for future unity as the Six.

'War' between the Inner Six and Outer Seven promptly began. The Seven call the Six scornfully a 'rich man's club'. The Six have 170 million people, and their gross national product, an enormous £52,000 million in 1958, is even larger today; the Seven are geographically not so centralized, less thoroughly industrialized, have only 86 million people, and in 1958 produced a gross national product of only £30,000 million. One reason why the Common Market is such an active issue in England is that a powerful body of opinion thinks that it is somewhat silly to have a trade war which will serve to divide Europe at precisely this time in the history of the world, when it needs most to be united. Liberals, some Labourites, and even a few Tories favour dropping the Seven, and joining up with the Six. But this will not be easy to do. The Commonwealth is still a terrific emotional as well as political and economic force to Britons. The Six, on their side, would like extremely to have the British in their ranks.

[1] But the EEC as such has no connection with NATO.

Meantime the paradox remains that England has the most European-minded government in its history, but is not a partner in what is probably the most consequential forward step ever taken towards European unity, prosperity, and peace.

FUNCTIONING OF THE EUROPEAN COMMUNITY

Both the Common Market and Euratom have their executives in Brussels; the Common Market headquarters are on the Avenue de la Joyeuse Entrée—the name seems to be a good augury, but it was purely an accident that the new organization is stationed there. A considerable bureaucracy has grown up; the Common Market secretariat numbers about eighteen hundred at the moment, and that of Euratom about six hundred—including research scientists.

Dr. Walter Hallstein, the head of the Common Market, was a professor of law when, some years ago, he was invited by Chancellor Adenauer to enter the German Foreign Office. He is fifty-one, and is highly articulate—to put it mildly—in French, German, and English; in fact, he is one of the comparatively few Germans who will discuss highly technical intricacies in French with a French colleague. Hallstein served in the German Army in World War II, and was taken prisoner by the Americans. Brought to the United States by his captors, he taught English in various prison camps, and finally emerged (1947) to join the law faculty at Georgetown University in Washington, D.C. Somewhat cold in manner, and anxious not to go too fast, he has great intellectual precision. Politics *per se* do not interest him much, but he is a devout internationally minded European.

President of Euratom is Étienne Hirsch, who was Monnet's first deputy on the Modernization and Reconstruction Programme (the Monnet Plan) which set out to put the French economy on its feet after the war. A French citizen of Jewish extraction, Hirsch is a warm, likeable personality, not yet fully tested politically, who has a wide range of intellectual interests. His chief assistants are an Italian, a Dutchman, and a German. Euratom is a very complex operation indeed. There are four uranium and thorium mines functioning in France, as well as deposits capable of exploitation in France, Italy, and West Germany; operating research centres are stationed at Grenoble and two other points in France, Rome and three other locations in Italy, West Germany (three installations), West Berlin (one), the Netherlands (two), and Belgium (one). As to experimental reactors, six are functioning in France, five in Germany, one in West Berlin, one in Belgium, and one in Holland. There are two power reactors in operation at Marcoule, the centre for all French experimentation in atomic energy, and two in Italy, one at Latina near Rome, one near Turin. Finally a dozen or more ore treatment plants as well as plants for the treatment of irradiated fissionable materials are functioning.

Headquarters of the Coal and Steel Community are in Luxembourg; the president of its High Authority is an Italian, Piero Malvestiti, who was formerly Hallstein's first assistant in the Common Market. The ECSC secretariat numbers about seven hundred, and has brought much vivacity to the life of Luxembourg. Whereas the Common Market has what is called a 'framework' constitution, that of the ECSC is more specific. It is the first supranational organization in history which has been empowered by its member governments to levy a European tax; this must not exceed one per cent of the value of its total annual production. The Common Market and Euratom are, in contrast, financed by allocations from the budgets of the six member governments. Hallstein, Hirsch, and Malvestiti hold equal positions in theory; there is no boss as among the three. Each of the three has a council of ministers, at which cabinet ministers of the national governments may also sit, depending on the subject under discussion.[1]

A Court of Justice which sits in Luxembourg has also been established; its president is a Hollander, Dr. A. M. Donner. Finally all organs of the European Community are responsible, in theory, to a single, common parliament which sits in Strasbourg, and meets as often as nine times a year. This grew out of the original 'Common Assembly' of the Coal and Steel Community, and is now known as the 'European Parliament'. It has 142 members, all of whom must be members of the six national parliaments represented. They do not, however, sit by

[1] For instance, the function of the Council of Ministers of the ECSC is 'to harmonize the national problems of the member states with the supranationalism of the High Authority'.

nation. Exactly as in the national parliaments, members belong to different blocs and parties. For instance, Italian, French, and German socialists sit together without regard to nationality, as do the conservatives.

The European Parliament meets in a building in Strasbourg called La Maison de l'Europe, which had previously been built for the Council of Europe. It has no legislative powers and, as of the moment, only slight political importance; yet it is a beginning. The present headquarters arrangements are not particularly unwieldy, but a suggestion was recently put forward by Dr. Franz Meyers, Prime Minister of North Rhine-Westphalia, for the creation of a new European Community 'capital' on a hundred-square-mile extraterritorial area where West Germany, Belgium, and Holland meet.[1] This calls to mind recent sensational proposals, launched in particular by the *Guardian*, to solve the Berlin crisis by moving the entire population of West Berlin, with its industrial and other equipment, bag and baggage, to a similar extraterritorial area.

OTHER EUROPEAN INSTRUMENTALITIES

1. *Western European Union*. This, which consists of the six Common Market countries plus the United Kingdom, dates from what is known as the Brussels Pact, signed in March, 1948. It was originally a defence arrangement, formed largely on the initiative of Anthony Eden, to bind the Western powers together. Then, when the European Defence Community, which envisaged the creation of a genuine pan-European army, was rejected, the Western European Union was inaugurated as a kind of temporary substitute. It still exists, but has scant importance now. Headquarters are in London, and the secretary-general is a Frenchman.

2. *The Council of Europe*. Essentially this derives from Sir Winston Churchill, who, as far back as 1946, was advocating reconciliation between France and Germany as the essential cornerstone of peace. It aims towards formation of a United States of Europe, and duplicates some of the membership of the European Parliament of the Common Market. The Council of Europe, broader in design than the European Parliament, has

[1] *Sunday Times*, August 28, 1960.

fifteen member states instead of seven, but it still is essentially a debating society without power to commit the member governments, and represents national rather than supranational views. Its president was John Edwards, a Labour member of the House of Commons, until his recent death, and the head of its permanent secretariat is an Italian, Ludovico Benvenuti. One of its auxiliary bodies is an interesting tribunal (devoted to 'the codification of international decency') called the European Court of Human Rights. Several countries now recognize the jurisdiction of this international court and it provides a forum—unique in European history—whereby a private citizen may bring action against his own sovereign government.[1]

3. *The Organization for European Economic Co-operation*, or OEEC—not, incidentally, to be confused with the EEC or European Economic Community. The OEEC, with its head-quarters at the Château de la Muette in Paris, and under British chairmanship, was originally set up in April, 1948, as a kind of executive agent for the Marshall Plan. It handed out the money. Originally it had, like NATO, fifteen members, and now has eighteen, including Spain and Switzerland. Jugoslavia is repre-sented by an observer. When the American aid programme wound up its activities, having spent £6,000 million, the OEEC continued to operate usefully, and became the essential mechanism for all manner of European financial and economic transactions. Now, as a result of initiative from Monnet and Douglas Dillon, who as American Ambassador to Paris had been intimately connected with its operations, it has been perpetuated in the form of a new body called the Organization for Economic Co-operation and Development. One obvious avenue for its future activity will be the administration of aid to underdeveloped countries.

4. *The General Agreement on Tariffs and Trade*, known as GATT. Twenty-three countries joined in 1948 to form this complicated organism, which is headquartered in the old League of Nations building in Geneva. Its members handle four-fifths of all world trade. In general what GATT tries to do is to ameliorate trade difficulties, and it relies on the old principle of most-favoured-nation treatment. This means that decisions have as a rule to be based on the lowest common denominator of

[1] The *Observer*, October 9, 1960.

acceptance, and this hampers progress. As Monnet says, 'Unanimity can be a killer.'

THE INDEFATIGABLE MR. MONNET

Jean Monnet, who recently turned seventy, is not only known as 'Mr. Europe'; he has been called the 'number one idea man of the continent', the 'chief merchandiser on the continent of social change', and 'the world's leading broker of ideas'. I have already listed some of his remarkable brain children. From first to last he has been a stimulator at large, an originator. Back in 1940 it was he who suggested to Winston Churchill the idea of a common Franco-British citizenship; twelve years later it was he who conceived the European Defence Community as a device for enabling a reformed Germany to rearm.

Monnet, born in Cognac and the scion of an illustrious family of French brandy manufacturers, has always been internationally minded; I have just come across a clipping from the *New York Times* (November 27, 1939), which describes him as a 'British' economist. He left school early, earned a fortune, and, no longer interested in acquiring money, became an assistant secretary of the League of Nations at the age of thirty-one. He took part in enterprises all the way from the Hudson's Bay Company to match factories in Sweden, and during the war was a purchasing agent in Washington for the French and British governments. His passport included a covering letter from Winston Churchill. I have already described enough of his postwar work to indicate the range of his activity. Lately he has set up an organization called the European Action Committee, which is devoted to lobbying for the creation of a United States of Europe.

Monnet's wife, a brilliant woman, is Italian; her name was Sylvia de Bondini, and she is a painter. Monnet met her some years ago when she was married to someone else. No divorce was possible under Italian law, and so Monnet—a practical man as well as an international visionary—contrived to take her to Moscow where, as it was once said, just marriage is grounds for divorce. She got a divorce promptly, and the Monnets have been happy ever since.

Edmond Taylor, writing recently in the *Reporter*, gave the best description of Monnet I have ever read.

Realism and flexibility are unquestionably characteristics of his powerful, complex mind . . . but it seems almost impossible to make any statement about him without immediately qualifying it somehow. In his personal habits . . . he is at once a sybarite and a Spartan, a finicky creature of delicate greeds, a sternly self-disciplined athlete who no longer smokes and rarely touches alcohol. . . . He loves authority and enjoys the limelight, but usually functions as a back room operator while others get the kudos or the blame earned by his ideas. He is courteous, arrogant, tyrannical, conciliatory, patient, and explosive.

When I last saw Monnet in Paris the main line of his talk was to emphasize the necessity of a long-range approach to matters of European unity. He said that such operations as the Council of Europe at Strasbourg represented, to his mind, an old-style method, that of trying to accomplish unity through political means. He wants to operate on a different level, and says, 'You can't change human nature, but you *can* change the attitude of people.' Psychological issues are what count. The Common Market treaties differ from any others in the history of the world in that they were not drawn up to fix up differences in the past, but to pave the way towards the future. There is a vast difference between a treaty of alliance, based on concepts of power, and those, based on the concept of unity, which become part of a 'process' leading to consolidation. Unity, he believes, can never be imposed by conquest; it can only come by evolution through co-operative means.

Monnet does not, unfortunately, get along well with General de Gaulle. This dates from the immediate post-war period, when Monnet, by aberration, supported a much flabbier man, General Giraud. European history might be quite different today if he had managed to bring de Gaulle, like Pleven, Mendès-France and Schuman, into his charmed circle. But de Gaulle hates anything that smacks of the supranational, and scorns Monnet for being an internationalist.

CHAPTER XX

Scandinavia—the Outer Bastions

TWENTY-FIVE years ago the Scandinavian countries were a refreshing pool of tranquillity outside the mainstream of European politics, untroubled by external events and devoted to their own rational, healthy, and fruitful development. Not quite the same thing can be said today, the obvious reason being the polarization of the world caused by the Cold War. The Scandinavian states are still healthy democracies, decently governed, modest, with social legislation more advanced than any country in the world except possibly New Zealand, but they are no longer isolated from the rest of Europe. Norway, Denmark, and Iceland are members of NATO; Finland is under strong Soviet influence; Sweden maintains a wary armed neutrality. World War I scarcely touched Scandinavia, but World War II brought a different story. The Nazis, as everybody knows, invaded and occupied Denmark and Norway in 1940, and the Russians fought Finland twice. The second Russo-Finnish War, known as the 'Continuation War', even caused a diplomatic break between Finland and the United States, and technically speaking Great Britain and Finland were, idiotically enough, at war for several years.

The Scandinavian countries are brothers—to paraphrase what I wrote in 1936—but, as is often the case with brothers, they are somewhat dissimilar in character. Denmark, the oldest kingdom in the world, is, speaking broadly, more 'continental' than Sweden and Norway—closer to the body of Europe. Denmark lives on butter, bacon and eggs, and is about twice the size of Wales, though its coastline, notched with indentations, is as long as that of European Russia. Sweden is a much larger country—the fourth largest in Europe, believe it or not—less intensively developed, living on water power and manufactured goods as well as on agriculture, and, in its northern emptiness, reminiscent of Alaska. The Swedes, by and large, are more formal than the Danes, stiffer, and more nationalist. The Norwegians, again speaking broadly, are more like the Danes than the Swedes, although Norway was part of Sweden till 1905. Norway is poorer than Sweden or Denmark, but not less sturdy. The Finns are a case apart, not merely because of the special characteristics of their topography, but because they derive from an altogether different stock. They have a strong Asiatic underlay, and their language belongs to the Finno-Ugric group. The old joke is that Finnish and Hungarian were once the same language, but that the Finns took all the vowels.

Sweden, Norway, and Denmark have closely interrelated royal families, and are members of a consultative group, the Nordic Council—Iceland and Finland too. Postal rates in Sweden, Denmark, and Norway are the same, the currency is more or less interchangeable, and the languages are similar. No slums; no illiteracy; powerful socialist parties; a high standard of living and the lowest infant mortality rates in the world; no delusions of national grandeur and genuine devotion to demo-cratic standards—these are all Scandinavian characteristics, just as before the war. But the aftermath of the war brought in new problems, issues, and developments.

*

As to Sweden (population 7 million, area 173,000 square miles), the dominant issues are defence, maintenance of its 'alliance-free status', and economic growth. One might also mention such items as that 60 per cent of the country is covered by woods and lakes, that the state religion is Lutheran but that all religions have freedom of status, and that its most distinguished citizen, after the incomparable Hammarskjöld, is probably Gunnar Myrdal, the sociologist who wrote the most commanding book on the Negro problem in the United States—*An American Dilemma*—ever written.

Sweden has had no war since 1814, a remarkable record, and the chief preoccupation of the country is to avoid being em-broiled in one. Its mechanisms towards this end are double. First, the policy of being altogether free of any political or military alliance that might produce entanglement. Sweden is a member of the UN and of several of its subsidiary bodies, but not of NATO. The Swedes were neutral in both world wars, but they are very firm to point out nowadays that their 'alliance-free policy' is not one of 'neutralism'; rather it is a positive policy—even potentially belligerent. If attacked, the Swedes will respond with vigour. Thus arises the second point. Sweden, although the figure is hard to believe, spends not less than 25 per cent of its budget on defence, a figure comparable to that of such 'non-neutral' powers as France, has what is probably the best army in Europe next to Switzerland and Jugoslavia, proudly possesses one of the two or three most powerful air forces in Europe, and is thinking of building its own defensive nuclear armoury. Another point is that the Swedes have constructed what are by all odds the most elaborate and ambitious underground air-raid shelters in the world—including enormous underground chambers hewn in the rock under parts of Stockholm—and its civil defence measures are probably more advanced than any other in Europe.[1]

In July, 1960, Dwight D. Eisenhower, speaking in Chicago, inadvertently caused a ferocious storm in all of Scandinavia, particularly Sweden, by referring to 'a fairly friendly European country' which had tried 'the experiment of almost complete paternalism' with the result that there had been a sharp rise in the suicide rate, 'lack of moderation', and more than twice American addiction to alcoholism. Obviously, although Denmark and Norway bristled, Sweden was Eisenhower's target, since he used the words 'fairly' friendly; this could only mean Sweden, since Norway and Denmark are American allies. The Swedes, as well as both the Norwegians and Danes, were quick to answer. One Norwegian newspaper said that Norwegians contemplating suicide got out of their predicament by going to the United States instead. Figures were adduced to deny Eisenhower's allegations. The highest suicide rate in the world is in West Berlin; Japan and Austria follow. The rate in Sweden is 19·9 suicides per 100,000 inhabitants, in the United States 10, and in Norway 7·4. As to beer consumption per inhabitant, the United States in 1954–57 consumed 63·9 litres per year, Sweden

[1] Legislation requires that every new building in Sweden must have an air-raid shelter in the basement capable of holding comfortably all the tenants.

28·7 litres, Norway 22 litres, and Denmark 0·8 litres. Sweden was, however, the leader in drinking hard liquor, with a consumption of 5·6 litres per inhabitant a year; the United States followed with 4·25, Norway with 2·23, and Denmark with 0·9.[1]

One of the pleasantest, most distinguished men in Europe today is Gustav VI Adolf, the King of Sweden, who was born in 1882 and did not ascend the throne until October, 1950, at the age of sixty-eight. His father, the estimable Gustav V, was long-lived. Next to Sweden, his chief interest is archaeology. Scandinavian monarchs are closely interrelated, and maintain cordial contact. Gustav VI Adolf's daughter, Princess Ingrid, is Queen of Denmark, having married Crown Prince Frederik IX of Denmark in 1935; he became king in 1947. Similarly, King Olaf V of Norway, who ascended the throne in succession to King Haakon VII in 1957, was married to Princess Martha of Sweden, who, before her death in 1954, spent much time in the United States and was well known in Washington. Of the three houses today the Swedish is the most regal. But all three kings comport themselves with democratic simplicity, and work in close harmony with socialist prime ministers; they are constitutional monarchs, and direct intervention in politics by any of the three would be impossible.

Tage Erlander, the Prime Minister of Sweden, was an editor by profession, and is distinguished by modesty, efficiency, and a nice hard-headedness. He was born in 1901. The circumstances of his official life are so informal that, when I called on him in Stockholm, I suddenly found myself, without being brought in by anybody, in a small, sunny, businesslike room; for a second I was not sure whether the man who rose to greet me (he was alone in the room) was the Prime Minister or one of his secretaries. No pomp in Swedish political circles! One question I asked Mr. Erlander was how it could be that Sweden, a small country, had no discernible fear of its elephantine neighbour, the Soviet Union. He replied quietly that the Swedes and Russians had had fights before, and that the Swedes had not come off too badly.

The Swedes have had a Social Democratic (socialist) government since the early 1930's. At present, following elections on September 18, 1960, the socialists are a minority by a slim

[1] New York *Post*, July 28, 1960.

margin, holding 114 out of 232 members in the Andra Kam-
maren, or lower house of Parliament. The government is,
however, outright Socialist, not a coalition. The opposition
parties are the Conservatives, Liberals, and Centrists. Together
these could out-vote the socialists—by one vote—but they have
not done so. The Communists are legal, got 3·4 per cent of the
vote in the last election, and have five seats in the Chamber.
Sweden takes its elections seriously, and politics are, in general,
restrained, orderly, and devoted to the common good. More
than 80 per cent of those eligible to vote did actually vote in
1960, one of the highest turnouts ever recorded in any country
in the free world.

One figure of consequence in Sweden is the veteran Foreign
Minister, Östen Undén, whose activity goes back to old League
of Nations days. He was a professor of international law by
vocation. No foreign minister in Europe is more subtle-minded,
rigid if need be, or tenacious.

*

Denmark, a member of NATO since its inception, has pronounced strategic importance because it controls the sea
approaches to the Soviet Union through the Baltic, and is a pivot
of the northern flank. The loyalty of the Danes to their international commitments, also their basic friendship for the West,
are unquestioned, but there are abundant neutralist tendencies
in the country. The Soviet Union continually tries to pry the
Danes out of NATO; the Danes resist these blandishments, but
at the same time seek to maintain as amicable relations with
Russia—also the satellites—as possible. They greeted the
Rapacki Plan as a constructive contribution, and H. C. Hansen,
the late Prime Minister and leader of the Social Democratic
party, recently paid a state visit to Belgrade. Denmark does not
allow the United States to maintain bases on its metropolitan
soil, and will have nothing to do with atomic weapons. On the
other hand, the United States is permitted to have an important
base on Greenland, which is part of Denmark, at the frozen
outpost known as Thule. This is a vital outpost in the American
ballistic missile early warning system. About six thousand US
troops are stationed there.

Denmark (population around 4·5 million, area 16,576 square miles) has, like Sweden and Norway, a middle-of-the-road socialist government which is long entrenched, enlightened, and effective. The social security programme is as advanced as any in Europe (nationalization is frowned upon, but there are strong economic controls); this is a welfare state *par excellence*, and one in which most citizens really enjoy life. The country lives largely on the export of fish and dairy products, but is rapidly becoming industrialized, and a lively economic boom is in progress.

The Social Democrats are the largest party, and won 76 out of the 179 seats in the Folketing, or Parliament, in a close election fought in November, 1960. Government coalitions usually include the Radical Liberal party, which represents rural elements (90 per cent of Denmark's tiny farms are cultivated by their owners), and a single-tax party known as the 'Liberal Georgists'. Denmark has a unicameral legislature. The single-taxers were wiped out in the last election, and the Radical Liberals, who are lukewarm about NATO, lost substantially. At the moment, the government has a majority of exactly one, and the balance of power is held by the representatives of Greenland and the Farö Islands, each of which is allotted two seats. On the opposition bench are, to the right, the Conservative and 'Moderate Liberal' parties with a total of seventy-five seats, which represent the business class, urban property owners, and the shipping interests. On the left are the Communists, who can be troublesome in Denmark. However, the Communist party split recently. A group known as the Socialist People's party, led by Aksel Larsen, takes a 'national' Communist line and stands moreover for nuclear disarmament. The worst sin of Communism, as was once said by a distinguished observer, is its exploitation of idealism; the major line of the Danish Communists is to exploit the latent pacifism of the people and try to draw left-wing socialists out of the Social Democratic party. What has hurt the Communist cause in Denmark more than anything since the war—this is true in the other Scandinavian countries as well—is Hungary. People, no matter how far on the left, simply could not stomach the massacre of Hungarian workers by the Red Army. The Hungarian affair was, in fact, the direct cause of the Larsen split. The Larsenists have eleven seats in the present Chamber, the official Communists none.

Viggo Kampmann, a vigorous Social Democrat, is Prime Minister. The Foreign Minister, a relative newcomer named Jens Otto Krag, who served in the Danish diplomatic service in Washington for a time, is one of the most discerning and competent in Europe. His wife, it happens, is a celebrated Danish film star, and is one of the prettiest young women ever known in a country famous for pretty women.

Several curiosities about Denmark should be noted. One is that for more than four hundred years—since 1513, to be specific —monarchs have alternately been named Christian and Frederik. There have been ten Christians, nine Frederiks. Another is that 9 per cent of all Danish births are illegitimate, and one out of every five marriages ends in divorce. This divorce rate is, however, not so high as that in the United States—where divorce terminates one out of 3·7 marriages.

Denmark has a remarkable institution known as the Ombudsman, as has Sweden. The function of the official who holds this post is to be a kind of protector-at-large for the citizenry *vis-à-vis* the state. Anybody who thinks that he has been treated unfairly by a court or who otherwise believes himself to be the victim of injustice may appeal to the Ombudsman, who at the moment is Professor Stephen Hurwitz. He has no judicial powers, but can bring grievances to sharp public attention, and it is his duty to do so. Any Dane jailed for any offence or incarcerated in a mental home has the right to appeal to the Ombudsman direct, without censorship. Other countries might well think of adopting this unique institution devoted to the permanent upholding of civil rights, and Norway is to do so soon.[1]

*

Iceland, a most peculiar little country (population around 180,000, about the same as that of Cambridgeshire; area 39,709 square miles, which is roughly the size of Ireland and Wales combined), has three principal issues: NATO, economic development, and fisheries. Government is by coalition, in which the socialists share. Four principal parties are represented in the unicameral parliament, or Althing: the Independents and the Progressives on the conservative side, and the Social Demo-

[1] The *Observer*, April 10, 1960.

crats and Communists on the other. The Communists, disguised under the name Labour Alliance, won 16 per cent of the vote in the 1959 elections, and have seven seats out of forty. The President of the Republic is Asgeir Asgeirsson. The Prime Minister, a member of the Independent party, is Olafur Thors (his brother is Ambassador to Washington), and the Foreign Minister, a Social Democrat, is Gudmundur I. Gudmundsson; all are worthy men. Ministers usually double up on portfolios, as in Luxembourg, because available personnel is scant.

The correct name of this little country, 'the most westerly in Europe', is Lydveldid Island; its history is ancient, its heritage distinguished, and its people isolated, inbred, and clannish. Iceland has no military establishment whatever, although its fishing fleet is armed. Also, uniquely in the world, it has no railways—or even navigable inland waterways. Travel is by bus or plane. Iceland has at one time or another been administered by both Norway and Denmark, but nationalist sentiment, fed by the ancient Icelandic sagas among other things, has always been spirited. The Danes recognized Iceland as a sovereign state in 1918, but both countries continued to be united under a common throne; in 1944 Iceland became a completely independent state, entered the UN two years later, and is an original NATO member.

The presence of American military installations at Reykjavik, the capital, has caused vehement controversy. Plenty of Icelanders, even if they are friendly to the United States, do not want their island to become nothing more than an American flat-top, and, in one angry period, all political parties in Iceland except the Independents joined to demand American withdrawal—throw the United States out. But when the Korean War came, Icelandic sentiment changed somewhat. Even so, a bitter election was fought on the issue of 'American occupation' in 1956; then occurred the Hungarian revolt. As a result of this the Icelanders modified their point of view again, and the American troops on Iceland (about four thousand) now rest there amicably. As to NATO, there can be no question of active Icelandic participation on the European mainland since the country has no armed forces, but its location gives it lively strategic importance; it commands the waterways near Greenland and the Farö Islands, which are essential paths for American

Navy forces, including Polaris-equipped submarines, *en route* to Arctic and Norwegian waters. Recently the US transferred one of its mobile early warning radar squadrons from Argentia, Newfoundland, to Iceland.[1]

Strange as it may seem, the nearest thing to armed conflict that has taken place in Europe since the Hungarian insurrection came in 1958 in consequence of an angry quarrel over fishing rights between Iceland and Great Britain. Ninety-five per cent of Icelandic exports are fish and fish products, and the catch is vital to the life of the nation; but the British also do much lucrative fishing near Iceland. To give themselves more room, the Icelanders extended the conventional three-mile limit for territorial waters to four miles. A dispute with the British followed, which a conference on the Law of the Sea held at Geneva in 1958 did not resolve. Then Iceland extended its limit to twelve miles. The British refused to accept this, since it seriously interfered with their catch, and their fishing vessels penetrated inside the twelve-mile limit, under protection of the Royal Navy; when Icelandic patrol ships tried to drive the British trawlers out, British warships intervened.[2] Two years later, after a second Geneva conference, the United Kingdom withdrew its naval forces, and a compromise is being worked out. An incidental point is that not less than one-quarter of Icelandic exports go to the Soviet Union. Another point is that the British faced an analogous situation over fishing rights *vis-à-vis* the Danes in the Farö Islands, which was settled without recourse to a threat of arms by either side.

*

We proceed now to Norway, as incorrigibly independent-minded, attractive, and idiosyncratic a country as any in the world. Until 1814, Norway was part of Denmark; it then became linked with Sweden, and did not finally become independent until 1905. A Danish prince, by name Carl, was elected King of Norway—one of the few sovereigns in the world

---

[1] Hanson W. Baldwin in the *New York Times*, December 19, 1960. One incidental point is that when NATO meetings are held in Paris or elsewhere, the Icelandic delegates attend political sessions but not military sessions.

[2] *An Atlas of World Affairs, op. cit.*, p. 58.

to reach his throne by such a means—and reigned for fifty-two years until his death in 1957, under the name of Haakon VII. Norway is the first country in the world in production of electricity, and has an extraordinarily long coastline; it has the fourth largest merchant fleet in the world, and lives mostly on sea and forest products. Only a minute 3 per cent of its area is arable, but its gross national product in 1959 was £1,700 million, a respectable enough figure for a country (area 125,064 square miles) with less than half the population of New York City—3·6 million. It produced a magnificent resistance movement during World War II, and one of its most distinguished citizens is Trygve Lie, first secretary-general of the United Nations. One curiosity is that, as a result of the Russian seizure of Petsamo from Finland, it has a common frontier—122 miles long—with Soviet Russia. Another is that, like the USA and Sweden, it once endured the agonies of prohibition, and still another is that it is obligatory for the king, of whom there have only been two in the modern period, to be a Lutheran. Both the king's daughters have, incidentally, married commoners.

Politics in Norway are stable, and the major parties agree on foreign policy. The government, not a coalition, is a straight-out Social Democratic ministry under the Labour party, which has 78 seats out of 150 in the Storting, or Parliament. Labour has, in fact, dominated Norwegian politics since 1935, and has never varied from a policy of middle-of-the-road progressivism, in which economic controls, planning, and high taxation play a role. The Communists are legal, and have one seat in the Storting. There are two conservative parties, one known as Liberal. The Prime Minister, Einar Gerhardsen, is well regarded, and his Foreign Minister, Helvard M. Lange, resembles to a degree Undén in Sweden, although he is younger —proficient, forward-looking, and both agile and tough in protecting his country's interests. Mr. Lange is generally credited with the accomplishment of having influenced Denmark and Iceland, as well as Norway, into joining NATO. His father won a Nobel Peace Prize, and—he lived in Britain for some years—he was once a member of the British Labour party.[1]

Norway is probably more solid on NATO than Denmark, but

[1] William L. Shirer, *The Challenge of Scandinavia*, p. 106.

not by much. Neutralist sentiment, despite an unalterable emotional kinship with the West, is pronounced. No American bases are permitted in Norway, although the United States has certain 'facilities' on Norwegian landing-fields; for instance, the ill-fated U-2 flight in May, 1960, was to have terminated in Norway. When the Soviet Union, following the U-2 flight, threatened to bomb any bases from which hostile action against the USSR was mounted, the Norwegians became considerably agitated. Subsequently Mr. Lange, though he is a firm supporter of NATO, asked Norway's allies 'not to strain the relationship between his country and the Soviet Union with incidents like the U-2 flight', and pointed out that Russia has 'legitimate security needs, which merit respect', and which Norway, a country with a common frontier with the Soviets, must regard carefully. The Rapacki Plan aroused much interest in Norway, and most Norwegians hope earnestly for a *détente* between the USSR and the Western powers.

*

Finally, Finland. This tough, worthy little state (area 130,148 square miles, population 4·4 million) is not, as I mentioned at the beginning of this chapter, Scandinavian in the true sense, but is strongly linked to Scandinavia, in particular to Sweden. The President of the Republic and the dominant political personality is Urho Kekkonen, who was elected in 1956 for a six-year term. He came into the news in remarkable circumstances when, just before the UN General Assembly in 1960, Khrushchev invited himself to Helsinki to help celebrate his sixtieth birthday. As a matter of fact, he knows Khrushchev well, and regards him highly; he had previously paid several state visits to Moscow, and Khrushchev and Bulganin visited Finland in 1957. The Finnish government, under Prime Minister Vaino Johannes Sukselainen, is a minority cabinet representing the Agrarian (moderate conservative) party, which has forty-seven seats out of two hundred in the one-chamber Eduskunta, or Parliament. But the biggest party is—a highly important point—the Finnish People's Democratic Union with fifty seats, a front organization for the Communists. The Social Democrats, who hold a quarter of the vote, are split between the regular variety, led by the anti-Communist veteran and grand old man of the country, Vaino Tanner, and the Skogist group, named after a dissident leader, Amil Skog. As to the Communist front party, it has not been a partner in any government coalition since 1948, despite its numerical strength, but it influences heavily most of the abstruse political manœuvring that goes on.[1]

Finland has all manner of peculiarities and distinctions. It was strongly under Swedish influence for centuries, but was annexed by Czarist Russia in 1809 and did not win national freedom until the Bolshevik Revolution in 1917. Swedish-speaking Finns still comprise 8 per cent of the population. The country has 55,000 lakes (which take up 9 per cent of its total area), and there are no fewer than thirty thousand islands off its coast. One-third of Finland lies above the Arctic Circle. Helsinki, like Copenhagen, is one of the most delightful small capitals in the world, and the Finns were the first people in Europe to give votes to women.

Finland, avowedly neutral, is not a member of NATO, and has close, intricate relations with the Soviet Union. The USSR is, after the United Kingdom, its principal customer. The Russians are careful to preserve the proprieties *vis-à-vis* Finland —some people say, in fact, that Finland is deliberately 'maintained' by the Russians as a showpiece, in order to demonstrate that they have no aggressive intentions towards small neighbouring democracies—and in 1955 made the considerable gesture of returning the Porkkala naval base to Finland. This, which they had seized in World War II, altogether dominates the military approaches to Helsinki, and the Finns were relieved to have it back. Then in 1960 the Soviets agreed to start negotiations for the return to Finland of the Saimaa Canal, an inland waterway important to the Finnish forestry industry, which they had also taken over in 1944. Finally, the USSR has, at the moment of writing, indicated that it will not object to entry by Finland into the Outer Seven—the European Free Trade Association—which the Finns want very much to join. Altogether Mr. Khrushchev is being conciliatory in the extreme to Finland, partly because he wants to counterbalance NATO influence in Scandinavia as a whole. In spite of all this, relations with Russia continue to be Finland's principal problem, and the

[1] 'Finland; A Survey, 1957-1960', *World Today*, January, 1961.

Kremlin could re-exert its stranglehold on the country at almost any time.

*

So now, coming to the end of this long and complicated European roundabout, we reach the Soviet Union and the bristly figure of Mr. Khrushchev, who dominates so much of European thought.

CHAPTER XXI

Khrushchev at the Summit

I HAVE attended a good many Press conferences in my time, some of them remarkable, but never one like that at the Palais de Chaillot in Paris, on Wednesday afternoon, May 18, 1960, when Nikita Sergeivitch Khrushchev tore open a grave for the Summit Conference, buried it, and, during two hours and forty-two minutes of outraged frenzy, spat venomously on the remains. Nobody among the three thousand or more journalists and officials who were present is ever likely to forget the experience, probably the most astounding one-man performance ever seen on a political stage—sordid, hair-raising, and unutterably bizarre.

My wife and I had lunch with David Douglas Duncan, the photographer, in the Crillon bar and left in a hurry to get to the Palais de Chaillot in good time. Of course, the audience was too big for any of the halls normally utilized for Press conferences, and the entire immense open lobby of the building, something like a concourse, was used instead. By the time we arrived it was half full; we dragged folding chairs from anterooms and pushed them forward. The hall filled up quickly; the atmosphere was electric, like that at Madison Square Garden before a really big fight. Acoustics were terrible and people behind us kept shouting '*Assis!*' as, from time to time, others rose in their excitement.

This was journalism in the modern age—no doubt about it. The square, hooded snouts of TV cameras protruded everywhere, and long rubber cables slithered over the floor. It was even possible to retreat to the far end of the hall and, while Khrushchev was speaking, take your choice of watching him in the flesh or, much more comfortably, seeing him on a TV screen at the identical instant. As far as I could tell, security arrangements had completely broken down. Nobody looked carefully at anybody's credentials, and it would have been easy for an intruder to have fired a shot or tossed a bomb. One extraordinary thing about Khrushchev is his obliviousness to security precautions. He is an obvious fatalist, and, unlike Stalin, must have been born without fear.

The Soviet Prime Minister entered the long, hot, noisy chamber, swirling with cigarette smoke, quivering in the light of sunbeams penetrating through broad windows, on time to the minute, and took his place on a dais flanked by Foreign Minister Andrei Gromyko, the Soviet Ambassador to Paris, by name Vinogradov, and none other than Marshal Rodion Y. Malinovsky, the Soviet Minister of Defence. Malinovsky, sitting there rigidly, looked like a grey-blue thumb.

Khrushchev rose to speak, and, as almost everybody will remember, was truculent, scornful, cocksure, diabolically clever, and, as usual, full of his own peculiar brand of peasant earthiness. When he was booed he said contemptuously that the demonstrators must be West German 'riff-raff' who had somehow escaped from Stalingrad, and whom Dr. Adenauer had shipped to Paris. But he was obviously stung by the boos and hisses and, as Russians always do, instantly projected the insult in the personal sphere to a political level. It was the Soviet Union that was being booed, not merely Mr. K., and he began at once to rant about victory in 'the great October Revolution', the 'leadership of the great Lenin', and so on. He always beats a subject to death. On this occasion, for two or three moments, he could not let alone the fact that he had been booed, and exclaimed, 'This booing heartens me, heartens and gratifies me. . . . I am speaking of this German riff-raff and not of the great German people. . . . I shall not conceal my pleasure. . . . I like coming to grips with the enemies of the working class and it is gratifying to me to hear the frenzy of these lackeys of imperialism.'

There were two celebrated passages about, of all things, cats. The first came in answer to a question as to whether or not Mr. K. still hoped for another Summit Conference in the future. He answered in the affirmative, but then added that there were difficulties, one of which was 'American aggression':

Ladies and gentlemen, we all have mothers, you all do, too,

otherwise you could not have come into this world. I remember during my youth—I was born in a very poor family, and it was only very rarely that my mother could buy us some cream, but sometimes when she did our cat would creep up and eat some of the cream and steal some of the cream. Then my mother usually took the cat by the scruff of the neck and gave it a good shaking, and in the end would poke its nose into the cream to make it understand that such stealing was not allowed. Would it be better, ladies and gentlemen, to grab the American aggressors by the scruff of the neck also and give them a little shaking and make them understand that they must not commit such actions of aggression against the Soviet Union?

Towards the finish he became more moderate:

I want to end by saying that the Soviet Union will continue to adhere to the policy of peaceful coexistence between the two systems, the capitalist and the socialist. We will continue to pursue the policy of peace, aimed at solving all questions at issue by negotiations.

Winding up, he permitted himself a mild joke—that it was time to adjourn because the interpreters were getting tired. They were working overtime, he said, and he wanted to respect the labour code! The mob began to scatter. I escaped from the building, and took a taxi back to my hotel. The driver said cynically, 'They'll be calling the Chaillot the "Palais de Khrushchev" before very long.'

*

So, in this crepuscular blaze, ended the aborted Summit. Five years of scrupulous, painstaking effort by the governments of the United States, the Soviet Union, the United Kingdom and France went for nothing. All the tentative good will laboriously built up so assiduously went down the drain—at least for the time being. It seemed, after a period of relative respite and amelioration, that the cold war would resume with full severity. The unprecedented trip taken by Mr. Khrushchev to the United States in 1959, culminating in the conversations with President Eisenhower at Camp David, lost its meaning. Eisenhower's own trip to Russia, which had been scheduled for June, 1960, was called off when the Soviet Premier, with maximum rudeness, withdrew the invitation. And, let it not be forgotten, Mr. K. had looked forward to the Eisenhower visit as something supremely important, and the President, if he had reached Moscow, would have received there one of the most triumphant —and masterfully organized—receptions in contemporary history, if only because he would have been greeted as a symbol of peace.

Khrushchev had worked strenuously for a Summit for years, and wanted it desperately. Why, then, did he do what he did in Paris? *Why* did he torpedo the Summit, and by so doing murder his own dream?

Hundreds of thousands of words have been written about this, and the whole subject still calls forth blistering controversy. But, though they are interlocking factors, the main reason is simple enough. Given the background, Khrushchev's behaviour was not so irrational as it may have seemed to be. Mr. K. wrecked the Summit because of the U-2 affair. It is quite possible, as several commentators have pointed out, that the Summit Conference would have been a failure even if it had taken place, because of a misunderstanding between Khrushchev and Eisenhower as to exactly what had taken place at Camp David in reference to Berlin, but it certainly would have *met* at least if the U-2 had not made its overflight. The U-2 gave the Russian Premier a convenient pretext for behaving as he did, but it was much more than a mere pretext. Khrushchev destroyed the Summit because of a young man named Francis Gary Powers.

U-2

We do not have the space to go into the story of the U-2 at length. Scraping it to the bare bones, we have the following. On Sunday, May 1, a special type of Lockheed single-pilot plane capable of sustained flight at extremely high altitudes, and known as the U-2, which was based on Adana, Turkey, and piloted by Mr. Powers, took off from a base near Peshawar, Pakistan, for a photographic-espionage flight over the Soviet Union. It was a kind of glider; ironically, the 'U' stands for 'utility'. It was shot down near Sverdlovsk, the great Soviet industrial and mining city in the Urals, after it had been in flight some 1,250 miles. We do not know at what altitude it was shot down—or precisely how. The U-2, flying at seventy thousand feet or even higher, was believed to be altogether immune from any kind of attack. The Russians assert that it was intercepted by rocket fire. Possibly it had a flame-out, was forced to descend to a vulnerable altitude, and was then shot down. Of course, it was totally unknown to the world at large that the United States had, in circumstances of absolute secrecy, been operating U-2 flights for almost four years, and that there had been no fewer than thirty successful flights over Soviet territory.

On Tuesday, May 3, American officials in Turkey announced that 'a plane belonging to the National Aeronautics and Space Administration' had been missing since May 1 'on a flight from Incirlik Air Base near Adana'. This appeared to be a routine item, and caused little stir. But it is still not clear why the US authorities chose to let the cat out of the bag with this brief announcement. It gave the Russians a chance to set a trap with sharp teeth. Moreover, it was misleading. The plane may have belonged to the NASA, but it was being operated by the Central Intelligence Agency, and even if it had taken off from Incirlik, it was nowhere near Turkish air space when it was brought to earth. Then on Thursday, May 5, came a corrosive sensation. Prime Minister Khrushchev, addressing a meeting of the Supreme Soviet in Moscow, announced that an American plane which 'bore no identification signs' had been caught in a flagrant violation of Soviet air space, and had been summarily shot down. An immense hullaballoo followed.

Meantime Washington issued a 'cover' story to 'explain' the flight. The NASA, a civilian agency charged with American space projects, announced—also on May 5—that one of its U-2 research aeroplanes, in use since 1956 in a 'continuing programme to study gust-meteorological conditions found at high altitudes', had been missing since Sunday, when its pilot reported that 'he was having oxygen difficulties over Lake Van, in Turkey'—a blatant lie. The announcement stated further that the pilot was a civilian, that his plane was unarmed, that he 'might have blacked out from lack of oxygen', and that, as a result, his aircraft 'might have continued automatically towards the Russian border'. Of course, Washington assumed that Powers must be dead. One of their announcements even gave out his name—which subsequently made it impossible for them to attempt to disclaim him. Still pretending innocence, the US sent a note to Moscow asking for details of the occurrence, and, as a hedge towards future eventualities, announced that the American government had grounded for fifteen days all 'foreign-based U-2 weather observation planes' in order 'to permit checking of their equipment'.

Then, falling more deeply into the trap, the State Department attempted to nullify the storm caused all over the world by Khrushchev's revelation by stating flatly the next day (May 6) that 'there was absolutely no—NO—deliberate attempt to violate Soviet air space . . . and had never been'.[1]

This played perfectly into Mr. K's tricky hand. Speaking again to the Supreme Soviet on Saturday, May 7, he gave out full details of the U-2 flight, announced that the plane had not been too badly damaged when it landed, produced some of the photographs it took, and, above all, revealed that Mr. Powers, far from having been killed in the crash or having killed himself subsequently as good spies are always supposed to do, was very much alive—a prisoner in Soviet hands, who had already given the Russians a detailed account of his activities. Moreover, he produced a fantastic array of paraphernalia Powers was carrying, including Soviet roubles, foreign money, gold, arms, a suicide kit, a Russian phrase book, and a handful of watches and rings! The CIA equips its emissaries well.

All this, obviously, blew up the American cover story, and the United States found itself humiliatingly embarrassed. Khrushchev, with maximum cleverness, had withheld news that Powers was alive until Washington fell into his neatly contrived trap. To this day some of the tangles that followed have not been completely unravelled. Khrushchev flamingly denounced the United States and told Turkey, Pakistan, and Norway (to which country Powers was *en route*) that they would be held severely to account if they continued to participate in 'hostile acts against the Soviet Union'. On the other hand, a highly suggestive point, he was extremely careful to give President Eisenhower opportunity for disowning responsibility for the flight. He intended, of

---

[1] Authority for most of this chronology is the *New York Times*. Also see the *New Republic*, May 23, 1960, Douglass Cater in the *Reporter* (June 9, 1960), and Henry Brandon in the *Sunday Times*, May 29, 1960.

course, to make copious use of the U-2 incident for both political and propaganda purposes, but he still most earnestly wanted the Summit Conference to take place, and tried to manœuvre so that the President himself could wriggle off the hook. Washington's response was confusing; various agencies of the American government haltingly told conflicting stories. On May 7 the State Department announced that as a result of an inquiry ordered by the President, 'it has been established that . . . there was no authorization for any such flights as those described by Mr. Khrushchev'. However, it proceeded to admit that, 'in endeavouring to obtain information now concealed behind the Iron Curtain, a flight over Soviet territory was *probably* [italics mine] undertaken by an unarmed civilian plane'. In other words the US seemed to be admitting that U-2 flights took place, but 'without authorization'; that is to say, the highest authorities of the American government did not know what was going on in this most sensitive of spheres. This made everything worse. So, on May 9, Secretary of State Herter announced that the President *had*, after all, known about the flights—moreover, that they would continue. On Wednesday, May 11, Eisenhower assumed personal responsibility for the incident, which Khrushchev had desperately hoped he would *not* do, at almost the very moment that Mr. K., in Moscow, held an informal Press conference at which he showed correspondents the wreckage of the U-2 and some of its equipment.

Meantime international tension mounted furiously. The French and the British, it seemed, had never been informed in detail about the U-2 operations and were naturally apprehensive as to the course of events with the Summit scheduled to open on the Monday following. Khrushchev kept on blasting away at Turkey, Pakistan and Norway, and the Norwegians felt it necessary to protest to the United States about the original schedule for the flight. The Pakistanis were particularly dismayed. All over the world, nervousness increased. Some people scoffed at the implications of the affair, but then Khrushchev scored another point by asking what the American reaction would have been if a Soviet espionage plane, in the week before the Summit, had been shot down over Omaha or Kansas City.

The first phase of this sorry story came to an end when, after various hesitations and equivocations, Mr. Herter reversed himself, and, after arrival in Paris, announced that American overflights above Russia had been suspended and would not be resumed. But this came too late to save the conference. Khrushchev, far from being mollified, exploded in exacerbated polemics as soon as he reached Paris, and demanded, as a price for taking part in the Summit, that the United States apologize for its 'aggression' and punish those responsible.

*

Post-mortems on the American side were vigorous. James Reston, writing in the *New York Times* on May 21, broke through a cloud of propaganda designed to protect the President by saying flatly, 'Mr. Eisenhower was responsible, directly or indirectly, for the greatest series of humiliating blunders suffered by the United States in a decade.' Senator Fulbright, reporting to the Senate, said that 'we forced Khrushchev to wreck the conference by our own ineptness', and cited two cardinal blunders among others: (a) the order to put the U-2 into flight on May 1 so close to the Summit date; (b) the disastrous decision whereby the President himself assumed personal responsibility for the flight.[1] Normally governments— in particular, heads of state—simply deny all knowledge if they are caught in a spy affair.

Walter Lippmann wrote in the New York *Herald Tribune*:

> We must remember that when the plane was captured, Mr. Khrushchev opened the door to the President for a diplomatic exit from his quandary: he did not believe, said Mr. K., that Mr. Eisenhower was responsible for ordering the flight. . . . The diplomatic answer would have been to say nothing at the time, or at the most to promise an adequate investigation of the whole affair. Instead Mr. Eisenhower replied that he *was* responsible, that such flights were necessary, and then he let the world think, even if he did not say so in exact words, that the flights would continue. This locked the door which Mr. Khrushchev had opened. It transformed the embarrassment of being caught in a spying operation into a direct challenge to the sovereignty of the Soviet Union.

[1] Mr. Fulbright even said, 'It is difficult to see how anyone could have been expected to act substantially different from the way Chairman Khrushchev acted under the circumstances which confronted him in Paris.'

Adlai Stevenson, speaking at a Democratic dinner in Chicago, said that although it was Mr. Khrushchev who wrecked the conference, 'we handed him the crowbar and the sledge-hammer'. Mr. Stevenson's analysis follows:

We sent an espionage plane deep into the Soviet Union just before the Summit meeting. Then we denied it. Then we admitted it. And then when Mr. Khrushchev gave the President an 'out' by suggesting that he was not responsible for ordering the flight, the President proudly asserted that he was responsible. . . . Next we evidently reconsidered and called off the espionage flights. But to compound the incredible, we postponed the announcement that the flights were terminated just long enough to make it seem that we were yielding to pressure, but too long to prevent Mr. Khrushchev from reaching the boiling point.

Still another eminent American put it this way:

The Administration first issued a lie; then a set of contradictory statements; third, an over-frank confession of our guilt; and finally and belatedly an announcement of the suspension of the flights.

Who said this? None other than the junior Senator from Massachusetts—John F. Kennedy.[1]

We revert now to the question put forward earlier—why did Khrushchev exploit the U-2 incident to the extent that he did? This is particularly puzzling because the Soviet high command certainly knew that previous overflights had occurred. In fact, Khrushchev publicly mentioned one as having taken place on April 9. Obviously the Powers plane could not have been tracked and intercepted with such precision if the Russians had not been lying in wait for it. The Soviet Prime Minister was, in view of this, asked at his May 18 Press conference why, since he knew about the flights, he had not protested to President Eisenhower about them when he visited the United States. Khrushchev's reply is interesting:

I will answer that question with pleasure. When we were talking in Camp David with President Eisenhower, I almost opened my

[1] Senator Kennedy also stated on May 30 that he would not approve resumption of espionage flights if he became President. Shortly after his inauguration in 1961 he reaffirmed this policy.

mouth to make that statement. I was on the point of making it, because the atmosphere there was so convivial, and with President Eisenhower calling me, telling me to call him 'my friend' in English and calling me, using the same word with regard to myself in Russian. And then, thought I, why not raise the matter with this friend of mine? But then I became apprehensive. I thought there was something 'fishy' about this friend of mine, and I didn't approach the subject, and it turned out that I was right, because when we caught them red-handed, they say that they are not thieves, it is just their thief-like policy, that is all.

At this point came Mr. K's second reference to cats:

This recalls to my mind what we used to do in the Donbas when I was a young boy. Whenever we caught a cat in the pigeons' loft, we would catch the cat by the tail and bang its head against the wall. That is the only way that it could be taught some sense.

Later, when Khrushchev had proceeded to the phase of talking about Eisenhower with open contempt—for instance, as a golf player fit only to run a children's home—he was asked again why Russia had not protested about the flights and replied:

We had no material *evidence* to prove such intrusions, and the Soviet government considered therefore that it would be a waste of time to issue protests.[1]

Here indeed is the crux of one aspect of the matter. After the Powers flight Mr. K. had a *corpus delicti*—the proof, the goods. Moreover, although the Russians had been aware of the over-flights, they did not know *what their results were* until the Powers films were developed. Apparently it had never dawned on them that the terrain of the Soviet Union could have been—and obviously had been—mapped with such terrifyingly comprehensive and detailed accuracy. Khrushchev discovered suddenly that the United States knew infinitely more about Soviet military, nuclear and other installations than anybody in Russia had ever conceived, and, naturally, since a large part of Russian bluster is founded on weakness and fear, this gave fresh fuel to his rage.

But why, granting the above, did he bother to come to Paris

[1] *New York Times*, May 29, 1960.

at all? If a definite decision had been taken in Moscow—before Saturday, May 14—not to take part in the conference, why did he not simply announce this from the Kremlin and stay at home? Surely a double answer applies here. First, he had been presented—gratis—with a magnificent forum for spilling out effective propaganda. Second, by making the affair a public issue, he hoped to split the Western Allies. But de Gaulle and Macmillan kept their heads. There is a third possibility as well, though it is difficult to credit—namely, that Khrushchev, totally misunderstanding American temperament and character, *may* have thought that Eisenhower would accept his ultimatum, apologize, and otherwise fulfil his impossible conditions, although full acceptance of these would have meant that Eisenhower would have had to punish himself or, at the least, throw Allen W. Dulles, head of the CIA, in jail.

Now as to other factors:

1. Khrushchev had publicly expressed admiration for Eisenhower in effusive terms, and was, as mentioned above, preparing for him what would certainly have been one of the greatest demonstrations of welcome in political history. There is no record of any head of a Communist state talking about any head of a capitalist state in terms as warm, even affectionate, as Khrushchev used about Eisenhower until the eve of the Summit. He positively cooed with the 'Camp David spirit'. Moreover, he was on record with innumerable statements about the bright prospects of peaceful coexistence. Therefore when Eisenhower took responsibility for the U-2, several complementary factors entered into play. First, Khrushchev felt betrayed and was, beyond doubt, crushed with personal disappointment. Second, his prestige was gravely shaken. Against considerable opposition, he had staked a great deal on friendship with the President and trust in him. Now his hopes were shattered, and his colleagues in the Kremlin could taunt him for his *naïveté* and departure from the normal Party line. Therefore he had to be doubly ugly, doubly violent, in his behaviour at the Summit, in order to dissociate himself from Eisenhower. His attitude was, 'Treat me like a dumb *muzhik*, and I'll show you how a *muzhik* can behave!'

2. China probably played a role. Immediately after his return from Washington Khrushchev had proceeded to Peking, where

Mao Tse-tung is supposed to have received him with marked coolness. The Chinese leader even spoke of 'certain people' who had been 'misled into trusting Eisenhower'.[1] So Mr. K. felt impelled to prove to Mao, as to the Kremlin Stalinists, that he was back on the right track, and that everything that had gone wrong was Eisenhower's fault.

3. Nobody to this day knows precisely what happened in regard to Berlin at Camp David. Eisenhower, a nice man, wanted to be nice, and, almost beyond doubt, Khrushchev interpreted either the sense or the mood of what he said as indicating that the West might be prepared to make large concessions on Berlin. Misunderstandings of this kind are a frequent result of informal personal contact between leaders. Diplomacy, as Harold Nicolson once wrote sapiently, should be the art of negotiating *written* agreements. Subsequently, when it became clear before the Summit that the United States had not the faintest idea of changing its course on Berlin, Khrushchev became enraged. His policy of relying on Eisenhower had failed, as his colleagues in Moscow were no doubt quick to point out. But Berlin *alone* would not have caused the breakdown.

4. 'The secret of Russian fury, Russian indignation, over the U-2 is Soviet *fear of war*.' I heard this remark in London shortly after the Summit breakdown. Its author was one of the wisest and most discerning Russians I know—not a Communist—and it tells much. Russia has always been extraordinarily sensitive to anything that touches on its sacred soil. One could go into examples from time immemorial. Moreover, secrecy plays a role in Russian administration to a degree scarcely understandable in the West. The Powers plane was a symbol of invasion, nothing more nor less, and it was prying into secrets and disturbing precious security as well. Khrushchev had to show his people that he was not afraid of the Americans, no matter how the illusion of Soviet invulnerability was disturbed by the U-2 episode.

Somewhat lamely, Americans in Paris during the Summit talked about the fact that Khrushchev had mentioned the 'internal political needs of the Soviet Union' during his Palais de Chaillot speech, an unusual thing to do, and was moreover invariably accompanied on public occasions by the stout and

[1] The *Observer*, May 22, 1960.

formidable-looking Marshal Malinovsky. Thus it was often intimated that the real motives for Khrushchev's behaviour were political disaffection at home, together with restiveness in the Red Army. This, in turn, was supposed to be the result of resentment at the drastic way Khrushchev, to save money and to relieve the labour shortage, has pared down the numerical strength of the Soviet armed forces. In particular some 250,000 Red Army officers have been displaced, and the army itself cut by 1·2 million men.

All that one can say to this is that, at the moment, no jot of evidence has come to the surface which supports these suppositions. It is entirely possible that Khrushchev may confront serious domestic trouble in time. But it seems almost inconceivable, in view of events during the past months, that military disaffection could have had much, if anything, to do with the Summit. Malinovsky is an out-and-out Khrushchev man, neither ambitious nor distinguished by much independence of mind. Probably Khrushchev brought him to Paris as a witness to confirm to the Kremlin what had happened—also as a symbol demonstrating Russian military might to the West.

THE REALM OF RESULTS

Finally, results. Khrushchev certainly got one thing at least— suspension of the overflights. On the other side of the fence, it is equally clear that, since 1956, the CIA had superintended one of the most stupendous espionage jobs in history, which must have collected an inestimably valuable mass of material about Soviet industrial and military installations—perhaps about similar installations in other Communist countries as well.

Set against this is the possibility that, having been amply alerted by the U-2 fiasco, the Russians have been busy ever since changing the locations of such installations as they can move, and the fact that, since the flights have not been resumed, we have no ready means for investigating such alterations.

In the political field there can be little doubt that the United States in particular and the Western Allies in general suffered an embarrassing defeat. To many citizens the revelation that the United States was willing to utter flagrant lies on a matter of supreme public interest was a severe disillusion. But spying is, and always has been, dirty work. Certainly never in history has there been such a piquant example of the pot calling the kettle black. It is, indeed, laughably ironic that the Soviet Union, a power more addicted to espionage than any other in the world, should of all countries have taken the holier-than-thou position of being an 'innocent' plaintiff in the Powers case. However, it cannot be gainsaid that the West suffered. Papers like the *Sunday Express* talked about 'an utterly unnecessary and stupidly provocative flight', and warned its readers that the fate of the world was 'in the trigger-happy fingers of a handful of American generals'. In a more serious sphere the alarm and embarrassment caused to various American allies must be reckoned with. American prestige fell substantially in various quarters of the world. Marshal Malinovsky, on his return to Moscow, announced that he had given orders to the Soviet rocket forces to strike instantly at any base from which any foreign aircraft infringed on Russian air space or that of Soviet allies. Thus the issue of American bases was dramatized everywhere, tendencies to neutralism increased, and among other things this led to the humiliating cancellation of President Eisenhower's scheduled visit to Japan.

On the other hand, over-all dislocations have not been so severe as might have been expected. Observers thought, immediately after the Summit break-up, that the Russians might move against Berlin, but, as was mentioned many pages earlier in this book, Khrushchev made a speech on his arrival in East Berlin which was remarkably temperate on the whole. Negotiations between the United States and the Soviet Union were slowed down, but did not break off. There was no diminution of activity in such fields as cultural exchange or American tourist traffic into Russia. The cold war is still going on, but for the moment it did not become much hotter. Finally, the collapse of the Summit probably had some value to the West in that it showed once and for all—if we still needed to know—the formidable character of the Khrushchev leadership.

THE PAVLOV ANALOGY

On May 18, 1960, *The Times* printed a remarkable letter from Dr. William Sargant, a distinguished British professor of psychological medicine, which pungently expressed the view that Khrushchev's behaviour in Paris, as well as analogous Soviet behaviour elsewhere, was based on the theories of Dr. Ivan Petrovich Pavlov, the renowned Russian physiologist who died in 1936. Pavlov, who won a Nobel Prize back in 1904, was the originator of the theory of the conditioned reflex—whereby dogs, as an example, salivate or have other physical reactions in response to such stimuli as the ringing of bells or mild electric shocks. Pavlov, even though he was never a Communist, worked for many years under the Communist system, and has become a major Soviet hero since his death. It was certainly not news that the Russians often employ the conditioned reflex principle in their educational and propaganda techniques. Push a button: a robot works. This is to over-simplify the Pavlovian concept, but there is no doubt that the Pavlov techniques have for a long time been a kind of psychological underpinning to much of the practice of the Soviet régime—for instance brainwashing.

Dr. Sargant went further. He suggested that Soviet statesmen of the present day were deliberately using Pavlovian methods to break down the 'nervous stability' of the bourgeois West, just as they have learned precisely how to break down nervous stability in dogs and other animals and thus produce in them 'states of uncontrollable neurotic excitement, which may lead later on to hysterical and submissive behaviour, and finally even to depressive apathy'.

The theory is an elaboration of the technique of 'blow hot, blow cold'. The Russian practice is to give 'positive and negative signals' calculated to make the British and American Press and public 'as bewildered, confused and suggestible as . . . Pavlov's dogs'. Russian policy, Professor Sargant proceeded, may seem 'absolutely bewildering to the Pavlovian uninitiated'. But Pavlov provides a clue that it would be well to take seriously. The Russians project lightning-quick changes of signal as a coldly calculated, deliberately planned exercise in psychological warfare, in order to baffle opponents, break down resistance, and make sure that we—the equivalent of the unhappy dogs in Leningrad—are mesmerized into ineffectiveness or even incoherence.

The Sargant letter produced a sheaf of lively and provocative replies. Dozens of experts—ranging from other scientists to diplomats and military men—wrote their observations to the letter column of *The Times*. One of Dr. Sargant's suggestions was that an effective answer to the Soviet technique would be to ignore it. This, several commentators suggested, was not sufficient defence. Escapism, in other words, is no solution. Other correspondents pointed out that the Sargant argument is somewhat far-fetched, in that the western peoples have not by any means been conditioned 'by a uniform series of stimuli'. One writer who joined the dispute in *World Today* went so far as to say, probably with tongue in cheek, that it might be the erratic behaviour of the *West* which the more truly represented Dr. Pavlov, and that the Soviet Union was the real victim, about to fall prey to 'mental confusion and ultimate breakdown'.

The following letters reflect different points of view in the columns of *The Times*:

> Surely Dr. Sargant's analysis of Russian methods . . . carries a lesson for the citizens of all bureaucratic-ridden, over-governed countries, including the United Kingdom. It is that the co-operative and conscientious dog always gets the cruellest treatment.

And:

> I think a spy is a valuable, though unrecognized, public servant. He should be praised for helping to avoid surprise and even to prevent wars. . . . Traditionally he went on foot; then on a horse; then in a motor-car; and now in an aeroplane. Why all this fuss about one of the oldest and most useful professions in the world?

Perhaps the last word belongs to a correspondent, A. D. Ingram, who wrote on May 24: 'I think it should be remarked that Mr. Khrushchev's recent behaviour is really less reminiscent of Pavlov than of Pavlov's dog.'

All this being said, we should reiterate, on a serious level, that Soviet policy has for years been distinguished by a phenomenal amount of tactical zigzagging, whether or not Pavlov is responsible. Pressure and seeming relaxation are employed turn by turn. Examples are available in realms all the way from Laos and Cuba to the current negotiations for a nuclear test ban.

KHRUSHCHEV AT THE UN

After the Paris Summit Mr. K's next *coup de théâtre* was his

twenty-five-day performance at the UN General Assembly in
New York in September-October, 1960. This marked his second
visit to the United States, and he came (by slow boat) un-
invited; rather, he appointed himself chairman of the USSR
delegation to the Fifteenth Assembly, and thus could not be kept
away. American authorities restricted his movements to Manhattan and the Soviet enclave on Long Island. This, even if it
was an annoyance, did not daunt him, and from his Park Avenue
balcony he made naughty little quips about being under 'house
arrest'.

Seldom in memory has there been such a *mélange* of odd fish
and international celebrities gathered in one city at the same time
—Castro, Nasser, Nehru, Sukarno, Nkrumah, Tito, Gomulka,
Macmillan, Hammarskjöld, Eisenhower—but Khrushchev was
the star. I watched him closely at several receptions, including one given by the Indians, one by the Indonesians. The
picture was always the same. No matter who else turned up, few
guests had eyes for anybody except Mr. K. He would bounce
into the room, pudgy and smiling, tiptoeing, leaning forward
earnestly, alert and attentive, to be swallowed up instantly by a
pushing, shouldering mob of journalists, other guests, and
kibitzers. One of Khrushchev's prime qualities, which all true
stars have, is magnetism. Not only for what he is but for what he
represents, people break their necks to get a close glimpse of
him, or overhear a private word.

In New York, Mr. K. was obnoxious, obstreperous, and out-
rageous—a scamp. He was also earthy, good-humoured on
occasion, resilient, unquenchable, ribald, tenacious, and a man
with a positive genius for saying the last word. He was odious,
but in some monstrous way not unattractive. His volatility was
a challenge. At times he seemed to have forgotten all about the
Summit four months before, and it did not even occur to him
that there were good reasons why President Eisenhower, whom
he had wantonly insulted, might not be happy to receive him.
Having done his best to destroy Hammarskjöld, a signal
wickedness, he embraced him cordially at a cocktail party the
next day. His relations with the United States had never been
more strained, but he did his best to crush James J. Wadsworth,
the American Ambassador to the UN, with a jovial bear hug—
but Wadsworth, who weighs 240 pounds, was too stout for

him to embrace—when they encountered one another at a reception.

One evening when journalists asked Mr. K. to say something about disarmament, a reporter for the New York *Herald Tribune* wrote that he at once 'innocently made a show of searching his pockets, thus to indicate that he had no gun, no bomb, no rocket'. He did, however, produce a small penknife. Opening it with a flourish he chortled, 'How can anybody puncture such a sack as Wadsworth with a little thing like this?' A few days later, he was capable of publicly calling an innocuous Filipino delegate a 'jerk', described the Security Council as a 'spittoon', and, as has become famous, tore off his shoes during a speech at the Assembly, waving them and banging with them on his desk.

Khrushchev in shirt sleeves conducted nocturnal interviews from his perch at the Soviet Embassy with newspapermen clamouring on the street twenty feet below, sang one night a few bars of the Communist hymn, 'The Internationale', and even, in a mock gesture of respect, pretended to be leading an orchestra and 'conducted' a passage or two from 'The Star-Spangled Banner' when he heard it across the street. He said that Eisenhower's speech to the General Assembly was 'soft music without content', suggested that a well-known correspondent of the *New York Times* should run for President of the United States, and solicitously asked Miss Marguerite Higgins of the New York *Herald Tribune*, who had recently given birth to a child, whether the infant was a boy or a girl. He joked with Edmund Stevens, the correspondent in Moscow of *Time*, about his beard, compared some hostile demonstrators on the street to the material that one may find under a horse, and, when he was roundly booed by a group of fashionable dowagers at the Hotel Plaza, roundly shouted 'Boo!' to them in return.

He scooted up to Harlem to visit Castro, denounced the Monroe Doctrine, promised to 'launch rockets if the United States attacked Cuba', and said that factories in the USSR were turning out space missiles 'like sausages'. He conceded that the police in New York behaved well, in the manner of good police everywhere, said that he felt that he ought to stay long enough in America to justify his expense account, announced after a private talk with Mr. Macmillan that 'our noses and hands are still in the same place', told journalists that he did not expect to start a war that night so that they could go home and sleep in peace, denied that he had destroyed the spirit of Camp David, said that it didn't matter if he was still in the United States at election time since he couldn't vote, and, when a reporter asked him if the Russian government was elected by the people, replied, 'Didn't you know that in our country we have no trousers to wear? Really, run quick and find out.'

He shouted jovially, 'Down with Gromyko!' when Gromyko, his Foreign Minister, was unaccountably late for some function, teased several of his Communist colleagues for being fat, said that if the US tried to intimidate him or 'sink his ship' he would go down to the bottom dragging America along, bored the General Assembly for two and a half dreary hours on disarmament, accepted an Indian pipe of peace from an American well-wisher, announced that he was for both the Pirates and the Yankees (the World Series was going on), said that he would sit down alone in a locked room with Eisenhower 'for as long as was necessary' to achieve an agreement on disarmament, and, when he was asked one morning if he had slept well, replied with emphasis, 'As always!'

Behind this fantastic mumbo-jumbo there were, of course, serious realities. Khrushchev did not come to the UN to be a vaudeville performer, but to attain concrete political objectives. First, he wanted to make use of the UN as a forum for propaganda purposes. Second, he wanted to seize, if possible, leadership of the Afro-Asian bloc, in which he was not successful, and to force a reorganization of the UN Secretariat, which he has so far failed to achieve. Third and above all, his antics were so dramatically overstressed if only because he wanted to show the West—and also the Chinese—that he was still *the* leader of the Communist world today.

CHAPTER XXII

More About Mr. K.

NIKITA S. KHRUSHCHEV, the foremost political personality
in the world today after John Fitzgerald Kennedy, was born on
April 17, 1894, in a hamlet called Kalinovka, near Kursk, close
to the Ukraine. Khrushchev is, however, Russian in origin, not
Ukrainian as is sometimes thought. At the moment of writing
his jobs are three: First Secretary of the Central Committee of
the CPSU (Communist Party Soviet Union), Chairman of the
Council of Ministers of the Union of Soviet Socialist Republics
(that is, Prime Minister), and Chairman of the Party Bureau for
the RSFSR (Russia proper). Thus he controls both party and
state, and is undisputed leader of the largest political organism
in the world, which covers one-sixth of the land surface of the
globe.

No man of politics has ever had his name spelt in so many
ways in so many different languages:

French:	Khrouchtchev
German:	Chruschtschow
	(but in Viennese newspapers this sometimes becomes Chruschtchew)
Italian:	Krusciov or Kruscev
Spanish:	Khrushchev
Portuguese:	Khruchtchev
Dutch:	Chroesjtjew
Swedish:	Chrusjtjov
Danish:	Chrustjov
Polish:	Chruszczew

The British popular Press incontinently lops off a few h's and
spells him simply 'Kruschev'. Gutter newspapers in America

call him 'Khrush', 'Krush', or even 'Krushy', and he is universally known, even in the most respectable circles, as 'Mr. K.' He is also variously pronounced. In Russian the correct pronunciation is 'crew-shove', with an accent on the 'shove'. Most Europeans alter this to 'cruse-shove'. To call him 'crew-*shef*' or 'crews-chef' is, to purists, incorrect.

Khrushchev's father was a miner who eked out a living by shepherding flocks; the family was dirt-poor. He had practically no education as a child, and Edward Crankshaw, one of the best-informed British authorities on Russia, says in *Khrushchev's Russia* (page 52) that he still *could not read or write at twenty-three*. Another authoritative British expert, writing anonymously in the *Observer* (May 15, 1960), says flatly that he first learned to read at the age of twenty-six. If this is true one can say fairly that the need to have formal education in childhood may be exaggerated, or, at the least, that Khrushchev's capacity for absorbing education as an adult was little short of spectacular. There may be gaps in his knowledge, but he is extraordinarily well informed on a large variety of subjects, and, even if his use of language is pedantic on occasion, few politicians have ever learned to express themselves with more articulateness, command of idiom, and punch. Incidentally, his love of peasant tales and vast fund of folklore and proverbs, which he quotes abundantly, are characteristic of one who has learned by ear in childhood, not from books.

The Russian Revolution came in 1917, when Khrushchev was twenty-three. He was a locksmith by trade, and also worked as a shepherd. He joined the Bolshevik forces, did well, and immediately after the civil war was sent to a party school in the Donbas region. Here some elements of education were pumped into him, and he was sent thereafter to a Workers' School at the Donetz Industrial Institute. Then in 1929, when he was thirty-five, he entered the Stalin Industrial Academy, now called the Moscow Industrial Academy, in Moscow for further study. As I pointed out in *Inside Russia Today*, this habit of picking out promising young men and giving them opportunity for specialized adult education is a characteristic—and admirable—Soviet trait.

In the 1930's Khrushchev rose like a rocket. He became a strong party member, lifted himself in the hierarchy and, when he was still under forty, was secretary of the Moscow District

Party Committee, a vital post. One of his sponsors, a man whom he later deposed, was Lazar M. Kaganovich, a historic early figure of the Revolution. By 1939 Khrushchev had become a full member of the Politburo, now called the Presidium, the ruling body of the party, and he has been a member of this organization, the most important in the USSR, ever since. He was the first man ever admitted to this holy of holies who grew up after the Revolution, and, as such, has always symbolized the new generation of leaders. He has no record of pre-Soviet activity and, as has been aptly stated, is 'totally a product of the Soviet era'.

When World War II broke out he was chief of the party in the Ukraine; he was promptly made a lieutenant-general in the armed forces, and took part both in the formal defence of Stalingrad and in guerrilla fighting in the neighbourhood. While still retaining the Ukraine post, he maintained his position as head of the party organization in Moscow as well and, in the immediate post-war period, divided his time between Moscow and Kiev, the capital of the Ukraine. He was responsible for the odious anti-Stalinist purges that afflicted the Ukraine after the war, managed to avoid being purged by Stalin himself, and advanced to become one of the half-dozen Kremlin leaders closest to Stalin in the ugly period when Russia was ruled by black terror and when the cold war got under way, between 1946 and 1953.

But the Kremlin guards its secrets well. When Stalin died on March 5, 1953, after thirty solid years of iron rule, Khrushchev was little known outside Russia and not particularly well known —except in the inner circle—within the country. The turning point of his life came immediately after Stalin's death. The full story of what happened is still unknown. But a decision was reached by those closest to Stalin, probably while his body was still warm, to abolish one-man rule, establish collective leadership, and reinstate the *party* as the chief organ of Soviet power. A motive for this was self-protection; the epigones huddled together to keep safe. For many years Stalin had not ruled through the party at all, but through the police and his own sinister private secretariat. Now a triumvirate was formed to *reinstitutionalize* the régime; it consisted of Vyacheslav M. Molotov, the former Prime Minister, Georgi Malenkov, who had been Stalin's principal secretary for years, and the notorious Lavrenti P. Beria, the boss of the secret police. Khrushchev himself was not, in the first instance, a member of this triumvirate. He was, however, still party boss in both Moscow and the Ukraine, and was given the job of superintending arrangements for Stalin's funeral. Malenkov became both Prime Minister and head of the party, as Stalin had been, on March 9. He held this double post for only eight days, however. Then, in circumstances which have never been satisfactorily explained, he decided to give up the party secretaryship but to remain Prime Minister. Malenkov must have known that the first of these positions held vastly more power than the second; therefore the supposition is that he was forced to divide his functions. By whom? We do not know. But we do know that it was Khrushchev who replaced him in the party post, and, a few months later, Mr. K. was formally installed as First Secretary of the CPSU, which job he still holds, and which is the most powerful in the Soviet Union. All of Khrushchev's subsequent career derives from this.

Malenkov, as Prime Minister, was much weakened. The triumvirate was now a quadrumvirate. But soon Malenkov, Molotov and Khrushchev turned like jaguars on Beria; he was arrested, condemned to death, and shot on Christmas Eve, 1953.

This ended the era of outright police rule, and the way was now open for the rubbery Khrushchev (one of his nicknames in Moscow is the 'Football'), with his unparalleled powers of manœuvre and political sense, to consolidate his own position. Malenkov was deposed as Prime Minister in February, 1955, and was replaced by the celebrated Marshal Nikolai Bulganin, one of Mr. K's closest associates; Malenkov himself was demoted to become Minister of Electric Power Stations. Next came the crisis of June, 1957, when Khrushchev, in one remarkable swoop, got rid of Molotov, Kaganovich, Shepilov, and several other semi-titans, when they were attempting to get rid of *him*. Malenkov was dispatched to exile in a remote eastern region and put in charge of a factory there, and Molotov was eventually made Ambassador to Outer Mongolia—also a long way from Moscow. Interestingly enough, none of those whom Mr. K. displaced were, so far as we know, sentenced to any term of imprisonment; certainly none were shot. Khrushchev was able to nip the Malenkov-Molotov plot in the bud by his control of the *party* apparatus, even though old-line Stalinists resented—and may still resent—his attitudes and policy. The next step came when Marshal Georgi K. Zhukov, Minister of Defence and boss of the Red Army, was sensationally eased out of office in October, 1957. Many so-called experts on Soviet affairs had held for a long time that Zhukov 'ran' Khrushchev; they were wrong. Mr. K. now had the field to himself, and in February, 1958, replaced the placid Bulganin as Prime Minister. Though he was sixty-four, he had never until that minute held anything but a party post—he had never been a cabinet minister or head of a government department.

For several years, however, it had been clearly apparent to those who had eyes in their heads that it was he who was running Russia. The 1958 reshuffle did no more than eliminate Bulganin and make the structure tidier.

PERSONAL

Many years ago I wrote: 'Stalin is about as emotional as a slab of basalt. If he has nerves, they are veins in rock.' Khrushchev, by comparison, is a kind of monstrous jellyfish with every tentacle flickering and vibrating, like antennae. This is not to say that he isn't tough. All of us in the western world have good reason to know how tough he is.

One aspect of his character can be clarified by keeping in mind always that he is, above everything, a peasant—cunning, tenacious, glib, impertinent, proud—always so proud!—with a gift for coarse repartee and wearing chips on his shoulders as big as epaulets.

Then, too, one should not neglect his irascibility. When Mr. Macmillan, visiting Moscow on the trip which opened the way to the Summit Conference, happened one morning to say that he had a high regard for Chancellor Adenauer, Mr. K. at once erupted into fury—so much so that the visit came close to being terminated on the spot. Also, once more, we must mention his outrageousness. Who but Khrushchev, on a trip to Yugoslavia, would confound the Yugoslav authorities by inviting all the plain-clothes men assigned to guard him, who had been pretending not to be plain-clothes men, into his chambers to have a round of convivial drinks? Who else, when he went to England, would have thought of bringing a live bear cub as a gift to the Queen?[1] And what other Communist leader would have said in his first public speech in New York, 'If you like capitalism—and I know that you like it—carry on and God bless you!'[2]

When Khrushchev first emerged on the public scene and made his first forays abroad, usually in company with Bulganin, who looks like a derelict Virginia landowner addicted to mint juleps, people were apt to think that he was a clown, a drunkard, a buffoon. He likes to drink and has certainly been drunk on occasion; but just as certainly he is not a drunkard. And, behind the fireworks, his hard core of belief and utter fixity of aim were always evident if you chose to look for them. Also, nobody should minimize his intelligence. Crankshaw tells a characteristic little story in *Khrushchev's Russia*. The Prime Minister, engaging a group of Western diplomats in discussion at a Moscow reception, clearly bested them. 'Look at me!' he proceeded to exclaim. 'Here am I, a simple Communist. I worked with my hands. I never went to school. You great gentlemen went to the best schools in the world. You are trained professionals. And yet I make rings around you. Tell me why!'

Mr. K's basic sources of power are, I should say, five. First, the sheer force of his personality combined with his painstakingly well-informed and ruthless control of the party machine. Second, the fact that most Soviet citizens are better off materially than they have ever been before. Third, he symbolizes termination of the terror—release from the depravities of Stalin's police. Fourth, he stands for peace, which every Russian wants. Fifth, he personifies vividly the stamina and extraordinary singleness of purpose of the Soviet régime.

He was thickly tarred with Stalin's evil brush, but, next to the evolution whereby he replaced Malenkov as first secretary of the party in 1953, the major landmark of his career was certainly the spectacular six-hour speech he made to the Twentieth Party

---

[1] The *Observer*, May 15, 1960.

[2] Of course, this remark must be judged in its context. Khrushchev also said, 'I speak bluntly so that you will know who you are dealing with. Such clarity improves relations. But remember that a new social system, the socialist system, has come into being. It is already treading on your heels and we are reckoning on overtaking and outdistancing you.'

Congress in February, 1956, in which he repudiated the Stalinist cult of personality, re-expressed the policy of collective leadership, and, making sensational disclosures about the Stalinist terror, drew the veil off some of the most heinous of his predecessor's crimes.

What Khrushchev hates most is NATO and the American overseas bases, because these confront him with the possibility of retaliation in the event of war. What he fears most, basic American strength apart, is West German rearmament. What he wants most, next to Soviet advance, is disarmament. What annoys him most is Berlin, with the UN secretariat a close second.

Finally, accomplishments. The broadest of these is, as indicated above, the process whereby 'socialist legality', as the Russians call it, has replaced one-man totalitarian rule. The labour camps have been largely broken up, the administration of justice has been reformed, the secret police no longer hold power both universal and unpredictably capricious, and rule by *overt* terror has ceased—although plenty of Soviet citizens still shake in their boots at the mention of a policeman.

Khrushchev has promised the Soviet people that they will within a few years pass the United States in *per capita* butter, milk and meat production—which may or may not happen—and has done something, although not nearly enough, to make more consumer goods available to citizens at reasonable cost. Soviet production of such articles as bicycles, shoes, watches, radios, cameras, et cetera, has mounted. Then, too, Mr. K. put in motion an elaborate procedure for decentralizing industry, and has opened 87·5 million acres of land in Kazakhstan to agriculture in the ambitious and hazardous 'Virgin Lands' development. Also he has put Soviet theory on a new tack by repudiating to a degree two formerly basic Marxist tenets—'that parliamentary government is never anything more than a mockery, and that violence is essential for the transformation of society.' Finally, as is well known, he has scrapped the Leninist hypothesis that war between the Communist and capitalist countries is inevitable, and espouses (on his own terms, of course) the cause of 'peaceful', competitive coexistence.

DE GAULLE ON KHRUSHCHEV

When President Charles de Gaulle visited New York in April, 1960, the following colloquy took place at a Press conference:

Q. A fundamental question, Mr. President, do you consider Khrushchev a man of good will, or does it make no difference?
A. I have had the advantage of having personal contacts with Chairman Khrushchev recently when he was in France. We have talked a great deal and at great length on all the subjects in which the world is concerned and even passionately interested in at the present time. If you would like to know what I can say about the impression I drew from these contacts, I would tell you that Mr. Khrushchev seemed to me to be a strong personality. He is a man who has fought all his life for his ideas, and that has necessarily left a mark on him.

Actually I have the impression that at the level where he finds himself, he realizes, and he has realized, that the problems of the world are perhaps less simple than one thinks when one considers them from a single point of view. Moreover he is a man who is very knowledgeable on current problems, very well informed of people and things. In short . . . I do not think that the Soviet Union could be represented by a man who better expresses what Russia is today, which, in my opinion—and this is my opinion—is no longer the Russia of yesterday, not even the Russia of ten years ago.[1]

THE PARTY, COLLECTIVE LEADERSHIP, AND THE SUCCESSION

Of the tetrarchs and thanes who surrounded Stalin twenty-five years ago, only one survives in an important post today—the pertinacious Anastas I. Mikoyan, who is still a first deputy chairman of the government. Mikoyan, an Armenian, was born in 1895. It was he who visited the United States in 1959 to prepare the way for Khrushchev's trip. He is high in both government and party councils but would, in the view of most, be impossible as a successor to Mr. K. no matter how much Mr. K. likes and admires him because (*a*) he is too old; (*b*) his interests are too specialized; above all (*c*) he is an Armenian. The Soviet Union could no more have an Armenian prime

[1] *New York Times*, April 26, 1960.

10*

minister today than the Israelis could have an Arab or the South Africans a naked Zulu, even though Stalin was a Georgian and although the government makes great play with the thesis that all the constituent republics of the USSR have equal rank.

Three other veterans survive, but their importance is limited. Kliment E. Voroshilov, the former war lord, is over eighty, and not in good health; he was replaced lately as chairman of the Presidium of the Supreme Soviet (i.e. titular 'president' of the country) in June, 1960, by the steeply rising Leonid I. Brezhnev. Another old-timer is Otto V. Kuusinen, born in 1881, a Finn who is a Communist theoretician of commanding prestige despite his age. The third, Nikolai M. Shvernik, was chairman of the Supreme Soviet before Voroshilov; his career has been based largely on trade union activity. He was born in 1888, joined the Bolsheviks when, a boy of seventeen, he was a workman in a metallurgical factory, and, many years later, was the *only* important member of the All-Union Council of Trade Unions to survive the Stalin purges.

All the other demigods of Stalin's day are dead or totally devoid of power with the possible exception of Molotov, seventy, who recently was removed from his post in Outer Mongolia and transferred to Vienna as Soviet representative on the International Atomic Energy Agency. Kaganovich, who was for many years the only Jew in the Politburo, lives in 'retirement' somewhere, as does Zhukov, and Malenkov is manager of a power station at Ust-Kamenogorsk in Kazakhstan, several thousand miles away from Moscow. Any list of leading Bolsheviks a quarter of a century ago would have included Trotsky, Zinoviev, Kamenev, Smirnov, Sokolnikov, Serebryakov, Pyatakov, Andreyev, Eikhe, Kosior, Ordzhonikidze, and Zhdanov, who was being groomed as Stalin's successor. Also there were military men like the celebrated Marshal Tukhachevsky. Of all these, Zhdanov was the only one who died a natural death—and perhaps his wasn't *too* natural. All the others were executed after the great treason trials in 1936 and 1937, or were subsequently liquidated in the purges, or, like Trotsky, were otherwise assassinated.

Of leaders today, the most interesting and important are probably Frol R. Kozlov, Alexei N. Kosygin, Leonid I. Brezhnev, and, in a different category, Mikhail A. Suslov. The first three are out-and-out Khrushchev men. Kozlov, a man in his early fifties, was a textile worker by trade who, among other things, has been party boss in Leningrad, Minister of State Farms, and Premier of the RSFSR (Russia proper). He is vigorous, personable, and practical. In a party shake-up in June, 1960 Khrushchev took him out of the government sphere to give him a leading post in the party—presumably to widen his experience—and he is now a secretary of the CPSU Central Committee. Kozlov, like Mikoyan, visited the United States in 1959; when Vice-President Nixon went to Moscow, this was to return the Kozlov visit. Recently Khrushchev told Averell Harriman that he had picked Kozlov as his successor.

Kosygin, also a practical man and an able citizen, was born in 1905, and became a member of the Council of Ministers (under Stalin) when he was only forty-one. He was mayor of Leningrad for a period, and at one time or other has been Minister of Textiles, Light Industry, and Finance—also, like Kozlov, a premier of the RSFSR. Planning has always been his major interest, and for many years he was a leading executive of the State Planning Commission, which runs the *Gosplan*. In 1960 Kosygin moved over to take Kozlov's post as a First Deputy Prime Minister of the government. One theory is that, if anything happens to Khrushchev, these two other K's will attempt to run the show together, with Kozlov in charge of party affairs and Kosygin as Prime Minister.

Still another 'K.' should be noted—Iosif I. Kuzmin, also a member of the 'technical aristocracy' like Kosygin, a bureaucrat who has risen out of the new managerial class. Born in 1910 in Leningrad, he worked as a machinist, and became an engineer. He rose to be chairman of the *Gosplan*, and was the first man in Soviet history to be made a deputy prime minister *before* becoming a member of the party Presidium. Another rising star is the youthful Dmitri S. Polyansky, born in 1917, the new Premier of the RSFSR. Several interesting shifts occurred in reshuffles in 1959 and 1960. Two men who had been Khrushchev handymen for years were eliminated from the party Presidium, Nikolai I. Belyayev and Alexei I. Kirichenko, long-time boss of the Ukraine. Another good friend, Yekaterina A. Furtseva, was dropped from her secretaryship of the party, and transferred to the government as Minister of Culture. She is the leading woman member of the government. Still another party secretary, Averky B. Aristov, was shifted abroad to be Ambassador to Poland, and others who held positions close to the top were demoted, like Nikolai G. Ignatov and the fierce, venerable theoretician Pyotr N. Pospelov. At present there are only five party secretaries—Kuusinen, Kozlov, Brezhnev, Suslov, and Nuritdin A. Mukhitdinov, an Uzbek who is one of the few representatives of the 'new' nationalities to be a full member of the Presidium.

Brezhnev, the 'President' of the USSR, was for some years boss of Kazakhstan, although he was born (1904) in Moldavia near the Rumanian frontier far on the other side of the Soviet Union. He has always been predominantly a party specialist, and has been a full member of the Presidium since June, 1957. He is tough, able, and very close to Mr. K. Also several younger men of the inner circle should be mentioned—Georgi A. Zhukov, a former *Pravda* correspondent who is now in charge of cultural relations abroad, with cabinet rank (the USSR cabinet is cumbersome, with no fewer than sixty-five members); A. N. Shepelin, the former head of the Komsomols, who is now chairman of the Committee on State Security and is thus boss of the new generation of police; and, perhaps most important of all, Alexei Adzhubei, editor of *Izvestia*, who is Mr. K's son-in-law and who seldom leaves his side.

Finally, Suslov. He differs from everybody else on this list because, first, he is an old-line theoretician who has never held a government job, and, second, is the last avowed Stalinist to survive in an important post. The son of a peasant, he rose in the conventional way through the Komsomols, and has been a party member since 1921. A dry-minded fanatic, Suslov is harsh, stubborn, and an intellectual of intellectuals. He has always been a propaganda specialist; for a time he was director of *Agitprop*, the Soviet propaganda machine, and was once editor of *Pravda*. He represents the extreme right, and despite his unpopularity, total lack of political magnetism, and paucity of experience in the hurly-burly of governmental manœuvre, he is often thought of as a serious candidate for the succession. Probably Khrushchev keeps him on, even though they take opposite stands on most issues, because he carries great weight with elder members of the party machine and surviving Stalinist bureaucrats.

Khrushchev himself, when asked about his team, is apt to shrug questions off. A reporter inquired of him during his visit to New York 'who ran the store' while he was away; he replied, 'My grandsons—Nikita, Alexei, and my third grandson, who is also a Nikita.'

*

Mr. K. certainly runs the Soviet Union today, but it is important to point out that government is still collegial. Khrushchev dominates, but he dominates through consultation: there is no doubt that, in the last analysis, he is 'accountable to a power entity',[1] namely the 135 members of the Central Committee of the party and its Presidium (14 full members, 7 alternates). He can bully the party; cajole it; pack it; talk it into doing things it does not like; and conduct extraordinarily intricate manœuvres within its body—but he cannot ignore it. One proof of this is that, if government were *not* collective, Khrushchev would not dare leave Moscow so often and for such extended trips. Dictators never let their thrones get cold. Stalin did not leave Russia more than once or twice in thirty years. But Mr. K. sails all over the place without care, to the most distant points, which can only mean that he has no fear of being eliminated in his absence—also that the régime has been institutionalized to the extent that his associates can take important routine decisions no matter where he is.

As a matter of fact, not merely has the dictatorship become liberalized, but severe opposition may be expressed to the Prime Minister on occasion. To the surviving Stalinist element Mr. K. is still a highly unorthodox type, and the right-wing dogmatists, like Suslov, have never accepted fully his volatility, tendency to improvise, and willingness to negotiate with heretics like Tito. To some extremists he is practically a Trotsky.

There are several dangerous points at issue. One is China. The Chinese Communists, dogmatists to the bone, can still quote the orthodox litany of Marx and Lenin, which Khrushchev cannot, because he has cut himself off from the support of traditional dogma. Second, agriculture. Two disastrous crop failures in a row have come to the Virgin Lands, and agriculture is, as always, the sorest subject in the Soviet Union. If further

[1] Richard H. Rovere, 'Letter from Below the Summit', *The New Yorker*, May 28, 1960.

crop failures should occur in Kazakhstan or elsewhere Khrushchev might very easily find himself in grave trouble. Finally,
quite without regard to dogma or concrete issues, there are
always questions of power politics to consider—outs wanting
to be in. All this being said, Khrushchev is an extremely wary
operator, his control of the party machine is firm, and he
dominates most of his fellows like a giant among pygmies.

ALTERATIONS IN THE SOVIET PATTERN—
ALSO FIXITIES

Surely I have written enough in this and the preceding chapter,
together with passing references elsewhere in this book, to indicate the depth, breadth, and comprehensiveness of changes that
have come to the Soviet Union since I wrote *Inside Europe* a
quarter of a century ago. Stalin is dead, and the power of the
secret police, a state within a state, has been broken. The USSR
has increased in size at the expense of various neighbours, and is
flanked on the west by a glacis of satellites with the result that
Soviet power now stretches to the Danube and the Elbe. The
ebullient Khrushchev, following the monolithic bleakness of his
predecessor, has done much to revivify the economy, give special
emphasis to education, encourage technical processes, improve
the standard of living, and encourage—to a degree—contacts
with the world outside. De-Stalinization has brought substantial
juridical and other reforms, and, as I once heard it put, 'the
atmosphere is lighter even if the system is the same'. The
difference between Moscow in 1935, when I visited it at the
beginning of the grimmest period of the Stalin dictatorship, and
when I returned in 1956, was, in some spheres, that between
night and day. Then in a very brief span Russia has advanced
to become the second industrial and military power in the world,
and, what with the Sputniks and Luniks, the first power (at least
at the moment of writing) in the exploration and conquest
of outer space.*

* Major Yuri A. Gagarin circled the earth (25,000 miles) in 108 minutes on
April 12, 1961, in a five-ton Soviet space capsule launched into space by a multi-
stage rocket with 750,000 pounds of thrust—the first man in history to make a
successful orbital flight. Twenty-three days later, on May 5, Commander Alan B.
Shepard, Jr., piloted the first American flight into space, reaching a height of 115
miles and traversing 302 miles in 15 minutes. There was, however, no attempt to
put Shepard into orbit—*Publisher's Note.*

On the other hand, Russia has *not* changed in several respects. The régime is still one capable of the infamy of suppressing the Hungarian revolt, and, on a different level, of forcing a man like Boris Pasternak to surrender the Nobel Prize and persecuting his friend and companion, Madame Ivinskaya, and her daughter. The de-Stalinization process may, in time, produce a certain amount of democratization, but, viewed in the light of today, the Soviet Union under Mr. K's collective leadership is still the most tightly sealed, totalitarian and oligarchical state in the world, China excepted. And, even if the Russians hope for a disarmament agreement and general amelioration of relations with the West, their methods of negotiation are still devious, absolutist, and based to an almost fantastic degree on stubborn obstructionism.

ANOTHER WORD ON MR. K. AND THE CHINESE

China is outside the province of this book, but one cannot discuss Russian fundamentals without passing reference to the Chinese. Disagreement, bad feeling, even tension, have distinguished relations between the Soviet Union and Communist China for several years. Partly the reasons are emotional; there are few lasting friendships between Goliath and Goliath. China, by far the largest country in the world in terms of population, has 650 million people and increases this enormous total, almost a quarter of that of the entire earth, by roughly 25 million a year; calculations are that the population will be a thousand million by 1980. Russia, by contrast, though by far the largest country in the world in area, has only around 210 million people, and the birth-rate is not particularly high. Also the USSR suffered tremendous casualties in the war, and Stalin, immediately after the war, refused to release young men from the Red Army; hence comparatively few children were born in age groups approaching maturity today.

The Soviet Union still considers itself to be a 'senior partner' of the Chinese, as I have reason to know on high authority, but the fantastic Chinese birth-rate automatically constitutes a challenge. Where, since China is barely able to feed itself, are the surplus Chinese going to go? One possibility is Siberia next door, to say nothing of Kazakhstan, both of which are sparsely populated. Another challenge is industrialization. China does not seriously approach the USSR in extent of industrialization as yet, but it is advancing rapidly; one forecast is that within twenty years it will have as large a steel production as the whole of western Europe. A third element of challenge is possible competition between the two giants for influence in Afro-Asian territories. Here the Chinese have a curious psychological advantage in that they are not *white*.

On the ideological plane the issue between Russia and China is specific, and we have already alluded to it in these pages. The Chinese take the old Leninist view that war between capitalist and Communist states is inevitable, and that the Khrushchev policy of so-called peaceful coexistence makes little sense. Here I am compressing drastically a subject of inordinate doctrinal complexity, which has many qualifications; but the main line of Chinese policy holds that the 'imperialist' powers can be conquered only by overt revolutionary struggle. The Russians take a somewhat different view. Khrushchev thinks that war is no longer inevitable or necessary, largely because Communist strength—in Russia, the satellites, and elsewhere—has advanced so swiftly. He thinks that capitalism will fall of its own weight, when people throughout the world discover, as he assumes that they will, that the Communist system works 'better' and brings them more. Therefore, active propagation of Communist ideas by naked revolutionary agitation is not worth the risk of provoking a retaliatory war with nuclear weapons. Of course, this does not keep the Russians from seizing any seemingly safe opportunity for exploiting local situations in countries like Iraq, Laos, or the Congo. Khrushchev certainly wants peace—if only to improve the Soviet standard of living and thus make his régime stronger—but he plays both sides of the street.

One reason why the Chinese are willing to take risks is that they would probably suffer much less than Russia in the event of nuclear war. First, their enormous population would in theory enable them to stand huge losses better than any other country. If the Soviet Union lost 200 million people it would be wiped out; if China lost a similar number there would still be 450 million Chinese left. Moreover, industrial targets in China are sparse and scattered. But Russia could—again in theory—lose most of its vital industrialization at a stroke.

On a more concrete and immediate level, the Chinese have several complaints *vis-à-vis* the Soviet Union. (1) First, the bomb. Russia has refused so far to give China atomic weapons or any nuclear equipment except one small experimental reactor.[1] (2) India. The Soviet Union took an extremely dim view of the Chinese penetration of Tibet and further Chinese machinations along the Himalayan frontier, and the Chinese resented it hotly that their ally did not come to their support. (3) The Russians give the Chinese a good deal of technical aid, but China considers that it is being 'starved' in this respect, and wants more. (4) The Chinese would like to give more active support to sub-merged Communist parties in the western world, and dislike it bit-terly that Soviet economic assistance is going to bourgeois states.

One further word about the bomb. Many observers think that, even without Soviet help, the Chinese have already produced their first nuclear bomb, or are about to do so. China has good scientists and technicians, and it is not particularly difficult to make a bomb nowadays. After all, it was the Chinese who invented gunpowder! One reason why the USSR is willing to discuss nuclear testing and favours a test ban (on its own terms) is that this might make it illegal for China to join the nuclear 'club' and begin testing on its own.

Why, in view of these and other circumstances, do not the Russians force a showdown with China? The chief reason is that an open split would irreparably damage Communist prestige, and probably make China a neighbour even more dangerous than it is now. Why do the Chinese not force a show-down with the Russians? The answer could not be simpler: they are almost totally dependent on Russia for industrial supplies. Nowhere else can China obtain commodities that are absolutely essential to its military and industrial programme, ranging from machine tools to aviation petrol. But nowadays the Soviets do not give the Chinese more than the bare minimum—enough to keep them going but not enough to enable them to surpass Russia's own industrial capacity.

Still one more cogent point is that Khrushchev's flirtations with the West are probably motivated partly by fear of China. He doesn't at all relish being at the mercy of Mao Tse-tung some fine day, and good relations with the West would give

[1] *Sunday Times*, August 20, 1960.

him a kind of backstop. This is one reason why he says he wants a successful Summit Conference.

Mostly Khrushchev minimizes his difficulties with the Red Chinese and implies that differences of opinion do not matter much. He said recently, 'It is impossible to lead all the socialist countries and Communist parties from any single centre. What is more, it isn't necessary.'[1] A temporizer as always, he refuses to align himself publicly with any criticism of the Chinese, as for instance from Yugoslavia, and at the same time keeps warning Mao discreetly that 'China could not stand alone against the capitalist world'. All this came to a head at a Congress of the Rumanian Workers Party in Bucharest in June, 1960, attended by Ping Chen, the Mayor of Peking and a member of the Politburo of the Chinese People's Republic, as well as various European leaders like Kadar, Ulbricht, and Gomulka. These latter all firmly supported Khrushchev on peaceful coexistence, agreed with him that a new world war would be madness, and even applauded when he went so far as to say that some of Lenin's theses were 'outdated and should be interpreted in the light of modern world conditions'. The Chinese listened hard, but said little. Khrushchev's speech was dismissed in a single paragraph by newspapers in Peking. Then evidences of tension rose, Russian technicians were reported to be leaving China in substantial number, important Chinese newspapers gave vent to such opinions as that there could be no departure from fundamental Leninist principles under any circumstances, that wars against imperialism were justified, and that there could be no peace except by 'elimination' of the capitalist system everywhere in the world. Next, as if the Chinese thought that they might be going too far, there came a cut-back. On October 22 the four chief Peking leaders—Mao Tse-tung, Liu Shao-chi, the President of the Republic, Prime Minister Chou En-lai, and the veteran revolutionary Marshal Chu Teh—sent a joint message to Khrushchev describing the Soviet Union as the 'inspirer and leader of the Communist world', and reiterating the 'monolithic solidarity' of the two Red partners.

Then occurred the 'Communist Summit' Conference in Moscow in November, 1960, attended by delegates of Communist parties in no fewer than eighty-one countries. The sessions, held

[1] Harrison E. Salisbury in the *New York Times*, January 29, 1961.

in the utmost secrecy during the commemoration of the forty-third anniversary of the Russian Revolution, lasted three weeks; twelve of the thirteen Communist countries in the world were represented, together with sixty-nine Communist parties in other countries; all told, the conference is supposed to have spoken for 36 million members of the Communist party the world over. The single hold-out was Yugoslavia. The chief Chinese delegate was Liu Shao-chi, the Chinese head of state. The result was a draw, which it took a twenty-thousand-word manifesto to express. The Chinese agreed to accept Khrushchev's position on peaceful coexistence and his thesis that war between Communism and the West was not inevitable; in return the Russians made a statement—the importance of which depends on future interpretation—to the effect that they would proceed 'strongly and uncompromisingly with their determination to do everything in their power, short of war, to accelerate the speed of revolution'. Moscow interpreted this as a Khrushchev victory. At any rate he avoided an open break with China, and, today, here the matter rests.

CHAPTER XXIII

Satellites and Soviet Policy

THE easiest way to seize the extent and variety of the Soviet dominion in Europe is to draw up a simple tabulation, as I did in *Inside Russia Today*. The satellite 'empire' in Europe consists of the following countries:

	Area (sq. miles)	Population
Albania	10,629	1,400,000
Bulgaria	42,796	7,629,254
Czechoslovakia	49,330	13,560,000
German Democratic Republic (East Germany)	41,645	17,300,000 (including East Berlin)
Hungary	35,911	9,929,000
Poland	120,358	28,997,000
Rumania	91,654	18,059,000
	392,323	96,874,254
And in a special category:		
Yugoslavia	98,674	18,380,000

How may one categorize these states in order of subservience to the Kremlin? Czechoslovakia is probably the most loyal of the lot, if only because most Czechoslovaks hate and fear Germany so fiercely. Also the Czechoslovak leadership is still predominantly conservative in the Communist sense, although its most extreme Stalinists, like Rudolf Slansky, the former party secretary, were liquidated some years ago; above all, it wants to go slow on 'reform' in order to obviate the possibility of explosions like those in Poland and Hungary. Next, the East Germans. The German Democratic Republic, as I have already mentioned in these pages, is a real country even if it is thoroughly subjugated under Ulbricht, who takes the straight

Kremlin line although he has substantial authority on his own; moreover, the Russians maintain strong Red Army forces on East German soil, which are a deterrent to disaffection. Then, too, the perennial Berlin crisis tends to tie East German leadership to Moscow. Third, Rumania, if only because it is geographically vulnerable and could not dare to be 'revisionist' even if it wanted to be. Fourth, Bulgaria. The Bulgars have a sturdy independence of spirit but also they have been distinguished throughout their whole history by a strong pro-Russian tradition, and this plays a role. Fifth, Hungary. Here, too, historical factors are involved. The patriotic revolt of October, 1956, was mercilessly extinguished by Soviet tanks, but Hungarian national instincts are still strong, and Hungary is, in several respects, a question mark. Its leader, Janos Kadar, even if he is a subservient Kremlin tool now, had a long Titoist (i.e. nationalist) history, and was in fact imprisoned and tortured by the Stalinists who ruled Hungary after the war. Sixth, Poland, which has such vibrant independence of spirit that it can scarcely be considered to be a true satellite at all. Seventh, Albania, a special case. Finally, Yugoslavia, which, although Communist, is neutral and not in the Kremlin fold.

All these countries have robust and lively nationalist traditions, and, even though the Kremlin controls them all (except Albania, Poland to an extent, and of course Yugoslavia), many of their separatist differentiations and characteristics survive. Poland, as I have written elsewhere, is still effervescent, volatile, and romantic; Czechoslovakia is still bourgeois, stolid, and obedient. No two peoples could differ more than the Albanians —primitive highlanders who have never been part of the European enlightenment at all—and the East Germans, with their formidable intellectual and technical prowess. Moreover, national frictions still exist under the surface, although the Russians have smoothed over most of them. Yugoslavs and Bulgarians still hate each other, and from time immemorial Rumanians have been despised by almost everybody. Yugoslavs and Albanians have been at odds since Turkish days, and Rumania and Bulgaria have never been particularly close or friendly. One curious point is that the Bulgars, by and large, are traditionally pro-American (as well as pro-Russian) and ardently seek more contact with the United States.

The Russians exert political dominance through several instruments. One is the Warsaw Pact of June, 1955. This was launched as a counter-move to NATO, and binds all the satellites (Yugoslavia excepted) to the Kremlin in military arrangements. Second, the so-called Council for Mutual Economic Assistance, known as COMECON, which includes East Germany, Poland, Czechoslovakia, Hungary, Rumania, and Bulgaria, as well as the USSR, and aims to correlate economic activity among the satellites, minimize competition, share markets, and in general improve trade. Roughly it corresponds to the Common Market of the West.

Some points in general: (1) The satellites dislike extremely being called satellites. They claim to be independent 'people's republics' on their own. (2) All are totalitarian dictatorships, but they insist that they are 'democracies'. (3) They cost the Soviet Union large sums in economic and other aid; running an empire is an expensive business. (4) They are of the utmost strategic value to the Soviet Union by reason of their geographical position as buffer states. (5) The lesson of Hungary is that any attempt at revolt will be put down by force. (6) Circumstances vary country by country, but, surprising as it may be to many, economic conditions in several are not so bad as might be thought. A case could be made that Poland under Gomulka has done more for the poorest peasantry, the serfs, than Poland under Pilsudski. (7) The fact that several countries had sordid reactionary governments before the war does not justify repression by governments today; all it does is indicate one reason, among others, *why* the present Communist installations were able to seize power. (8) Not a single government in the entire area could possibly survive a free vote of its people today. *Every* Communist régime would be kicked out at once.

FELLOWS IN THE NEST

East Germany has already been described in Chapter V above. Let us glance now at the other European countries in the Soviet sphere.

Poland. The main point to stress is, of course, the intense vivacity and virility of the Polish spirit, and its relative freedom from Kremlin strictures. Poland is the only Warsaw Pact member with substantial civil liberties—which is the more remarkable because it is the only state in Europe flanked by the Red Army on both sides. Perhaps the best way to express the delicate relation between Warsaw and Moscow is to say that the Kremlin leaves Poland alone on domestic matters, in return for Polish agreement and co-operation in foreign affairs. There are subtleties to watch. Gomulka will never be a Kremlin slave or puppet; on the other hand, he is a perfectly definite Communist, and his government is a definite Communist government even though it differs from all others in the amount of freedom it permits its citizens. Gomulka makes his own revisionist policy, but he is not necessarily anti-Kremlin.

Just the same, this little story was frequently told in the pre-Summit era. Eisenhower, Khrushchev and Gomulka are summoned to the bar of heaven; St. Peter gives each a wish. Eisenhower wishes for the total, immediate destruction of the Soviet Union—and promptly the Soviet Union disappears from the face of the earth. Khrushchev similarly requests the total obliteration of the United States, and—presto!—the United States disappears. St. Peter then turns to Gomulka, asking him what *he* wants. The Polish leader leans back with a happy sigh, murmuring, 'A cup of tea.'

Wladyslaw Gomulka, First Secretary of the Politburo of the PZPR (Polska Zjednoczona Partia Robotnicza, Polish United Workers party), is one of the half-dozen most important men in contemporary Europe. Of peasant stock, he was born in 1905; his father worked in an oil refinery, and young Gomulka started life as a manual labourer. He struggled for an education, rose through the labour unions, became an influential figure in the Socialist party, and in time turned to Communism. He was several times imprisoned by the Germans. After World War II he became general secretary of the Polish Workers party, and advanced quickly on the stormy national scene. But, despite tribulations, his essential characteristics never changed; he has always been professorial in manner, aloof, and angular, with a peculiar spry pepperiness. He almost never receives outsiders. He has a fanatically disciplined, one-track mind. Also he is packed with guts. He took sides with Tito when Yugoslavia broke with the Kremlin in 1948, was dismissed from power as a result by the Stalinists then in command in Warsaw, and spent several years in jail. Then he recanted, and was eventually released. In June, 1956, occurred the 'Bread and Freedom' riots in Poznań, and the country came near to exploding. Everybody knew that Gomulka was the most vital and commanding authority in the country. He defied the Kremlin and, despite extreme Soviet pressure, was able to seize rule on October 21, and make his own kind of Communist régime. Khrushchev flew urgently to Warsaw, and attempted to make Gomulka withdraw under the threat of armed force. Gomulka stood firm, Khrushchev receded, and overnight Poland found itself miraculously free of 'the entire apparatus of Soviet control'.[1] Khrush-

[1] *Sunday Times*, December 4, 1960.

chev did not want to risk an open insurrection like that which came to Hungary a few days later, and Gomulka has been in command in Poland ever since.

Structurally the Polish government is built on the Moscow pattern, with the all-powerful Politburo of the PZPR holding ultimate authority behind the *sejm* (parliament) and governmental façade. Parties other than the PZPR are, however, permitted to exist, like the United Peasant party and the Democratic party. But these work closely with the PZPR and are members of the 'Front of National Unity', which the PZPR altogether dominates. Issues are several. Poland, despite an extensive industrial programme, is still 47 per cent agricultural, and collectivization of agriculture has been a problem from the beginning. The independent-minded Poles simply would not accept collectivization; at peak only 12 per cent of the total arable land of the country went into collective farms, and this has shrunk to 1 per cent today. Some 13 per cent of the land is, however, organized into state and other public farms. Second, religion. Poland is a profoundly Roman Catholic country. As early as December, 1956, two months after he took power, Gomulka hammered out an agreement with Stefan Cardinal Wyszynski, who had been imprisoned under the previous régime, whereby religious teaching would continue to be permitted in the church schools, but there have been tense quarrels between state and church recently. Early in 1961 the Vatican asserted that the original accord had 'disintegrated'. Third, consumer interests. As in the Soviet Union, a major Polish problem is allocation—what percentage of the national effort shall go into heavy industry, what for consumer goods.

The United States has given Poland aid amounting to £152 million since 1956; Poland is the only Warsaw Pact power which accepts American aid (that is, is allowed by the Kremlin to accept it), and America's giving it is sound policy, if only for the reason that it tells the Poles that the Americans are friends eager to show admiration for their dauntless spirit and indomitable effort to build as much of a life as they can despite the iron embrace of the Soviet Union.

After Gomulka, the most prominent Pole is the Prime Minister, Jozef Cyrankiewicz, one of the ablest of all personalities in eastern Europe. He was for many years a left-wing Social

Democrat and member of the PPS, Polish Socialist party, and, when he became Prime Minister in 1947, was not a Communist. He was born in Cracow, the heart of Polish culture, and is a man replete with force, magnetism, and colour. Cyrankiewicz is about fifty; his wife is a well-known actress, and he likes mountain climbing, fast cars, and good food and drink. The Germans caught him in the war, but did not know who he was; he escaped, and helped organize the Polish underground. He was imprisoned for a time at Oświęcim (Auschwitz), lost his hair there as a result of privation, but miraculously survived. Violent, unending hatred of the Nazis and the Gestapo is still a major chord in every satellite, particularly Poland.

Czechoslovakia. This dour, hard-working little country, with an area of just under 50,000 square miles, is vital to the Soviet empire for several reasons. It is close to the West, its people are educated, and the economy is advanced. Czechoslovakia is the only Communist state in *central* as apart from eastern Europe, except the German Democratic Republic; its western tip is only 250 miles from the Rhine. As to economics it is—again with the exception of East Germany—the most highly industrialized of all the satellites, the most prosperous, and the one with the highest standard of living. Great factories like Skoda in Pilsen are prime suppliers of munitions, as well as much else, not merely to other countries in the Communist bloc but to states far afield like the United Arab Republic, Indonesia, and Guinea.[1] Also Czechoslovakia has aptly been called the most 'tragic' satellite. It was the only one which was a true democracy before the war; hence, its people really lost something when the Communists took over. Poland and Hungary were dictatorships in the 1930's, with strongly entrenched feudal interests; reactionary landowners held a fantastically disproportionate amount of economic power, and millions of landless peasants were a submerged class. But the Czechs were democratically governed, under statesmen like Dr. Eduard Beneš, and had made a model land reform. This was a decent, modern, modest, well-run state.

Moreover, the Communists took Czechoslovakia (February, 1948) by means of internal conspiracy and a *coup d'état*. There was no civil war, and the Red Army played no direct role. The country was not conquered; it was betrayed. On the other hand,

[1] *Time,* July 4, 1960.

the Communists had become the largest single party in the country in elections held in 1946, with 38 per cent of the vote and 114 deputies out of an Assembly numbering 300. The prime ministership and several other important ministries were held by Communists. One important actor in the smooth, bloodless coup which gave them complete power was Dr. Zdeněk Fierlinger, a former Czechoslovak Ambassador to Austria and the Soviet Union, who was an extreme left-wing Social Democrat, not a Communist at all. He is speaker of the National Assembly today, and if nobody is listening people still call him 'Dr. Quislinger'. The Communists are, parenthetically, somewhat sensitive about the manner in which they won Czechoslovakia. As recently as May, 1960, the Prague government demanded an official apology from Mr. Herter, the American Secretary of State, when he stated that the Czechoslovak Communists had seized power 'by force'.[1] Also they are still sensitive about the tragic death of Jan Masaryk, who, a few weeks after the coup, jumped from his bathroom window in the Czernin Palace in Prague, or was pushed out of it. Masaryk, a brave, honest, turbulent, and impulsive man, was Foreign Minister in the Communist-led government. He was, as everybody knows, a son of Thomas G. Masaryk, one of the great men of this or any other country, who founded the Czechoslovak state.

Lesser folk rule today. The President of the Republic, who is also First Secretary of the Central Committee of the Communist party, is Antonín Novotný. He has held the presidency since 1957, the party secretaryship since 1953. He was born near Prague in 1904, and was a locksmith by trade; he has been a party member since 1921, endured various vicissitudes including imprisonment by the Nazis during the war, and takes an all-out Russian line. His position on domestic matters is such that, as a British observer put it recently, the Czechs are just now 'catching up with the Twentieth Congress and the post-Stalin thaw'. Of all the men in Khrushchev's team who spoke at the UN in 1960, Novotný was the dullest.

One geographical curiosity is that Czechoslovakia, like Norway and Hungary, has today a short common frontier with the USSR. For strategic reasons the Soviet Union annexed the

[1] *New York Times*, May 22, 1960.

eastern stub of the country, once known as Sub-Carpathian Ruthenia, after their armies moved into it in World War II. The Russians call it Trans-Carpathia, and it marks the extreme western projection of Soviet territory into Europe.

Hungary. The fact may be hard to believe, but Hungary is the satellite which, next to Poland, probably has the best record in civil liberties and the freest spirit. Of course, 'best' does not necessarily mean much by Western standards, and 'freest' is a strictly comparative term. Nevertheless Hungary today is considerably more relaxed than it was under the detested régime of Matyas Rákosi in the late forties and early fifties. Rákosi, who was both Communist Prime Minister and first secretary of the party, was, I think, the most malevolent character I ever met in political life. After some years a combination of pressures, both from Budapest itself and from Khrushchev in the Kremlin, forced him out. This was like pulling a stopper from a boiling bottle, and the Hungarian uprising of October, 1956, was the direct result.

Dozens of pages could be written about this heroic tragedy. The revolt was not officially anti-Communist at the beginning— although it was certainly anti-Russian; the upheaval began as a kind of civil war between competing Communists. Imre Nagy, the new Prime Minister, was a Titoist; the unspeakable Ernö Geroe, who had succeeded Rákosi as party boss, was Stalinist to the core. There were two separate Soviet interventions. The second came after Nagy, thinking that he had won, renounced the Warsaw Pact, declared Hungarian neutrality, and asked protection from the United Nations. This was too much for Moscow to accept, because if the Hungarians were allowed to wrest themselves completely free from Kremlin control, the whole Soviet position in eastern Europe would have collapsed, and Poland and the other satellites would probably have been lost. Also Khrushchev's position in Russia would have been gravely compromised. So, on November 4, the Russians let loose their tanks, and the Hungarian patriots, for all their magnificent and stubborn bravery, were beaten down.

Janos Kadar, who became both first secretary of the party and Prime Minister after these searing events, is still the first man in the country, and is an odd fish indeed. Twice he has committed appalling acts of betrayal. About forty-eight, he was born of peasant stock; for a time he earned a living as a tram conductor. He rose in the trade union movement, joined the Communist underground during the Horthy dictatorship after World War I, and sat out World War II in Budapest although almost all other Hungarian Communists of the period had escaped to Moscow and were living there in safety.

Kadar, like both Gomulka and Novotný, was imprisoned for a time by the Nazis, and, when the Communist régime was established in Budapest after the war, rose to be Minister of the Interior. As such he played a substantial role in the sensational trial of Josef Cardinal Mindszenty in 1948. In 1949 the most brilliant of modern Hungarian leaders, Laszlo Rajk, the Foreign Minister, was arrested on charges of Titoism. Kadar and Rajk had been intimate friends and colleagues. Kadar told Rajk that his life would be spared if he confessed; Rajk promptly did so, whereupon Kadar double-crossed him and had him shot. Then, in 1951, Kadar was in turn arrested by the Rákosi government. He spent three years in jail; his fingernails were torn out by the Rákosi-Stalin police, and one persistent story is that he was castrated.[1]

Came the rising in October, 1956. Kadar, who had been released from prison, at first joined the Freedom Forces. But, when Soviet tanks began crashing through the Budapest streets, he changed sides, joined the Russians, and presently became head of the new government. For Soviet purposes he was an admirable 'front'. Then came the second double-cross. Kadar promised Nagy, who had taken refuge in the Yugoslav legation, a safe conduct if he would give himself up. Nagy did so; promptly he was betrayed, kidnapped by the Russians, deported to Rumania, and, in June, 1958, tried and shot—an episode of unparalleled infamy. No wonder Kadar today looks like a man pursued by shadows, a walking corpse.

Enough on Kadar. We must have another word about the so-called thaw proceeding in Hungary today. Intellectual life is lively, though not so lively as in Poland, writers long buried have sprung from their hibernation, police rule has been much ameliorated, and people are given more to buy, although the

[1] Some of these details come from a brief biography in the New York *Herald Tribune*, September 18, 1960. Also see Mitchel Levitas in the New York *Post*, September 29, 1960.

general economic level is probably not quite so high as in Czechoslovakia. On the other hand, the collectivization of agriculture has been forced through relentlessly to virtual completion, and 90 per cent of all arable land is now in the 'socialist sector'. Collectivization, which had to be given up in Poland (also Yugoslavia), has won the day in Hungary. One ugly note in another field is that, even today, patriots who took part in the uprising are still being plucked out of hiding, tried, and, in some cases, given long prison terms or shot.

Government, as in Czechoslovakia, follows the Soviet model closely. The Communist party is, with no holds barred, the boss, although it had to be reconstituted from top to bottom after its disintegration during the revolt. Its new name is Hungarian Socialist Workers party (HSWP), and its membership is about 430,000, half what it was under Rákosi. Purging, in other words, has been drastic. The analogous Polish and Czechoslovakian parties are much bigger. Recently I asked a man well informed on eastern Europe and of notably impartial mind what result, in his opinion, a free vote in each satellite would bring. Estimates: Poland, 60 per cent against the régime; Czechoslovakia, 70 per cent; Rumania and Bulgaria, probably 80 per cent; East Germany, 85 per cent; Hungary, 95 per cent.

Rumania. This has been called the 'softest' of the Soviet marionettes. Before the war I knew Bucharest well—'a little Paris', gay, silken, and almost inconceivably corrupt. Few travellers report it as being gay or silken today, but the third characteristic probably still applies. There are several curiosities here: this is the only Communist country where a Romance language is spoken, and it is the only one where a Communist government was organized under a bourgeois king. When a remarkable character named Petru Groza set up a coalition régime dominated by the Communists (Groza himself was, however, not a Communist), young King Michael, the son of the celebrated Carol II, still sat on the throne. This was in 1945. But Michael was forced to abdicate in 1947, following some exceptional strong-arm work by the late Andrei Vyshinsky, the Soviet Foreign Minister of the day, and the Rumanian People's Republic was established.

Rumania, which is about three times the size of Scotland, has another distinction unusual in eastern Europe—it is a rich country spilling over with a profusion of oil, grain, timber, minerals, and other natural resources. Collectivization of agriculture is 81 per cent accomplished. One striking item is that the Rumanians, a leisurely people even under Communism, have what is by all odds the longest-range planning mechanism in the world. Not content with a four-, five-, six- or seven-year plan, they have a *sixteen*-year plan, the span of which is 1960-75. One other item out of the ordinary has to do with tourists. All the satellites except Albania cordially welcome American tourists, and do their utmost these days to entice them in, as indeed does the Soviet Union itself; but the hospitable Rumanians go further than the others. Visas are given to Americans automatically—gratis and on request—something unusual in a Communist state. The cost of tours has been cut down, the local currency is made available to tourists at a special rate, any amount of money may be brought into the country, and any tourist buying anything in Rumania can take it out without paying any export fee.[1]

Rumania is a straight-cut Communist dictatorship on the Russian pattern, but its government has curiosities too. At the top of the 'legislative' structure is the Grand National Assembly, with 437 members; this has a Presidium consisting of a chairman and twenty-one associates, who are known in bulk as 'the Collective President of the Rumanian People's Republic'. Few countries have an executive body with no fewer than twenty-two pairs of eyes, twenty-two pairs of ears, and, in short, twenty-two heads. Behind this is, of course, the Rumanian Workers party (RWP), the only political party permitted in the country. The first secretary of the party, and the man who without question rules the country, is Gheorghe Gheorghiu-Dej, who was once a Tito deviationist. For a time he was Prime Minister as well as first secretary, and has several times alternated between these posts. In most Communist countries, except Hungary and also the Soviet Union itself, where Khrushchev is both Prime Minister and party leader, the top jobs in government and party go to different people, because this is supposed to emphasize the principle of collective leadership.

Mr. Gheorghiu-Dej, a handsome man in his late fifties, is Moldavian by birth. He rose out of the working class, and has

[1] New York *Herald Tribune*, June 24, 1960.

always been a strong party man. Like practically all Rumanians
—again we see here a variant from the stereotyped Communist
pattern—he is supposed to be indulgent in temperament. He
accompanied Khrushchev to New York in 1960, a few months
after being his host at the Rumanian Party Congress in
Bucharest.

Communism came to Rumania, as it did to all the satellites,
for a variety of reasons. One was, of course, occupation by the
Red Army; also special local circumstances played a role. I wrote
in *Behind the Curtain* in 1948:

> The traditional curse [of Rumania] is that greedy landlords and
> politicians, dishonest and venal almost beyond belief, have always
> sucked it dry, leaving nothing but a rind for the peasants and
> workers in the towns. . . . In the past twenty years Rumania has had
> at least half a dozen different dictatorships, ranging from exercises
> in Graustarkian extravaganza to outright Fascism of a type worse
> than in any country in the world except Germany itself. . . . So
> Communism had a particularly soft and ready field in Rumania.
> There comes a time when even Zenda must get down to facts and
> figures. Feudalism; laws which made trade unions a crime; royal
> scandals; no tradition of decency in the public administration; a
> debauched judiciary; political apathy by the educated; fantastic
> displays of overt luxury by a fat crust of rich—all this existed.

Bulgaria. The titular boss of Bulgaria is Todor Zhivkov, first
secretary of the party, who was recently described in a British
newspaper, quoting an American source, as 'fat, apprehensive,
cold, conceited, and stupid', with 'evil eyes'. In his late fifties,
he was a printer by trade; he rose slowly in the Communist
underground, and distinguished himself as a Partisan in World
War II. Behind him is a man named Vulko Chervenko, a former
Prime Minister and head of the party, who, as a result of complicated manipulations, has found it prudent to step behind the
scenes. Chervenkov is a last-ditch, old-style Stalinist, who had
large influence and prestige partly because his brother-in-law
was the celebrated Georgi Dimitrov, the hero of the Reichstag
fire trial in Germany in 1933. Dimitrov dominated Bulgarian
affairs in the period immediately after the war.[1]

Government is, in theory, run by an instrument known as
the Fatherland Front. As in Poland, several other political

[1] *World Today*, January, 1960.

parties apart from the Communists are permitted to exist and
have representation in the Fatherland Front and government,
but these have no effective power. Bulgaria has an ugly,
complex party history. In 1947 Nikola Petkov, leader of the
National Agrarian Union, a non-Communist left-winger and
the biggest man in the country, was purged and executed at the
instigation of Dimitrov. Three years later, Traicho Kostov, the
second-ranking Communist, was, like Petkov, put on trial, found
'guilty' on trumped-up charges, and duly shot. The trial, which
was totally superintended by Stalinists, was designed to link
Kostov and his group with nationalist, revisionist Communists
in Yugoslavia. One result was that the United States broke off
diplomatic relations with Bulgaria (1950), and these were not
resumed until ten years later.

There was sharp irony to the Kostov trial, because Dimitrov
himself had met Marshal Tito in Bled, Yugoslavia, in 1947, and
the two leaders worked out provisional plans for a fusion of
Yugoslavia and Bulgaria into a new state, to be called the Union
of South Slav People's Republics, which Albania was to have
joined later. Tito was to have become Prime Minister of this
amalgamation, with Petkov as his deputy. Such a merger would
have made good sense; it would have helped to solve the
Macedonian problem, a Balkan bugbear for generations, and
laid the framework for a genuine Balkan federation. But the
Kremlin thought that such a bloc would give too much power to
the local satraps. Dimitrov was sharply rebuked by Moscow,
and he recanted and apologized; Petkov was 'eliminated by
shooting'. Then, for different reasons, came the great, rasping
break between the Kremlin and Tito the next year.

One reason why the Communists, following occupation of
Bulgaria by the Red Army, were able to seize power was the
good record of the Communist resistance against the Axis. The
Communists played their cards with great skill. The pattern is
familiar. First, a broad coalition was set up embracing all the
leftist parties; second, rigged elections were held which the
Communists won; third, the Communists enlarged themselves
by absorbing the Social Democrats and other left-wing parties;
finally, a new national 'front' was created and the transfer of
power became complete. Thus Bulgaria, a stalwart little country,
peopled by decent, frugal citizens almost all of whom have

profound democratic instincts, went down the drain. Bulgaria today has been influenced to an extent by Chinese developments. Agriculture, which is 85 per cent collectivized, was reorganized in 1959 into a system bearing resemblance to Chinese 'communes'. Also pressure was put on to increase economic expansion at an extraordinarily rapid pace, in an effort calling to mind the Chinese 'Great Leap Forward'.

One striking development has been the transformation of the Bulgarian beaches on the Black Sea into a kind of Soviet Florida; here are hotels, sanitaria, rest-houses and the like for the *élite* of the Communist bloc all over Europe. Another item is that, in the summer of 1960, the Bulgarian government deposited eleven hundred pounds of attar of roses in a London bank, as collateral for financial transactions. Attar of roses, one of the principal Bulgarian exports for many years, is valued at £600 a pound, and the Bulgarians keep stocks of it in banks in France, Switzerland and the United States.[1]

Albania. Here we have a puzzle. This Lilliputian country, only twice the size of Northern Ireland, and with a population little greater than that of Glasgow, is a kind of Communist outhouse—the real end of the line. It lies, however, on the Adriatic, which gives it a certain strategic importance. There are Soviet submarine 'pens' at Saseno. The strange fact is that Albania, small as it is, has dared to take an independent line *vis-à-vis* the Russian colossus, which, if the two countries were contiguous, could extinguish it with the drop of a finger. This is because, of all things, Albania has seemingly adopted a strong pro-*Chinese* course, and is even regarded as Mao Tse-tung's 'first outpost' on the continent of Europe.

Several reasons may be adduced for this, but none are altogether satisfactory. One is that Albania, a miserable, grimy little dictatorship, deplores the general loosening-up that has come with de-Stalinization. More suggestive is the traditional Albanian dislike and fear of Yugoslavia. Khrushchev has, by fits and starts, sought to heal the breach between the Kremlin and Yugoslavia, whereas the Albanians want the quarrel to remain open. Peking takes a bitterly anti-Yugoslav line, and this appeals to the Albanians. Enver Hoxha, the Albanian party secretary and dictator, who has been called the 'last avowedly Stalinist

[1] *New York Times*, August 23, 1960.

chief of state in Europe', has always hated Yugoslavia. Hence
when the break between Tito and the Kremlin occurred, he
'developed an almost fanatical admiration for Stalin, who had
forced Tito out of the Cominform fold'.[1] Finally, the Albanians
have no frontier with any other Communist state except Yugoslavia, and are totally isolated geographically from the mainstream of satellite developments; therefore, their sensitiveness
to things Yugoslav is augmented.

This does not, however, make an altogether adequate
explanation. The Bulgars also dislike the Yugoslavs, and are
also inclined to take a somewhat Stalinist line; but they have not
become partners of the Chinese.

In any case events speak for themselves. Albania was the only
satellite state not represented at the recent Bucharest Congress,
and was the only European satellite to send an emissary to the
Chinese National Day celebration on October 1, 1960. The
Chinese have lent Albania tidy sums of money, interest-free,
and, although their own grain shortage is acute, have bought
European grain and given it to the Albanians after a recent crop
failure. On the other hand, the Albanian Prime Minister,
Mehmet Shehu, attended the UN Assembly in New York in
1960 with Khrushchev.

Albania, the correct name for which is Shqiperia, is 73 per
cent Moslem; it is the only European state both Moslem and
Communist. It has had an outright Communist régime since
1948, and, like most of the other satellites, operates under a one-
party system; the sole party is the Albanian Workers party,
Partija e Punes. Communism came to Albania by methods which
are—or should be—familiar: abolition of the monarchy, creation
of a suitably disguised party apparatus, formation of a temporary
coalition, and 'free' elections. The job was made easier because
there was no Albanian government in exile; the land had been
run over and terrorized by the Germans after years of colonial
exploitation by Italy, and no effective political body existed
except the Communists, who were an important element in the
resistance. Albania was, in short, a vacuum, and Moscow moved
right in.

General Hoxha, a picturesque figure who has been in power
since November 29, 1944, is little known to the outside world.

[1] C. L. Sulzberger in the *New York Times*, March 6, 1961.

He was born of bourgeois stock, something unusual among Communist leaders, and was educated in France, where he was converted to Communism. Returning to Albania he became a teacher; he lost his job because he refused to join the local Italian-dominated Fascist party, and set up a secret Communist cell in a tobacco shop. Then, with the advent of World War II, he organized the National Liberation Movement, became secretary-general of the Communist party underground, and, when he was still in his mid-thirties, emerged as the commander-in-chief of the Albanian armed forces. At present he holds none but a party post, but he has at one time or other been Prime Minister, Foreign Minister, and Minister of War.

Mehmet Shehu, his Prime Minister, is also colourful. He is the son of a Moslem priest, fought in Spain with the International Brigade, was educated subsequently in Moscow, and speaks good English.

The United States does not recognize Albania, and has no diplomatic relations with it. Recently General Hoxha accused Yugoslavia and Greece of a plot, made in conjunction with the American Sixth Fleet and 'Albanian traitors who had taken refuge in Yugoslavia', of a conspiracy to overthrow his régime.

YUGOSLAVIA, A SPECIAL CASE

Yugoslavia, with its eighteen million people crowded into an area less than 100,000 square miles, has had three names since its foundation in 1919. One of its fathers was Woodrow Wilson. Originally it was called the 'Kingdom of Serbs, Croats, and Slovenes'; the name 'Kingdom of Yugoslavia' replaced this in 1929, and, in 1945, under Tito, the 'Federal People's Republic of Yugoslavia' was established. Like that of the Soviet Union, the structure of government is federal, and consists of six 'People's Republics'—Serbia, Croatia, Slovenia, Bosnia-Herzegovina, Macedonia, and Montenegro. As a matter of fact, despite the celebrated break with the Kremlin, Yugoslavia has closer resemblances to Russia itself than any other satellite. It is soundly Slav in fundamentals, but, with Albanian, Hungarian, and Turkish minorities, to say nothing of the Catholic Slovenes and Croats, it has a variegated and colourful texture. Its people are at once brawny and animated—a tough, brusque, lusty folk.

The Yugoslavs made their own heroic resistance in World War II, and got little assistance from the Soviets. One curiosity is that its hard-grained army contains a substantial number of women troops—the only army in the world except that of Israel that does so.

Marshal Tito is, of course, the boss. When I saw him in 1960 for the first time since meeting him in Zagreb twelve years before, I thought that he seemed younger—slimmer, muscular, solid of cheek, fresh of eye, with hair only slightly grey and sparkling white teeth. He has been President of both the Republic and the Federal Executive Council since the state was formed, and Secretary-General of the LCY (Union of Communist Yugoslavia) for years. Thus he is at once head of state, government, and party, of which the last is—as always with Communist régimes—the most consequential. Tito may have split with the Kremlin on certain issues, but one should never forget that he is first, last, and all the time a Communist—from some points of view a 'better' Communist than Khrushchev. His accomplishments have been considerable. One, largely forgotten nowadays, is that he has to all intents and purposes ended the ravaging quarrel between the Serbs and the Croats which tortured the Yugoslav state during the first forty years of its existence. Early tendencies to separatism on the part of the Macedonians, Dalmatians, Bosnians (who are largely Moslem), and the turbulent idiosyncratic mountaineers of Montenegro have also been for the most part forgotten.

The outline of Tito's career is so well known that we may be brief. Of Croat origin, he was born near Zagreb on May 25, 1892, and was named Josip Brozovic, later shortened to Broz. He assumed the *nom de révolution* 'Tito' many years later. No doubt he chose 'Tito' by accident or because it was a name simple, forceful, and easy to remember. But there have been all manner of elaborate theories to explain the choice. One is that he named himself after the Roman emperor Titus, or after St. Titus, an early Balkan missionary; another is that the initials stand for 'Secret International Terrorist Organization', and still another is that the sound 'Tito' resembles that of the Yugoslav words, 'you' and 'do', and the legend arose that, when Tito gave orders in the old days, his followers got into the habit of calling him by a similar locution.

He was one of fourteen brothers and sisters, eight of whom died in childhood—sufficient motivation for a revolutionary.[1] He followed his father's trade, became an apprentice to a metal-worker, and worked as a locksmith briefly.[2] He managed then to reach Vienna, where he studied at the university. Drafted into the Austro-Hungarian Army in World War I, he saw prolonged service, and was captured by the Russians; he was a Communist long before this, but residence in the Soviet Union confirmed his convictions, and he learned party methods in Moscow. He did not return to Yugoslavia until 1923. Becoming secretary of the Metal Workers Union in Belgrade, he was sentenced to five years in jail for underground revolutionary activity; then, during World War II, he became a triumphant guerrilla commander. He organized the National Liberation Movement, rose to the top, and eventually liquidated opponents like his rival, General Draja Mikhailovic, who was accused of having collaborated with the Nazis.

Tito probably would not be where he is today had it not been for Winston Churchill. First, Mr. Churchill sent his son, Randolph, as well as other British agents, to make secret contact with him during the bitterest and most furious phase of the Resistance struggle against the German invader. The worthy Randolph, at great risk, was parachuted into Tito territory. The elder Churchill, never wanting in political sense, caught on at once to the fact that Tito was the only personage who counted in Yugoslavia, conferred with him in Naples in dramatic circumstances, conceived a romantic admiration for him, and backed him to the limit. Then, after the war, it was largely Churchill's influence which led to Allied recognition of the Tito régime, even though this meant the eclipse of King Peter II. Not often does Mr. Churchill take sides against a king, but the circumstances were extremely special.

One of Tito's pronounced characteristics since he emerged into fame has been that he is always neatly dressed, and some-times wears flamboyant uniforms. No doubt he is compensating for the extreme poverty of his youth, to say nothing of the ragamuffin days in the underground. His personality has

---

[1] *New York Times*, September 20, 1960.

[2] Too much should not be made of this, but it is weirdly interesting that Khrushchev, Novotný, and Kadar were also locksmiths.

changed little with the years, and he is still a man proud, stubborn, boyish, patient, and, above all, courageous.

The Yugoslav rupture with the Kremlin became known on June 28, 1948. Simmering months of tension—Stalin was, of course, still alive—led to the schism. Tito and his men were accused by Moscow of various derelictions, and, after the exchange of an extraordinarily interesting and acrimonious correspondence, were expelled from the Cominform. The Yugoslavs, it is interesting to recall nowadays, did their best not to be expelled; their letters addressed to Moscow from Belgrade were far from being intransigent and, at the beginning, were almost meek. Time and time again the Yugoslavs sought to point out their staunch, fervid loyalty to Communism and the Soviet Union. But they refused to recant from their 'heresy', and Tito stoutly set forth his view that 'national and international exigencies compelled them [the Yugoslavs] to develop socialism in their country in a *somewhat different form* [italics mine] from that attained in the Soviet Union'.

It is interesting that, twelve years later, Khrushchev—operating *vis-à-vis* the Chinese—has precisely taken over this formula, and ardently espouses it. He himself has become a Titoist to an extent, which is one reason why Peking is so angry with him.

Khrushchev, as a matter of fact, was probably on Tito's side all the time, although he could not say so while Stalin was alive. But as soon as he had begun to establish himself in power he opened negotiations of reconciliation with the Yugoslavs, who, meantime, had been subject to unspeakable vilification by the Soviets. Khrushchev, Bulganin, and Mikoyan journeyed to Belgrade in May, 1955, and an armistice was patched up. The Yugoslav dictator returned their visit in June, 1956, and Khrushchev and Tito issued a joint declaration stating that it *was*—after all—possible for different countries to pursue 'different roads to socialism'. Since then Soviet-Yugoslav relations have, as an official document puts it, 'oscillated'. A ruder way to express this would be to say that Mr. K. and Mr. T. have kissed, broken, and made up several times. After the Gomulka *coup* and the Hungarian revolution in October, 1956, their relations deteriorated; in fact, the Russians accused the Yugoslavs of responsibility for 'fomenting' these disorders. The

Kremlin cut off credits to Yugoslavia, and otherwise sought to punish it. Then Khrushchev and Tito met again in Rumania in 1957, and resumed co-operation. Another quarrel followed, and Tito refused to attend the celebration of the fortieth anniversary of the Bolshevik Revolution in Moscow. In retaliation Russia and the 'loyal' satellites boycotted Yugoslavia and, once more, venomous polemics were resumed. But in October, 1960, Khrushchev and Tito had cordial talks at the UN meeting in New York. Subsequently Tito declared that Belgrade and Moscow had 'identical views on the most important issues of the day', and Khrushchev told an interviewer, 'Yugoslavia is neutral, but I believe it would fight on the Soviet side if the USSR were attacked.'

One result of this continuing fracas has been to throw Tito into close touch with the other neutrals: he has built up intimate relations with Nasser, Nehru, and Sukarno, and has made two extended trips to the uncommitted nations of the Afro-Asian bloc, visiting Burma, Ethiopia, Ceylon, and the Sudan, as well as India, the United Arab Republic, and Indonesia. Aid to the uncommitted nations is, he thinks, imperative, and he probably agrees with Mr. Nehru that the orderly development of undeveloped states constitutes the greatest single problem in the world today, next to disarmament. The United States, it would seem, has not taken Tito seriously enough, exploited his neutralist position to sufficient advantage, or conducted policy *vis-à-vis* the Yugoslavs with much subtlety or skill. It was generally understood that the Marshal would be invited to visit the United States after settlement of the Trieste dispute with Italy, but no invitation was forthcoming. In October, 1960, Tito cooled his heels for several weeks in New York, but was never invited by President Eisenhower to Washington. On the other hand, it should be pointed out that the United States has granted Yugoslavia more than £350 million in economic aid since the split with the Cominform, and an era of fruitful political relations may well begin as a result of the appointment of George Kennan as American Ambassador to Yugoslavia by the Kennedy administration.

*

Tito is sixty-eight and, although his health could not be better, the question of succession must be faced. The man likeliest to take over from him is Edvard Kardelj, a Slovene about fifty, who for years has been the chief theoretician of the Yugoslav Communist party. He is not particularly popular, but his competence is universally respected. At present Kardelj is vice-president of the Federal Executive Council, a member of the Executive Committee (Politburo) of the LCY, and secretary-general of the Socialist Alliance, as the party's mass front organization is called. He was for many years Foreign Minister. Kardelj limps, and it is popularly supposed that, during one period in prison, under the old Serb régime, his toes were broken by police inquisitors. Another highly influential man is General Aleksander Rankovic, around fifty, a former Partisan fighter with Tito (as was Kardelj), who was Minister of the Interior for many years. His mother and wife were both murdered by the Gestapo during the German occupation. A third eminent personage, Milovan Djilas, a Montenegrin, fought for the Loyalists in the Spanish Civil War, and subsequently became one of the closest of the early Tito coadjutors. But Djilas, a fiery character, kept getting into trouble for ideological deviations, and in 1959 was arrested, tried, and put into jail. While imprisoned he wrote a book, *The New Class*, which bitterly characterized the Yugoslav régime as a 'totalitarian tyranny', whereupon his jail sentence was extended. But he was released in 1961.

CODA

At last, concluding this long chapter, we return to the USSR itself. To recapitulate: the essence of Soviet foreign policy under Khrushchev is simple enough. The Russians certainly do not want war, if only because they might well lose it; and certainly in the event of nuclear war they would be bound to suffer enormous, catastrophic damage, and their precious industrialization, which is their principal accomplishment, would be put back many years, if it survived at all. What they do want is *to win the world without a war*. Thus arose the policy of 'peaceful' coexistence, a device based not only on a genuine desire for peace for its own sake but on the theory that a peaceful world gives them better opportunity to pursue their long-range aims. Peaceful coexistence does not, in the official words of the manifesto of December, 1960, issued after the eighty-one-nation Communist conference in Moscow, mean the 'conciliation of bourgeois ideologies'. On the contrary, it implies 'intensification of the struggle of the working class for the triumph of socialist ideas', since it is avowedly competitive. Mr. K. has even said that peaceful coexistence gives the Soviet Union 'the right to make capitalist countries jump about like fish in a frying pan',[1] although this remark is probably little more than an expression of bravado and extravagance.

On a more concrete, immediate level, Soviet policy has several bases, as I wrote in *Inside Russia Today*. First, perpetuation of the régime. Second, efforts to nullify or counteract American superiority, and to weaken the United States as a potential antagonist. Third, as to the rest of the world, pick up pieces where they fall. What Khrushchev hates most is NATO and the American system of overseas bases, because these confront him with the possibility of retaliation. What he fears most, basic American strength aside, is West German rearmament. What he wants most, next to Soviet advance, is disarmament. What annoys him most is Berlin.

What is not simple is to summarize what American policy is —or should be. Of course we want peace, as do the Russians; moreover, we are open to reasonable exercises in compromise and accommodation. Nevertheless the United States—the western world as well—finds itself often in an intolerably awkward position. We have launched several policies. We tried containment, but this can scarcely be said to have worked, in view of the fact that Russian power and influence have steadily expanded, e.g. in Africa and Asia. 'Massive retaliation' was another policy; America still has immense striking power and ability to retaliate if the need arises, but massive retaliation as a threat had to go out of the window as soon as it became clear that Soviet nuclear strength was equivalent to ours—perhaps superior.[2] Does this mean that we are now obliged to meet the Russians on their own chosen field, and play the game according to their rules? Are we merely to be the fish in the

[1] *Guardian*, March 2, 1961.
[2] C. L. Sulzberger in the *New York Times*, March 18, 1961.

frying pan? Of course not. The crucial problem for the western world is how to co-exist with the Soviet Union without weakness or appeasement, and establish a concordance without surrender. We must engage and compete with them and win, that is keep our world from falling into Soviet hands. Also we must maintain our own house in good order and play cleaner, which is not always easy in view of Soviet techniques of stirring the pot, evasion and provocation. Certainly peace is preferable to war; harmony is preferable to disruption; agreement is preferable to chaos; a *détente* is preferable to tension. But these are not the only reasons why the United States must accept the Soviet challenge no matter where it lies, at the same time trying to mantain reasonably correct relations. If we did not, it would mean that we knew that we were beaten—which we are not.

CHAPTER XXIV

A Few Paragraphs in Conclusion

So we approach the end. We have discussed briefly the differences between the Europe of today and that of a quarter of a century ago, and have inspected the contemporary political situation in countries throughout the continent. It remains to pull a few loose ends taut and staple the whole cloth together.

First, most European leaders are oldish men today. Adenauer is 85, de Gaulle is 70, Macmillan is 66, Gronchi is 73, Franco is 68, Tito is 68, Khrushchev is 66. There are few questions more pertinent, or more difficult to answer, than what will happen in Germany after Adenauer dies, or in France with the passing of de Gaulle. In Great Britain and the Soviet Union the question is perhaps not quite so vital, because in both these countries the *system* will presumably carry on without much dislocation—needless to say, a different system. The fact remains that a change of leadership is inevitable in every important European country within the next decade—perhaps sooner. This in turn means that a new generation of rulers is bound to reach power in the near future, with consequences that are largely unpredictable.

Second, the most pressing and difficult problem in Europe is, after disarmament, Berlin and the future status of Germany. The West, for reasons amply discussed in these pages, has to stay in Berlin; the East (so it feels today) has to push us out. Berlin, cut in half, symbolizes Europe cut in half. It reflects the whole cold war in miniature, and is also a sharp crystallization of the fact that this is veritably a two-power world.

Third, the Western alliance takes severe beatings on occasion, as over Suez, but is still intact. De Gaulle wants more prestige, more power and illumination, for France; Adenauer is terrified that the United States and Britain might, under certain circum-

stances, modify their position on West Germany to buy a
general European settlement. Why, despite these and other
frictions, is the Western alliance likely to remain solid? The
reasons are complementary: (1) Western Europe, in the event
of Soviet attack, could not survive without the assistance of
American power, which is now concretely represented on the
European continent itself; (2) the American position in the
world struggle *vis-à-vis* the Soviet Union would be hopelessly
prejudiced if western Europe were to be lost. So it is to the
advantage of both sides of the Atlantic to hold together.

Fourth, the basic line-up is still USA-Canada-UK-France-
West Germany-Spain-Portugal-Italy-Greece-Turkey-Benelux-
Norway-Denmark against the USSR-China-Poland-East Germany - Czechoslovakia - Hungary - Rumania - Bulgaria - Albania.
Analysis of the comparative strength of each bloc—in population, area, natural resources, gross national product, military
prowess, et cetera—is not altogether comforting. Five countries
are neutral—Austria, Eire, Switzerland, Sweden, and Finland.
Yugoslavia is in a category all its own. It should also be pointed
out that Spain is not a member of NATO, and that Portugal
carries little weight as an ally. Finally, there are decided
neutralist tendencies in several of the NATO countries,
although these are not decisive at the moment—Denmark,
Norway, Iceland, and even Great Britain—also Cyprus. Greece
is pretty much a question-mark in the long run, and Turkey is in
a state of revolutionary—or counter-revolutionary—flux.

All this being said we should make another point, *fifth*, that
the future of Europe may well depend on events outside Europe.
This is partly because England, France, Belgium, and the
Netherlands have surrendered much (in some cases all) of their
former imperial position in colonial territories. Thus a large
segment of the world has become neutralist or uncommitted
overnight, and governments in several newly free countries are,
to say the least, not yet fully seasoned or responsible. Which
way are they going to go? What will be the effect on the world
balance of power if part of Africa, let us say, goes Communist,
or succumbs to chaos? What will be the future of Laos or the
Congo? And what may not happen in Cuba or elsewhere in
Latin America? Above all, the new African and Asian states do
not want to take sides if this entails danger to their newly won

freedom. It must be faced that half the countries in the UN today, perhaps more, are neutralist, and vigorously hope to remain so no matter what pressures are evoked by the acrid struggle between the USA and the USSR.

Sixth, the several forces tending to assist and encourage European unity, like Euratom, the European Coal and Steel Community, and the Common Market, are encouraging developments. Forces also exist which tend to impede unity, such as British aloofness to the Common Market design and the easily abraded nationalist pride of General Charles de Gaulle. Nationalism is, it goes without saying, still a powerful and pervasive force almost everywhere in Europe. Yet western Europe has probably moved closer towards economic unity in the last twenty-five years than in the previous five hundred, and the beginnings of integration on the political level are almost sure to follow. It is a striking fact that the frontiers of the Common Market are almost precisely those of the empire of Charlemagne, except for the boot of Italy.

Seventh, democratic impulses are, by and large, comfortably in the ascendant in western Europe. England and the Federal Republic of Germany have healthy two-party systems; France and Italy are ruled by loose centre coalitions. De Gaulle is on top in France and Adenauer in West Germany, but not by any reasonable definition could either be called a dictator. A quarter of a century ago the entire continent, except for the United Kingdom, France, and the neutral states, was ruled by totalitarian dictators; today only two remain in the Europe of the West, Franco and Salazar, and both are isolated from the main streams of European development.

Finally, I can only repeat what I said at the beginning of this book, this tentative attempt to compare the Europe of twenty-five years ago with the Europe of 1961. General war is unlikely because an attack on the West does not suit Russian or Communist interests. Mr. Khrushchev can be extraordinarily disagreeable and obstructionist and he acts with pure peasant nastiness on occasion, as at the UN in 1960; his long-range politics obviously represent a severe threat to the democratic way of life throughout the world, but he is not a Hitler, who actively wanted war, not a bloodthirsty or criminal paranoiac. But if global war should, despite everything, come through blunder or miscalculation, the world will be confronted with a possibility never before known in history—total annihilation. Professor Einstein was once asked what the weapons of World War III would be. He replied, 'I do not know. But I know what the weapons of World War IV will be—rocks.'

Acknowledgments

THE idea for this book came from Hobart Lewis of *Reader's Digest*, and I want to thank him. He proposed a brief trip to Europe for an article which would compare the continent as it was in 1936 to what it is today—little anticipating that I would turn out, after some months of struggle, the longest article (it ran to some 42,000 words) the *Digest* has ever received. Then Cass Canfield of Harper's and Hamish Hamilton in London, my publishers, suggested that I add to this material and extend it into a full-length book. They had, in fact, been urging me to do a new *Inside Europe* for many years. So the seventh book in the *Inside* series now appears. It is approximately three times longer than what I wrote for the *Digest*.

During the trip Jane Perry Gunther and I took to Europe to gather material we were stoutly helped by scores of friends old and new. It would be pretentious to list their names, and so I must content myself with a broad general acknowledgment. I would, however, like to mention one generous friend, my old colleague M. W. Fodor, who gave us the benefit of his acumen and store of wisdom accumulated over many fruitful years. Also I owe cordial thanks to Alice Furlaud, my secretary, who struggled amiably and ably with various stages of my disorderly manuscript.

I have tried to keep footnotes to the minimum, and, since I did little research in books, I do not include a bibliography—the first *Inside* book that does not contain one. For updating I used standard sources, and again let me limit myself to a broad general acknowledgment. Such publications as the *New York Times*, the New York *Herald Tribune*, the *Observer* and *Sunday Times* of London, the *New Statesman*, the *Guardian* (Manchester), the *Economist*, *Foreign Affairs*, the *Reporter*, *Life*, and *Time*, among others, were indispensable. Also I want to express my obligation to two admirable reference works which are perhaps not so well known as they should be, one small in size,

An Atlas of World Affairs, by Andrew Boyd (Praeger, New York, 1957), and one very large, the newly published and useful *Worldmark Encyclopedia of the Nations* (Worldmark Press, Inc., and Harper & Brothers, New York, 1960), as well as to *Political Handbook of the World*, published annually by the Council on Foreign Relations, New York. Also, as always, I have used freely *Current History*, various pamphlets published by the Foreign Policy Association (New York), and in particular *World Today*, the admirable monthly publication of the Royal Institute of International Affairs, London.

Finally, I have had the privilege of access to a number of invaluable documents issued by an official—but confidential—source.

Index

Reims, 90
Reinhardt, Max, 171
Religion, in Belgium, 105; in England,
223; in Germany, 30; in Netherlands,
113; in Portugal, 122; in Spain, 133
Renard, André, 111
Renault company, 83, 84, 98
Reporter, 108n, 256, 276n
Republican party, in France, 87; in
Italy, 138
Republican People's party, 164, 166
Rerum Novarum, 121
Resistance, 83, 84, 85, 86, 88, 89, 146,
147
'Return of the Warrior', 72n
Reunification of Germany, 23–4
Reuter, Ernst, 55
Reykjavik, 265
Reynaud, Paul, 85
Rhee, Syngman, 169
Rhineland, 22, 26, 28, 29, 34, 43
Rhodes, Cecil, 15
Rhoendorf, Germany, 19–20, 22, 23,
27, 28
Ringstrasse, 171
Rise and Fall of the Third Reich, The,
240n
Risorgimento, 138
Robles, Jose Maria Gil, 134
Rome, 90, 122, 140
Rommel, Erwin, 240
Roncalli, Angelo Giuseppe, 150
Roosevelt, Franklin D., 209, 215
Rosebery, Lord, 219
Rotterdam, 113
Rousseau, Jean Jacques, 181
Rovan, Joseph, 28n
Rovere, Richard H., 301n
Royal Air Force, *see* RAF
Royal Question, 105–7, 110
Royaume de Belgique, 105
Ruhr, 29, 43, 46, 246
Rumania, 13, 45, 309, 310, 318–20
Rumanian Party Congress, 306, 320
Rumanian Workers party, 306, 319
Russell, Bertrand, 201
Russia, 9, 80n, 214, 237, 291; and
Adenauer, 25; and Austria, 173; and
Brandt, 57; and Denmark, 262; and
East Berlin, 48, 49, 57, 61–9; and
England, 25, 198; and Finland, 13,
258, 267, 269; and FLN, 96; and
Germany, 32, 37, 38, 42–5, 49, 59–
69; and Greece, 158; Gronchi and,
141–2; and Hungary, 13, 263, 302;
and Iceland, 258; and NATO, 96;
310; and Netherlands, 114; and nu-
clear weapons, 12, 203, 237, 243;
and Portugal, 122, 128; as power,
13; and Spain, 131; and Sweden, 261;

and Turkey, 168; and U-2 flight,
59, 168, 268, 274–80, 282, 283–4.
See also Communism, Communist
Party, Khrushchev, *and* peaceful co-
existence
Russo-Finnish War, 258

SAAR, 246
SAC, 200, 204
SACEUR, 204
Sahara, 89, 100
Saimaa Canal, 269
Saint-Cyr, 74, 92
St. Helena, 194n
Salan, Raoul, 92, 100n
Salazar, Antonio de Oliveira, 14, 71,
120–1, 122, 123ff
Salisbury, Lord, 214, 223
Salten, Felix, 171
Sandys, Duncan, 182, 225
San Francisco, 15, 245
Sanjurjo, Jose, 132
Santa Maria, 120, 126, 129
Saragat, Giuseppe, 55, 138, 148
Sardinia, 40
Sargant, William 284–6
Sarper, Selim, 167
Sartre, Jean-Paul, 99
S-Bahn, 49, 54
Scandinavia, 112, 158, 242, 258ff
Scelba, Mario, 149
Schaerf, Adolf, 176–7
Schaumburg Palace, 20
Schaus, Eugene, 118
Schauspielhaus, 62
Schiele, Egon, 171
Schirdewan, Herr, 66
Schlegel, August, 28
Schleswig-Holstein, 30
Schmid, Carlo, 36, 41
Schnitzler, Arthur, 171
Schumacher, Kurt, 40, 56, 66
Schuman, Robert, 85, 246, 257
Schuman Plan, 26, 85
Schuschnigg, Kurt, 174, 177
Scotland, 189
SED, 49, 64
Segni, Antonio, 149
Segura y Saenz, Pedro Cardinal, 133
Senegal, 102
Separatist movement, 22
Serbia, 324
Serebryakov, 298
Sergeant rockets, 241
SHAPE, 204, 238, 242, 243, 244
Shaw, G. B., 212
Shehu, Mehmet, 323, 324
Shepelin, A. N., 300
Shepard, Alan B., 302n
Shepilov, Dimitri T., 293